Microsoft® SharePoint® 2010: Business Connectivity Services

Penelope Coventry
Brett Lonsdale
Phill Duffy

Published with the authorization of Microsoft Corporation by:
O'Reilly Media, Inc.
1005 Gravenstein Highway North
Sebastopol, California 95472

ISBN: 978-0-735-66018-2

1 2 3 4 5 6 7 8 9 LSI 6 5 4 3 2 1

Printed and bound in the United States of America.

Microsoft Press books are available through booksellers and distributors worldwide. If you need support related to this book, email Microsoft Press Book Support at *mspinput@microsoft.com*. Please tell us what you think of this book at *http://www.microsoft.com/learning/booksurvey*.

Microsoft and the trademarks listed at *http://www.microsoft.com/about/legal/en/us/IntellectualProperty/Trademarks/EN-US.aspx* are trademarks of the Microsoft group of companies. All other marks are property of their respective owners.

The example companies, organizations, products, domain names, email addresses, logos, people, places, and events depicted herein are fictitious. No association with any real company, organization, product, domain name, email address, logo, person, place, or event is intended or should be inferred.

This book expresses the author's views and opinions. The information contained in this book is provided without any express, statutory, or implied warranties. Neither the authors, O'Reilly Media, Inc., Microsoft Corporation, nor its resellers, or distributors will be held liable for any damages caused or alleged to be caused either directly or indirectly by this book.

Acquisitions and Developmental Editor: Kenyon Brown

Production Editor: Kristen Borg

Editorial Production: Zyg Group

Technical Reviewer: Neil Hodgkinson

Copyeditor: Nicole Flores

Indexer: BIM Publishing Services

Cover Design: Twist Creative • Seattle

Cover Composition: Karen Montgomery

Illustrator: Rebecca Demarest

Contents at a Glance

Contents

What do you think of this book? We want to hear from you!

Microsoft is interested in hearing your feedback so we can continually improve our
books and learning resources for you. To participate in a brief online survey, please visit:

microsoft.com/learning/booksurvey

Chapter 6 Building Business Data Dashboards   161

Chapter 7 Using External Data with Office Client Applications 201

What do you think of this book? We want to hear from you!

Microsoft is interested in hearing your feedback so we can continually improve our
books and learning resources for you. To participate in a brief online survey, please visit:

microsoft.com/learning/booksurvey

Introduction

Microsoft SharePoint 2010: Business Connectivity Services helps small and medium-sized businesses as well as bigger organizations put their business data to work—and create valuable business solutions. Use Microsoft SharePoint Foundation 2010, Microsoft SharePoint Server 2010, or Microsoft SharePoint Online (part of Microsoft Office 365 cloud services) to unlock data and increase productivity.

Who Should Read This Book

The book is aimed at business users, project managers, architects, administrators, and decision makers who want to create solutions that are required to create, use, share, and find information using Microsoft SharePoint 2010 websites, where the information is not stored in Microsoft SharePoint 2010 SQL Server content databases. Led by SharePoint experts, you'll learn hands-on strategies for deploying business solutions that integrate data from business applications and databases using BCS.

Who Should Not Read This Book

The book is not aimed at developers; therefore, it does not cover in detail the creation of server-side code using Visual Studio. However, it does contain examples of client-side code (such as XSLT, JavaScript, and jQuery) that can be incorporated into business solutions using tools such as Microsoft SharePoint Designer 2010 to present and manipulate data exposed when using BCS.

Assumptions

This book assumes that you have a working knowledge of SharePoint 2010 and Microsoft Office 2010 client applications. If you need to learn how to use SharePoint 2010, we recommend that you read the following two books:

- *Microsoft SharePoint Foundation 2010 Step by Step* by Olga Londer and Penelope Coventry (Microsoft Press, 2011)

- *Microsoft SharePoint 2010 Plain & Simple* by Johnathan Lightfoot and Chris Beckett (Microsoft Press, 2010)

System Requirements

To use this book, you must have access to a server running SharePoint Foundation 2010, SharePoint Server 2010 or SharePoint Online. These product provide different Business Connectivity Service (BCS) capabilities that are explained in the book. Directions on how to install these products are outside the scope of the book. However, once you have access to one of these products, this book details how to configure and extend BCS.

The book uses the the Microsoft Adventure Works LT and AdventureWorks databases when creating a SQL Server external content type (ECT), external lists, and dashboards. You can download these databases from *http://msftdbprodsamples.codeplex.com*.

To use the companion content (sample files), you must have a development environment where Visual Studio and a SharePoint server product are installed on the same server. The requirements for developing SharePoint Solutions can be found at *http://msdn.microsoft.com/en-us/ee231582.aspx*.

Organization of This Book

This book provides a comprehensive look at the various SharePoint features you will use. It is divided into three parts.

Part I: Planning and Maintaining Business Connectivity Services

This part provides an introduction to Business Connectivity Services (BCS) and why you might want to use it. It details BCS terminology and the tasks that a SharePoint server administrator and business owner need to complete to enable users to present the external data within SharePoint websites.

Chapter 1, "Making SharePoint the Central Hub for Business," reviews how organizations have changed over the last 20 years with regard to business data, and how these changes led to organizations having pockets of data throughout their business processes. The chapter then explains how BCS can provide a uniform method of accessing data for all stakeholders in an organization.

Chapter 2, "Introducing Business Connectivity Services," introduces the types of solutions you can create with BCS and how you can plan and extend BCS. This chapter explores the BCS architecture and how it is divided into four layers: external system, connectivity, presentation, and tools.

Chapter 3, "Creating and Maintaining Business Data Connectivity Service Applications," first explains the SharePoint service application architecture and its effect on the deployment of BCS. The chapter then breaks down the server administration tasks to create and configure a Business Data Connectivity (BDC) service application, explains the security options, outlines how to configure the Secure Store Service, discusses modifications to the BCS throttling settings, and details the administration of BCS in a tenant environment.

Chapter 4, "Defining External System Connections Using SharePoint Designer," helps you hook up external data with SharePoint and Office applications with the creation of an external content type (ECT). The chapter explains that while you can use other tools to create an ECT, SharePoint Designer provides you with a wizard to easily define the BDC model, ECT, BDC objects, and operations that you are allowed to perform on the external system.

Part II: Presenting External Data

In this part, you'll learn how to extend the user experience to display and manipulate content from an external system in Office 2010 client applications and websites built on top of SharePoint 2010.

Chapter 5, "Creating External Lists and Using External Data in Lists and Libraries," explains that the preferred method of displaying data from external data sources is to use external lists. The chapter helps you use both the browser and SharePoint Designer to create external lists, and finishes by showing you how to use external columns in SharePoint lists and libraries.

Chapter 6, "Building Business Data Dashboards," explores how to build business data dashboards using Business Data Web Parts and other Web Parts, and how to configure them in an effective way.

Chapter 7, "Using External Data with Office Client Applications," helps you use external data within Microsoft Office applications, such as Microsoft Word, Microsoft Outlook, Microsoft SharePoint Workspace, and Microsoft Access, as well as how to modify external list forms with Microsoft InfoPath Designer 2010.

Chapter 8, "Finding Information from External Systems," provides tools and strategies that allow organizations to provide their users with the ability to search for all relevant business data, whether it is stored within SharePoint SQL content databases or outside SharePoint. This chapter explains the search options available, depending on the version of SharePoint 2010 that you are using.

Chapter 9, "Using External Data in User Profiles," explains how you can use BCS to populate user profile data that exists elsewhere within your organization, and explores how this benefits an organization when using SharePoint 2010 features such as people search and audience targeting. This chapter also explains how you can use Duet Enterprise to connect SharePoint 2010 and SAP solutions.

Chapter 10, "Exploring Office 365 and Connecting to External Data," helps you to connect SharePoint Online, which is part of Office 365, to external data. It compares the use of BCS SharePoint Online with dedicated SharePoint Online and with an on-premises installation of SharePoint 2010. The chapter finishes by describing how to build a SharePoint Online BCS solution.

Part III: Extending the Out-of-the-Box Business Connectivity Services Functionality

In this part, you'll explore the options you can use to extend BCS.

Chapter 11, "Using Client-Side Code and External Data," introduces the SharePoint 2010 Client Object Model and how you can leverage client-side code to create solutions to greatly extend how your organization works with line-of-business (LoB) data.

Chapter 12, "Building Server-Side BCS Solutions," introduces the use of Visual Studio to build SharePoint solutions, how to use Visual Studio to build solutions that execute code on SharePoint servers, as well as how to use Visual Studio to create and deploy BDC models.

The Appendix, "BCS Model Infrastructure," describes the BCS metadata object hierarchy and details the relationships among commonly used metadata objects.

Conventions

The following conventions are used in this book:

- Boldface type is used to indicate text that you type.

- The first letters of the names of ribbon tabs, dialog boxes, dialog box elements, and commands are capitalized. For example, the Save As dialog box.

- Keyboard shortcuts are indicated by a plus sign (+) separating key names. For example, Ctrl+Alt+Delete means that you press the Ctrl, Alt, and Delete keys at the same time.

About the Companion Content

We have included companion content to enrich your learning experience. The companion content for this book can be downloaded from the following page:

http://go.microsoft.com/FWLink/?Linkid=248519

The companion content includes the following:

■ The BDC model project used in Chapter 12, "Building Server-Side BCS Solutions."

■ The BDC model *.bdcm* file referenced in the Appendix, "BCS Model Infrastructure."

Acknowledgments

We'd like to include a special thanks to Kenyon Brown (O'Reilly Media senior editor), Neil Hodgkinson (technical reviewer), Kristen Borg (O'Reilly Media production editor), Nicole Flores (copyeditor), and all the people at O'Reilly who kept us on track and provided such excellent suggestions.

Writing a book is never easy and it places a considerable amount of strain on personal and professional lives. On many occasions while writing this book, we ignored our families and loved ones, even when we were supposed to be on holiday with them. So it is with our greatest appreciation and admiration that we say thank you to them.

Support and Feedback

The following sections provide information on errata, book support, feedback, and contact information.

Errata

We've made every effort to ensure the accuracy of this book and its companion content. Any errors that have been reported since this book was published are listed on our Microsoft Press site at *www.oreilly.com*:

http://go.microsoft.com/FWLink/?Linkid=248518

If you find an error that is not already listed, you can report it to us through the same page.

If you need additional support, email Microsoft Press Book Support at *mspinput@ microsoft.com*.

Please note that product support for Microsoft software is not offered through the addresses above.

We Want to Hear from You

At Microsoft Press, your satisfaction is our top priority, and your feedback our most valuable asset. Please tell us what you think of this book at:

www.microsoft.com/learning/booksurvey

The survey is short, and we read every one of your comments and ideas. Thanks in advance for your input!

Stay in Touch

Let's keep the conversation going! We are on Twitter:

www.twitter.com/MicrosoftPress

PART I

Planning and Maintaining Business Connectivity Services

CHAPTER 1

Making SharePoint the Central Hub for Business

In this chapter, you will:

- Review how organizations have changed their approach to business data over the last 20 years

- Understand why organizations have islands of data throughout their business processes

- Learn how a familiar application such as SharePoint can help resolve the problem of distributed data

- Learn how Business Connectivity Services can provide a uniform method of accessing data for all stakeholders in an organization

Before you learn how to use Business Connectivity Services (BCS) to make external data available to SharePoint, it is important to understand how and why the technology is so useful.

In this chapter, you will review a real-world company and how it changed in the early 1990s as a result of the evolution of email and the Internet, both of which made accessing data more efficient. You will then examine a real-world problem seen in many businesses today, where senior management and other business users often require business data to be available in a single location so that they can closely monitor all aspects of the organization. Having business data immediately available is important at any time, but especially so within a challenging economic climate.

Data is often spread across an organization in different systems and with different user interfaces, and accessing this data to provide business intelligence can be difficult. Getting the right data into the format you need can be challenging and time-consuming, especially when the data needs to come from several sources. It takes time to learn each system, and then additional time to take snapshots of data that soon becomes out of date. In the latter part of this chapter, you will explore how you can use BCS to bring business data into SharePoint to make business-critical and required information easily accessible. Finally, you will examine a realistic scenario using Adventure Works as an example of a modern-day business, and you will learn how BCS can be used to meet the needs of the Adventure Works business users.

Reviewing How Businesses Store Data

Let's start by looking at a real-world company and the changes it underwent in the 1990s with respect to business data. A global distribution company in 1993 provided storage and distribution of electronic components. The electronic components were packed within the warehouse and shipped to customers throughout the world. Over four years, this company experienced a huge change in the way that it operated, purely due to the development of computer software and how that software was used within each department.

In 1993, the company mainly used Windows 3.0 as an operating system, with only a handful of computers using Windows 3.1, which incorporated networking capabilities. The networking capabilities back then were primarily used for some file sharing, but mainly printer sharing. Besides that, some data was available on dumb terminals from a mainframe system based in the United States.

Teams of people within the organization worked on each customer contract, processing the orders. The order process typically involved receiving faxes of required goods from a customer and then typing the contents of the faxes into a spreadsheet, which was then printed and hand-delivered to the warehouse for packing. The address details for the delivery were then hand-typed again into another software application to produce the shipping label. Tracking the status of the order was usually carried out by telephone.

Soon, technology moved on and the organization began receiving orders by Electronic Data Interchange (EDI), which involved using a single computer to dial up to another computer via modem, in order to receive an electronic file containing the orders to be shipped. This data was then imported into an application called Wisdom.

Within a couple of years, customers were placing their own orders via a website. They used a custom application for the orders and warehouse shipping, which was replicated via an ISDN line to a central server, allowing the rest of the company to report on the data. Customers could track an order using their order tracking number on the website.

Technology evolved very quickly back then, which meant that businesses went from storing physical documents and mailing them when required, to electronic storage and email—within just a few years. Through the use of networking, relational databases, and Internet technology, customers and business users had a much better experience.

However, one big problem existed then and often still exists today: islands of data. For example, say a given tracking system in an organization works exceptionally well, but you want to get a big-picture view of what is going on in the organization. What if you need to know your revenue and profit for the quarter, along with the number of successful deliveries, the number of days your staff were absent, and so on? In the past, obtaining all that information often meant involving other people and departments, and receiving numerous spreadsheets all formatted differently; or you had to track down the information yourself, which meant gaining access to and learning lots of dissimilar systems. The data is out there, but it is separated out on various "islands" spread across different departments, technologies, and systems.

Each department and sometimes each branch of an organization may use its own system for business processes. You will often also find these systems duplicated within an organization with different technologies—for example, Adventure Works in the United Kingdom may use Microsoft Dynamics CRM for customer relationship management, while Adventure Works in the United States might use Salesforce.com. In addition, the human resources group might be using an Oracle application for personnel data, the accounting department may be using Sage for invoicing, and so forth. Each part of the business could be using an application designed specifically for its departmental business processes. It is logical that when you design a system, you are not designing it for the entire organization; rather, you are designing it for a business process, and for that reason, your organization uses great applications for its individual business processes. One issue with this approach is that your organization's departments may use dissimilar technologies for data storage, and each software application has a different user interface, reinforcing the islands of data problem.

To resolve this issue, you certainly don't want to create an application that is generic enough to provide all of the required services across the entire organization. You'll just end up with a jack-of-all-trades application that has fewer capabilities and functionality than the software designed to solve a particular business process. The solution to this problem lies in using Microsoft SharePoint and Business Connectivity Services (BCS) to provide a central hub for all of the business information within the organization.

Note Sometimes the "islands of data" issue arises as the result of a company acquisition—for example, a merger of two large airlines. When a merger such as this occurs, you will have at least two of everything to deal with: two CRM systems, two booking systems, two intranets, and so forth. BCS and SharePoint can bring these two sets of data together for reporting purposes.

Bringing Data Together in One Place with Business Connectivity Services

Today's businesses thrive on business intelligence. Business people want to be able to troubleshoot problems before they occur (and result in cash-flow issues or even a lack of demand for a specific product). The ability to quickly obtain this business-critical information is of great importance.

A good example of the use of business-critical information is illustrated in a story that comes from a member of the SharePoint community. This person is a business analyst whose job is to provide reporting capabilities for organizations. He was producing some charts based upon products and sales per store when his attention was immediately drawn to a line on a chart showing that sales of chewing gum in a particular store had suddenly stopped. Sales of this chewing gum brand went from hundreds of packages per day to zero per day. He thought this strange, as all of the other store branches were still selling the product successfully. He checked the stock levels at the store, which appeared to be fine, and the product was still current—yet this store had not sold a single pack of the chewing gum for three days. He called the store manager, who discovered that a poster had fallen from the wall and was covering the box of chewing gum. Without business intelligence, this issue might have gone unnoticed for weeks.

SharePoint can be used to bring information together into an easy-to-use, easy-to-navigate central hub of business data. The central hub provides you with the ability to search, view, modify, and report on information across your organization's data and even beyond, to data outside of your organization.

An Internet search engine is a good example of the central hub concept. You can use a single Internet search engine to search websites for data all over the world, regardless of where that data resides. As a user, you don't care what technology is used to store the data for Amazon or Expedia, for example, and you don't care what language was used to develop the website. All you care about is being able to see and retrieve the data quickly when you want it, via a familiar Internet search site.

Figure 1-1 shows how easy it is to get the information you want in a single place. From the Bing search engine, you can retrieve the weather report for your region without having to go to a specific website or television channel.

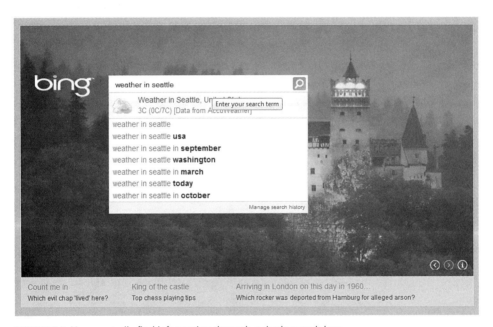

FIGURE 1-1 You can easily find information through a single search box.

You can also create a dashboard of information in some search engines, as shown in Figure 1-2. You could spend a good part of your day going to individual websites to check the weather, read the news, find the latest currency exchange rates, and so on. Sometimes it is more useful to have a single page where you can view all of this information at a glance.

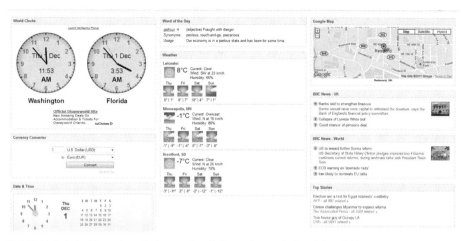

FIGURE 1-2 A dashboard can help you view information and absorb it quickly.

Most of the information in the dashboard in Figure 1-2 is driven through other websites. The data is stored somewhere, but most of the time you don't know or care where it is stored. Have you ever wondered where websites you visit get weather reports from, for example? The National Climatic Data Center (NCDC) and the National Weather Service (NWS) are two examples of weather information providers. The information from these providers is made available for use by news agencies and other websites.

Figure 1-3 shows an example of information aggregated from multiple data sources, which makes it convenient for people to find and use.

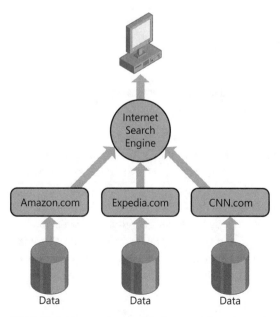

FIGURE 1-3 You can search data from an Internet search engine regardless of the technology used for the website and data storage.

Aggregating data from multiple external data sources is exactly what you can achieve with business data through SharePoint. SharePoint is quickly becoming a familiar interface within organizations, just as Bing and Google are familiar among users for searching the Internet and finding information. You can view SharePoint as a central hub of information, just like an Internet search engine. When you need to see your organization's data, you don't have to learn how to use all of the dissimilar systems the departments in your company use—you simply navigate to SharePoint to see a dashboard of information.

Figure 1-4 shows an example of such a dashboard. The dashboard brings external data into SharePoint from more than one data source.

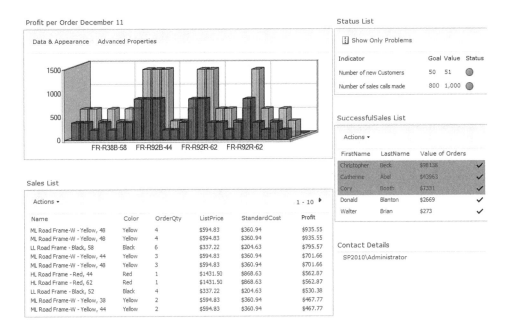

FIGURE 1-4 This SharePoint report page shows sales-related information from the Adventure Works SQL database via BCS.

Notice that the Business Connectivity Services (BCS) Chart Web Part is used to display product sales from the current quarter in a 3D bar graph. The bar graph shows the standard cost versus the list price of each order. Below that graph is a Business Data List Web Part that has been customized using SharePoint Designer 2010, showing the products ordered this month along with the quantity, standard cost, and list price. A custom column has been created that shows the list price multiplied by the order quantity minus the standard cost, multiplied by the order quantity. The cost columns are set in currency format using SharePoint Designer 2010, and the sort order is set to the Profit column in descending order. Lastly, the Web Part is configured to show only the 10 most profitable orders that were taken within this quarter.

In the middle-right of the dashboard is another Business Data List Web Part that is obtaining its data from a custom view within the Adventure Works database. The custom view displays the top five salespeople this quarter. Using SharePoint Designer 2010, the rows are formatted with conditional formatting showing those salespeople who achieved at least $5,000 worth of sales. The rows have a green background if that is the case.

Finally, in the top-right corner is a Status List Web Part displaying key performance indicators (KPIs). Unfortunately, the Key Performance List within SharePoint 2010 does not support external lists that contain external data. You can, however, configure SQL Analysis services to base your KPIs on. SQL Analysis Services is being used to determine the number of sales calls made and the number of new customers. This information is obtained from the Microsoft Dynamics CRM application, not the Adventure Works database. In this way, you can see that information from multiple external data sources can be mashed together or combined within a single dashboard to provide a useful view of live business information.

Using SharePoint as the Central Hub for All Your External Data Sources

To demonstrate how SharePoint can become the central hub for your organization's data, you'll work with a fictitious organization called Adventure Works Cycles throughout this book. Adventure Works Cycles is a large multinational company. The company manufactures and sells metal and composite bicycles to the North American, European, and Asian commercial markets. While its base operation is located in Bothell, Washington, with 290 employees, Adventure Works has several regional sales teams located throughout its market base.

Adventure Works uses a Microsoft SQL Server database to handle buying, manufacturing, and selling bicycles. Within the database, you will find all of the components that make up a bicycle, the cost of each part, and a list of the suppliers for each component. Members of the accounting department use the database primarily to work out the company's profit and loss based upon the sales of each product. The sales at each Adventure Works store are also recorded within the database so that sales information can be retrieved.

The Microsoft SQL Server database is not the only data store within the Adventure Works organization. Sales representatives use Microsoft Dynamics CRM to track and manage the relationship with each Adventure Works customer. In addition, the human resources group uses an Oracle solution to store information about each of the company's 290 employees. Within the Oracle solution is information about each employee, such as the employee's home address, next of kin, salary, skills, and résumé.

Figure 1-5 illustrates all the external data sources that Adventure Works would like to consolidate via SharePoint.

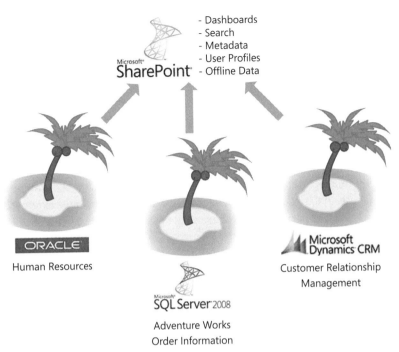

FIGURE 1-5 Adventure Works wants to use these external data sources within SharePoint to provide a common, more intuitive view of the external data.

In addition to building dashboards with external data via Business Connectivity Services (BCS) in SharePoint, you can perform the following tasks on all business data within your organization:

- Search external data.

- Browse external data.

- Use external data within Office documents and metadata.

- Update external data, including inserting, modifying, and deleting information.

- Display dashboards of data made up of charts and KPIs.

- Use external business data to populate SharePoint user profiles.

Through its investment in SharePoint, Adventure Works would like to make better use of the SharePoint product and use it as a central repository where users can obtain business information. Business information, in this case, is a broad category consisting of documents, spreadsheets, databases, websites, employee information, and much more.

You will focus on how you can make business data available to SharePoint throughout this book, but first you need to understand the company's requirements:

- Adventure Works has requested the ability to see who the top-performing salesperson is within the organization. Sales activity, such as the number of calls, is recorded within Microsoft Dynamics CRM, invoices and profit are stored within the Microsoft SQL Server database, and all of the employee information is stored within the Oracle solution. To determine the top-performing salesperson, you need to gather information from all three places. Using a Microsoft SharePoint site, you can connect to each data source and display a dashboard of information from all three data stores. The dashboard can show the highest sales activity within a chart, the largest single order from the Microsoft SQL Server database, and the location of each top-performing salesperson by using connections on the dashboard between the CRM and Oracle applications.

- Adventure Works wants to make business data available within client applications. Adventure Works uses Microsoft Office to produce letters to customers and order more stock from suppliers. The company performs further data analysis using Microsoft Excel. Using BCS, the external data from Microsoft Dynamics CRM, Microsoft SQL Server, and the Oracle application can be made available to Microsoft Office applications through the BCS Client Runtime. Chapter 6, "Building Business Data Dashboards," covers how to use BCS in Office client applications.

Figure 1-6 shows what using external data within a client application such as Microsoft Word looks like. After you complete a document, you can select the external data by clicking the relevant Quick Parts within the Word document.

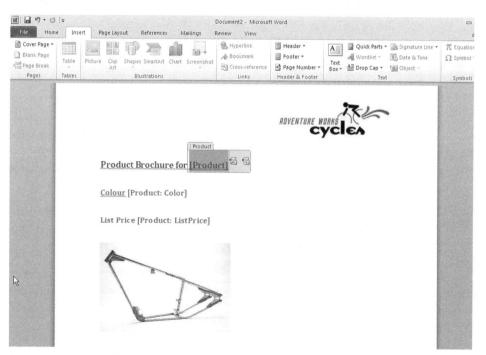

FIGURE 1-6 You can add the external data column to the body of a Microsoft Word 2010 document created from within a document library, allowing external data to be selected from the live external data source.

- Adventure Works would like users to be able to find product information using a search facility (see Figure 1-7). Rather than having the search functionality return product information from multiple sources, such as SharePoint lists, documents, and external data, Adventure Works requested a search page that shows results only from the external databases.

FIGURE 1-7 A single search box in the SharePoint Enterprise Search Center allows you to search external data sources together with or seperately from other data sources, such as documents or list items.

- Adventure Works would like to improve upon the findability of documents. Currently, documents are stored in folders within document libraries, and the libraries have taken on the same poor structure as the folders on the file server, including duplicate folders and subfolders created in the wrong locations. Adventure Works would like users to be able to find documents more easily, using metadata that is consistent with the external data sources.

- Each department of Adventure Works would like a team site with an announcements list. The announcements should be aggregated from each of the subsites and displayed in a single location. Some announcements are not of interest to everybody within Adventure Works, however, so the announcements should be targeted. To avoid duplicating the personnel information within the Oracle database, Adventure Works would like the SharePoint user profiles within SharePoint to be populated with the department users work in, who they report to, and what skills they have. This will allow audience targeting to be more effective.

- Adventure Works is considering the possibility of hosting SharePoint online with Office 365. The company would like to know how to make its business data available to SharePoint in the future, even if the data resides on the premises and SharePoint is hosted in the cloud.

Throughout this book, you will learn how to fulfill the Adventure Works requirements, along with how to connect to the external data systems and administer BCS to ensure that security and performance requirements are also met.

Building New Solutions

SharePoint is a big investment within an organization due to the need to purchase hardware, software licenses, training, and consultancy. It is therefore sometimes incorrectly assumed that SharePoint should be able to provide everything the organization needs going forward. SharePoint becomes the automatic solution to every problem.

As powerful as it is, SharePoint cannot do everything. It does not replace relational database technology, spreadsheets, or file systems. It often happens that after adopting SharePoint, companies move all their files from the file system into SharePoint, and SharePoint lists are used for data storage. File systems still have their place, as many organizations have extremely large files (such as video files) that are just too big to upload and download on a daily basis. Although SharePoint is not necessarily the place to store such files, it can make your file shares available, helping to make SharePoint the central hub for business information.

This book focuses on new business solutions. After your organization has made a big investment in SharePoint, if you require a new business solution such as a help desk application, the answer that you hear might be to use SharePoint. Is SharePoint the right tool for a help desk application? Maybe. But you still need to analyze all of the help desk applications available and consider them against developing a custom solution versus using existing technology within your company. You might find that SharePoint lists, InfoPath forms, and Workflow provide you with the solution that you require. That said, you might also find that the type of data you want to gather is more suitable for storage in a relational database than in SharePoint lists, or that the chosen help desk solution already uses a relational database back end.

The point is that if you decide to use SharePoint to build all your future solutions, you are likely to be disappointed. SharePoint cannot replace Microsoft Excel or Microsoft SQL Server, but it makes for an excellent tool to expose Microsoft Excel spreadsheets and Microsoft SQL Server databases to users. While SharePoint now offers IDs for documents and list items, it cannot reproduce the relationships required in a relational database management system and, for that matter, it cannot match the performance.

Your organization should still carefully consider its software choices, but keep in mind that even if you opt for an off-the-shelf application that uses a relational database back end, you can make that data available to SharePoint. For example, the help desk team will use the help desk application on a daily basis to receive trouble tickets, escalate tickets, and report bugs. SharePoint can be used to display dashboards showing how many tickets were resolved successfully last month, how many times the service-level agreements were broken, and which employee handled the most tickets.

Although you can't use SharePoint to resolve every business problem that exists today, you can often use it as part of a new system. SharePoint is many things to many people, and it is a difficult product to describe. Using SharePoint as a central hub of information for existing systems as well as future systems will at least make information more accessible.

Summary

This chapter presented an overview of the business problems that Business Connectivity Services (BCS) resolves. These business problems include the fact that organizations often contain lots of data that is stored in dissimilar systems and databases throughout different departments. You learned that by using BCS, you are able to aggregate these external data sources into one familiar application, such as Microsoft SharePoint.

In this chapter, you learned how the problem of isolated data sources came about and also how it can be resolved. The chapter introduced the fictitious company called Adventure Works that you will be working with throughout the book. Some of the business problems that Adventure Works would like to resolve with BCS were highlighted.

This chapter has provided a foundation for subsequent chapters to build on, to show how some of the services BCS has to offer can help a real-world organization.

CHAPTER 2

Introducing Business Connectivity Services

In this chapter, you will:

■ Learn what Business Connectivity Services is and the types of solutions you can create with it

■ Explore the Business Connectivity Services architecture

■ Learn how Business Connectivity Services connects to external systems

■ Overview how to extend Business Connectivity Services

■ Plan for a Business Connectivity Services solution

Chapter 1, "Making SharePoint the Central Hub for Business," discussed the frequent problems enterprises have when integrating disparate business data. Many organizations see Microsoft SharePoint as yet another silo of information that can only exploit data stored in lists and libraries. However, by using Microsoft Business Connectivity Services (BCS), an organization does not need to move all its data into SharePoint to build integrated business solutions, bringing together the business processes and the business data in a familiar user experience.

BCS—the evolution of the Business Data Catalog, which was shipped with Microsoft Office SharePoint Server 2007—is a key feature of SharePoint 2010. First introduced in the Enterprise edition of Microsoft Office SharePoint Server 2007, Business Data Catalog enabled you to integrate data stored in SharePoint with data from line-of-business (LoB) applications and other enterprise and Web 2.0 data sources. It allowed you to connect to business data from back-end systems and then, by using prebuilt Web Parts, you could display information from these external data sources on dashboards without the need for coding.

With Microsoft SharePoint Server 2010, these features have been enhanced. BCS is now available in the base product, Microsoft SharePoint Foundation 2010, and SharePoint Online, which is part of Microsoft Office 365.

This chapter introduces some key elements of BCS and forms the foundation of the rest of the book. You'll learn about BCS, look at its architecture and how it connects to the external system, and consider its security implications. This chapter also introduces the integration of BCS with Microsoft Office client applications and examines how you can use BCS features to build composite solutions and dashboard pages, making SharePoint and Office a simpler and more cost-effective platform to integrate with your business data. The rest of the book explores each of these areas in detail, showing how BCS can help you mitigate the frequent problems enterprises have when integrating disparate business data, as discussed in Chapter 1.

What Is Office 365?

Office 365 is Microsoft's cloud-based software as a service (SaaS) offering that consists of Microsoft Office Professional Plus, Microsoft SharePoint Online, Microsoft Exchange Online, Microsoft Lync Online, and Microsoft Office Web Apps. Office 365 allows you to collaborate and access email, web conferencing, documents, and calendars from anywhere you have access to the Internet. There are two versions of Office 365: Standard and Dedicated. The Standard version is hosted on shared (multitenant) servers and consists of a number of plans. Plan P is aimed at small businesses with fewer than 50 employees, and Plan E accounts are for larger organizations, as well as educational organizations. The Dedicated version of Office 365 is hosted on server hardware that is dedicated to a particular customer and is intended for organizations with at least 20,000 users. You can find more information about BCS with SharePoint Online in Chapter 10, "Exploring Office 365 and Connecting to External Data."

What Is Business Connectivity Services?

Business Connectivity Services (BCS) in SharePoint 2010 enables integration with line-of-business (LoB) applications and other external data sources. As mentioned previously, BCS is built on the SharePoint Server 2007 Business Data Catalog technology. It bridges the gap between the various applications that an enterprise uses for surfacing key business data, from platforms such as Siebel, CRM, and SAP or data stored in a mainframe such as an AS/400 system, to SharePoint sites, lists, search functions, user profiles, and Microsoft Office applications.

As noted in Chapter 1, many companies have invested a lot of time and money into the LoB systems that manage their business, with each LoB system having its own specialist and set of management tools. The data from the external system is typically business critical, yet it cannot be used by the end users who need it. Those end users who can access the LoB system data have to contend with multiple different user interfaces (UIs) with an array of terminology. Typically these end users have undergone training in each UI and have developed their own cheat sheets to translate terms in the UIs into their everyday business speech.

The aim of BCS (and any solutions you build with BCS) is to simply streamline the access to external data for end users who need to use it. That is, BCS connects with the external systems and exposes the external data either in SharePoint or in Office applications, such as Outlook 2010, Access 2010, and SharePoint Workspace 2010.

When using BCS, organizations no longer have to train their developers and end users in multiple systems. Professional developers need to learn only one method of developing against the external systems: the BCS application programming interfaces (APIs). End users can exploit their knowledge of SharePoint and Office applications to use LoB data in their business decisions.

Types of BCS Solutions

Solutions that bring together data from a number of systems to assist in the automation of a business process are known as *composites* in SharePoint. BCS is a key component in building composites. BCS solutions can be divided into three types, as shown in Figure 2-1.

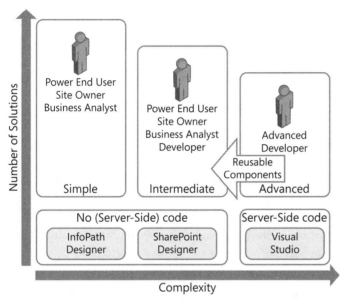

FIGURE 2-1 The three types of BCS solutions are simple, intermediate, and advanced.

- **Simple** Built using the out-of-the-box capabilities within SharePoint. Connecting Office applications to external lists exposes the external data, such as when you use a Quick Part in Word 2010. Many of these simple solutions require that the definition of how to connect to the external system is already in existence. The solution is built almost entirely using the ribbon in the browser or Office applications.

- **Intermediate** Built by power end users, site owners, or business analysts. Such users, termed "citizen developers" by Gartner, Inc., operate outside the scope of IT, work in the business domain, and can use the WYSIWYG tools to create new business applications for consumption by others.

Citizen developers use a combination of technologies, such as InfoPath forms, webpages, workflows, and integration into Office applications, such as Outlook task panes or Word documents. Citizen developers know what they want to achieve, they understand their business needs, and with a bit of SharePoint knowledge, they can wire together the business processes or sets of tasks.

Intermediate solutions are more complex than simple solutions, and they may involve the use of Office application macros or the manipulation of XSLT using the code view of Microsoft SharePoint Designer 2010. Therefore, citizen developers may initially need some training or help from the organization's central SharePoint team, particularly if they have never used SharePoint Designer or InfoPath Designer before.

> **Note** Gartner, Inc. reports that citizen developers will build at least 25 percent of new business applications by 2014 (see *www.gartner.com/it/page.jsp?id=1744514*) and warns that IT departments that fail to capitalize on the opportunities that citizen development presents will find themselves unable to respond to rapidly changing market forces and customer preferences.

- **Advanced** Built by the IT department and professional developers, involving the development of reusable components to augment simple and intermediate solutions or solutions that require a deep knowledge of architectural concerns and a formal code, test, deploy, and support management process. Such reusable components could include .NET assembly connectors to connect, aggregate, and transform data from external systems, custom Web Parts, custom workflow actions that can be used from within SharePoint Designer, code for InfoPath forms, or extensions to the browser UI. Many of these components can only be developed with the use of Visual Studio.

IT departments will need to differentiate between the types of solutions citizen developers can create and those that the IT department should develop. When this identification process is completed successfully, it should free up IT resources for more complex problems.

Although many business users will have developed complex solutions with, say, Excel, that involved thousands of rows of data, the simple and intermediate types of BCS solutions will be based around forms or business processes. While many users in an organization may not have the specific data skills to build solutions in Excel or Access, they may have the SharePoint skills to create SharePoint solutions in which BCS defines data from multiple external systems. Because users will see little difference in creating solutions where data lives within SharePoint databases and solutions where data is stored in external systems, they are likely to promote the use of BCS related solutions throughout the organization.

The increased use of citizen developers to create business solutions may be new to an organization and will instigate a user adoption strategy as well as an education program. This education program will be focused more on introducing and managing the changes in the way the business will work going forward than enhancing skill sets. Other organizations may assimilate the use of SharePoint and its tools into their formal/informal reengineering process. Whichever way an organization chooses to introduce SharePoint and BCS, it should not be seen by end users as another task for them to complete in their already busy day; rather, end users should be encouraged to view the use of these technologies as a new way of working, so they can accomplish more in the same amount of time.

Many of the most successful SharePoint solutions are built by the users who use them: the citizen developers. The solutions are successful because the citizen developers know what they want to achieve, they are using the solutions as they develop them, and they can resolve any problems, including issues that can only be uncovered by using the solution. Citizen developers find that there is no need to provide feedback to others or raise incidents with their organization's help desk. These citizen developers are probably very passionate about their own SharePoint solutions. Therefore, when an organization encourages citizen developers to instigate the business reengineering process, it is more likely that other users in the organization will adopt the solution, as one of their own developed it, and that person knew the business requirements and experienced firsthand the issues of the solution.

Key to the success of this paradigm shift is that organizations need to take the citizen development strategy into consideration with any development process. That is, any SharePoint-related development project needs to add to the list of citizen developer tools, continuing the SharePoint philosophy of self-service for end users, content owners, business owners, and site owners.

By using the different types of BCS solutions, an organization can accomplish the following objectives:

- Reduce or eliminate the code required to access LoB systems.

- Achieve deeper integration of data into places where an end user works.

- Centralize deployment of data source definitions for use by both BCS and Office applications.

- Reduce latency to access and manipulate data. After a data source is defined in the BCS repository, it will be immediately available to the web applications associated with that particular BCS service application.

- Centralize data security auditing and connections.

- Perform structured data searches.

The Structure of a BCS Solution

Both SharePoint Designer and Microsoft Visual Studio 2010 enable users to model how to connect with external business systems. Once a BCS model is created, the data from the external system can be surfaced within the browser or Office application. Then, depending on the operations defined within the model, the end user can manipulate the external system data with full create, read, update, and delete (CRUD) operation support. The definitions within the BCS model enable full integration into SharePoint Server 2010, such as surfacing data from an external system within search or a user's profile.

Note One feature often cited as new for BCS in SharePoint 2010 is the ability to write back to external systems. You could create SharePoint Server 2007 Business Data Catalog data source definitions that allowed you to update or insert data into the external data sources; however, none of the out-of-the-box Web Parts exposed this feature. You needed a developer to create a custom Web Part to match the data source definition.

A BCS solution can be divided into four layers:

- **External System** Layer that contains the external content.

- **Connectivity** Layer that connects the presentation layer with the external system. It uses different types of connectors depending on the interfaces supported by the external systems, together with information defined in an XML file, known as the Business Data Connectivity (BDC) model, to read and write data to and from the external system.

- **Presentation** Layer that extends the user experience (UX) to display and manipulate content from external systems in Office 2010 client applications and websites built on top of SharePoint 2010.

- **Tools** Layer used to develop solutions and create the BDC model.

Figure 2-2 shows the high-level interaction among the four layers, SharePoint 2010, and Office applications.

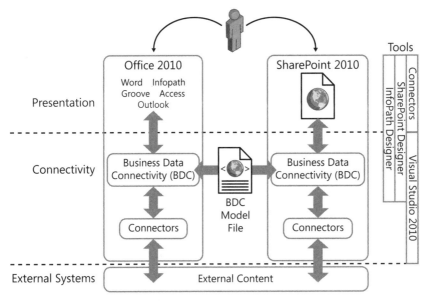

FIGURE 2-2 The high-level architecture of BCS.

External System

This layer contains the external data. Before using BCS, you should work with the owners of the external system to evaluate the best method to connect to it. There may be more than one method—for example, you may obtain the data from the external system by directly interrogating the database or by using a web services interface. If your external system does not have a compatible interface, you can develop your own BCS connector or expose the content as a web service.

Connectivity

This layer of BCS connects to the external systems and is referred to as Business Data Connectivity (BDC). (Note that this acronym was used in the previous version of SharePoint, where it represented the Business Data Catalog.) To connect to the external system, you need to define the location of the external system, the protocol to use, and the credentials. Once connected, you need to define the operations on the data that are allowed and the format of the data that will be returned. The operations that can be used on the external data and its format are defined in an external content type (ECT). The definition of the location of the external system together with the ECT is known as the *BDC model*.

The BDC model consists of XML declarations that describe the external system you want to access as well as the operations you want to perform on the external data. For example, you might want to read a data record, update one data record, or delete one data record. You can create the BDC model on a development or test SharePoint installation, and from there download and import it into the SharePoint production farm, a SharePoint installation that is installed on one or more servers that share the same SharePoint configuration database.

See Also *You can find detailed information on the BDC model XML schema in Appendix A, "BCS Model Infrastructure."*

All BDC models to be used within SharePoint are stored in a Microsoft SQL Server database created especially for the use of BCS, known as the metadata store or ECT repository.

Microsoft Office 2010 client applications can also use the BDC model. Office 2010 client applications only contain components to upload a BDC model, so Office 2010 client applications do not provide any management or configuration interface. With SharePoint 2010, however, you can use the SharePoint 2010 Central Administration website or Windows PowerShell to manage and configure the BDC model.

See Also *For more information about creating a BDC model, see Chapter 4, "Defining External System Connections Using SharePoint Designer."*

Presentation

BCS enables you to bring external data into SharePoint and Office and allows end users to gain insight into the underlying data in a reusable way. SharePoint uses the information in the BDC model to present the external data using external lists, the Business Data Web Part, external data columns, and external data search, as well as by using SharePoint Designer to create Data Form Web Parts (DFWPs) to display the data. Other Web Parts, such as the Chart Web Part, can also present external data.

Your professional developers could create new Web Parts to present the data, but typically your citizen developers will use tools such as the browser, InfoPath Designer, or SharePoint Designer. For example, in SharePoint 2010, you can display data from external systems on publishing pages, Web Part pages, and wiki pages. No matter which page you are working with, external data is exposed by using Web Parts. For example, external lists use Web Part pages to create views of the external data. These pages contain the XSLT List View (XLV) Web Part, or you can choose to use an InfoPath form or the DFWP. The XLV Web Part and the DFWP use XSLT, and you can use SharePoint Designer's WYSI-WYG editing pane as well as its code view to amend the code for these Web Parts.

 Note External data can also be exposed when you use SharePoint search or in a user's profile. Some of the search Web Parts also use XSLT to present a user-friendly view of the data.

External data can also be presented in Office 2010 client applications by connecting through SharePoint to the external systems or by using the BDC model to connect directly with the external systems.

See Also *You can find more information about how to present external data in SharePoint and in Office applications in Part II of this book.*

Tools

Both SharePoint and Office client applications provide programming interfaces that use BCS and allow professional developers to create solutions. SharePoint 2010 also provides tools for the power user, site owners, and business analysts—the citizen developer tools, such as SharePoint Designer and Microsoft InfoPath Designer.

You can use Visual Studio 2010 to create the BDC model, interact with the BCS program interfaces, and manipulate BDC objects. Third-party tools are also available for you to work with, and you can even use an XML editor, such as XML Notepad 2007 or Notepad, to create a BDC model.

Interaction Between the Layers

There is a close symmetry between the BCS architecture of a SharePoint installation and Office 2010 applications. The Office 2010 client applications do not have a BDC metadata store, but they have a BDC client-side cache that is used to store the BDC model when data from an external list is taken offline. If amendments are made while the client is offline, they are stored in the client data cache and committed to the external system when the client is next online.

The offline data from the external list is also stored in the client-side cache, within a SQL Compact Edition client database. When the user's computer is turned off, the BDC model and the offline external data is persisted.

Also, note in Figure 2-2 that Office 2010 client applications have their own connectors. When you switch from offline mode to online mode, the Office application connects directly to the external system without connecting through SharePoint. Access 2010 can import a client-side version of the BDC model, therefore it does not need to connect to SharePoint at all—it connects directly to the external system.

Alternative Methods of Connecting SharePoint 2010 with External Systems

SharePoint 2010 provides the following methods of integrating with data that is not stored in SharePoint:

- **Access Services**   This service application is available in the Enterprise edition of SharePoint Server 2010 and the P1, E3, and P4 plans of SharePoint Online. You can also create a Web Database by publishing a Microsoft Access 2010 database, where data held in Access tables is moved to SharePoint lists and forms and reports are created as webpages. You can then access the web database using the browser or the Access client application. You can find more information about using Access Services in the Microsoft paper "Improving the Reach and Manageability of Microsoft Access 2010 Database Applications with Microsoft Access Services" at *www.microsoft.com/download/en/details.aspx?id=19061*.

- **Visio Services**   This service application is available in the Enterprise edition of SharePoint Server 2010 and the E3 and E4 plans of SharePoint Online. It allows you to share and view Microsoft Visio 2010 web drawings (*.vdw* files) in the browser without the Visio client application or the Visio viewer installed on your local computer. The Visio web drawings can contain visuals that are linked to data from an external data source. Visio Services can fetch the data from these linked data sources and update the visuals of a Visio web drawing. Only Microsoft Visio Professional 2010 and Microsoft Visio Premium 2010 can publish Visio web diagrams to a SharePoint Server 2010 site. You can find more information about using Visio Services at *http://technet.microsoft.com/en-us/library/ee663482.aspx*.

- **Excel Services**   With this service application, you can publish Microsoft Excel 2010 workbooks to SharePoint 2010, which allows users to view and interact with the workbooks in their browser. First introduced in the Enterprise edition of SharePoint Server 2007, Excel Services is now implemented as a service application available in the Enterprise edition of SharePoint Server 2010. It consists of Excel Calculation Services, the Microsoft Excel Web Access Web Part, and Excel Web Services for programmatic access. Excel workbooks hosted in Excel Services can connect to external data using embedded connection definitions, or connection definitions can be stored in a data connection library. Excel Services is available in all plans of SharePoint Online, where it can connect only to data stored within SharePoint Online. You can find more information about Excel Services at *http://technet.microsoft.com/en-us/library/ee424405.aspx*.

- **PerformancePoint Services** PerformancePoint is available in the Enterprise edition of SharePoint Server 2010 as a service application. At the time of this writing, it is not available in any SharePoint Online plan. PerformancePoint Services allows you to monitor and analyze business information by providing tools to build dashboards, reports, scorecards, and key performance indicators (KPIs). All data used in PerformancePoint is classified as external data, including data stored in SharePoint lists or Excel files published to Excel Services. However, data stored within SharePoint can only be used in PerformancePoint in read-only mode. You can use PerformancePoint to connect to tabular data in SQL Server tables, Excel workbooks, and multidimensional (Analysis Services) data sources, and you can use a PowerPivot model built using the PowerPivot add-in for Excel as a data source. You can find more information about PerformancePoint Services at *http://technet.microsoft.com/en-us/library/ee681486.aspx*.

- **InfoPath forms** With InfoPath, you can create both forms and browser-based forms. Users entering data into forms require Microsoft InfoPath Filler 2010. For browser-based forms, users need only a browser and InfoPath Form Services. Form templates for both types of forms can be created using Microsoft InfoPath Designer 2010. Forms created using InfoPath can connect to data sources such as SharePoint lists or web services. Forms or browser-based forms can be saved in a SharePoint Form library. The ASPX pages in external lists that allow you to create, read, update, and modify data from an external system can be replaced with InfoPath browser-based forms.

- **InfoPath Form Services (IFS)** This service application enables InfoPath browser-based forms to be rendered in SharePoint 2010. This service is available only in the Enterprise edition of SharePoint Server 2010 and the E3 and E4 plans of SharePoint Online. However, in the Standard edition of SharePoint Server, a version of IFS is activated that allows you to use InfoPath workflow association and initiation forms. IFS is not a SharePoint 2010 service application, but it is configured at the farm level using the SharePoint 2010 Central Administration website. For more information about IFS, see *http://technet.microsoft.com/en-us/library/cc262498.aspx*.

- **Microsoft SQL Server 2008 R2 Reporting Services (SSRS)** When installed, this free add-in for SharePoint Technologies 2010 allows you to run SSRS Report Server within SharePoint 2010, where the SSRS reports, items, and properties are stored in SharePoint. Users can browse to SharePoint libraries to find the reports, and if they have sufficient permissions to use the Report Builder, they can create reports. You can find an overview of SSRS and SharePoint integration at *http://msdn.microsoft.com/en-us/library/bb326356.aspx*.

- **Data Sources gallery using SharePoint Designer** Using Microsoft FrontPage 2003, and then later Microsoft Office SharePoint Designer 2007, you could connect, present, and modify data from several types of external data sources using the Data Source Library and Data Source Details task panes. This method is still available with SharePoint Designer 2010 with the Data Sources gallery, which you can access through the Navigation pane. The Data Sources gallery replaces the Data Source Library task pane in SharePoint Designer 2007. The advantage of using BCS as opposed to the Data Source gallery in SharePoint Designer is that you define the external system and external content type (ECT) only once, and you can then use that ECT on many sites across all web applications that are associated with the BDC service application. The disadvantage is that ECT designers must be given edit permissions to the metadata store, which is a high level of security, whereas with the Data Source gallery you only need to be, for example, a site owner. In addition, you need to set other BCS security settings to allow users to access the external content. You can implement these settings using the SharePoint 2010 Central Administration website or Windows PowerShell. Setting the correct level of BCS security requires a level of collaboration between the ECT designer and the SharePoint farm administrator, which in a large organization are typically two different people.

Introducing the BCS Architecture

A SharePoint 2010 installation can consist of one or more servers, depending on the number of concurrent users to the SharePoint sites and the functionality they use. Such a collection of servers is called a SharePoint *farm*, and it uses a client/server architecture, as shown in Figure 2-3.

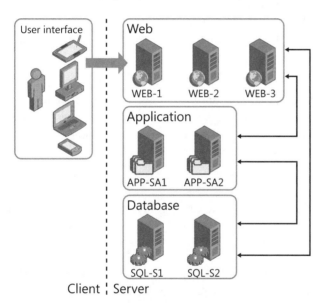

FIGURE 2-3 SharePoint 2010 is installed as a client/server architecture.

The server architecture consists of four tiers:

- **User interface** Hosts the applications that access the data from the external system. The UI applications run on the user's computer, laptop, tablet, or mobile device. These applications could be a browser; one of the Office client applications, such as Word 2010 or InfoPath Filler; a third-party application; or an application that your organization created.

- **Web** Hosts the IIS Web Server Infrastructure and ASP.NET Framework that SharePoint websites use. The first part of a SharePoint website—for example, *http://www.adventure-works.com* or *http://intranet*—maps to an IIS website, which in turn maps to what in SharePoint is known as a *web application*. This tier responds to requests from the user interface, and directs requests to the appropriate application server and obtains data from the database server. This tier, like the other two tiers, could consist of more than one server for resiliency and load reasons:

  - **Resiliency** If one server is lost, there is still at least one server that can respond to user requests.

  - **Load** If the requests from users cannot be serviced by one server, another server should be added to make the solution scalable. When this tier consists of more than one server, the load is balanced across the servers, and it appears to the world as if it is a single URL.

- **Application** Hosts services associated with SharePoint 2010 service applications. Service applications are a separate SharePoint 2010 functionality that allows you to manage and deploy a SharePoint installation in a service-orientated approach. In SharePoint Server 2007, these services were all grouped into Shared Service Providers (SSPs), which had severe limitations when trying to scale or deploy complex solutions.

  The web and application tiers can reside on the same server or servers; however, in larger deployments these two tiers may be installed on their own servers, where each application server may host one or more service applications. Before installing a multiserver SharePoint farm, a basic understanding of the service application architecture is necessary, as this will affect nearly every aspect of a SharePoint installation.

  SharePoint 2010 service applications include Business Connectivity Services (BCS), Managed Metadata Service (MMS), PerformancePoint Services (PPS), Office Web Apps, SharePoint Server Search Service, Secure Store Service (SSS), User Profile Service (UPS), and Web Analytics Service, as well as the client-related services, such as Access Services, Excel Services, and Visio Services.

  After the Business Data Connectivity (BDC) model is imported into the server running the BCS service application, the external data is made available to any web applications associated with that BCS service application.

  > **See Also** *For more information about BCS service applications, see Chapter 3, "Creating and Maintaining Business Data Connectivity Service Applications."*

- **Database** Stores the data required by the application and web tiers.

The server architecture can reside on one or more servers. The number of servers will vary from organization to organization and depend on a number of factors, such as the number of concurrent users, scalability, redundancy, resiliency, and the number of service applications used.

For example, when deploying SharePoint 2010 for evaluation or development purposes for a small number of users (for example, fewer than 100 users), the implementation could consist of one server. The single server, known as a single-server farm, would host the web, application, and database tiers. For between 100 and 1,000 users, where redundancy and resiliency are considerations, a four-server farm could be implemented, where two servers would host the web and application tiers and the other two servers would host a clustered or mirrored database server configuration—the database tier.

See Also *You can learn more about common ways to build and scale farm topologies, including planning which servers to start services on, at* www.microsoft.com/download/en/details.aspx?id=6096.

Connecting to Business Applications

The Business Connectivity Services (BCS) data connectivity layer, known as the Business Data Connectivity (BDC), uses connectors to access the external systems. The built-in connectors allow you to connect to databases, cloud-based services, Windows Communication Foundation (WCF) endpoints, and web services, as well as provide you with the ability to create new connectors, such as .NET assembly and custom connectors. These two connectors are created using Visual Studio. The .NET assembly connector is typically developed internally in an organization and allows a developer complete control over the operations with the external system with the code the developer writes. Custom connectors are typically developed by third-party companies so that the purchasers of the third-party solution can integrate the solution with a SharePoint installation.

Once SharePoint knows how to connect to an external system, then depending on the operations SharePoint is allowed, it can retrieve, modify, and create external data. An improvement in SharePoint 2010 is the introduction of batch and bulk operations for retrieving external data. When multiple documents are retrieved, it is also possible to retrieve the documents in chunks, which reduces the number of round-trips to retrieve the data.

The connection and data operation details are stored in the BDC metadata store, also known as the BCS database. In this database, SharePoint stores and secures external content type (ECT) and related objects defined in the BDC model, so this database is also known as the ECT repository. This database does not contain external data; it contains only information about the external system. The metadata store is accessed by the Administration and Runtime interfaces, as shown in Figure 2-4, which are discussed in more detail in the following sections.

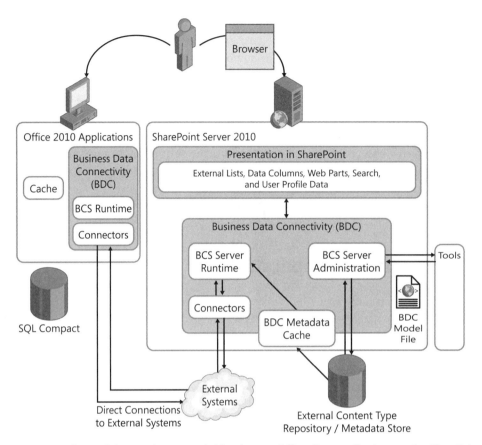

FIGURE 2-4 External data can be accessed either from an Office client application or using SharePoint.

BDC Administration

The Business Data Connectivity (BDC) interface creates, reads, updates, and deletes objects within the metadata store. All of the SharePoint 2010 built-in features use this interface. For example, when you use the SharePoint 2010 Central Administration website, the BCS administration webpages use the BDC interface to import the model, as does the external data picker in any of the business data Web Parts.

On a server hosting the BDC service application, the BDC layer stores in memory (caches) all the BDC model information, so most of the time a call to the administration interface will result in manipulating objects from the cache instead of making round trips to the SQL Server to access the ECT repository. If the BDC sees a change to one of the BDC model objects, it clears and then loads the cache.

Important A SharePoint 2010 timer runs once every minute on each server to look for any changes to the BDC metadata objects. If the logic within the timer job sees a change, it clears the cache and then reloads it. Therefore, after you change metadata, you must wait up to a minute for changes to propagate to all the servers in the farm. The changes take effect immediately on the computer on which you make them.

BDC Runtime

This layer is used to create, update, display, and edit the external content. External content is not saved in the ECT repository but is retrieved by the BDC server runtime using bulk load routines when the content is needed.

For example, if a user clicks a link for an external list, the BDC runtime is used to populate the default view of the external list. However, before the BDC runtime can populate the default view, it must first call the BDC Administration interface to find the location and format of the data from the BDC model, so that it can call the appropriate connector, which is the component that obtains the external data. This process causes network traffic between the web server and the servers that host the BDC service application. Examples of the built-in features that use the BDC runtime are external lists, business data Web Parts, the Retrieve data link, and the refresh icon in the external data column of a list or library.

The Office applications include a symmetrical BDC runtime to the BDC runtime that runs on the server. The BDC runtime, whether it is on the client or SharePoint 2010, uses the same connectors, so the client does not need to connect back to SharePoint to access the external data.

The BDC runtime provides an intuitive, "stereotypical," consistent object model, independent of the external system. Developers need to understand only the BDC Object Model to extract data from the external systems, whether they are developing code for the client or the server.

The BDC runtime consists of an infrastructure component to provide runtime connection management and shared security services to the external systems. Access to the external systems is the responsibility of the BDC connectors.

External Content Types

External content types (ECTs) are a new concept in SharePoint 2010 and are the building blocks of BCS, similar to the entity object in SharePoint Server 2007. ECTs refer to external data objects and define the fields, methods, and behavior of the data in SharePoint and Office client applications. Both read and write capabilities are included, along with batch and bulk operation support. ECTs are defined in the BDC model. The data objects defined by the ECTs can be displayed on SharePoint 2010 sites using Web Parts, external columns in lists, and libraries. Also, as the data objects are similar to content types, you can use them to create a specialized list, such as an external list, or in Office 2010 applications where ECTs are the framework for creating Office Business Applications (OBAs).

BCS Security

To create, modify, or delete the BDC model, or to access the data from the external systems, you will need to plan and consider security requirements. The security requirements of the external systems will usually be outside your control. Many of the external systems will have been installed in your organization before the installation of SharePoint, probably many years before SharePoint was even considered by your organization. You will need to work closely with the external system owners, and with your organization's security experts if you are in a highly regulated industry, as you develop SharePoint composite solutions.

Security requirements can be divided into two types: authentication and authorization. Authentication involves some type of system that provides a mechanism such that users can prove their identity. An authentication mechanism commonly used by large organizations is Windows authentication, where users are provided with a user name and a password. This approach could be augmented with advanced techniques, such as smart cards or fingerprint recognition. Windows authentication involves the installation of Active Directory (AD) within your organization and servers (domain controllers) whose role is to take requests from other servers in your organization to check that a user's credentials are valid. Once the requesting servers have received positive notification from a domain controller concerning the user's credentials, then the requesting server can authorize the user to perform actions based on the permissions granted to the user (authorization).

Authentication

A BCS solution involves a number of systems and each system has its own authentication method. A solution typically involves an end-user device, such as a laptop, desktop computer, mobile phone, or tablet, and on that device an application will run, such as a mobile phone application, an Office application, or a browser. A BCS SharePoint solution involves a SharePoint farm as well as the external system. Each one of these systems—end-user device, SharePoint, and the external system—will be able to use a number of authentication methods, such as Windows authentication, SAML token, or Windows Live ID.

In an ideal world, once a user has signed on to their device, there should be no need to have the user authenticate again. Such an environment, in which a user need only authenticate once no matter how many systems the user's application has to request information from, is known as single sign-on. Although over the years the authentication process has become increasingly transparent to the end user, it still doesn't happen by magic. In most BCS solutions, you will have work to do. If not you, then someone in your organization will need to understand the authentication methods.

For example, in an organization that hosts its own AD and SharePoint farm, the credentials that a user logs on to their computer with are used to authenticate with the web server—this is called *Windows authentication*. SharePoint, using the authorization settings for the user (for example, the site permission settings), allows the user to complete certain operations. In this scenario, the two systems involved—the user's computer and the SharePoint web server—share the same authentication method, and there is just one hop from the user's computer to the SharePoint server.

With a BCS solution, in the same scenario three systems are involved, as shown in Figure 2-5: the user's computer, the SharePoint web server, and the external system.

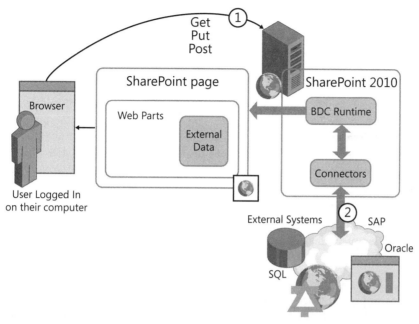

FIGURE 2-5 Displaying data from an external system requires two-hop authentication.

Even if the external system shares the same authentication method as the end-user device and SharePoint, when you try to pass a user's Windows authentication identification on to the external system, doing so will always incur a double hop: one hop from the client's computer to the SharePoint server, and a second hop from the SharePoint server to the external system. Unless SharePoint 2010 and the external system are installed on the same server, the user's credentials will not be successfully passed on to the external system. This is known as the *double-hop issue*.

 Note SharePoint 2010 and the external system are usually installed on the same server only in small organizations, or in larger organizations in a development, prototyping, or demonstration environment.

The workaround to the double-hop issue, where you want to use Windows authentication both for the SharePoint site and the external system, is to use Kerberos or an SSS service application.

The SSS service application is available with SharePoint Server 2010 and can be used with BCS to authenticate users with external systems. It supports access to external data by allowing you to map the credentials of SharePoint users or groups to external system credentials. The SSS application has its own database where the user credentials are encrypted.

Note Microsoft recommends using Secure Sockets Layer (SSL) when connecting end-user devices and SharePoint web servers, as well as SSL or Internet Protocol Security (IPsec) between servers running SharePoint and external systems, to ensure that sensitive data is not compromised.

Authorization

There are at least three levels of authorization with a SharePoint-based BCS solution:

- **SharePoint permissions** Sites are organized into site collections, and a site collection is a security boundary—that is, the top-level site of a site collection starts with its own unique security settings. When you create sites, by default they inherit the permissions of their parent site, which then percolates down to all lists, libraries, list items, and files within that site. When you create a page to display external data or when you create an external list, SharePoint permissions are used to control who can see that page or list. You can break the inheritance on your site so that pages and lists can have their own unique permission settings.

Note When you create an external list from an ECT, you cannot have unique permissions on items within the external list. You can have only per-item level permissions when the data resides within SharePoint. An external list presenting data held in the external system and only the external system can apply permissions on a per-item level.

- **BCS service application permissions** Since any BDC model could be extensively used through your SharePoint installation and could be a critical component to the day-to-day working of your organization, there is a mechanism to guard against accidental or malicious modifications to the model. The BDC service application also allows you to specify who can use the definitions to access the external data that the BDC model describes.

- **External system authorization** Most external systems have their own authorization settings determining who can see the data as well as who can view, create, manipulate, or delete the data.

When you create a SharePoint page to display or modify external data, the user experience will be a combination of these three levels of authorization. The user must have SharePoint permissions to the library where the page is stored. The user must have BCS model permissions for SharePoint to read the external system connection details and ECT information. Then the external system must allow the data to be retrieved for that user.

Also, once a BDC model is created, then the visibility of the external data is not limited to a single site. You can set permissions on the BDC model so that only a subset of users can see it, and those users may be site owners or list owners on other sites. However, without a full understanding of how you set up the authorization permissions, the users may decide to create solutions to use the data on their sites or within their lists with unexpected results. Other users on these sites may not have permissions to see the external data because of authorization settings at the BCS service application level or within the external system. These users on other sites may be presented with an error message, and then they might phone the help desk for support. Therefore, it is important to understand the security implications of your solution, not just on the site where you plan to create external lists and business dashboards, but also throughout all the web applications associated with the BCS service application where your model is stored.

See Also *For more information about configuring BCS security, see Chapter 3, "Creating and Maintaining Business Data Connectivity Service Applications."*

Taking External Data Offline

When connecting an external list to Outlook 2010 and SharePoint Workspace 2010, you may notice that you can take the external data offline. However, to take the external data offline, additional logic is required. This logic is provided by a Visual Studio Tools for Office (VSTO) ClickOnce deployment package, which is provided only in the Enterprise edition of SharePoint Server 2010. In SharePoint Foundation or the Standard version of SharePoint Server 2010, you cannot take external list data offline in Outlook 2010 or SharePoint Workspace 2010 unless you write your own code.

See Also *For more information about using VSTO with external data, see Chapter 11, "Using Client-Side Code and External Data."*

Extending Solutions

As previously explained in this chapter, Business Connectivity Services (BCS) allows you to connect to external data through SharePoint Server 2010 and surface the data in Office 2010 client applications, but that is just the beginning. By further extending the Office 2010 client that exposes the external data, you can create very rich, user-friendly, intuitive solutions. Once you've established the BCS connection, you can do a great deal more in the client applications to enhance the user experience.

For example, Microsoft Access 2010 makes connecting to external data easier than ever before. Access has always been a great landing pad for data. With Access 2010, Microsoft has built a new cached mode to dramatically improve the performance of connections to SharePoint lists. Additionally, Access can now slice, dice, and report on BCS data, just like any other linked table.

Although you can develop your own BCS connectors, most BCS development within an organization will concentrate on the presentation and manipulation of the data. With a web-based solution, you have the choice of developing logic that will run on the server, server-side code, or code that runs within the browser, client-side code:

- Server-side code is developed using languages such as C# and is available on web servers as precompiled dynamic-link libraries (DLLs). You can expose such code as controls that you can place on pages or activate as features at the farm, web application, site collection, or site (web scope) level.

- Client-side code is developed using interpretive languages, such as JavaScript, JQuery, and CSS, that are either embedded into HTML or sent to the browser in separate files. The advantage of using client-side code is that it allows the browser to respond to certain user actions, such as clicking a button, without the need to communicate with the server, providing a faster response and improved user experience. You can also add client-side code to pages using tools such as InfoPath Designer and SharePoint Designer.

See Also *You can find more information about how to extend the out-of-the-box BCS functionality in Part III.*

Planning to Use BCS

Whenever a solution is created that should be easily used by many people, whether it is a SharePoint-related solution or any other type of solution, the ease of use will come only if the architect of the solution has a deep understanding of the types of business scenarios it will be used for, information about the systems that store the business data, and knowledge of the skill set of the users. This is true for a Business Connectivity Services (BCS) solution as well. The person who architects the solution could be a business analyst, a citizen developer, a power end user, or a representative from the IT department, such as a developer.

A BCS solution consists of many components, and with good planning you can create an effective solution. The key to successfully using BCS is to create a Business Data Connectivity (BDC) model file that contains meaningfully named definitions that users can then use to expose the external data on their sites.

During the planning stages, you will need to liaise with a number of people, depending on your knowledge, the scope of the solution, and the number of external systems the solution will use. The solution can be very complex or simple. You need to give consideration to security, ensuring that users who should be allowed to use the data can use the data and that those users are not presented with permission-related error messages.

A BCS solution is not like a solution that can be created using the Data Sources gallery in Share-Point Designer. Such solutions tend to be created on a per-site basis, for a small set of users, by a person who knows the external system and knows the users who will use the solution. The creator of such a solution tends to also be a user of the solution and can tweak and readily extend the solution, creating other Data Source definitions as required using naming conventions that only the creator needs to understand.

If you plan to make heavy use of BCS within your organization, you will need a thorough understanding of BCS, which is the aim of this book. The project/program manager will have to create a communication plan so that end users adopt the solution. For example, the project/program manager will have to obtain the backing of the business owner; train the relevant citizen developers and help desk staff in the use of external lists, SharePoint Designer, and InfoPath Designer; and create electronic help or additional text on pages, such as any new pages you plan for the search center to inform users of the new search capabilities.

You may have to build a prototype that enables you to create the necessary business plan so you can identify whether the BCS solution is a SharePoint-related solution and/or an Office client application solution, whether users want to connect to the data using Outlook, and whether they want to take the data offline. You will need to identify if you can create the solution with only the out-of-the-box functionality or if you will need professional developer assistance.

In reading this chapter, you most likely have already identified some of the technical decisions and tasks you will need to complete when creating a BCS solution, including the following infrastructure and security-related tasks:

- Infrastructure

  - Determine which SharePoint servers will run BCS service application(s).

  - Consider whether you need more than one BCS service application.

  - Plan to include capacity and performance testing for solutions that will be used extensively. The BCS solutions you develop could result in a large amount of data being transferred from the external systems to the SharePoint servers. These solutions could increase workload on the external systems and SharePoint servers.

  - Add SQL database backup and monitoring processes and procedures for all new BCS and SSS databases.

  - For an Office client application solution, identify whether the functionality you plan to use requires the Enterprise edition of SharePoint Server 2010 and Office Professional Plus 2010.

- Security

  - Identify the authentication methods used by SharePoint and the external systems.

  - Determine whether the BCS solution will need to use the SSS.

  - Consider the need to secure communication between user devices and SharePoint servers and external systems for SharePoint-based solutions, or between user devices and external systems for Office client application solutions.

  - Plan permissions for the SharePoint site, BDC service application, and external system.

See Also *If you have not upgraded to SharePoint 2010, but you are planning to do so and you are currently using the Business Data Catalog in the Enterprise edition of Microsoft Office SharePoint Server 2007, refer to http://technet.microsoft.com/en-us/library/ff607947.aspx for more information about upgrading.*

Summary

Business Connectivity Services (BCS) allows you to hook up external data with SharePoint and Office applications, enabling either professional developers or citizen developers in your organization to quickly develop composite solutions. BCS is implemented as a SharePoint service application, which allows you to create an external system definition once, known as a Business Data Connectivity (BDC) model, and share these definitions with many sites. In addition, a SharePoint farm can host more than one BCS, and each one can be configured independently by different sets of administrators.

The BDC model consists of XML declarations that describe the external system you want to access as well as the external content type (ECT) that defines the operations you might like to use on this external data and its format. Once an ECT is defined, then using the browser or SharePoint Designer, you can manipulate the data from the external system as you do other SharePoint objects, such as lists and Web Parts, by using the external list, a new list type in SharePoint 2010.

You can extend the out-of-the-box BCS functionality using either client-side or server-side code. Client-side code can be developed using tools such as the browser, InfoPath Designer, or SharePoint Designer, whereas server-side code is developed using Visual Studio and deployed as precompiled dynamic-link libraries (DLLs).

SharePoint 2010 has tighter integration with Office client applications than in Microsoft SharePoint Server 2007 had with the Office client applications. You can use the BDC model to reveal external data in Microsoft Office 2010 applications, including Microsoft Outlook 2010, Microsoft Access 2010, Microsoft Workspace 2010, Microsoft Word 2010 and Microsoft InfoPath 2010.

Whether you create a SharePoint-related or Office client application BCS solution, you should consider the infrastructure and security implications, and plan the solution accordingly.

CHAPTER 3

Creating and Maintaining Business Data Connectivity Service Applications

In this chapter, you will:

- Understand the service application architecture and its effects on the deployment of Business Connectivity Services

- Understand Business Connectivity Services security options

- Create and configure a Business Data Connectivity service application

- Configure the Secure Store Service

- Use Windows PowerShell to administer a Business Data Connectivity service application

- Modify the throttling settings of Business Connectivity Services

- Administer Business Connectivity Services in a tenant environment

In SharePoint 2010, Business Connectivity Services (BCS) is managed using the Business Data Connectivity (BDC) service application, which can be shared between one or more web applications or between farms. As explained in Chapter 2, "Introducing Business Connectivity Services," the BDC service connects the presentation layer with the external system. It uses different types of connectors depending on the interfaces supported by the external systems, together with information defined in an XML file, known as the BDC model, to read and write data to and from the external system.

The BDC shared service is built upon the Microsoft SharePoint 2010 shared service architecture, and it is available in SharePoint Foundation 2010, both the Standard and Enterprise editions of Share-Point Server 2010, and SharePoint Online. Different sets of administrators can manage the shared service architecture independently using the SharePoint 2010 Central Administration website or Windows PowerShell.

In this chapter, you will learn how SharePoint uses service applications and its effect on the deployment of BCS. You will then learn how to create and manage BDC service applications, how to configure the security options, and how to administer BCS in a tenant environment.

What Are Service Applications?

SharePoint 2010 contains a number of shared service applications, each of which functions independently of each other, allowing you to install SharePoint in a service-oriented approach. These services include the following:

- Access Services

- Application Discovery and Load Balancer Service Application

- Application Registry Service

- Business Data Connectivity Service

- Excel Services

- Managed Metadata Service (MMS)

- PerformancePoint Service (PPS)

- Search Service Application (SSA)

- Secure Store Service (SSS)

- Security Token Service (STS)

- State Service

- Subscription Settings Service Application

- Usage and Health Data Collection Service

- User Profile Service (UPS)

- Visio Graphics Service

- Web Analytics Service (WAS)

- Word Automation Services

 Note In SharePoint 2010, InfoPath Form Services (IFS) is not implemented as a service application. It is a farmwide component, and you cannot share it across farms or partition it, nor can you create multiple InfoPath Form Services in one farm.

Microsoft Office SharePoint Server 2007 provided some of these services, but you could not install them independently of each other. In that version, the services were grouped into Shared Service Providers (SSPs), and you were severely limited when you tried to scale or deploy complex solutions.

Not all service applications are available in all versions of SharePoint 2010. Business Connectivity Services (BCS) and the Usage and Health Data Collection Service are the only service applications available in SharePoint Foundation 2010. Other service applications are provided by other Microsoft products, including Microsoft Office Web Apps (OWA), which enable users to access and do light editing and sharing of documents created with Microsoft Word, Excel, PowerPoint, and OneNote.

> **Note** You will need the Application Registry Service only if you upgraded from Microsoft SharePoint Server 2007 Enterprise Edition and used Business Data Catalog.

BCS and the Service Application Architecture

You can associate service applications with one or more web applications. For example, a Business Data Connectivity (BDC) service application can contain multiple BDC models, each defining connection and security details of several external systems. If you associate the BDC service application with the two web applications *http://portal.adventure-works.com* and *http://marketing.adventure-works.com*, as shown in Figure 3-1, all site collections within both web applications can access those definitions and present the data from those external systems, as long as the authentication and authorization requirements are met.

You can associate other service applications, such as the MMS service application, with the two web applications, making available terms from the term store and content types defined in the MMS service application.

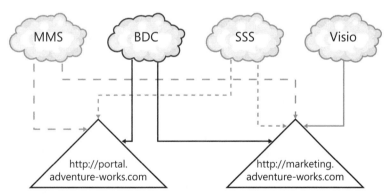

FIGURE 3-1 You can share one or more service applications between web applications.

Using Multiple Service Applications

You can have multiple occurrences of a service application. For example, you can create multiple BDC service applications: one that contains the definitions for external systems associated with the human resources department (for example, definitions for your organization's SAP or PeopleSoft system) and another that contains definitions to external systems that you want to present only on pages in your organization's portal web application. Similarly, you can have multiple MMS service applications: one global MMS service application for terms and content types applicable to all departments and divisions within your organization that you want to control centrally and another for each division within an organization (human resources, marketing, finance, etc.). You can configure each divisional MMS service application with its own term stores and content types, with the management of the term stores and content types delegated to the appropriate people within each division.

Also, some service applications allow multiple instances to be associated with one web application; the MMS service application is an example. All the MMS service applications could be associated with a web application—for example, *http://portal.adventure-works.com*. A divisional web application, such as *http://hr.adventure-works.com*, is associated with two MMS service applications: one containing organization wide terms and content types and one containing HR-related terms and content types, as shown in Figure 3-2. When two MMS service applications are associated with a web application, one has to be defined as the default.

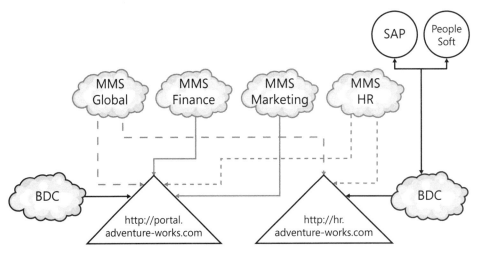

FIGURE 3-2 Service application instances can be shared between web applications.

Each BDC service application can have its own BCS administrators, who could be the business owners of the external systems and therefore familiar with the data held in the external system, the business processes that it supports, and security considerations. Each business team can control access to the business data without exposing the connection details of external system. As a result, each BDC service application can be administered in isolation and contain its own definition of external systems, external content types, and security settings.

Web applications can be associated with one or more BDC service applications. However, only the BDC service application that is specified as the default will be used. The second BDC service could be consumed through custom code.

Sharing Service Applications Across Farms

You can share service applications across SharePoint farms. The BDC service application is one of the service applications you can share across server farms, so you can manage it centrally and it can be consumed by web applications created on other farms. Table 3-1 lists the other service applications that can and cannot be shared across farms.

TABLE 3-1 Service applications that can and cannot be shared across farms

Can be shared	Cannot be shared
■ BDC	■ Access Web Services
■ MMS	■ Document Conversion
■ Search Services	■ Excel Services
■ SSS	■ PPS
■ UPS	■ Project Services
■ WAS	■ State Service
	■ Visio Graphics Services
	■ OWA Services

> **Note** To make a BDC service application available to be consumed by other SharePoint farms, you need to publish the BDC service application. You can find information about how to publish a BDC service application later in this chapter.

For example, in a large international organization, one farm could be hosting the BDC service application that contains all BDC models for all enterprise line-of-business (LoB) applications, plus a MMS service application that contains organization-wide terms and content types. Each country could host its own SharePoint farm, and web applications in those farms would use the central BDC and MMS service applications and service applications that have been created locally, as shown in Figure 3-3. Very large organizations could create a SharePoint farm with the sole purpose of hosting service applications that other farms consume—that is, the farm would host no web applications.

If you are considering such a configuration for your organization, you must ensure that the connectivity between the sites does not adversely impact the user experience. You will need to consider the retrieval of both the BDC model from the central BDC service application and the data from the external system. Once the BDC model is retrieved from the central BDC service application, it will be cached locally. The information in the BDC model will then be used by the local farms to retrieve data from the external systems—this too will be cached. There could be a long delay the first time a user requests a page that uses a Web Part that displays data from an external system. Subsequent requests will use the cached data and will be faster, but if the external data is rarely accessed, then users will always experience a delay.

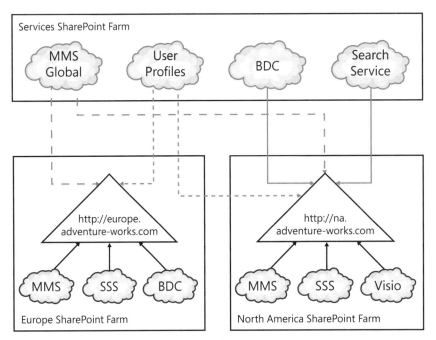

FIGURE 3-3 Service application instances can be shared between SharePoint farms.

Partitioning Service Applications

You can partition some service applications, and each partition can be used by one or more site collections when those site collections are hosted in a web application configured for multiple tenants. Each tenant, sometimes referred to as a customer, is identified by a computer-generated number known as a *subscription ID*. Subscription IDs can be created only when the Subscription Settings service is started.

> **Note** *Multitenancy* is the term commonly used to describe the isolation of websites in a hosting environment. It is the configuration used in Microsoft Office 365 SharePoint Online P and E plans.

Each tenant can have multiple site collections as well as a tenant administration site collection. Site collections belonging to the same tenant are known as *member sites*. The subscription ID is used to identify all the member sites belonging to the same tenant.

The BDC service application is one of the service applications that can be partitioned, where each partition can contain its own external system definitions. Each partition is associated with a subscription ID, which identifies those site collections that can use the partition's external system definitions. Figure 3-4 shows four tenants, each associated with its own subscription ID.

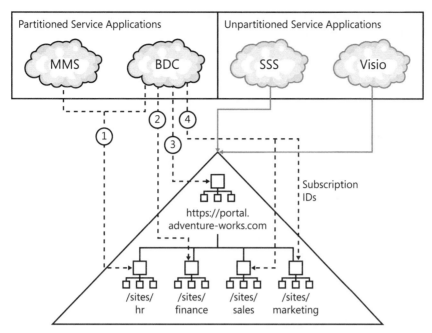

FIGURE 3-4 Service application partitions can be mapped to tenant site collections.

The BDC models uploaded into the first partition of the BDC service application can only be used by the member site */sites/hr.*

In Figure 3-4, note that the SSS application is depicted as unpartitioned. SSS can be used in a tenant environment. You create the SSS service application in the same way as in a nontenant environment, and you manage it using the Tenant Administration page. However, in a hosting environment such as Office 365, where each tenant may belong to a separate organization, it is not prudent to use SSS where credentials from one organization are saved in the same encrypted database as credentials from other organizations—therefore, companies who provide hosting solutions may not allow the use of SSS.

See Also *You can find information about how to administer a tenant environment later in this chapter.*

In Figure 3-4, each site collection is created below a managed path, *sites*, under the root-level site collection *http://portal.adventure-works.com*. To view the pages in the HR site collection, for example, users would use the URL *http://portal.adventure-works.com/sites/hr*. This is not the only way to deploy a multitenant web application.

SharePoint allows multiple root-level site collections, known as *host header site collections*. Each host header site collection can have its own top-level domain name that is independent of the web application where the site collections are stored. In SharePoint 2010, you can use host header site collections with managed paths and both HTTP and HTTPS protocols. Also, it is possible to configure site collections in multitenant web applications so that a mixture of host header site collections and web protocols coexist. The site collection structure could remain as shown in Figure 3-4, and then you could configure it so users refer to the HR site collection as *https://hr.adventure-works.com*, while the finance site's URL is *http://portal.adventure-works.com/sites/finance*.

See Also *You can find a poster summarizing the hosting environments and illustrating common hosting architectures on the Microsoft download site at* www.microsoft.com/download/en/details .aspx?displaylang=en&id=3326.

BCS and the Service Application Infrastructure

You can host service applications across one or more servers. SharePoint provides its own round-robin load-balancing mechanism to evenly distribute user requests across the servers running the service application code. In the case of the BDC service, the service application code then connects to the external systems to obtain the external data.

The service application infrastructure consists of the following:

- Service instances
- Service applications
- Service application proxies
- Service application groups
- Web applications

Service Instance

On each server, the process that runs service application code is known as the *service instance* or *service*. A SharePoint service instance is similar to a Windows service: each maps to an executable that performs specific functions, does not require user intervention, and runs for a long time.

Windows services include the Background Intelligent Transfer Service (BITS), DNS Client, Print Spooler, and Task Scheduler. A server administrator can start and stop Windows services using the Services Microsoft Management Console (MMC; *services.msc*) snap-in, which you can start from Administrator Tools on the Start menu or through the Services tab in Windows Task Manager. SharePoint service instances are not Windows services, however, and to manage them, you use the SharePoint 2010 Central Administration website or Windows PowerShell.

Before creating a service application, you must start the appropriate service on at least one SharePoint server in the farm. That is, to create a BDC service application, you must start a BDC service on at least one SharePoint server.

Note Not only service application executables run in service instances. Other functionalities also need to run as service instances, such as the Microsoft SharePoint Foundation Subscription Settings Service, which provides the functionality to create and manage the subscription IDs that allow you to deploy a multitenancy environment.

By starting the BDC service on a number of servers, you are distributing BDC service applications across those servers, providing redundancy and the ability to scale your solution to support more users. For example, you could start the BDC service on two SharePoint servers, and if one of these SharePoint servers was lost, this issue would be detected by the built-in load balancer in each Share-Point web server. All subsequent requests from the web servers for external data would be directed to the SharePoint servers that are running the BDC service.

 Note You can find the number of servers you need to run BCS service instances only by completing performance and capacity monitoring activities in your environment.

You can run only one BDC service per server, with such servers fulfilling the application tier role. If you create two BDC service applications, they both run in the same BDC service and have their own Windows Communication Foundation endpoint. As detailed in Chapter 2, a SharePoint server can fulfill both web and application tier roles. In large deployments, some SharePoint servers will be running only service application services. For example, the two application servers in Figure 3-5 are hosting a subset of service application services, including the BDC service, and the remaining services are hosted on the web servers.

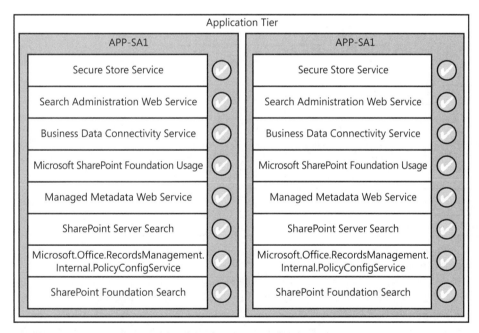

FIGURE 3-5 Service applications distributed over two application servers.

See Also *You can find more information to help you plan your service architecture at* http://technet.microsoft.com/en-us/library/cc560988.aspx *for SharePoint Server 2010 and* http://technet.microsoft.com/en-us/library/ff627854.aspx *for SharePoint Foundation 2010.*

Service Application Proxy

Most service applications require a service application proxy, also known as a service connection. A service application proxy connects the service application to a service application consumer, the web application.

Service Application Groups

Service applications are grouped together into service application groups. When you install Share-Point, there is one service application group: default. A service application can belong to more than one group. When you create a web application, you can select the default service application group or create a service application group, named custom, that is a specific collection of service applications for the web application you are creating, as shown in Figure 3-6.

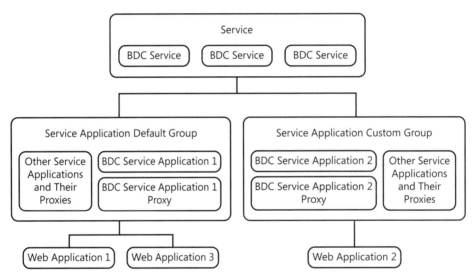

FIGURE 3-6 The interaction between BDC services, service application groups, BDC service applications, BDC service application proxies, and web applications.

All service applications are automatically added to the default group. If you are a member of the Farm Administrators group, you can add and remove service applications from service application groups at any time by using the link to the service application groups on the Service Application Associations page. To navigate to this page in the SharePoint 2010 Central Administration website, click Configure Service Application Associations under Service Applications on the Application Management page.

When you click a service application group name, a modal window showing the Configure Service Application Association page appears, as shown in Figure 3-7. All service applications are displayed on this page. Select the ones that you want in your service application group.

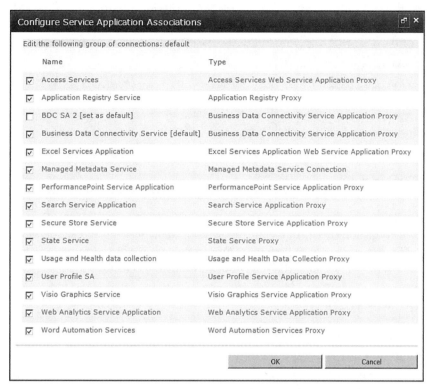

FIGURE 3-7 Associate service applications with service application groups on the Configure Service Application Associations page.

You can add more than one BDC service application to a service application group, but only the BDC service application configured as the default will be used. You are unable to create any new external content types (ECTs) or use any existing ECTs stored in the metadata store of the BDC service application other than the default.

If you set a different BDC service application as the default, then any external lists you created from ECTs saved in the previous BDC service application will not display any data, and an error message similar to "Entity (External Content Type) cannot be found with Namespace = 'http://Adventure-WorksSalesInvoicing', Name = 'AdventureWorks_Customers'." will display, together with a correlation ID, as shown in Figure 3-8. Select only one BDC service application in a service application proxy group.

FIGURE 3-8 An error message is displayed when an ECT for an external list cannot be found.

See Also *See the section "Troubleshooting Connection Problems" later in this chapter for information about correlation IDs and how they can help during troubleshooting.*

BCS Security Options

Chapter 2 introduced you to some security considerations when implementing Business Connectivity Services (BCS) in your organization and differentiated between authentication and authorization. In this section, you will take a closer look at both these processes, including the authentication modes and methods as well as the permission settings on Business Data Connectivity (BDC) objects stored in the BDC metadata store.

Authentication

Authentication is the process of verifying that a user is who they claim to be. Authorization is the process of finding out whether the user, once authenticated, is permitted to access the data. Access control is managing access to the business data exposed using BCS.

There are two authentication scenarios to consider with BCS. The first is SharePoint's use of BCS, exposing information on webpages, and the second is the use of BCS in Office client applications. Figure 3-9 shows the three major components: the Office client, SharePoint 2010, and external data sources.

Each lock in Figure 3-9 identifies a form of authentication, as follows:

- **Lock 1** Logging on to your computer using Windows credentials.

- **Lock 2** Authentication by Internet Information Services (IIS) on a SharePoint web server. When your SharePoint site is classified in the browser's intranet zone, you may be prompted for credentials; otherwise, the Windows credentials you used to log on to your computer are used to authenticate you. This experience could vary widely depending on the configuration of Internet Explorer. When the SharePoint site is configured for forms-based authentication (FBA), IIS will prompt for your credentials.

- **Lock 3** Authentication required when an Office application such as Outlook 2010 is configured to display contact information from a customer relationship management (CRM) or enterprise resource planning (ERP) system.

- **Lock 4** Authentication when SharePoint displays data on a webpage.

Locks 3 and 4 represent the additional security requirements that an external data source may impose.

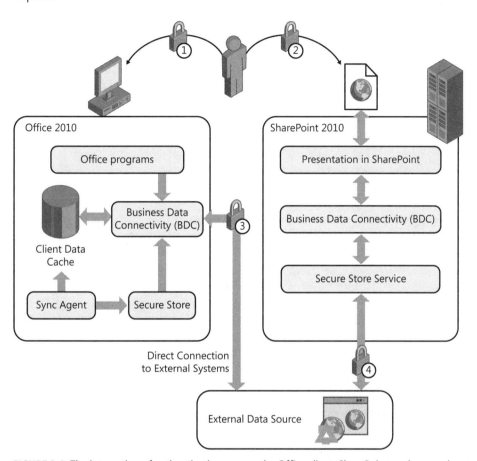

FIGURE 3-9 The interaction of authentication among the Office client, SharePoint, and external systems.

Authentication Modes

The two authentication modes in BCS are as follows:

- **Trusted Subsystem** The SharePoint web tier controls authentication and authorization, and retrieves data from the external systems using a fixed identity—that is, the SharePoint servers are a trusted subsystem. In the trusted subsystem model, an account is used to access the external system on behalf of all authenticated users or a set of users, so administrators do not have to specify on the external system the access rights for each user. The account can be the BDC service application pool ID or the credentials associated with a group target application ID retrieved from the Secure Store Service (SSS) database. If the external system is configured to use identify federation authentication, the user's identity is passed to the Secure Token Service (STS) to obtain the user's token or claim.

- **Impersonation and Delegation** This mode uses the authorization of the external system, which delegates authentication to the SharePoint web tier. The BDC service application's pool ID impersonates the user and connects to the external system on the user's behalf using Kerberos, the credentials associated with an individual target application ID retrieved from the SSS database, or the user's name passed as a parameter.

Table 3-2 details the benefits of these two modes.

TABLE 3-2 Trusted Subsystem vs. Impersonation and Delegation

Benefit	Trusted Subsystem	Impersonation and Delegation
Connection pooling	Yes	No
Could reduce licensing costs on the external system if it uses a product charged on a per-user basis	Yes	No
Less complex to use	Yes	No
Provides a single model for authorization	Yes	No
Supports scenarios in which there is no per-user authorization at the back-end	Yes	No
Allows per-user auditing at the back end	No	Yes

Authentication Methods

When you create the BDC model or external content type (ECT), you define the authentication method that the BDC runtime uses with the external system:

- **User's Identity (also known as *PassThrough*)** SharePoint sends the user's credentials to the external system, and the user is allowed or disallowed access based on those credentials. If you use Windows authentication and have a single-server SharePoint farm, and the external system is installed on that server, then using the user's identity works well. This method will not work in a multiple-server farm installation due to the double-hop issue (explained in Chapter 2), unless you configure Kerberos on your servers or configure your SharePoint web applications to use SSL. When using SSL, authentication of the user is completed at the server and not at the user's computer; therefore, there is only one hop from the computer that authenticates the user to the external system.

  The other disadvantage of using the user's identity for authentication is that if the external system is an SQL database, a new SQL connection pool is created for each user who is using the ECT to access the external content, which can cause performance issues. You can disable connection pooling, which can also affect performance.

- **Impersonate Windows Identity** A specific Windows user name is used to authenticate with the external system. This could be the same for all users—it could be a group ID, or there could be some mapping mechanism, so the user requesting the content from SharePoint is matched to a different Windows identity passed on to the external system. Using this and the next authentication method requires some mechanism to do the mapping. If you are using

SharePoint Server 2010, you can use an SSS application, or if you are using SharePoint Foundation or SharePoint Online, you can write your own equivalent system.

- **Impersonate Custom Identity** This method is similar to the previous authentication method, but this method does not involve Windows identities. The identities could be SQL user names or claims-based identities.

- **BDC Identity (also known as *RevertToSelf*)** SharePoint reverts to the web application's application pool identity to authenticate with the external system. This user name has a high level of privileges on a SharePoint installation. Any user who can create or edit a BDC Identity model can make themselves an administrator of site collection. Microsoft does not recommend the use of this authentication mode, and it is disabled by default, but you can enable it using code or Windows PowerShell. When a user tries to import or change the authentication mode to RevertToSelf, an error message displays, as shown in Figure 3-10 (in SharePoint Designer).

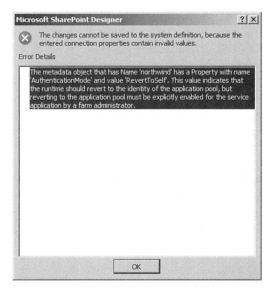

FIGURE 3-10 This error dialog box appears when a user attempts to change the authentication mode to RevertToSelf.

Table 3-3 shows the relationship between the authentication modes and methods.

TABLE 3-3 Relationship between authentication modes and methods

Mode/method	Trusted Subsystem	Impersonation and Delegation
User's Identity/PassThrough	No	Yes
RevertToSelf	Yes	No
Impersonation Windows/Custom - SSS Group Target Application type	Yes	No
Impersonation Windows/Custom - SSS Individual Target Application type	No	Yes

Client Authentication Considerations

When you configure a BCS solution for client applications, both the PassThrough and RevertToSelf authentication modes use the credentials the user entered when logging on to the computer to directly connect to the external system.

When the BCS solution uses SSS, client applications still connect directly to the external system but do not use the credentials stored in the SSS database, as passing credentials from the server for the client to use is seen as a major security risk. The first time a user tries to connect to the external system, the BCS code on the client will prompt for credentials for the external system. These credentials are saved in the Credential Manager, which is an application incorporated into the Windows client operating system. When the user subsequently accesses the external system, the credentials are retrieved from the Credential Manager.

Note To manage credentials stored on the client, navigate to the Control Panel, click User Accounts and Family Safety, and then click Manage Windows Credentials under Credential Manager.

On the server, when pages display data from external systems and SSS is configured to use the individual target application type, it is common practice to prompt users for their credentials for the external system. When BCS solutions involve both server-side and client-side presentation of data, users are prompted twice for the same credentials: once for the credentials to be stored in the SSS database and once for the credentials to be stored in the Credential Manager.

Important If SSS is configured to use the group target application type, however, the credentials that a group of users will use to authenticate with the external system is usually stored in SSS by an administrator. Users are still prompted when the client application connects to the external system, but in this scenario, users do not generally know the group credentials. This approach can cause problems and calls to the help desk, so organizations tend not to use the group target application type when the BCS solution involves client applications.

See Also *You can find more information on using SSS later in this chapter in "Configuring the Secure Store Service.".*

Authorization

Once a user is authenticated, the requesting server can authorize the user to perform actions based on the permissions granted to the user (authorization). The user's request to access external data is routed through a number of components:

- SharePoint site

- BDC metadata store

- BDC objects

- External system

Of particular interest in this section are the BDC metadata store and the BDC objects that it contains.

BDC Metadata Store Permissions

Farm administrators, SharePoint Windows PowerShell users and, depending on how the farm administrator has configured service applications, some application pool accounts, have full permissions to a BDC service application and thus to the metadata store. This level of access allows farm administrators to maintain or repair the BDC service application if necessary and enables them to deploy solutions packages that use BCS.

No other users have access to the metadata store, so once you have created the BDC service application, the next task is to set the permissions on the metadata store, as shown in Table 3-4.

TABLE 3-4 BDC metadata store permissions

Permission	Description
Edit	Users with this permission can create and amend BDC models, external system definitions, and ECTs. You should assign this permission to only highly trusted users, especially in a production environment. Users with this permission can see external system definitions created by other users, and this can be a security risk, as a malicious user can use the information in the external system definition to access and corrupt external content and adversely affect the running of the SharePoint installation.
	When you upload a BDC model from a development environment into a production environment, the security settings from the development environment may be included. Therefore, remove the Edit permissions from the BDC model for those users who created it in the development environment. If you do not have a development or prototype environment, then give users who create external system definitions and ECTs using either SharePoint Designer or Visual Studio Edit permission on the metadata store to create the ECT. Afterward, you can remove the Edit permissions on the metadata store but leave Edit permissions on the ECT.
Execute	There is no Execute or Selectable In Clients permission on the metadata store, but you can choose to propagate these settings to child objects in the BDC model, external systems, ECTs, methods, and method instances, and their child objects.
Selectable In Clients	
Set Permissions	Users with this permission can manage BDC service application permissions on the BDC metadata store, and by propagating a user's settings, the user can set permission on any object in the metadata store. This permission is usually given only to BDC service application administrators.

BDC Objects

The metadata store includes all the BDC models, external systems, ECTs, methods, and method instances defined for that BDC service application. These objects exist in a hierarchy that determines which objects can propagate their permissions to other objects.

The permission options are Edit, Execute, Selectable In Clients, and Set Permissions. For information about how you can use these permissions on each BDC object, see the TechNet article at *http://technet.microsoft.com/en-us/library/ee661734.aspx#Section4* and the Microsoft Business Connectivity Services Team Blog at *http://blogs.msdn.com/bcs/archive/2009/11/24/permissions-in-business-connectivity-services.aspx*.

Although farm administrators have full permissions on the metadata store, this level of permissions is not propagated to all objects in the store. For example, farm administrators do not have Execute permissions on any metadata store objects. Such accounts can create a BDC model with its associated external system definition and ECT, and they can even create an external list from those ECTs, but they cannot execute any of the operations on the external content. When the external list displays in the browser, an authentication error appears.

Creating BDC Service Applications

You can use the SharePoint 2010 configuration wizard, the SharePoint 2010 Central Administration website, or Windows PowerShell to create a Business Data Connectivity (BDC) service application. Using the SharePoint 2010 Central Administration website or Windows PowerShell, you can specify the SQL Server database name or use a preconfigured database name. When you use the configuration wizard, it automatically generates a BDC database name, which does not adhere to the naming standard that your database administrator uses.

To create a BDC service application using the SharePoint 2010 Central Administration website, follow these steps:

1. Under System Settings, click Manage Services on Server and ensure that the server where you want to start the BDC service is selected in the Server drop-down list. In the Action column, click Start for the Business Data Connectivity Service if it is not already started, as shown in Figure 3-11.

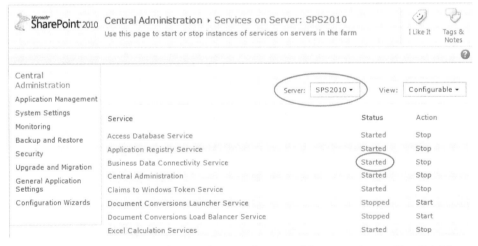

FIGURE 3-11 At least one BDC service must be started on one of the servers in your SharePoint farm.

2. In the left navigation pane, click Application Management, and under Service Applications, click Manage Service Application.

3. On the Service Applications ribbon tab, in the Create group, click New, and then click Business Data Connectivity Service.

4. On the Create New Business Data Connectivity Service Application page, type the name of the service application, the database server, the database name, the authentication method, and the user name and password if appropriate. You can also specify a failover server if you are using SQL Server database mirroring, as well as create or use an existing application pool, as shown in Figure 3-12.

> **Note** Application pools created for service applications can be used only by other service applications. They cannot be used as application pools for web applications.

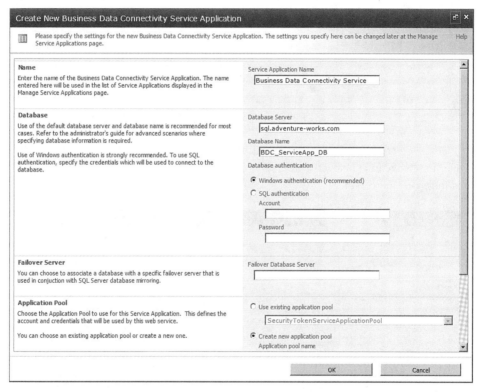

FIGURE 3-12 Enter the BDC service application settings on the Create New Business Data Connectivity Service Application page.

When you start a BDC service and create its associated service application, an IIS virtual application is created within the SharePoint Web Services IIS website. The SharePoint Web Services exposes a Windows Communication Foundation (WCF) web service, also known as the *service application endpoint*, as shown in Figure 3-13. The endpoint is used by SharePoint itself, and it can be used by your organization to develop new solutions. Such an endpoint is created by SharePoint on each server where the BDC service is started.

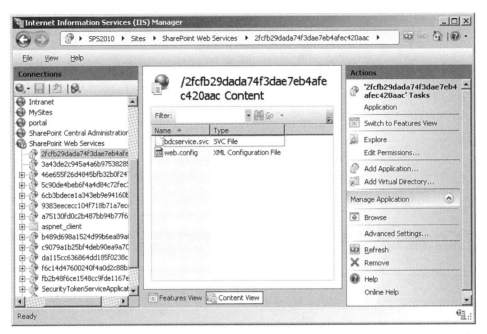

FIGURE 3-13 The BDC service application endpoint is created in the SharePoint Web Services IIS website.

Once you create the BDC service application, on the Service Applications page in the Central Administration website, below the BDC service application, you will see a BDC service application proxy, as shown in Figure 3-14.

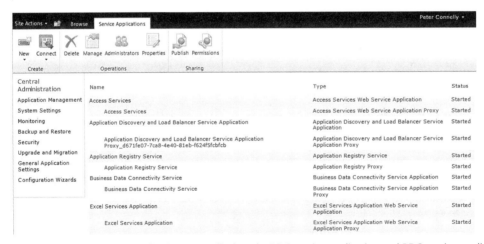

FIGURE 3-14 The Service Applications page displays the BDC service application and BDC service application proxy.

Configuring Business Data Connectivity Service Applications

Once you create the Business Data Connectivity (BDC) service application, you will need to complete the following administrator tasks:

1. Create BDC service application administrators.

2. Import the BDC model that contains the metadata information.

3. Set BDC metadata store permissions.

4. Configure profile page creation (SharePoint Server 2010).

5. Configure Secure Store Service (SSS) if you plan for any of the BDC models imported into the metadata store to use this authentication mechanism.

6. Deploy any custom business data solutions, such as dashboards.

Use the Service Application Information page, shown in Figure 3-15, to view, add, modify, and delete BDC models, external systems, and external content type (ECTs), as well as configure permissions. On SharePoint Server 2010, there is an additional group on the ribbon to manage ECT profile pages. The Service Application Information page displays information from the metadata store in three different views: BDC Models, External Content Types, and External Systems.

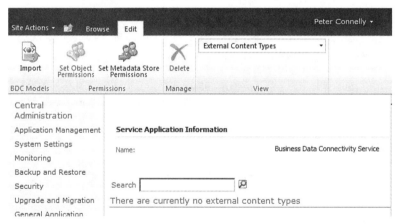

FIGURE 3-15 Use the Service Application Information page to manage BDC models, metadata store permissions, external systems, ECTs, and the profile page.

Creating a BDC Service Application Administrator

Once you create a BDC service application, you can delegate the administration of that service application to users. Such users will have access to the SharePoint 2010 Central Administration website; however, the webpages will be modified to display only the links (security trimmed) to allow them to manage only the service application.

 Note Only members of the Farm Administrators group are able to add or remove users as service application administrators. By default, the Farm Administrators group can manage all service applications.

To create or remove BDC service application administrators, follow these steps:

1. Navigate to the SharePoint 2010 Central Administration website, and click Manage Service Applications under Application Management.

2. On the Service Applications page, select the row of the BDC service application for which you want to create administrators.

 Note Do not click the name of the BDC service application, as that is a hyperlink that directs you to a page to manage the BDC service application.

3. On the Service Application ribbon tab, in the Operations group, click Administrators to display the Administrators for Business Connectivity Service page.

4. Enter the users who will manage the BDC service application in the first text box. You can use the People icon to validate each name you enter, or you can use the Address Book icon to search for a user.

5. Click Add. The username appears in the second text box.

6. In the third box, select Full Control, as shown in Figure 3-16.

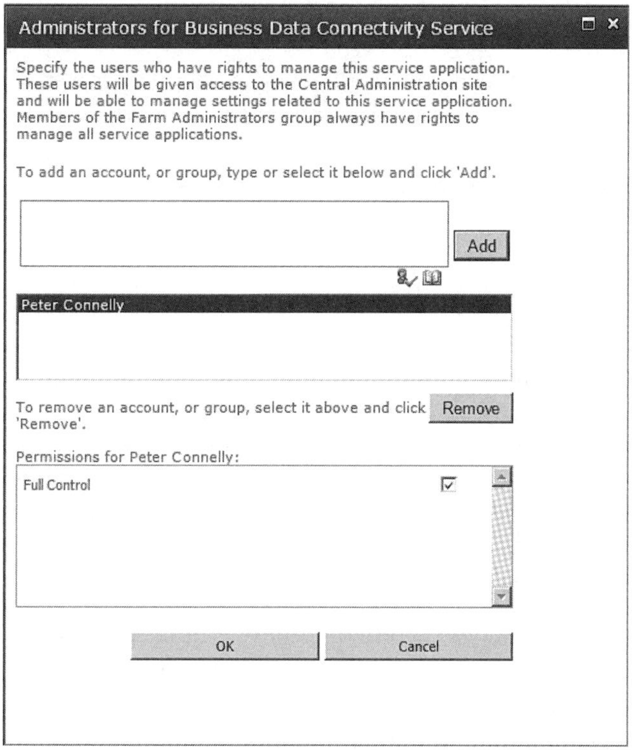

FIGURE 3-16 Use the Administrators for Business Data Connectivity Service page to add and remove users.

7. Click OK.

To remove a user as a BDC service application administrator, repeat steps 1 through 3 above. Then in the second text box, select the user you want to remove and click Remove.

Importing and Exporting BDC Models and Resource Files

ECTs are metadata objects defined in the BDC model XML file, which has the extension *.xml* or *.bdcm*. The BDC model is usually created by a business analyst, a developer, or a database administrator (DBA). Together, they have the knowledge of the external system or database, as well as how the business uses the data.

You can include resource information in the BDC model or in a separate resource XML file, which usually has an extension *.bdcr*. The creation of the base metadata information and the resource information is an important activity. You can create the base metadata information using the ECT Designer in SharePoint Designer 2010, Visual Studio 2010, an XML editor, Notepad, or a third-party tool. You can create or configure resource information after the BDC model data is imported.

Note You can only use SharePoint Designer 2010 to create a model XML file for SQL Server databases, web and Windows Communication Foundation (WCF) services, and .NET connectivity assemblies. For other types of external systems, edit the model XML file in Visual Studio 2010, an XML editor, or a third-party tool. For more information on creating BDC models with SharePoint Designer, see Chapter 4, "Defining External System Connections Using SharePoint Designer."

One purpose of the model is to describe how the BDC runtime will obtain the data from the external system—that is, it describes the interface. Another purpose of the model is to provide meaningful text in the browser to help users determine the data they require from the external system. The model describes what can be done with the browser and the relationships among the different types of data. For example, using BCS, you can create, read, update, and delete (CRUD) external data in SharePoint and Office client applications, if the external system supports the operations and is modeled appropriately in the BDC model.

Note Not all Office client applications can write to the external system, even though the external system supports the operations and they are correctly modeled in the BCS. For example, in Word 2010, BCS exposes read-only data in content controls that map to external data columns in a SharePoint document library, and you can import a BDS model into Access 2010 to create read-only tables. For more information, see Chapter 7, "Using External Data with Office Client Applications."

The BDC model contains a hierarchy of XML elements, each containing text or other elements that specify the external system settings and structure. The model must conform to the standards for well-formed XML, so all element names are case sensitive. The model must also conform to the schema described in the file *Bdcmetadata.xsd*. When you have a separate resource file, the schema definition file is *BDCMetadataResource.xsd*. Both files are stored in the TEMPLATE\XML SharePoint installation root folder, which by default is C:\Program Files\Common Files\Microsoft Shared\Web Server Extensions\14. A snippet of a BDC model is displayed below:

```
<LobSystemInstances>
        <LobSystemInstance Name="AdventureWorksLT">
          <Properties>
            <Property Name="AuthenticationMode" Type="System.String">PassThrough</Property>
            <Property Name="DatabaseAccessProvider" Type="System.String">SqlServer</Property>
            <Property Name="RdbConnection Data Source" Type="System.String">sql</Property>
            <Property Name="RdbConnection Initial Catalog"
Type="System.String">adventureworkslt</Property>
            <Property Name="RdbConnection Integrated Security"
Type="System.String">SSPI</Property>
```

```
            <Property Name="RdbConnection Pooling" Type="System.String">True</Property>
            <Property Name="ShowInSearchUI" Type="System.String"></Property>
          </Properties>
        </LobSystemInstance>
      </LobSystemInstances>
      <Entities>
        <Entity Namespace="http://AdventureWorksSalesInvoicing" Version="1.4.0.0"
EstimatedInstanceCount="10000"
                      Name="AdventureWorks_Customers" DefaultDisplayName="AdventureWorks
Customers">
          <Properties>
            <Property Name="OutlookItemType" Type="System.String">Contact</Property>
          </Properties>
          <AccessControlList>
            <AccessControlEntry Principal="contoso\peter">
              <Right BdcRight="Edit" />
              <Right BdcRight="Execute" />
              <Right BdcRight="SetPermissions" />
              <Right BdcRight="SelectableInClients" />
            </AccessControlEntry>
```

See Also *See Appendix A, "BDC Model Infrastructure," for more information on the BDC metadata object definitions.*

Importing a BDC Model

If you create a BDC model using SharePoint Designer or a third-party tool, or you need to transfer a BDC model from a development environment to a production environment, you can import the model file using the SharePoint 2010 Central Administration website as follows:

1. Navigate to the SharePoint 2010 Central Administration website, and under Application Management, click Manage Service Applications.

2. On the Service Applications page, click the name of the Business Data Connectivity service application where you want to import the BDC model. The BCS Application Information page appears, where you can manage permissions, export the BDC model, or delete the BDC model.

3. Click Import on the Edit ribbon tab to display the Import BDC Model page.

4. In the BDC Model section, click the Browse button to navigate to where the BDC model is located.

5. If you are importing a resource file, select the resources defined in your model file in the Advanced Settings section, as shown in Figure 3-17.

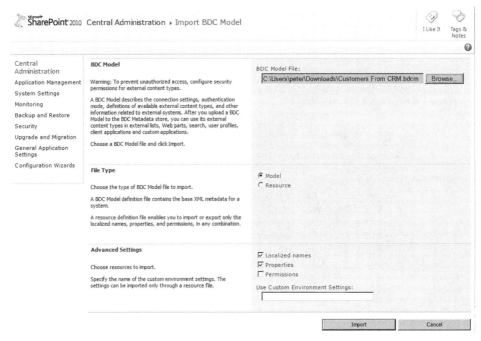

FIGURE 3-17 Select the resources defined in your model file on the Import BDC Model page.

Note When you choose to import permissions that are defined in your BDC model and an entry for an ECT already exists in the ACL, its value is overwritten with the permission information from the imported file.

6. Click Import.

The import process parses the file and validates it. If errors are found during the import process, additional information is displayed. You can find additional information in the Windows event logs and the SharePoint 2010 log file located at %ProgramFiles%\Common Files\Microsoft Shared\web server extensions\14\LOGS, where the relevant messages will appear in the Business Data category. You might have to pass this information back to the user who created the BDC model.

A successful import will result in the message "Application definition was successfully imported." The import process can identify any deficits in the BDC model, in which case you will see the message "Application definition was successfully imported" together with any warnings issued, similar to the page shown in Figure 3-18.

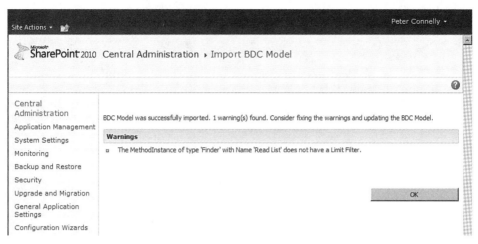

FIGURE 3-18 The import validation process can provide warning messages.

During the import process, SharePoint 2010 separates the external system details from the ECT information. You can then configure the appropriate access rights to users according to the business requirements using the Set BDC Metadata Store Permission command in the ribbon.

Exporting a BDC Model

To export a BDC model, follow these steps:

1. On the Service Application Information page, on the Edit ribbon tab, in the View group, select BDC Models from the drop-down list, as shown in Figure 3-19.

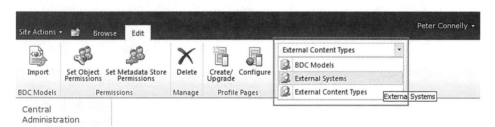

FIGURE 3-19 Use the drop-down list to manage BDC models, external systems, and ECTs.

2. Click the BDC model you want to export, and then select Export BDC Model from the drop-down list, as shown in Figure 3-20. When BDC models are displayed, on the Edit ribbon tab three commands are visible in the BDC Model group: Import, Delete, and Export.

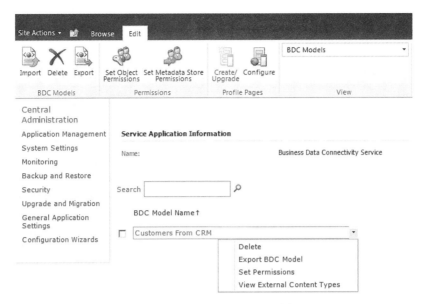

FIGURE 3-20 Use the drop-down list to export a BDC model.

 Note You can also use the drop-down list to delete the BDC model, set permissions on the BDC model, or view the ECTs defined in the BDC model. When you delete a BDC model, all ECTs and external data sources that are defined in the BDC model and that are not also contained in another model are deleted along with the BDC model.

3. On the Export BDC Model page, in the File Type section, select the type of BDC model file to export (Model or Resource), and then in the Advanced Settings section, select the resources and environmental settings to export.

4. Click Export.

Setting BDC Metadata Store Permissions

The BDC model and resource files are stored in the BDC metadata store. Users must have Edit permissions on the BDC metadata store to create, import, export, or remove files from the BDC metadata store. This level of permissions is usually assigned to BDC service application administrators.

As described in the "BCS Security Options" section earlier in this chapter, you can set permissions on the following objects:

- Metadata store

- Model

- External system

- ECT

Setting permissions on the BDC metadata store should be one of your first tasks after you create a BDC service application. To do so, follow these steps:

1. Navigate to the SharePoint 2010 Central Administration website, and under Application Management, click Manage Service Applications. On the Service Applications page, click the name of the Business Data Connectivity Service for which you want to manage permissions to display the Service Application Information page.

2. On the Edit ribbon tab, in the Permissions group, click Set Metadata Store Permissions to display the Set Metadata Store Permissions page, as shown in Figure 3-21.

3. Enter the appropriate users or groups and assign the appropriate permissions. Permissions set at this level can be copied to any model, external system, or ECT stored in the metadata store for this BDC service application.

4. Click OK.

 Note To create a BDC metadata store administrator, select Edit, Execute, Selectable In Clients, and Set Permissions, and then select the check box Propagate Permissions to All BDC Models, External Systems, and External Content Types in the BDC Metadata Store. This overwrites any existing permission settings.

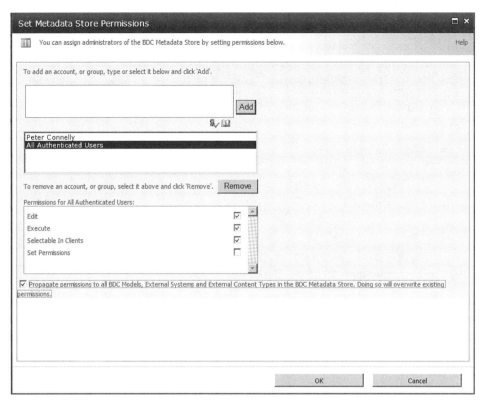

FIGURE 3-21 Use the Set Metadata Store Permissions page to configure permissions for users and groups.

Follow these steps to set permissions on one or more models, external systems, or ECTs:

1. On the Service Application Information page, on the Edit ribbon tab, in the View group, select BDC Models, External Systems, or External Content Types from the drop-down list. The page displays only objects of the type you have chosen.

2. Select the objects you want to modify, and then click Set Object Permissions, on the Edit tab, in the Permissions group.

3. On the Set Object Permissions page, enter the appropriate users or groups and assign the appropriate permissions.

Permissions set at this level can be copied to any child objects. For example, if you are setting the permissions for external systems, then permissions can be propagated to all ECTs that belong to the external systems. Be aware, however, that doing so will overwrite existing permissions.

When you import or create a BDC model—especially if you have chosen to copy all permissions to descendants at the metadata store level—you should set the permissions appropriate to the business requirements. This is also true when you create an ECT using SharePoint Designer. Ask the metadata store administrator to set permissions on your newly created ECT. Failure to do so could result in data from the external source not displaying whenever the ECT is used. The lack of data from the external system on a page could also include you when you visit the page. Using SharePoint Designer, you connect directly to the data source using a specific authentication method. Using the ECT to display data will always go through the metadata store, so you need access to the ECT and you need to meet the authentication criteria defined to view/modify/delete external data.

Once you have created the BDC model or ECT and set permissions on that object, you can create a profile page for the ECT.

Configuring Profile Page Creation

You use the profile page to display a single row of data from an external system defined by an ECT. For example, where you have created an ECT to display the customer table from your CRM system, the profile page for the customers' ECT would display the details for one customer. You do not create a profile page for each customer; instead, when you pass a customer ID to the profile page, it pulls the customer details from the CRM system and displays information about the customer, such as the customer's name, address, country, telephone number, and any other properties or fields that are defined in the BDC model.

In SharePoint Foundation and SharePoint Online, you must build these profile pages yourself and place controls or Web Parts to display the data. In SharePoint Server 2010, you can create profile pages with one click of a button using the SharePoint 2010 Central Administration website or Share-Point Designer.

See Also *You can find information about creating profile pages using SharePoint Designer in Chapter 5, "Creating External Content Types and Using External Data in Lists and Libraries."*

The website that hosts the ECT profile pages can be different for each BCS service application in a SharePoint farm. You first create a site that will host the profile pages and set the permissions so that any user who will create profile pages must have the Add and Customize Pages permission right on that site. All users who have access to the data from the external system can also access the profile pages created in this site. Read-only permission is usually sufficient for such users.

> **Important** If you create a new web application to host the profile site, ensure that the web application is associated with all BCS service applications that will create profiles on that web application.

After you have set permissions on the BDC metadata store, follow these steps to configure profile page creation:

1. Navigate to the Service Application Information for the BDC service application that you need to configure.

2. On the Edit ribbon tab, in the Profile Pages group, click Configure to display the Configure External Content Type Profile Page Host dialog box, as shown in Figure 3-22.

3. Select Enable Profile Page Creation and type the URL of the site where the profile page will be hosted.

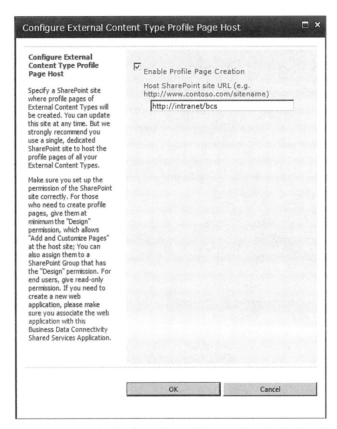

FIGURE 3-22 Use the Configure External Content Type Profile Page Host page to configure where profile pages are created.

4. Click OK.

Creating a Profile Page

Once you import a BDC model, you should consider creating a profile page for each ECT that it contains. If you are using the Enterprise edition of SharePoint Service 2010, it is easy to create a profile page using either SharePoint Designer or the SharePoint 2010 Central Administration website. For more information on creating a profile page, see Chapter 5.

Configuring the Secure Store Service

When using Business Connectivity Services (BCS), you will often create solutions where the current SharePoint user is known differently or has a different user name in the external system. If you are using SharePoint Server 2010, then you can use the Secure Store Service (SSS) with BCS to authenticate users with external systems. You can also use SSS to overcome the double-hop issue, which was explained in Chapter 2.

Note SSS replaces the Microsoft SharePoint Server 2007 single sign-on (SSO) feature.

SSS is a service application, just as BCS is. It provides a database to store user credentials and a mechanism to map SharePoint user credentials with credentials used by the external system. Even though user credentials stored in the database are encrypted, Microsoft recommends that the SSS database be deployed to a different SQL Server instance than the instance where the rest of your SharePoint databases are deployed.

In addition, Microsoft recommends that you use Secure Sockets Layer (SSL) when connecting end-user devices and SharePoint web servers, and that you also use SSL or Internet Protocol Security (IPsec) between servers running SharePoint and external systems to ensure the security of sensitive data. The encryption of data is particularly important if the credentials are passed as clear text between the SharePoint servers and the external system.

Note The BCS component within Microsoft Office clients uses the Windows Credential Store as a Secure Store provider.

In SSS terminology, each external system that you want to authenticate is known as a *target application* and is represented by a target application ID. When a user requests content from an external system, the Business Data Connectivity (BDC) runtime reviews the BDC model. If the external system uses a target application ID, then the ID the user used to log on to SharePoint (step 1 in Figure 3-23) is passed to the SSS application (step 2 in Figure 3-23), which uses the information in the SSS database to match the logged-on user name with credentials that can be used with the external system. The matched credentials are then used to authenticate the external system (step 3 in Figure 3-23), and the external system also uses these credentials to identify the user's access rights in the external system. The returned data is then incorporated into the SharePoint page and rendered in the user's browser.

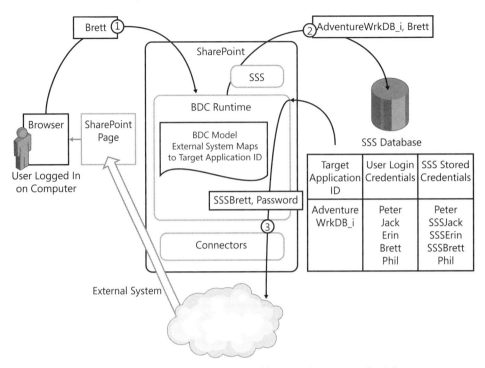

FIGURE 3-23 Use SSS to map logged-on user names with external system credentials.

SSS uses two types of authentication with external systems:

- Individual A one-to-one mapping, where every SharePoint user needs a unique user name in the external system

- Group A many-to-one mapping, where multiple users can access an external system using one user name

Although user and group credentials are usually stored in the form of a user name and password, some external systems require additional information, such as a database name. SSS allows you to create the necessary fields to pass to the external system.

Creating a Secure Store Service

Creating an SSS service application is very similar to creating a BDC service application. Follow these steps on the SharePoint 2010 Central Administration website:

1. Under System Settings, click Manage Services on Server, and then on the Services on Server: *<server name>* page, click Start to the right of Secure Store Service. Repeat this step for each server where you want SSS to run.

2. On the Application Management page, under Service Applications, click Manage Service Applications and create a new SSS, providing a name for the service application and a database name, and selecting an application pool or creating a new one, as shown in Figure 3-24.

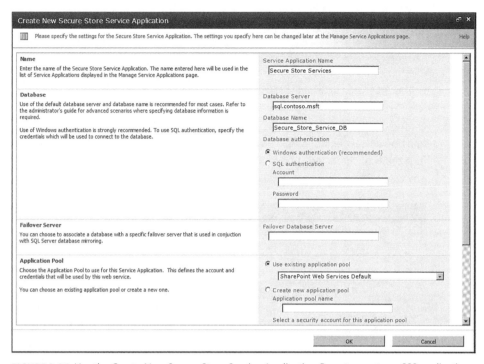

FIGURE 3-24 Use the Create New Secure Store Service Application Page to create an SSS application.

You can also use the Create New Secure Store Service Application page to enable auditing and specify the number of days the audit logs will be saved in the SSS database, after which they will be purged. The audit log is saved in the SSS database, so if at any time you need to set the database to read-only, you must first disable auditing. Otherwise, the following error message displays when an attempt is made to use the credentials within the SSS database: "Cannot complete this action as the Secure Store Shared Service is not responding. Please contact your administrator."

3. Click OK to create the SSS application and the service proxy.

4. From the Manage Service Applications page, click the SSS service application you created in the preceding step, and then on the Edit ribbon tab, in the Key Management group, click Generate New Key, as shown in Figure 3-25.

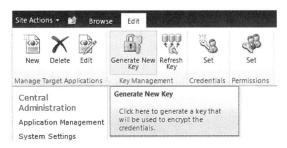

FIGURE 3-25 Use the Generate New Key command to create an encryption key.

5. On the Generate New Key page, type a pass phrase, as shown in Figure 3-26. This pass phrase must be at least eight characters in length, and it must contain at least three of the following four types of characters: uppercase, lowercase, number, or any of the special characters " ! " # $ % & ' ( ) * + , - / : ; < = > ? @ [\ ] ^ _ ` { | } ~ .

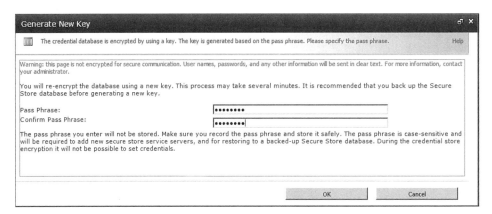

FIGURE 3-26 Use the Generate New Key page to enter a pass phrase.

Note The pass phase is used to encrypt the SSS database, but it is not stored. Therefore, if you want to refresh the key in the future, you must save the pass phrase entered. Refreshing the key propagates the encryption key to all servers in the farm. You can generate a new key at any time.

6. Click OK.

Using the Secure Store Service

To use SSS, first create a target application that represents the external system. Once you create this application, you can associate it with a BDC model or an ECT, or use it with other service applications that access external content, such as Excel Services or Visio Services.

Creating a Target Application ID

Create a target application as follows:

1. Display the Secure Store Service Application page by clicking the SSS service application on the Manage Service Applications page, and then on the Edit ribbon tab, in the Manage Target Applications group, click New.

2. Three pages are used to create a new secure store target application. On the first page:

    a. In the Target Application ID text box, type a name that represents the external system, such as **AdventureWksDB**. You cannot modify this name once it is created. This name will be passed as a parameter in URLs, and it is referenced in the BDC model, so do not include spaces or characters that are not allowed in URLs, such as $ & + , / \ : ; = ? @ " < > # % { } | ~ ^ [ ] '.

    b. In the Display Name text box, type a name that will be used for display purposes, such as **Adventure Works Database**.

    c. In the Contact E-mail text box, type an email address. Usually this is the email address of the business owner or the business analyst of the external system.

    d. In the Target Application Type drop-down list, select Individual if each user has an account in the external system, or select Group if the external system uses one account for all users. By using a naming convention for the target application ID, you can quickly identify the application type when looking at the BDC model. For example, AdventureWorksDB_i would indicate that the target application ID is to be used where every user has their own external system credentials.

    e. Leave None selected for the Target Application Page URL, as shown in Figure 3-27, so credentials that will be used to access the external system will be entered by the SSS administrator. Select Use Custom Page if you are going to create a webpage for users to enter the credentials for the external system. When you select Use Default Page, Share-Point generates a webpage that can be used to enter credentials. When you select a Target Application Type of Group, you can only select Use Custom Page or None.

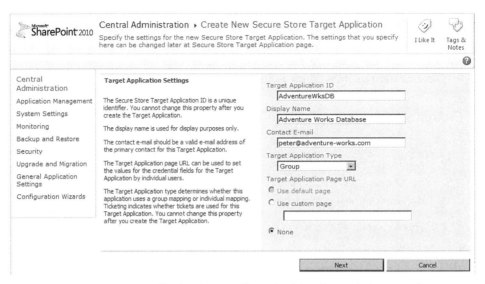

FIGURE 3-27 Create a target application ID to specify credentials to be used when accessing an external system.

  f. Click Next.

3. On the second page, you specify the number of fields required by the external system, as shown in Figure 3-28. All the fields created on this page are required when a user or the target application ID administrator creates the credentials.

FIGURE 3-28 Enter the credential fields for your external system.

Note Select the field type that matches the authentication method used by the external system. For example, if the external system is a database hosted by SQL Server, SQL Server supports two types of authentication: Windows and SQL authentication. By default when SQL Server is installed, only Windows authentication can be used. If your SQL Server is configured to use SQL authentication, and you want to use an SQL user ID as your user credentials, then select the field types User Name and Password in place of Windows User Name and Windows Password.

4. To navigate to the third page, click Next, and then in the Target Application Administrators text box, enter the users who administer the SSS setting for the external system. If you select Group as the Target Application Type, then a Members text box displays where you can enter those users or groups, as shown in Figure 3-29. These users will be able to map to the group credential that provides access to the external system.

FIGURE 3-29 Enter SSS administrators for the external system and users who are allowed access to the external system.

5. To create the target application ID, click OK.

You can modify the target application ID, its display name, contact email, administrators, and members once these have been created, but you cannot amend the following fields:

- Target Application ID

- Target Application Type

- The number of credential fields, their field names, or their field type (however, you can change the field property that controls whether to mask the text typed when entering the credentials).

Note By using an Active Directory (AD) group to identify users who can access the external system, you can reduce maintenance of the target application ID by the designated administrator.

Setting Field Credentials

To set the credentials used by the external system, you can use the default or custom page, if that was selected for the target application ID. Alternatively, on the Secure Store Service Application page, select the target application ID, and then on the Edit ribbon tab, in the Credentials group, click Set. You can also use the drop-down list associated with the target application ID to set the credentials, as shown in Figure 3-30.

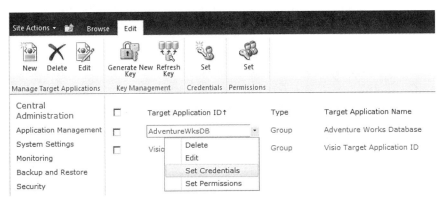

FIGURE 3-30 Use the Secure Store Service Application page in the SharePoint 2010 Central Administration website to set the target application ID credentials.

On the Set Credentials for Secure Store Application page, enter the user name for the external system, the password and confirmation of the password, and values for any other field you defined when you created the target application ID, as shown in Figure 3-31.

If the user name field is a Windows user name, then the name you type must be a valid AD user name of the format *<domain name>\<user name>*, such as **AdventureWrks\SSSBrett**. The credential owners will not be able to directly access the information you enter on this page; the BDC service application and the SSS application will use the user name and password on behalf of the credential owners. And, of course, the external system owner will use the user name to allow access to the content stored in the external system.

Notice the warning at the top of the page (shown in red text in the interface). User names, passwords, and any other information that you enter on this page are passed as clear text.

Once you click OK, the values you typed in the fields are stored in the SSS database. If you select Individual as the Target Application Type, you are asked to supply the credential owner. Normally, the target application administrator does not manually add every individual user as a credential owner using this page, but instead provides the link to the default or custom webpage and allows users to specify the external system credential information that they have been provided with.

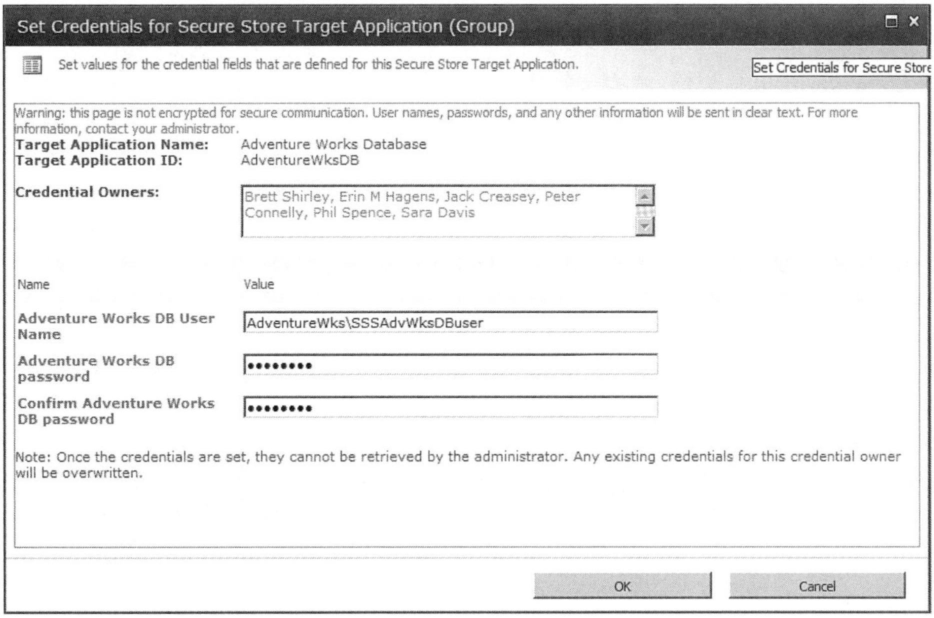

FIGURE 3-31 Set the values for the credential fields as defined for the SSS target application.

Whether you choose Individual or Group as the Target Application Type, if your organization implements an account policy that forces you to change the password for the credentials stored in the SSS database on a regular basis, then you will need to display the Set Credentials page and enter the new password.

The URL page for the default page is *http://<website>/_layouts/SecureStoreSetCredentials. aspx?TargetAppID=<TargetAppID>*, where *<website>* is the name of any website within a web application associated with the SSS service application and *<TargetAppID>* is the target application ID, such as AdventureWksDB. When a user clicks the link to the default page, a modal window may display stating that there is a problem with the website's security certificate, as shown in Figure 3-32. Again, this is a warning that the information entered will be sent in clear text.

FIGURE 3-32 SSS displays a warning message when information will be sent in clear text.

Click Continue to This Site to display SSS Set Credentials page.

If you try to display the default page for a group target application ID, a modal window displays an SSS error that access is denied for the target application, as shown in Figure 3-33.

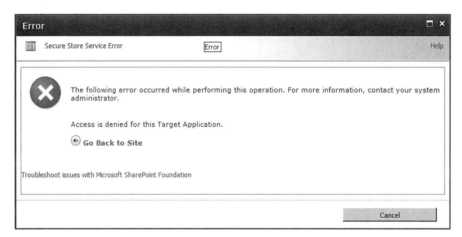

FIGURE 3-33 An SSS error appears when you try to display the default page for a group target application ID.

Note The default page is an application page, so there is only one instance of that page per SharePoint farm installation. Application pages cannot be modified using SharePoint Designer. If you do not like the default page, you can create a custom page. You can create a custom page using SharePoint Designer, store it in a content database or package it as a solution, and deploy it to each server in the farm. You can also have a custom page for each target application ID.

When the BDC model or ECT uses an individual target application ID to display the contents of the external system, such as when a user displays an external list created from the ECT and credentials have not been provided, then no data will be retrieved. A webpage displays with a Click Here to Authenticate link, which when clicked displays either the default or custom page depending on the configuration of the target application ID, allowing the user to enter the appropriate credentials.

Troubleshooting Connection Problems

When the credentials provided do not have access to the external system, an error message similar to the following displays and a correlation ID is provided: "The query against the database caused an error." This is a generic error message. The correlation ID is a hyphenated number, known as a globally unique identifier (GUID), and it will look similar to the following: aac9af1d-e90c-45f7-b590-650cf1b659d5. The GUID will help you identify the cause of the problem, and you can use it in the ULS logs to find further information about the error. The ULS logs are stored on servers in the log folder within the 14 hive. Microsoft provides the ULSViewer tool, which displays the entries in a user-friendly format and can be downloaded from *http://archive.mdsn.microsoft.com/ULSViewer*. The ULS log entry generated when the credentials stored in the SSS database do not have access to the external system is shown in Figure 3-34.

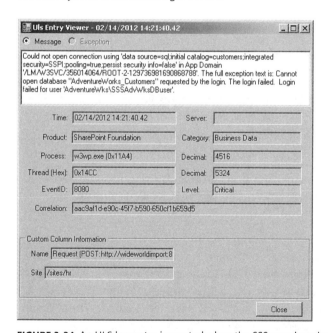

FIGURE 3-34 An ULS log entry is created when the SSS saved credentials do not have access to external system.

Configuring an ECT to Use Secure Store Service Credentials

Before you can create an ECT using SharePoint Designer, you first define a connection to the external system, where you provide the connection properties and the credentials that should be used. For example, for a SQL Server connection, you use the SQL Server Connection dialog box to provide the database server and database name. You then select the type of credentials you will use to connect to the SQL Server. Two impersonated identity options map to credentials stored in the SSS database:

- Connect with Impersonated Windows Identity Use this option if you create a target application ID, where the field types for user name and password are Windows User Name and Windows Password.

- Connect with Impersonated Custom Identity Use this option when you use other field types.

Once you select the identity type, in the Secure Store Application ID text box, type the name of the target application ID, as shown in Figure 3-35.

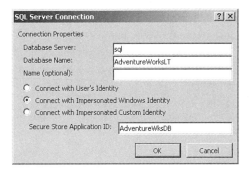

FIGURE 3-35 To use SSS target application IDs, select either of the impersonated identity options.

Note Throughout this book, you will use the Microsoft Adventure Works LT database when creating a SQL Server ECT. You can download this database from *http://msftdbprodsamples. codeplex.com*. See Chapter 4 for information about how to create ECTs for SQL Server databases.

After you create the ECT, you can modify the connection properties by clicking Edit Connection Properties on the External Content Type ribbon tab, in the Connection Properties group. The Connection Properties dialog box displays, as shown in Figure 3-36, where you can also configure a secondary Secure Store application ID.

You use the secondary Secure Store application ID when the ECT uses a web service or a .NET assembly connector, and the ECT operations are defined to use the optional filters, user name, and password. When the ECT is used to access the external system, values from the SSS database for the fields User Name and Password are passed as input values to the external system. The ability to pass the user name and password as input values can be very useful when connecting to an external system such as a web service, where custom HTTP headers and SOAP headers can pass user name and password information.

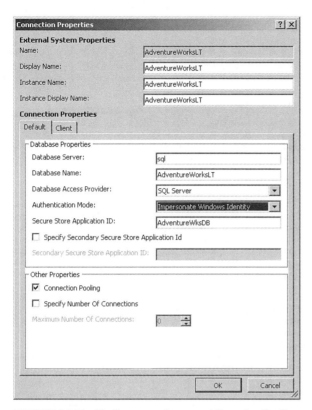

FIGURE 3-36 Modify the connection properties using the Connection Properties dialog box.

See Also *You can find information about custom HTTP and SOAP headers at* http://msdn.microsoft.com/ en-us/library/bb802855.aspx *and how to use SSS with .NET connectors at* http://msdn.microsoft.com/en-us/ library/ff798272.aspx. *For details about how to build .NET assembly connectors, see Chapter 12, "Building Server-Side BCS Solutions."*

Using Windows PowerShell to Administer BCS

SharePoint Foundation 2010 contains over 240 SharePoint-related Windows PowerShell cmdlets, and SharePoint Server 2010 contains over 530. Help is built in within Windows PowerShell. For example, for more information about the cmdlets relevant to Business Connectivity Services (BCS), start the SharePoint 2010 Management Shell as an administrator, and use a command similar to the following to list all Business Data Connectivity (BDC)-related cmdlets:

```
Get-Help *SPBusiness*
```

The preceding command generates the following output:

```
Name                                Category   Synopsis
----                                --------   --------
New-SPBusinessDataCatalogServi...   Cmdlet     Creates a new Business Data Conn...
Set-SPBusinessDataCatalogServi...   Cmdlet     Sets global properties for a Bus...
New-SPBusinessDataCatalogServi...   Cmdlet     Creates a new Business Data Conn...
Get-SPBusinessDataCatalogThrot...   Cmdlet     Returns the throttling configura...
Set-SPBusinessDataCatalogThrot...   Cmdlet     Sets the throttling configuratio...
Get-SPBusinessDataCatalogMetad...   Cmdlet     Returns a Business Data Connecti...
Set-SPBusinessDataCatalogMetad...   Cmdlet     Sets the value of a property or ...
Grant-SPBusinessDataCatalogMet...   Cmdlet     Grants a right to a principal fo...
Revoke-SPBusinessDataCatalogMe...   Cmdlet     Revokes a right to a principal i...
Import-SPBusinessDataCatalogModel   Cmdlet     Imports a Business Data Connecti...
Import-SPBusinessDataCatalogDo...   Cmdlet     Imports a .NET Connectivity asse...
Export-SPBusinessDataCatalogModel   Cmdlet     Exports a Business Data Connecti...
Remove-SPBusinessDataCatalogModel   Cmdlet     Deletes a Business Data Connecti...
Remove-SPSiteSubscriptionBusin...   Cmdlet     Removes the Business Data Connec...
Export-SPSiteSubscriptionBusin...   Cmdlet     Exports all data from the Busine...
Import-SPSiteSubscriptionBusin...   Cmdlet     Import-SPSiteSubscriptionBusines...
Clear-SPSiteSubscriptionBusine...   Cmdlet     Deletes all data from the Busine...
Copy-SPBusinessDataCatalogAclT...   Cmdlet     Copies a set of permissions of a...
Enable-SPBusinessDataCatalogEn...   Cmdlet     Activates an External Content ty...
Disable-SPBusinessDataCatalogE...   Cmdlet     Deactivates an External Content ...
```

 Note You can find all Secure Store Service (SSS)-related cmdlets by typing **Get-Help *securestore***.

You can then type the following to find more information about a specific cmdlet:

```
Get-help Get-SPBusinessDataCatalogMetadataObject
```

Learning the cmdlets and the logic you need to create a robust set of commands comes with experience and testing. Many administrative tasks will require only one line of code. For example, use the following command when you want to list all BDC service applications and the names of their databases:

```
Get-SPServiceApplication | where {$_.typename -like "*business*"} | select Name, Database
```

Other administrative tasks require a couple lines of Windows PowerShell. For example, when you want to enable the RevertToSelf authentication method, you first obtain a reference to the BDC service application that you want to manage, and then you complete the administrative task on that service application.

Other tasks require a number of lines of code. Do not expect to correctly create a Windows Power-Shell sequence of commands on your first attempt. It is often helpful to draw a diagram detailing the logic for the set of commands.

In most cases, when you try to complete BCS-related administrative tasks using Windows Power-Shell, you will need to use the SharePoint BDC cmdlets displayed previously, plus other SharePoint cmdlets. You may find that you sometimes have to reference the SharePoint namespace, similar to when a developer creates a program to do such tasks. In such instances, you may have to refer to the SharePoint 2010 software developer kit (SDK) or engage the help of a developer.

See Also *For more information about Windows PowerShell and SharePoint 2010, see* Microsoft SharePoint Server 2010 Administrator's Companion, *by Bill English, Brian Alderman, and Mark Ferrarz (Microsoft Press, 2010), Chapter 5, "Using Windows PowerShell to Perform and Automate Farm Administrative Tasks," and* http://technet.microsoft.com/en-us/library/ee661742.aspx.

Enabling the RevertToSelf Authentication Method

By default, the authentication method RevertToSelf is disabled. Microsoft recommends using the RevertToSelf authentication method only in a production environment, when all the following conditions are true:

- You are using SharePoint Foundation 2010.

- You do not have resources to create a custom SSS.

- You trust all of the people who use SharePoint Designer as completely as if they were Share-Point administrators.

- The application pool account is locked down such that the attack surface exposed to a malicious user of SharePoint Designer is limited.

Use Windows PowerShell as shown in the following example to enable RevertToSelf, where the variable *BDCName* is the name of your BDC service application:

```
$BDCName = "Business Data Connectivity Service";
$bcs = Get-SPServiceApplication | where {$_.displayname -eq $BDCName};
$bcs.RevertToSelfAllowed = $True;
```

Although the BDC server runtime would use the application pool ID to retrieve data from the external system no matter which user wants to display the external content, remember that you can use permission settings on the BDC service application to restrict access to the external content.

Importing a BDC Model

You can use the SharePoint 2010 Central Administration website to import a BDC model, as shown in the following code:

```
$catalog = Get-SPBusinessDataCatalogMetadataObject -BdcObjectType catalog '
   -ServiceContext http://intranet
Import-SPBusinessDataCatalogModel -Identity $catalog -Path c:\adventurewksCust.bdcm;
```

If the preceding set of commands is successful and there were no warnings or errors, you will see no output. You should check that the model successfully loaded and that you can use the ECTs that the model may contain. To display all BDC models in the BDC metadata store, type on one line the following command, using the URL of your own web application:

```
Get-SPBusinessDataCatalogMetadataObject -BdcObjectType Model '
   -ServiceContext http://intranet -Name "*" | select Name
```

To display all the external systems in the BDC metadata store, and to display the type of external system together with its entities (ECTs), use this command:

```
Get-SPBusinessDataCatalogMetadataObject -BdcObjectType LoBSystem '
   -ServiceContext http://intranet -Name "*" | select Name, SystemType, Entities
```

The output will look similar to the following:

```
Name                           SystemType Entities
----                           ---------- --------
SharePointDesigner-adve...                Database {SharePointDesigner-ad...
AdventureWorksLT                          Database {AdventureWorks_Custom...
SharePointDesigner-adve...                Database {SharePointDesigner-ad...
adventureworksdw                          Database {AdventureWksDW_Employ...
```

Modifying External System Throttling

External system throttling is enabled by default to prevent denial of service (DoS) attacks. You are most likely to see the effect of this feature if you created no limit filter on the BDC model and the retrieval of data from the external system is taking too long. Each BDC service application can have a number of throttle configurations, and each configuration can be tuned to a throttle type and/or scope, where the five throttle types are as follows:

- **None**   No throttle type specified

- **Items**   The number of external content type (ECT) instances returned, such as the number of customers or employees

- **Size**   The amount of data retrieved by the BDC runtime in bytes

- **Connections**   The number of open connections to a database, web service, or .NET assembly

- **Timeout**   The time until an open connection is terminated, in milliseconds

The five throttle scopes refer to the external system connection type and include the following:

- **Global**   Includes all connector types, such as database, web service, Windows Communication Foundation (WCF), and .NET assembly connectors, except for custom connectors

- **Database**

- **WebService**

- **WCF**

- **Custom**

Not all combinations of throttle types and scopes are defined when you first create a BDC service application. The rules are as follows:

- Global Scope, Throttle Type Connections

- Database Scope, Throttle Type Items, and Timeout

- WebService Scope, Throttle Type Size

- WCF Scope, Throttle Type Size, and Timeout

You can retrieve and amend the throttling rules by using the Business Data Windows PowerShell cmdlets, as shown in the following examples, where the variable *BDCName* is the name of your BDC service application.

```
$bdcproxy = Get-SPServiceApplicationProxy | where {$_.displayname -eq $BDCname};
```

To display the throttling configuration for a BDC service application, type the following command on one line:

```
Get-SPBusinessDataCatalogThrottleConfig –ServiceApplication $bdcproxy `
  -Scope Global –ThrottleType Connections;
```

The output from the command is as follows:

```
Scope       : Global
ThrottleType : Connections
Enforced    : True
Default     : 200
Max         : 500
```

The output displays five properties. The three properties that you can amend are:

- **Enforces** Defines if the rule is enabled

- **Default** Affects external lists and custom Web Parts, although custom Web Parts can override this value and therefore can present more data than external lists

- **Max** The limit used when custom Web Parts override the value in the Default property

To disable a throttling rule, type the following command:

```
Get-SPBusinessDataCatalogThrottleConfig -ServiceApplication $bdcproxy `
    -Scope Global -ThrottleType Connections | Set-SPBusinessDataCatalogThrottleConfig `
    -Enforced:$False;
```

To modify a throttle rule, type this command:

```
$dbrule = Get-SPBusinessDataCatalogThrottleConfig -ServiceApplication $bdcproxy `
    -Scope Database -ThrottleType Items;
$dbrule | Set-SPBusinessDataCatalogThrottleConfig -Maximum 2000000 -Default 5000;
```

Administrating BCS in a Tenant Environment

You can create a tenant environment that can host multiple tenants in SharePoint Foundation and is available for you to create if you are using SharePoint Server, Standard or Enterprise edition, and SharePoint Online. There are four components to a SharePoint 2010 multitenant installation:

- **Services**   These applications are partitioned and nonpartitioned.

- **Feature packs**   A subscriber can use only those site or web-scoped features defined in the feature pack.

- **Multitenant admin site**   Each tenant has its own tenant administration site that allows the owners of the tenant to create sites, create site collections, manage user profiles, and so on. You create this site from the Tenant Farm Administrator site template.

- **Multitenant member sites**   All site collections that form part of one tenancy are associated together by a subscription, and so a tenant is also known as a subscriber. The subscription key, also known as the subscription ID, is a GUID used to map features, services, and sites to a tenant, and also to partition service data.

The SharePoint 2010 Central Administration web application does not expose all the tasks needed to create a multitenant environment. You use Windows PowerShell to create the multitenant service application, admin site, subscription ID, feature packs, and association of site collections to a specific subscription. SharePoint provides a number of Windows PowerShell cmdlets to manage site subscriptions. To find more information about these cmdlets, type the following:

```
Get-Help *spsitesub*
```

This code outputs:

```
Name                                  Category  Synopsis
----                                  --------  --------
New-SPSiteSubscription                Cmdlet    Creates a new site subscription.
Get-SPSiteSubscription                Cmdlet    Returns the site subscription fo...
Remove-SPSiteSubscription             Cmdlet    Removes data stored in a subscri...
Get-SPSiteSubscriptionConfig          Cmdlet    Returns the configuration proper...
Set-SPSiteSubscriptionConfig          Cmdlet    Sets the configuration propertie...
Remove-SPSiteSubscriptionSettings     Cmdlet    Removes the settings service dat...
Export-SPSiteSubscriptionSettings     Cmdlet    Creates a backup file of site su...
Import-SPSiteSubscriptionSettings     Cmdlet    Restores a backup of subscriptio...
New-SPSiteSubscriptionFeaturePack     Cmdlet    Creates a new SharePoint Feature...
Get-SPSiteSubscriptionFeaturePack     Cmdlet    Retrieves available SharePoint F...
Remove-SPSiteSubscriptionFeatu...     Cmdlet    Removes a SharePoint Feature set...
Add-SPSiteSubscriptionFeatureP...     Cmdlet    Adds a feature to a SharePoint F...
Remove-SPSiteSubscriptionFeatu...     Cmdlet    Removes a feature definition fro...
Remove-SPSiteSubscriptionBusin...     Cmdlet    Removes the Business Data Connec...
Export-SPSiteSubscriptionBusin...     Cmdlet    Exports all data from the Busine...
Import-SPSiteSubscriptionBusin...     Cmdlet    Import-SPSiteSubscriptionBusines...
Clear-SPSiteSubscriptionBusine...     Cmdlet    Deletes all data from the Busine...
Set-SPSiteSubscriptionEdiscove...     Cmdlet    Sets properties for the eDiscove...
Get-SPSiteSubscriptionEdiscove...     Cmdlet    Displays the eDiscovery hub for ...
Get-SPSiteSubscriptionEdiscove...     Cmdlet    Displays the search scope for th...
Get-SPSiteSubscriptionMetadata...     Cmdlet    Returns the site subscription co...
Remove-SPSiteSubscriptionMetad...     Cmdlet    Removes site subscription config...
Set-SPSiteSubscriptionMetadata...     Cmdlet    Sets the site subscription confi...
Add-SPSiteSubscriptionProfileC...     Cmdlet    Adds a new site subscription to ...
Set-SPSiteSubscriptionProfileC...     Cmdlet    Sets the parameters of a site su...
Remove-SPSiteSubscriptionProfi...     Cmdlet    Deletes a site subscription from...
```

To create a tenant environment:

1. Create an AD account and register it as a managed account for the subscription service application.

2. Create a web application where all the tenant's site collections will be created.

3. Create managed paths for the tenant's site collections.

4. Start the SharePoint Foundation Subscription Settings Service on one of the servers in the farm.

5. Create a Subscription Settings service application.

The last two tasks have to be completed using Windows PowerShell. For each set of tenants, using Windows PowerShell, create the following:

- A subscription.

- A tenancy administration site in its own site collection.

- Feature packs, which you then associate with the subscription (optional).

- A partition of a service application (optional).

- One or more tenant site collections. You can also create these using the top-level site of the tenant's administration site collection.

See Also *You can find more information about how to create a multitenant environment with SharePoint 2010 at www.harbar.net/articles/sp2010mt1.aspx.*

Creating a PartitionMode BDC Service Application

To create a new Business Data Connectivity (BDC) service application in PartitionMode, start a BDC service instance on one server in the farm like any other service application, and then create the BDC service application. You can complete both of these tasks using Windows PowerShell, as shown in the following code:

```
Get-SPServiceInstance |
where{$_.GetType().Name -eq "BdcServiceInstance"} | Start-SPServiceInstance'

$BDCName = "BDC SA PartitionMode"
New-SPBusinessDataCatalogServiceApplication -PartitionMode -Name $BDCName
    -ApplicationPool "SharePoint Web Services Default" -DatabaseName "BDC_PartitionedDB"
```

This command creates a BDC service application and its proxy, and includes the proxy in the default proxy group. If you delete the service application proxy that is created automatically, you must consequently delete the service application as well. Recreating the service application is the only way to create a service application proxy in partition mode.

After provisioning the BCS service application in partition mode, you will no longer be able to manage the service from the SharePoint 2010 Central Administration website—you must navigate to the BCS Management page from the Tenant Administration site. Remember, however, that only the BDC service application set as the default in the proxy group is used by web applications. Therefore, if a BDC service application already exists when you create the PartitionMode BDC service application, although it is added to the default proxy group, it will not be set as the default, and you will get an error when you try to administer it from the Tenant Administration page.

Note With other service applications, the SharePoint cmdlet to create the service application will not create the service application proxy or add it to the default proxy group. For those service applications, you use either the relevant SharePoint cmdlets or the SharePoint 2010 Central Administration website.

Managing BCS from the Tenant Administration Site

To manage the partition of the BDC service application associated with a tenant, navigate to the Tenant Administration site, and then under System Settings, click Manage Business Data Connectivity, as shown in Figure 3-37. A page similar to Figure 3-15 displays, where you can manage BDC models, external systems, external content types (ECTs), metadata store BDC object permissions, and the configuration and creation of profile pages.

FIGURE 3-37 Use the Tenant Administration website to administer BCS.

If your SharePoint solution is hosted in a tenant environment, you do not have access to the servers and cannot run the SharePoint cmdlets. If your company is the hosting organization, then you can manage the PartitionMode BDC service application using Windows PowerShell as you would a non-PartitionMode BDC service application, except the service context will be a tenant site collection—either the tenant administrator site collection or the site collection of a member site—and not the URL of a web application. To import a BDC model, you use the following code:

```
$catalog = Get-SPBusinessDataCatalogMetadataObject -BdcObjectType catalog '
    -ServiceContext http://intranet/tenant/T1admin
Import-SPBusinessDataCatalogModel -Identity $catalog -Path c:\adventurewksCust.bdcm;
```

Summary

The Business Connectivity Services (BCS) connectivity layer is provided by the Business Data Connectivity (BDC) service application, which is a Microsoft SharePoint 2010 service application and can thus take advantage of the service application architecture. A SharePoint 2010 farm can host a number of BDC service applications that can be independently configured by different sets of administrators using the SharePoint 2010 Central Administration website or through Windows PowerShell.

Once you create the BDC service application, you need to complete a number of tasks before the data in the external system can be used:

- Create BDC service application administrators.

- Import the BDC model that contains the metadata information.

- Set BDC metadata store permissions.

- Configure profile page creation for the Enterprise edition of SharePoint Server 2010.

- Configure the Secure Store Service (SSS) application if you plan to have any of the BDC models imported into the metadata store use this authentication mechanism.

The chapter also discussed external system throttling, which is enabled by default to prevent denial of service (DoS) attacks.

CHAPTER 4

Defining External System Connections Using SharePoint Designer

In this chapter, you will:

- Create and manage external content types using SharePoint Designer

- Create and modify data connections

- Create and maintain data source operations

- Export external content types

Business Connectivity Services (BCS) allows you to hook up external data with SharePoint and Office applications, enabling either professional developers or citizen developers in an organization to quickly develop composite solutions. To connect to the external system, the location of the external system, the protocol to use, and the credentials must be defined. Once connected, you need to define what operations on the data are allowed and the format of the data that will be returned. The operations that can be used on the external data and its format are defined in an external content type (ECT). The definition of the location of the external system together with the ECT is known as the Business Data Connectivity (BDC) model.

ECTs are a new concept in SharePoint 2010 and are the building blocks of BCS, similar to the entity object in SharePoint Server 2007. ECTs refer to external data objects and define the fields, the methods, and what a user can do with the data in SharePoint and Office client applications. Both read and write capabilities are included, along with batch and bulk operation support. You need to define the external system and ECT only once, and then you can use that ECT on many sites across all web applications associated with the BDC service application.

See Also *You can find information on BDC service applications and how to associate them with web applications in Chapter 3, "Creating and Maintaining Business Connectivity Services Service Applications."*

To create the BDC model, ECT, and BDC objects, you have a choice of tools: Microsoft SharePoint Designer 2010, Microsoft Visual Studio 2010, and third-party tools, and you can even use an XML editor, such as XML Notepad 2007, or a regular text editor, such as Notepad. The advantage of using SharePoint Designer is that it provides users with a wizard that, when configured, generates the XML that defines the BDC model, ECT, BDC objects, and operations. The user, however, does not need to learn the BDC XML schema to define the connection details to the external system.

See Also *For detailed information about the BDC model XML schema, see Appendix A, "BCS Model Infrastructure."*

Creating ECTs Using SharePoint Designer

Before you can create an external content type (ECT), you must create a Business Data Connectivity (BDC) service application, and the BDC service application administrator must set edit permissions on the BDC metadata store for users of SharePoint Designer who will be creating ECTs. This is a high level of privileged access to the entire store; therefore, if a SharePoint Designer user is only going to modify an existing ECT, then the BDC service administrator can remove the edit permission on the BDC metadata store and just give the user edit permission on the ECT.

To create an ECT, you need to complete the following tasks:

1. Identify the external system that contains the data needed by your solution, the business users who will use your solution, and the access those users will need. If you are not familiar with the external system, you will also need to engage the help of the business owner/analyst.

2. Provide a name, display name, and namespace for the ECT.

3. Define the external system connection.

4. Define the operations to create, read, update, and delete (CRUD) content stored in that external system that is needed for your solution, including setting filters and defining the association operation.

5. Generate profile pages and actions if required.

6. Save and test the ECT by presenting the data from the external system, using external lists, using external columns in existing lists, and using Business Web Parts or presenting external data from within an Office application.

    See Also *You can find information about the different methods you can use to present external data in other chapters in Part II of this book.*

7. Liaise with the BDC service application administration to configure the permissions on the ECT so that necessary business users can see content from the external system.

SharePoint Designer provides two pages to configure an ECT: the Summary View and the Operations Design View. You can switch between these two pages using the Summary View and Operations Design View commands in the Views group on the External Content Types ribbon tab. You will use these two pages to create the ECT, its connection to the external system, and the operations that can be used to access the external data in the external system.

Using the ECT Summary View

The Summary View page is divided into a number of areas, which work together with a context-sensitive ribbon tab. Before you can use the ECT Summary View, you need to start to create an ECT. Then you can use the ECT Summary View to define the ECT's name, display name, and namespace, and configure it for use with Office applications.

Create an ECT

To create an ECT, follow these steps:

1. Open SharePoint Designer, and then open a SharePoint site in the web application associated with the BDC service application where you have edit permissions on the BDC metadata store.

2. In the Navigation pane, click External Content Types to open the External Content Types gallery, as shown in Figure 4-1. The ECT gallery lists ECTs you have permission to see. The gallery may be empty if no ECTs have been created or if you do not have permission to view any. On the context-sensitive ribbon tab for the ECT gallery, you can create new ECTs and external lists, edit or delete an ECT, and export one or more ECTs in a BDC model.

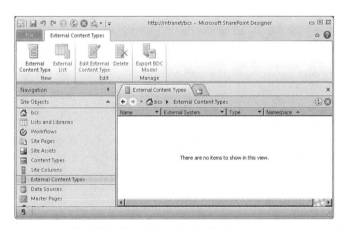

FIGURE 4-1 The ECT gallery in SharePoint Designer is empty when no ECTs have been created or you do not have permission to view any.

When the ECT gallery is empty, the only command active on the External Content Type ribbon tab is External Content Type in the New group—that is, you can only create new ECTs. Once an ECT is defined and is displayed in the ECT gallery, you can then use the ribbon to create external lists from an ECT, edit or delete an ECT, or export the BDC model that contains one or more ECTs. To select more than one ECT, select one ECT and then hold down the Shift or Ctrl key to select other ECTs, as you would when selecting multiple files in Windows Explorer.

3. On the External Content Types ribbon tab, click External Content Type in the New group. The Summary View of the ECT is displayed with an asterisk on the workspace label, as shown in Figure 4-2.

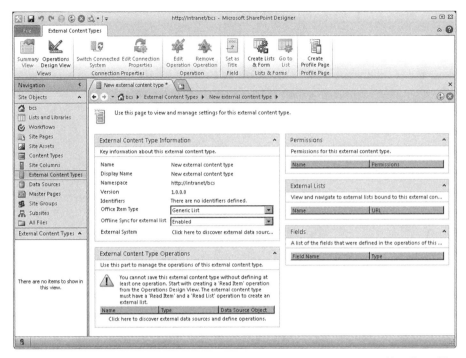

FIGURE 4-2 An asterisk on a workspace tab indicates that your changes are stored locally and have not been saved to the SharePoint server.

The asterisk identifies that you have not saved the ECT to the server. You have several ways of saving an ECT back to the BDC metadata store:

- Click the floppy disk icon in the Quick Access bar.

- Right-click the ECT workspace label where the asterisk is displayed, and click Save.

- Use the keystroke Ctrl+S.

Areas on the Summary View Page

The Summary View page consists of five areas:

■ **External Content Type Information** is where you enter key information about the ECT, such as the name, display name, namespace, version, and identifiers; select an Office item type; enable Office Sync for external lists; and configure the connection options to the external system.

■ **External Content Type Operations** allows you to manage the operations for the ECT.

■ **Permissions** allows you to view the permissions settings for the ECT.

■ **External Lists** allows you to view and navigate to external lists using the ECT.

■ **Fields** displays the fields that are defined for the operations for the ECT.

External Content Type Information area   Before configuring the connection details to the external system, you should name the ECT, select whether the external content is compatible for any Office format and, if you are using the Enterprise edition of SharePoint Server, choose whether users are allowed to take the content offline. You can set these properties in the External Content Type Information area:

■ **Name** Enter the name of the ECT, such as AdventureWorks_Customers or AdventureWorks_Sales. The ECT name is usually a short but meaningful name that preferably does not contain spaces. You cannot save an ECT until it has a name. Once you have saved the ECT, you cannot change the ECT name in SharePoint Designer; however, you can change the ECT display name. If you do name the ECT incorrectly, you can export the ECT as part of a BDC model, alter the XML in the file (for example, in Visual Studio), and then reimport the BDC model into the BDC metadata store. This will create a new ECT. You can then remove the misspelled ECT, but note that this will impact any external lists you have created from the misspelled ECT. An ECT is identified internally by a unique reference number, known as a globally unique identifier (GUID), which is generated using the name of the ECT and its namespace.

> **See Also**   *You will learn about exporting and importing the BDC model later in this chapter.*

■ **Display Name** This is the name displayed in the External Content Type Picker dialog box, as shown in Figure 4-3. If you do not enter a display name, then the ECT name is used as the display name. You should enter a name that your users can relate to, as the External Content Type Picker dialog box is used when creating external lists and external columns and configuring Business Web Parts. It is stored in the BDC metadata store as a Unicode string with a maximum length of 255 characters.

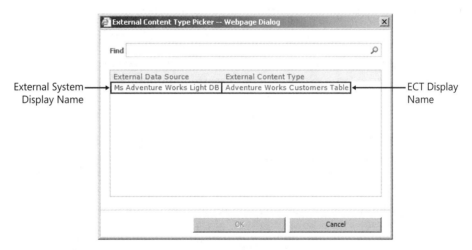

FIGURE 4-3 The External Content Type Picker dialog box uses the external system display name and the ECT display name.

- **Namespace** By default, the namespace is configured as the URL of the website where you are creating the ECT. The External Content Types gallery in SharePoint Designer displays ECTs grouped by the name of their namespace, and you should change the namespace to a name that represents the business purpose of the external data—for example, http://Adventure-WorksSalesInvoicing for all ECTs that relate to sales data for a company, no matter which data source they come from, or for all ECTs that you create from the same data source (for example, all ECTs based on the AdventureWorks database). As the namespace is a URL, it should not include spaces or characters such as $ & + , / \ : ; = ? @ " < > # % { } | ~ ^ [ ] '.

- **Version** This string field has the format 1.0.0.0. SharePoint Designer will automatically increment the fourth digit each time you save the ECT, but if you make a major update, such as changing the external content source for the ECT, then the second digit is incremented. When either of the first two digits is changed, it is considered a breaking change, and any external lists built previously will not work. Specifically, the pages that were created to display or modify the contents from the external system will not work, such as views or forms, whether they are ASPX pages or InfoPath forms.

Multiple versions of an ECT can be stored in the metadata store, but only the active version is used. When SharePoint Designer creates a new version, it automatically makes the ECT version that it is creating the active version, and it deletes previous versions of the ECT.

When you use the SharePoint 2010 Central Administration website to import a BDC model that defines a new version of an ECT, the new version is activated. The version number is not automatically incremented, however, when you use the SharePoint 2010 Central Administration website, previous versions of the BDC model will be deleted. To view all versions for an ECT, use the following Windows PowerShell code:

```
Get-SPBusinessDataCatalogMetadataObject -BdcObjectType Entity ‘
   -ServiceContext http://intranet ‘
   -Name AdventureWorks_customers  -Namespace http://adventureworkscustomers;
```

To delete the current version, first deactivate it, activate the previous version, and then delete the version you wish to remove, as shown in the following code, where the variable *$ecta* references the ECT you wish to activate, and the variable *$ectd:* references the ECT you wish to delete.

```
$exta = Get-SPBusinessDataCatalogMetadataObject -BdcObjectType Entity ‘
   -ServiceContext http://intranet ‘
   -Name AdventureWorks_customers -Namespace http://adventureworkscustomers | ‘
   where {$_.version -eq “1.6.0.0”};

$extd = Get-SPBusinessDataCatalogMetadataObject -BdcObjectType Entity ‘
   -ServiceContext http://intranet ‘
   -Name AdventureWorks_customers -Namespace http://adventureworkscustomers | ‘
   where {$_.version -eq “1.6.1.0”};

$ectd.Deactivate();
$ecta.Activate();
$ectd.Delete();
```

Note If an ECT has no active versions, then the ECT will not be visible when you use the SharePoint 2010 Central Administration website. If no ECTs are listed, it does not mean that there are no ECTs—just that there are no active ECTs. In SharePoint Designer, if an ECT exists but there is no active version, then the ECT displays in the ECT gallery, but when you click the ECT in the workspace, a message appears stating that SharePoint Designer cannot display the item.

To delete all but one version, use the following code:

```
Get-SPBusinessDataCatalogMetadataObject -BdcObjectType Entity '
    -ServiceContext http://intranet '
    -Name AdventureWorks_customers  -Namespace http://adventureworkscustomers |
    foreach { if ($_.version -ne "16.0.0.0") {
        $_.delete();
    }};
```

When you have deleted all versions of an ECT, you should ensure that the BDC metadata store does not contain any BDC models that are no longer needed. You can delete BDC models using the SharePoint 2010 Central Administration website or Windows PowerShell. Remember, an ECT is defined by its name and namespace, so different versions of the same ECT could have been defined in different BDC models. Also, a BDC model can contain more than one ECT, so take care when deleting BDC models.

- **Identifiers** This column or field name contains a unique identifier for each item of data returned from the external system. When you use a database as your external source, this field is usually designated as the primary key. The column could contain a business unique number, such as a Social Security number, or it could be a number that the external system automatically generates, such as a GUID when using Microsoft SQL Server. You can choose the identifier when you create operations to access the external source. You create operations in the Operations Design View. When you first create an ECT, you have not selected either the external system or operations, therefore no identifier is set, and the message "There are no identifiers defined" appears.

- **Office Item Type** If you want to display external data in an Office application, you can choose one of five options from the drop-down list: Generic List or one of the four Office item types (Appointment, Contact, Task, or Post). The Office item types are aimed at Microsoft Outlook 2010.

When you connect the external list to Outlook, the external content can be shown in the contacts, calendar, mail, or task pane, as well as in the SharePoint External Lists folder. If one of the external content fields is mapped to the Office email property, you can send an email to a person whose details are stored in the external system.

See Also *You can find more information on connecting external data with Office applications in Chapter 7, "Using External Data with Office Client Applications," and Chapter 11, "Using Client-Side Code and External Data."*

When an Office item type is selected, you will need to map a field or fields from the external data source to an Office property when you create the Read Item operation. Each Office item type has mandatory properties that you must map to a data source field, as shown in Table 4-1. Also, you can choose mappings only for those fields that have a compatible Office properties data type, shown in parentheses in the table.

TABLE 4-1 Office properties that need to be mapped to data source elements

Office item type	Mandatory Office properties
Appointment	Subject (String), Start (DateTime), End (DateTime)
Contact	LastName (String) or FullName (String)
Task	Subject (string)
Post	Subject (string)

- **Offline Sync for external list**   Use this option if you want to connect any external lists created from the ECT to either Outlook or Microsoft SharePoint Workspace 2010. The Sync To SharePoint Workspace and Connect To Outlook commands can be found when displaying an external list in the Connect & Export group on the List ribbon tab. If you do not see these commands, check this setting within SharePoint Designer. The logic to take the data offline is provided by a Visual Studio Tools for Office (VSTO) ClickOnce deployment package, which is provided only in the Enterprise edition of SharePoint Server. With SharePoint Foundation and some Office 365 plans, you cannot take external list data offline in Outlook or SharePoint Workspace.

- **External System**   Use this option to define the external system authorization details and the external system details, such as the database server name, database name, and database access provider, for both SharePoint and when the external data is accessed using an Office application. When an ECT is first created, the hyperlink Click Here to Discover External Data Sources and Define Operations is displayed. Click this hyperlink to display the operations design view.

Permission area and permission implication for SharePoint Designer   This area on the Summary View displays the permission settings for the ECT. These settings are retrieved from the BDC metadata store. You cannot set the ECT permissions from SharePoint Designer—you need to use the SharePoint 2010 Central Administration website, Windows PowerShell, or a third-party tool or develop your own code against the BDC Administration application programming interface (API).

See Also *You can find more information about how to configure permissions using the SharePoint 2010 Central Administration website in Chapter 3.*

Each object stored in the BDC metadata store has an access control list (ACL) that specifies which users and groups have permissions on the objects. Out of the 13 BDC metadata objects, only the external system, ECTs, and the BDC model permissions can be set using the SharePoint 2010 Central Administration website. A professional developer can set the permissions using code for ECT operations and instances of those operations that specify how to use the operation by using a specific set of default values. Only five BDC metadata objects can have their own controllable ACLs: the external system, BDC model, ECTs, operations, and operation instances. These objects are referred to as *individually securable metadata objects*.

All other objects obtain their permissions from their parent object. For example, associations, actions, and identifiers cannot be assigned permissions directly but take their permissions from their parent ECT. However, by default, permissions do not propagate from one individually securable metadata object to another, so an ECT operation does not inherit its permissions from its ECT, unless the propagate check box is selected. However, if permissions are propagated from an ECT, all operations and operation instances for that ECT receive the new permissions, replacing the permissions originally set on those individually securable metadata objects.

You can set the following four permissions on the BDC metadata store and BDC metadata objects:

- Edit

- Execute

- Selectable In Clients

- Set Permissions

Not all permissions are applicable to all objects. For example, enabling the Execute and Selectable In Clients with the BDC metadata store or the external system has no effect. However, setting these permissions at the BDC metadata store or external system level and selecting the propagation check box can be useful when you do not want to individually configure ECTs or operations for these two permissions. There isn't Edit permission on the ECT, but setting the Edit permission on the ECT is useful, so users of SharePoint Designer can create and modify objects that the ECT contains, such as operations, actions, and associations.

When you create an ECT with SharePoint Designer, you need to define an external system, which you can do using SharePoint Designer. When you save your newly created ECT, a BDC model is created. To create a definition for an external system, a BDC model, and an ECT, you must have Edit permissions on the BDC metadata store. However, the ECT will inherit permission settings only from the BDC metadata store, if the permission settings were configured to propagate. It is possible that you can create an ECT, and an external list from that ECT, but you may not be able to view data that the external list should display. Once an ECT is created, you can check the information in the Permissions area to see if the ECT inherited permissions from the BDC metadata store, as shown in Figure 4-4. If the Permissions area is empty or you do not have Edit, Execute, and Selectable In Clients permissions, you should contact your BCS administrator and ask them to set the permissions for you and for users who should access the external data.

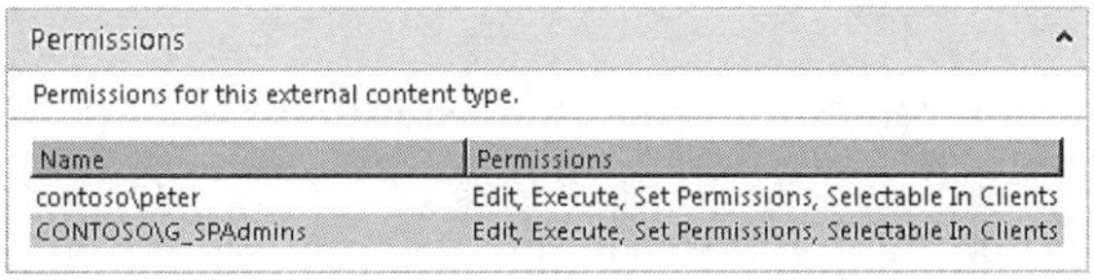

FIGURE 4-4 Use the Permissions area on the Summary View to identify the permissions set for the ECT.

To work with external data in SharePoint Designer and then test your ECT by displaying content from the external system in external lists or Business Web Parts, you will need the permissions shown in Table 4-2.

TABLE 4-2 BDC permission levels and what they mean for users using the SharePoint 2010 Central Administration website, SharePoint Designer, or the browser

Tasks to complete	Permission	Permission to be set on BDC metadata objects
Create a new or import a BDC models or create an external system	Edit	BDC metadata store
Edit and use an external system, including making the external system visible to SharePoint Designer on the Operations Design View	Edit	External system
Edit BDC models	Edit	BDC model
Export a BDC model	Edit	BDC model and all external systems in the model
Create a new ECT	Edit	External system
Use the ECT picker (for example, to create external lists and external columns, or when using Business Web Parts)	Selectable In Clients	ECT
Edit an operation	Edit	Operation
Execute operations or operation instances that allow you to complete CRUD operations on the external data	Execute	Operation and method instances of the ECT

Microsoft recommends that users of SharePoint Designer not be given the Set Permissions permission. Also, to help ensure a secure solution, SharePoint Designer should be used to create ECTs in a test environment in which Edit permissions can be assigned freely. When you deploy the tested solution to a production environment, you should remove the Edit permissions to help protect the integrity of the external data. In a development environment, give users who build ECTs with SharePoint Designer all four permissions, and give to other users all but the Set Permissions permission on the metadata store, and propagate permissions to all BDC models, external systems, and ECTs in the BDC metadata store.

External Lists area   This area lists external lists that were created from the ECT. Only the external lists created in the site opened in SharePoint Designer appear in this area; external lists created on other sites are not displayed. If one external list appears in this area, then the Create Lists & Forms command is active on the Externals Contents Ribbon tab in the Lists & Forms group.

When you select an external list in this area, the Go to List command in the Lists & Forms group becomes active, and when clicked, this command opens a new SharePoint Designer workspace tab to display the list settings page for the external list.

External Content Types Operations area   You can use this area together with the Edit Operation and Remove Operation commands in the ribbon to manage the operations of the ECT. The ribbon commands are not active unless you click an operation, as shown in Figure 4-5.

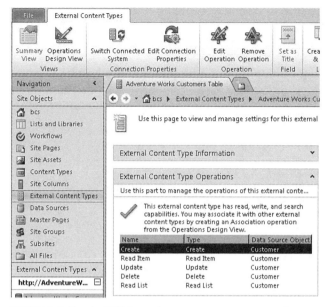

FIGURE 4-5 Use the ECT Operations area to manage operations.

With a newly created ECT, no operations will exist, and you will need to use the Operations Design View to create new operations.

Fields area   This area displays the fields that were defined in the operations for the ECT.

Using the Operations Design View

Now that you have created an ECT and given it a display name and a namespace, you will want to select the external data source if previously defined or define a new content source, which you can do on the Operations Design View. You can display the Operations Design View in one of two ways:

- On the External Content Types ribbon tab, in the Views group, click Operations Design View.

- On the Summary View, within the Key Information About This External Content Type area, to the right of External Systems, click Click Here To Discover External Data Sources And Define Operations.

The Operations Design View, as shown in Figure 4-6, consists of an area where you can add, remove, and explore data connections, and a second area where you can manage operations for the ECT.

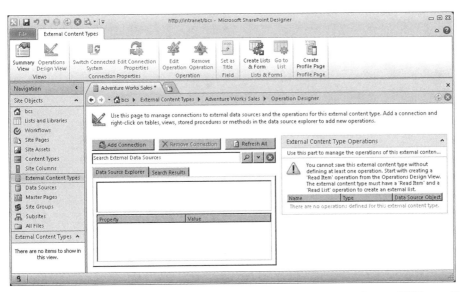

FIGURE 4-6 Use the Operations Design View to manage data source connections and ECT operations.

In a new installation of SharePoint, whether it is SharePoint Server, SharePoint Foundation, or Office 365, the Operations Design View will not list any data connection for you to select. The next task is to create a data connection.

Using the Summary View and Operations Design View Ribbon Tabs

The Summary View and the Operations Design View share the same context-sensitive ribbon tab named External Content Types. It consists of six groups, and the commands in each group will be active depending on the components selected within areas of the page.

Views

Use the two commands in this ribbon group to switch between the Summary View and the Operations Design View.

Connection Properties

The two commands in this group, Switch Connect System and Edit Connection Properties, can only be active on the Summary View. These commands allow you to reassign the ECT to another compatible external system or to edit the connection properties to the external system.

Operation

The two commands in this group are always active on the Operations Design View, but they will be active on the Summary View only if you select an operation in the External Content Type Operations area.

Field

This group contains only one command, Set as Title, which is active only on the Summary View and when a field is selected in the Field area. All SharePoint lists and libraries share a common column: the Title column. During a search, when an item or a file meets the search criteria, the contents of the Title column are displayed. Although it is not mandatory that you map an ECT field to the SharePoint Title property, if you plan to configure SharePoint so that it indexes the external content, then you should map a field in the Field area to the Title property.

Lists & Forms

This ribbon group contains two commands.

- The Go to List command is active only on the Summary View and when an external list is selected in the External Lists area.

- The Create Lists & Form command is active if there is at least one external list created for the ECT on the site that is opened in SharePoint Designer. When you click this command, the Create List and Form dialog box opens, as shown in Figure 4-7. Here you can either create a new form or create a new external list.

See Also *You can find information on creating external lists in Chapter 5, "Creating External Lists and Using External Data in Lists and Libraries."*

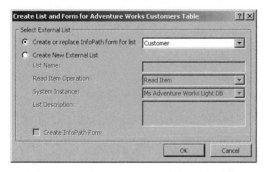

FIGURE 4-7 Use the Create List and Form dialog box to create new forms or new external lists.

When you select the Create or Replace InfoPath Form for List option, you can select any external list that is created on the site from the ECT. When an external list is created, a number of pages are created: one page to display the items returned from the external content, and three form ASPX pages depending on the operations defined for the ECT that allow you to create a new item, display all the fields for one item, or edit the fields for one item. These ASPX pages, like other SharePoint lists, are created under the list and are named *DispForm.aspx*, *EditForm.aspx*, and *NewForm.aspx*. They contain the XSLT List Form Web Part.

Using the Create List and Form dialog box, you can create InfoPath-equivalent forms for the three ASPX form pages. Three ASPX pages (*displayifs.aspx*, *editifs.aspx*, and *newifs.aspx*) are created, and each contains an InfoPath Web Part to display the newly created InfoPath form. The InfoPath form, named *template.xsn*, and the three ASPX pages that host the form are created in the Item folder under the list. You will find no reference to the InfoPath form on the external list settings page. You have to use the All Files option in the Navigation pane in SharePoint Designer to navigate to the Item folder, as shown in Figure 4-8.

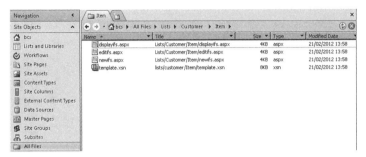

FIGURE 4-8 To modify the InfoPath form *template.xsn*, use the All Files option in the SharePoint Designer Navigation pane.

Profile Page

In this ribbon group, you will see one command: Create Profile Page. This command is applicable only in the Enterprise edition of SharePoint Server. Prior to using the Create Profile Page option, the BDC service application administrator must configure a SharePoint site where the profile pages will be created. Microsoft recommends that you use a single dedicated SharePoint site to host the profile pages for all your ECTs. You also need to ensure that the permissions on the site are set up correctly. Users who will use the profile page to display all the fields associated with an ECT need read-only permissions. Users who create profile pages will need to be mapped to the Design permission level, which includes the Add and Customize Pages permission.

See Also *For information on defining the SharePoint site to host profile pages, see Chapter 3.*

When you click Create Profile Page, SharePoint automatically creates a page in the designated hosted site, under a subfolder of the _bdc folder. The subfolder name takes its name from the ECT namespace, such as http__AdventureWorksSalesInvoicing. The page is named *<ECT name>_n.aspx*— for example, *AdventureWorks_Sales_1.aspx*, as shown in Figure 4-9.

FIGURE 4-9 Profile pages are created in the designated SharePoint site.

Note When you delete ECTs, their respective profile pages are not deleted. Using SharePoint Designer and the All Files object in the Navigation pane, you can delete profile pages that are no longer needed.

At the same time that SharePoint creates the profile page, it also creates an external data action named View Profile. This external action is the default action for the ECT, so when a user clicks an external data item, for example, in a list with an external column, the list item menu, also known by developers as the edit control block (ECB), displays at least one item: the link to the default action, View Profile, as shown in Figure 4-10.

FIGURE 4-10 The View Profile link on the list item menu for an external item redirects you to the profile page.

See Also *You can find more information on external actions in Chapter 5.*

You should define all the operations your solution needs, including filters and the association operation, and save the ECT before you create a profile page. Also, if you click Create Profile Page a second time, an Overwrite Profile Page dialog box opens, as shown in Figure 4-11. This dialog box states that the ECT already has a default action at the profile page host site and asks if you want to overwrite it.

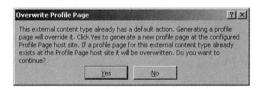

FIGURE 4-11 This warning message appears when you create a profile page and one already exists.

The profile page uses two Business Data Web Parts, Business Data Item Builder and Business Data Details, which are available only in the Enterprise edition of SharePoint Server 2010 and in the Office 365 E3 and E4 plans.

You can also have SharePoint automatically create a profile page for an ECT using the SharePoint 2010 Central Administration website. The ribbon on the Central Administration website is trimmed to not display this option on a SharePoint Foundation installation. However, SharePoint Designer will display the command on whatever version of SharePoint is installed.

On a SharePoint Foundation installation, when you click the Create Profile Page ribbon command, a Microsoft SharePoint Designer dialog box opens that states the server could not complete your request, but it does not provide any details as to why the request could not be completed. A second dialog box then opens that states the expected changes to the ECT could not happen and you should create the profile page again! Ignore these messages. SharePoint can't automatically create profile pages using SharePoint Foundation 2010 or on most Office 365 plans. You can manually create a profile page for an ECT using the Data Form Web Part and BDC actions.

Creating and Modifying Data Connections

Out of the box, SharePoint provides a number of connectors that the Business Data Connectivity (BDC) server runtime can use to connect to the external system. These connectors define the types of data sources that an external content type (ECT) can connect to:

- Databases

- Cloud-based services

- Windows Communication Foundation (WCF) endpoints

- XML web services

- .NET assembly that can gather data from multiple sources

- Custom external systems that have nonstatic interfaces that change dynamically

On the Operations Design View, click Add Connection to display the External Data Source Type Selection dialog box, as shown in Figure 4-12.

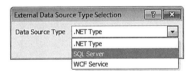

FIGURE 4-12 Select the data source type for your external system.

In Figure 4-12, notice how SharePoint Designer can only define external systems that use the data source types SQL Server, .NET Type, and WCF Service.

Defining a SQL Server Database Connection

When you select SQL Server as your data source type, the SQL Server Connection dialog box opens, as shown in Figure 4-13. The SQL Server data source type is the easiest of the three data source types to configure in SharePoint Designer.

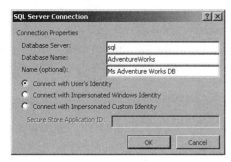

FIGURE 4-13 Enter details on how to connect to an SQL database and the authentication credentials to be used.

Note You can use the out-of-the-box database connector to connect to databases stored in SQL Server, Oracle, MySQL, or any other database system that uses the ODBC connector. However, SharePoint Designer generates only the necessary methods to connect to an SQL database. You will need to create these ECTs by exporting a SQL Server ECT from SharePoint Designer and amending it, or using Visual Studio or a third-party tool.

In the SQL Server Connection dialog box, type the name of the SQL Server, the name of the database (such as AdventureWorksLT or AdventureWorks), and a display name, labeled as optional in the dialog box. The display name appears in the ECT picker that is used by site and list owners and users who create dashboards using the Business Data Web Parts.

Note This book uses the Microsoft AdventureWorksLT or AdventureWorks database when creating SQL Server ECTs. These SQL Server ECTs are used in subsequent chapters to create external lists, external columns, and dashboards using Business Data Web Parts. If you want to create ECTs exactly as described in this chapter, you can download these databases from *http://msftdbprodsamples.codeplex.com*.

Authentication

Select the authentication method you are going to use to connect to the SQL Server. SharePoint Designer will use these credentials to directly connect to the external system. It will not go via the BDC service application on the server, as you cannot save the ECT to the BDC metadata store until at least one operation—the Read Item operation—is created, and the SharePoint Server cannot access the external data store until the ECT is in the metadata store. You can later change these settings to suit your authentication needs for the external system when the ECT is stored in the BDC metadata store.

Of the four authentication methods detailed in Chapter 3, the SQL Connection dialog box only allows you to select the user's identity, also known as PassThrough, Impersonated Windows, and Custom identities. Later, when you configure the credentials that the BDC model should use, you will be able to select the BDC identity known as RevertToSelf. However, remember that this authentication method is disabled by default, and if you want to use it, you need to use Windows PowerShell to enable it.

If you do choose one of the impersonation authentication methods at this point, then you need to supply the SSS Target Application ID for the external system. As SharePoint Designer is going to connect directly to the external system, when the impersonation methods are selected, a Connection Validation dialog box appears that states Wait While Your Connection Is Being Validated, followed by a BCS Secure Store dialog box, as shown in Figure 4-14.

FIGURE 4-14 When you use impersonation authentication methods, you are prompted for credentials that SharePoint Designer can use to directly connect to the data source.

Data Source Explorer

Once your credentials are authenticated by the external system, the external system will inform SharePoint Designer about the tables you are authorized to access, including views and stored procedures. SharePoint Designer will then display this information in the Data Source Explorer, as shown in Figure 4-15. When you select a stored procedure that requires input or output values, the name of the property and the property type are displayed in the bottom text box.

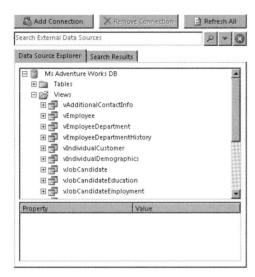

FIGURE 4-15 Use the Data Source Explorer to find the table, view, or routine that you want to act as an external data source for your ECT.

> **Note** Once you add a connection in SharePoint Designer, on the View External Systems page in the SharePoint 2010 Central Administration website, you will see listed an external system named *SharePointDesigner-<Connection Name>-<User who created connection>-<GUID>* (for example, *SharePointDesigner-Ms Adventure Works DB-peter-44418237-5d92-462x-9d58-ab283793de24*). This external system is not connected to any BDC models or ECTs that you subsequently create.

Defining a WCF Service Connection

When you select Windows Communication Foundation (WCF) Service as your data source type, the WCF Connection dialog box opens, as shown in Figure 4-16. You can use this data source to connect to WCF services and XML web services, also known as SOAP services. WCF services usually end with an .svc extension, and XML web services, if created using ASP.NET, end with an *.asmx* extension. Microsoft has provided a number of services for SharePoint with *.svc* and *.asmx* extensions, but none of them are BCS compatible.

See Also *You can find information on creating a BCS-compatible WCF service in Chapter 12, "Building Server-Side BCS Solutions."*

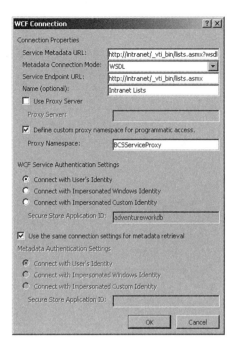

FIGURE 4-16 Enter details about how to connect to a WCF service and the authentication credentials to be used.

To complete the connection definition, supply the following information:

- **Service Metadata URL** This information allows SharePoint Designer to receive the metadata/schema for the service so that the Data Source Explorer can be populated with web methods. You can then use these methods to create the ECT operations. For an XML web service *?wsdl* is appended to the URL, and for a WCF service */mex* is appended to the URL.

- **Metadata Connection Mode** You have the option of using either WSDL or MEX. Select WSDL if your data source uses XML web services; select MEX if your data source uses WCF.

- **Service Endpoint URL** SharePoint will use this URL to connect to the data source when displaying an external list, using an external column, or displaying data in a Business Data Web Part.

- **WCF Authentication Settings** These options are the same as those you see when creating an SQL data connection.

Although doing so is optional, you should provide a name for the service, as this name appears in the ECT picker. You may also need to define a proxy for SharePoint to access the data source. This information will be provided by your developer if the WCF service is developed in-house, or in documentation provided by a third party.

Defining a .NET Assembly Connection

When you select .NET Type as your data source type, the .NET Type Selection dialog box opens, as shown in Figure 4-17. You can only select .NET connectors that are already deployed to the SharePoint server.

FIGURE 4-17 Select a .NET assembly from those that have already been deployed.

.NET assembly connectors are one of two types of BCS connectors that can be created with Visual Studio; the other is a custom connector. .NET connectors are typically developed internally to an organization to a particular instance of an external system, such as your own Exchange system that has all your organization's configurations and settings. This connector gives you complete control over the operations on the external system with the code you write.

Custom connectors are typically developed by third-party companies so that the purchasers of the third-party solution can integrate the solution with their SharePoint installation. For example, a third party may develop a custom connector that connects to any Exchange system.

Modifying a Data Connection

Once you have created a connection, the next step is to create one or more data source operations, and then you can configure the data connection you would like SharePoint or an Office client to use to connect to an external data source. Switch to the Summary View by using the command on the External Content Types ribbon tab in the Views group. You can display the Connection Properties dialog box in one of the following two ways:

- On the External Content Types ribbon tab, in the Connection Properties group, click Edit Connection Properties.

- In the ECT workspace, in the External Content Type Information area to the right of External System, click the hyperlink that has the name of your data source. If you provided the optional name—display name—then that will be the name used for the hyperlink.

The Connection Properties dialog box, shown in Figure 4-18, allows you to configure the connection details for SharePoint (the Default tab) and for Office client applications (the Client tab).

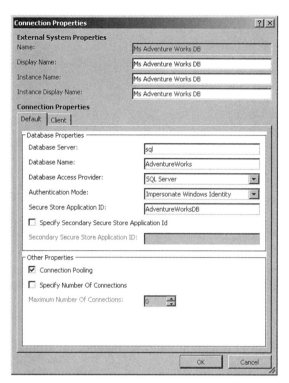

FIGURE 4-18 Use the Connection Properties dialog box to define the data connection for the ECT.

The Connection Properties dialog box for the WCF services provides different properties to an SQL connection as well as additional properties that are not present when you first add a data connection. For example, you can select whether the web service supports claims authentication.

Creating and Maintaining Data Source Operations

Once you have defined the external system authorization and connection details, you can define the ECT's CRUD operations that you want to execute on the external data source. SharePoint Designer provides you with an operations wizard to create the different access methods you want for your solution. The operations wizard consists of three pages:

- **Operation Properties** On this page, you enter the operation name, operation display name, and operation type. When you create operations for a database external data source, you have an option to create all operations by running the operations wizard once. In this scenario, the operation properties are automatically generated and the operation names will be Create, Read Item, Update, Delete, and Read List, and the operation display name will be of the format *<ECT Name><Operation Name>* (for example, AdventureWorks_Customers Read Item). When you create an external list from an ECT, a default view is created using the operation display name.

- **Parameters** On this page, you can select those fields known as elements you use in your solution. The Properties section displays properties you can modify for each data source element, including the identifier name, the field name, and the name of the field when it is displayed in the browser. You must select at least one field that will be shown in the external item picker control.

- **Filter Parameters** Use this page to optimize the amount of data returned from the external system.

To start the operations wizard and create the necessary operations, follow these steps:

1. On the Operations Design View, in the Data Source Explorer, expand the appropriate data source node by clicking the plus sign (+) to the right of the data source name, such as Ms Adventure Works DB, and then expand Tables, Views, or Routines. In this example, you are creating operations on a view.

2. Right-click the view for which you want to create a BDC model, such as vSalesPersonSalesBy-FiscalYears, and then click the operation for the methods you want to create.

   Depending on the methods exposed by the external system and the data source, you can create individual operations: Read Item, Read List, Create, Update, and Delete. For a database data source, you can create all operations, as shown in Figure 4-19.

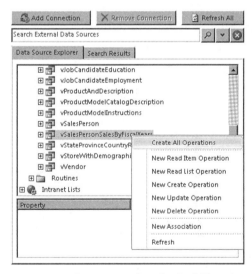

FIGURE 4-19 Create operations for the ECT on the selected data source.

To save the ECT, you must create at least one operation: Read Item. If you want to use the ECT to create an external list, then you need two operations: Read Item and Read List. These operations allow users to easily view the content from the external data source but not update, modify, or delete the data. The ECT is not connected to the data source until one operation is defined. If you try and save an ECT without creating an operation, an error dialog box opens, as shown in Figure 4-20.

FIGURE 4-20 You cannot save an ECT until at least one operation is defined.

When you choose to create one or all operations, the three-page operations wizard opens, as shown in Figure 4-21. Each page contains a section at the bottom that displays issues, warnings, and errors as you configure the operations.

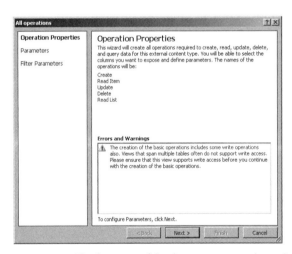

FIGURE 4-21 The first page of the three-page operations wizard.

The three pages of the operations wizard are as follows:

- **Operation Properties** When you create one operation, you can use this page to set the operation name and operation display name. If you choose all operations, then the operation properties are automatically generated, and this page is for information only. The operation names will be the name of the operation, such as Create, Read Item, Update, Delete, and Read List, and the operation display name will be used when views and forms are created for external lists.

- **Parameters** Use this page to select those fields known as elements that you want to use in your SharePoint solution. You can modify each data source element, including the identifier name, the field name, and the name of the field when it is displayed in the browser.

- **Filter Parameters** Use this page to add your own throttling conditions to your solution, which will optimize the time it takes to return the data from the external system. Remember, external content is not saved in the BCS database; rather, it is retrieved by the BDC server runtime when needed.

Once you have configured the operations for the data source, you have created a BDC model, and when you click the Save command, the BDC model will be stored in the BDC metadata store.

Defining Parameters for an Operation

The second page of the operations wizard allows you to map fields from the data source to BCS-related properties. Most options on this page of the wizard are self-explanatory, but a few need further clarification. By selecting the appropriate BCS property on this page, you make it easy for your users when working with data external to SharePoint.

Identifier

You must select at least one field that should be used as an identifier (primary key) that uniquely identifies an item from the data source. In the left box under Data Source Elements, select the field you want to use as the identifier, and then in the right box under Properties, select Map to Identifier, as shown in Figure 4-22.

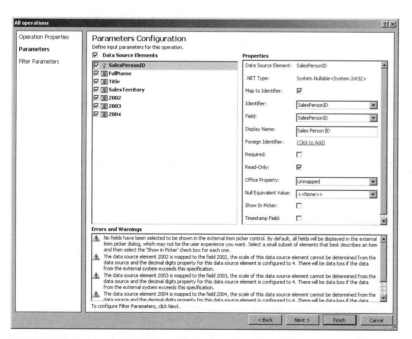

FIGURE 4-22 On the second page of the operations wizard, select an identifier for the external data source.

Show In Picker

By default, all fields will be shown in the external data item picker when list owner adds an external data column to a list or library. If the table, view, or routine returns a large number of fields, displaying them all in the external item picker will confuse users. Therefore, it is best to select a small set of elements that best describes an item. For the vSalesPersonSalesByFiscalYears view, for example, you might want to select FullName, Title, and SalesTerritory to show in the data item picker.

Office Property

If you selected an Office item type on the Summary View, you will use this page to map the external content data fields to Office properties. For example, say you are creating an ECT for the Customer table in the AdventureWorksLT database. You then create an external list from that ECT and want to connect it to Outlook, so each customer in the Customers table is recognized by Outlook as a contact, and you can use a customer's email address when you want to send a message to that person without having to copy all the customers from the AdventureWorksLT database.

First, create an ECT with the name AdventureWorks_Customers, and create all operations on the Customers table. A Contact Office item type must have a data source field mapped to either the Last-Name or FullName Office property. When the second page of the operations wizard displays, in the bottom Errors and Warning box an error message is displayed stating that this is a requirement.

To map data source fields to an Office property, under Data Source Elements select Last Name, ensuring you have not cleared the check box, and then under Properties in the Office Property list select Last Name, as shown in Figure 4-23.

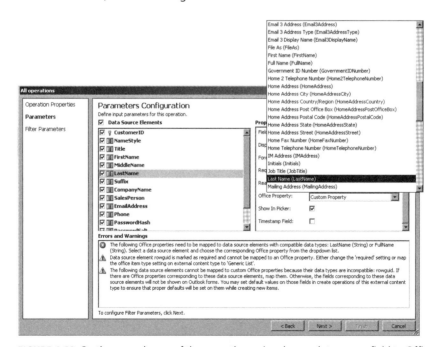

FIGURE 4-23 On the second page of the operations wizard, map data source field to Office properties.

Repeat the previous step to map the following data resource element to the matching Office properties in Table 4-3.

TABLE 4-3 Data source element to Office property mappings

Data source element	Office property
First Name	First Name (FirstName)
Title	Job Title (JobTitle)
MiddleName	Middle Name (MiddleName)
Suffix	Suffix (Suffix)
CompanyName	Company Name (CompanyName)
EmailAddress	Email 1 Address (Email1Address)
Phone	Business Telephone Number (BusinessTelephoneNumber)

The Office mapping form is part of the Read Item operation, so if you wish to modify these settings once an ECT is created, modify the return parameter properties of the Read Item operation. You can also change the Office item type on the summary page once an ECT is created.

Understanding Filters

The filter types available depend on the operation. For the Read List operation in SharePoint Designer, the filters are Comparison, Limit, Page Number, Timestamp, and Wildcard, as shown in Table 4-4. The value you specify for any of these filter types is passed to the external system, and external data items are returned if they meet the criteria. You can achieve the same effect by using the Filter section when configuring views on the external list, but defining an external data filter reduces network traffic and workload on the SharePoint servers.

TABLE 4-4 BCS filters available in SharePoint Designer

Filter name	Description
Comparison	Specified on the Read List operation and used by the external system to compare a value with a value in a particular field, for example, SalesTerritory = Northeast.
Limit	Specified on the Read List operation and used to limit the number of external data items returned.
Page Number	Used when a Read List operation returns multiple pages and you want to display only one page of external data items. Page numbers start at 0.
Timestamp	Used with the Read List operation to return only external data items that have changed since the previous time that the Read List operation was called.
Wildcard filter Wildcard	For string data types, use the Wildcard filter type, as this will internally translate to a like clause in queries to get the data.

See Also *When creating your ECT using Notepad, Visual Studio, or a third-party tool, more BCS filters are available, as described in the MSDN article "Types of Filters Supported by the Business Data Connectivity Service," at* http://msdn.microsoft.com/en-us/library/ee556392(office.14).aspx.

If you are going to configure SharePoint to index the external data source, then the default finder method (that is, the first Read List operation you create) will be used for this purpose. To ensure that SharePoint indexes all the data items from the external data source, you should not configure a filter on that operation. However, if more than 2,000 data items are returned when using the default find method on an external list, an error message is displayed.

To create a limit filter either for a Read List operation or when you have selected to create all operations, follow these steps:

1. On the Filter Parameters Configuration page of the operations wizard, click Add Filter Parameter. Then under Properties, click Click to Add to display the Filter Configuration dialog box.

2. Select New Filter and type a meaningful name, such as Top 100 Sales. In the Filter Properties section, select a filter type of Limit and click OK. The Filter Configuration dialog box closes and under Properties, Top 100 Sales: Limit is displayed to the right of Filter.

3. Under Properties, in the Default Value list, highlight the text <<None>> and type **100**, as shown in Figure 4-24.

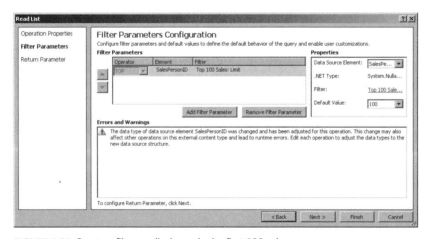

FIGURE 4-24 Create a filter to display only the first 100 sales.

Creating other Read List filters follows a similar process. To create a wildcard filter, choose fields that contain values, where users may want to use the search options Starts With, Ends With, Contains, and Equals. Figure 4-25 shows the Filter Configuration dialog box for a Wildcard type. The Default Value on the Filter Parameters Configuration page would be set to an asterisk.

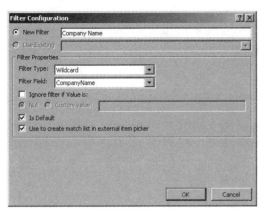

FIGURE 4-25 Use the Filter Configuration dialog box to create a wildcard filter.

When you create more than one filter, you can choose whether you want the filters combined or OR'd, as shown in Figure 4-26. The user will be doing a wildcard search on the company name or filter by SalesPerson.

FIGURE 4-26 You can combine filters.

You can also create filters on the Read Item, Create, Update, Delete, and Association operations. For these operations, the filter is defined for the input parameters—that is, the input parameters are used to pass data to the operation. The filter types available for these operations are shown in Table 4-5.

TABLE 4-5 Filters used as input values to the operations Read Item, Create, Update, Delete, and Association

Filter name	Value to be passed to operation
Last ID Seen	Identifier of last item read. Used to return chunks of data.
Password	These two filters are used together with the Secondary Secure Store Application check box on the Connection Properties dialog box. The Username and Password filters will use Secure Store to fill in the correct data before making the operation call. This option is used when a service account is used to authenticate with the external system for performance reasons. When one account is used to access the external system, no matter the number of users who connect to the external system, all user connections are pooled to the single logon account. Then, values passed as these filter values are used to authenticate.
User Name	
User Context	Identity of the user who called the operation. Use this if a service account or a group ID is used to authenticate with the external system.
Secure Store Token	Used to supply a Secure Store Token, which is similar to a claim.
User Profile	Profile of the current user.
Activity ID	GUID that represents the current operation context. In SharePoint Foundation, it uses a correlation ID.

Note Only trust filters that are used to pass security information when they come from SharePoint. When an Office application can directly connect to an external source, the filter values can be changed.

The amount of data returned from the external system is not solely controlled by the filter. BCS throttling is enabled by default to prevent denial of service (DoS) attacks. You are most likely to see the effect of this feature if no limit filter is created. In this case, you will see only a subset of the external data items, or when the BDC runtime attempts to retrieve data from the external system, it may time out due to the large amount of data it is trying to retrieve.

By default, the number of external data items returned from a database query is limited to 2,000, with a database connection timeout of 60 seconds. A WCF connection is not limited by the number of items, but by the size of the data returned. The default size for a WCF connection is 3 MB, with a connection timeout of 60 seconds.

See Also *For more information on BDC throttling, see Chapter 3.*

Creating Associations

You can create associations when there is a relationship between two ECTs, such as customers and orders: each customer may have one or many orders. This is known as a *one-to-many relationship*. These two ECTs could define data from the same or two different external systems. The customer details could be stored in a CRM system, with the order details in a separate external system. Defining an association in an ECT documents this relationship. You must create an association if you wish to use the Business Data Related List Web Part to provide a relationship—a Web Part connection—between itself and a Business Data List Web Part, or when you customize a solution for Office applications, such as adding a custom task pane to Outlook, where the task pane shows both customer details and all active orders for that customer.

Note You do not need to create an association in an ECT if you plan to use a Data Form Web Part (DFWP) to link data sources or when joining or merging data and displaying the data in a DFWP. Using a DFWP with external data is detailed in Chapter 5.

To create an association, you must have at least one field that is common to both ECTs, for example, so that orders can be identified with a unique customer. Usually the relation is configured such that the customer field in the orders ECT uses the same value that is the primary key field in the customers ECT. The customer field in the orders ECT is known as a *foreign key*. In the Adventure-WorksLT database, the primary key in the Customers table is CustomerID, and the foreign key in the SalesOrderHeader table is CustomerID. It is common practice to design tables so that the primary key and the foreign keys have the same column names—this helps identify relationships between tables. You can also create cascading associations. An example of a cascading association is when a customer has many orders and each order consists of many products.

You can use SharePoint Designer to create one-to-many associations when the relationship is defined using foreign keys in database tables or views, including self-referential associations (relating instances of the same ECT). When you are using database views or a web service method, the external system needs to have a stored procedure or method that accepts the primary key from the parent ECT as a foreign key for the child ECT.

You can use alternate tools to create other relationships, such as one-to-many and many-to-many relationships when foreign keys are not used or where a primary key is made from multiple columns, known as a *composite key*.

Note When you create an association between two ECTs, SharePoint 2010 cannot ensure data referential integrity between the two ECTs, unlike the linking of two tables in a relational database where business logic can used.

The trick to creating associations is to create the association on the ECT that is on the many side of the many-to-one relationship—that is, the ECT where the foreign key is used. This ECT is known as the *child* ECT. For example, using the customer and orders scenario, create the association on the orders data source.

In the following example, you will create an association between two ECTs using tables from the AdventureWorksLT database: an ECT named AdventureWorks_Customer, based on the Customer table, and an ECT named AdventureWorks_Orders, based on the SalesOrderHeader table.

1. In the External Content Types gallery, click the ECT where the foreign key is defined, such as AdventureWorksLT_Orders, and then go to the Operations Design View for the ECT.

2. In the Data Source Explorer, expand Adventure Works LT DB, and then expand Tables. Right-click SalesOrderHeader, and then click New Associations to open the Association Wizard. This wizard consists of four pages: Association Properties, Input Parameters, Filter Parameters, and Return Parameters.

Note An association is an operation, just as Read List is an operation. An association is also known as the *AssociationNavigator* method.

3. In the Association Name box, type **GetOrdersForCustomer**, and in the Association Display Name box, type **Get Orders for Customer**.

4. To the right of Related External Content Type, click Browse to open the External Content Type Selection dialog box, as shown in Figure 4-27.

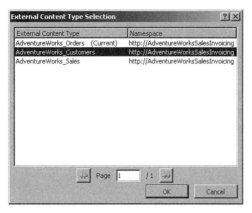

FIGURE 4-27 Select the related ECT.

5. Click AdventureWorks_Customer from the External Content Type picker and then click OK. The External Content Type Selection dialog box closes, and on the Association Properties page, under Related Identifier, CustomerID appears and is automatically mapped to the foreign key for the AdventureWorks_Orders ECT, as shown in Figure 4-28.

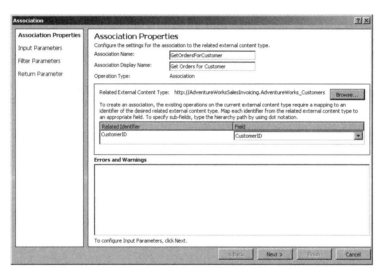

FIGURE 4-28 The Related Identifier (from the Customers table) is related to the field CustomerID in the SalesOrderHeader table.

6. Click Next to display the Input Parameters page of the Association Wizard. Under Data Source Elements, click CustomerID, and then under Properties, select the check box Map to Identifier, as shown in Figure 4-29. The error message in the Errors and Warnings box disappears.

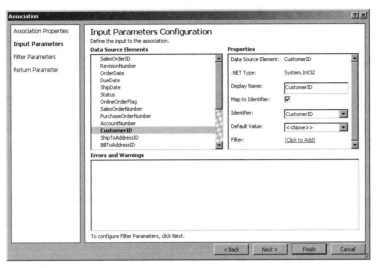

FIGURE 4-29 Mark the CustomerID as an Input Identifier (foreign key).

7. Click Next twice. The Return Parameter Configuration page of the Association Wizard displays. Under Data Source Elements, select SalesOrderID. Do not clear the check box, and under Properties, select the check box Map to Identifier if it isn't already selected, as shown in Figure 4-30.

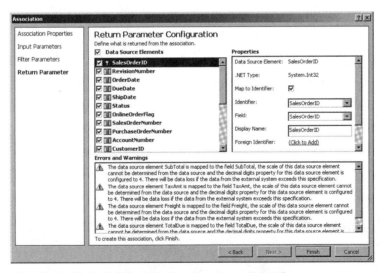

FIGURE 4-30 Mark the SalesOrderID as the returned identifier.

8. Click Finish to close the Association dialog box. In the External Content Type Operations area, the GetOrdersForCustomer association is listed, as shown in Figure 4-31.

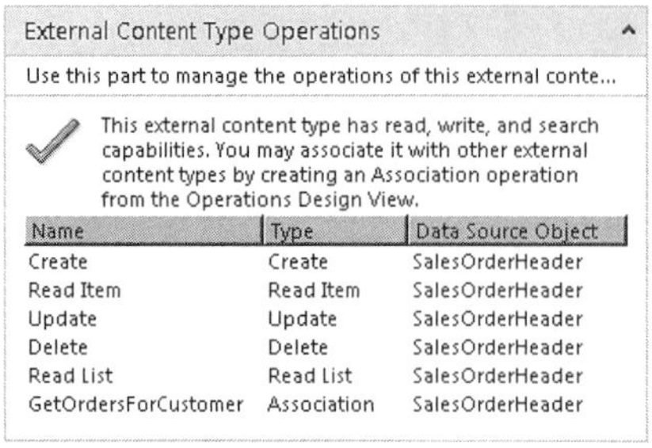

FIGURE 4-31 The ECT Operations area now lists an association operation.

You can also set or define associations when creating or modifying the Read List operation on the Return Parameter Configuration page of the operations wizard. On the child ECT, select the data source element that is to be the foreign key, and then under Properties, to the right of Foreign Identifier, click Click to Add.

Once you define an association, if you create the profile page for the parent ECT, a Business Data Related List Web Part is added to the page for each child ECT associated with the parent ECT. When the profile page is displayed, it will automatically display related data defined in the child ECT, as shown in Figure 4-32.

FIGURE 4-32 Create the profile page after creating associations. The profile page will then contain related data from the child ECTs.

On database-based ECTs, you create the association on a table—the same table used to create the other operations. For web service or WCF-based ECTs, you create the association on the appropriate web method. You can also add filter parameters to a database-based ECT association, but not on a WCF-based association. Reverse associations, where you provide an order ID and return the customer associated with that order, cannot be created on a database-based ECT.

Operation Considerations

The Read List operation is also known as the Finder method, as it finds and returns one or more external data items, also known as an entity instances from the external data source. The Read List operation is used to create external lists, and it is also used in the Business Data Web Parts and search. You are not limited to creating only one operation of each type. The first Read List operation you create will be marked as the default Finder method. When you create subsequent Read List operations, on the first page of the operations wizard a check box displays that enables you to mark the new Read List operation as the default Read List operation, as shown in Figure 4-33.

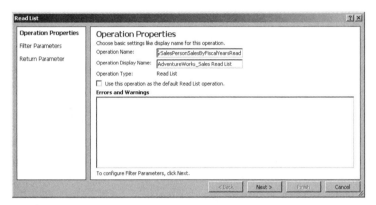

FIGURE 4-33 Use the check box to set a Read List operation as the default Read List operation.

The Read List operation used by search is also known as the root Finder method. You could create two Read List operations, one as the default Finder method (used by external lists) and the other as a root Finder method (used by search). However, the SharePoint Designer operations wizard does not allow you to do this, so if this functionality is required, you have to export the ECT, amend it, and import it.

Other developers may use different names for the operations created by SharePoint Designer—for example, the Read Item operation is known as the *SpecificFinder* method, Create as Creator, Update as Updater, and Delete as Deleter. A developer using Notepad, Visual Studio, or a third-party tool to amend the BDC model can create other operations, such as the *AccessChecker* method, which can be used to check whether a user has rights to access an external data item.

To modify an operation, in the External Content Type Operations area on the Summary View or the Operations Design View, either double-click the operation or select the operation. Then on the External Content Types ribbon tab, in the Operation group, click Edit Operation.

If you have elected to create all operations together, you may need to revisit some of the operations for the following reasons:

- You want to change the operation name and display name to be more meaningful to users. For example, when you create an external list from the ECT, the default view's page name and display name use the name and display name of the default Read List operation. The default view on other types of SharePoint list is *AllItems* with a display name of All Items; therefore, you might want to rename the Read List operation's name to match, or you can rename the page to *AllSales* or *All Sales*. You should make this change prior to creating external lists. If you make this change after creating external lists, it will not affect already created list views.

- On the Read Item and Read List operations, you may want to return only those data source elements you want displayed in the external list or Business Data Web Part. Although you can configure the external list view or the properties of the Business Data Web Part to display a limited number of the elements, for performance reasons and to minimize the amount of network traffic, it is best to configure the ECT to bring across to the SharePoint servers only wanted elements from the external data source.

Exporting ECTs

External content types (ECTs) are metadata objects defined in the Business Data Connectivity (BDC) model XML file, which usually use the extension .bdcm. You or other users who create an ECT using SharePoint Designer may not have created it on the SharePoint installation where it is to be used. You may have created it on a development or a prototype environment, so you will need to export it. Another reason to export a BDC model is that you may have created one for use with an Office application. You do have mechanisms available for exporting a BDC model from one SharePoint system to another (default export) and to an Office application (client export).

You can use the SharePoint 2010 Central Administration website or SharePoint Designer to export BDC models, but you can only use the SharePoint 2010 Central Administration website to import a BDC model. Also, you cannot use the SharePoint 2010 Central Administration website to export the client version of a BDC model. Whichever environment a BDC model is planned for—SharePoint or an Office application—again, you must test it once you have imported it into that environment. To export a BDC model from SharePoint Designer, follow these steps:

1. In the External Content Types gallery, click the icon to the left of the ECT you want to export. You can select more than one ECT by holding down either the Ctrl or Shift key as you would in Windows Explorer. Then on the External Content Types ribbon tab, in the Manage group, click Export BDC Model to open the Export BDC Model dialog box.

2. In the BDC Model Name text box, type a meaningful name, such as **AdventureWorks-CustOrders**. In the Settings List, select the type of BDC model you want SharePoint Designer to create.

3. Click OK, and save the file.

See Also *You can find information about how to import a BDC model into SharePoint in Chapter 3. For examples of importing a BDC model for use in an Office application, see Chapters 7 and 11.*

Summary

Business Connectivity Services (BCS) allows you to hook up external data with SharePoint and Office applications. You use external content types (ECTs) to define how to connect to the external system, the connector to use, and credentials. You define in the ECT the operations you can use on the external data and its format. Using SharePoint Designer, you can define six operations: Read List, Read, Create, Delete, Update, and Association.

For performance reasons, such as limiting the amount of data transferred across the network and the load on the SharePoint servers, you should consider using filters when you define ECTs.

Once you have defined an ECT, you can use it to present data to end users. You can use the ECT to create external lists, to create external columns in SharePoint lists and libraries, and on pages with the use of Business Data Web Parts and the Data Form Web Part. You should define all the operations your solution needs, including filters and the association operation, and save the ECT before creating external lists or the profile page.

To uniquely identify an ECT, the ECT name and namespace are internally combined. The ECT name and the namespace, together with the operation names, will be visible to users. If you change either of these properties, any external list, Business Data Web Part, or external column that used the previous name will no longer work.

PART II

Presenting External Data

CHAPTER 5

Creating External Lists and Using External Data in Lists and Libraries

In this chapter, you will:

- Create and use external lists

- Use external data in lists and libraries

- Use external data actions

In Chapter 4, "Defining External System Connections Using SharePoint Designer," you learned how to create and maintain external content types (ECTs). Once an ECT is created, you can then create solutions with that ECT using the browser or Microsoft SharePoint Designer 2010. You can also create custom Web Parts or Windows Forms applications with Microsoft Visual Studio 2010 that can access the data defined in the Business Data Connectivity (BDC) metadata store, which is where ECTs are stored.

No matter which version of SharePoint 2010 you have installed, the preferred method of displaying data from external data sources is to use external lists. Depending on the operations you have specified in the ECT, the external list can provide create, read, update, and delete (CRUD) capabilities. The external list can also be added to a SharePoint page as an XSLT List View (XLV) Web Part and you can then configure additional columns, conditional formatting, sorting, and grouping in the browser and in SharePoint Designer.

 Note If you have Microsoft SharePoint Server 2010 Enterprise Edition, you can also use the Business Data Web Parts. For more information about these Web Parts, see Chapter 6, "Building Business Data Dashboards."

You create external lists using the browser, SharePoint Designer, Windows PowerShell, or code.

Creating and Using External Lists

External lists are created from external content types (ECTs). Each external list contains a number of pages that allow you to create, read, update, or delete data from the external system that you can connect to using the ECT. The pages created when an external list is created are dependent on the operations defined in the ECT. Pages that display multiple items from the external system are called *views* and are based on the Read List operation defined in the ECT. Pages that allow you to create a new item in the external system, modify an external data item, or display an external data item are called *forms*. To create an external list, the minimum operations you have to define on an ECT are the Read List operation and the Read Item operation.

Creating an External List

Before you create an external list, you must complete the following tasks:

- Create an ECT that exposes the data from the external system. You will find details on how to create an ECT in Chapter 4.

- Ensure that the Business Data Connectivity (BDC) service application administrator gave you the Selectable In Client permission on the ECT and the Execute permission on the operations and method instances defined by the ECT. The Selectable In Client permission allows you to use the ECT picker so you can choose the ECT to build the external list. The Execute permission allows you to execute the ECT operations to complete create, read, update and delete (CRUD) operations on the external data. You can find more details about security options in Chapter 3, "Creating and Maintaining Business Data Connectivity Service Applications."

- Create a list in the site where you want to create the external list. Creating an external list is no different from creating any list within a SharePoint site—that is, you must have the Manage Lists permission at the site level. On a team site, this permission is usually incorporated into the Full Control permission level, which is mapped to the site's Owners SharePoint group. On publishing sites, the Design permission level also includes the Managed Lists permission, and the Design permission level is mapped to the Designers SharePoint group. So unless you have created your own SharePoint groups and permission levels, you must be a member of the site's Owners group or Designers group, or you must have your user ID mapped to either the Full Control or Design permission levels.

  See Also *You can find more information about SharePoint groups and permission levels in the book* Microsoft SharePoint Foundation 2010 Step by Step *by Olga Londer and Penelope Coventry (Microsoft Press, 2011).*

- Activate the site feature Team Collaboration Lists if you plan to create an external list using the browser. When you use SharePoint Designer to create an external list, this feature does not need to be active.

- Ensure you are able to access the content in the external system. You may not have to do anything special to access the content stored in the external system, as the BDC service application administrator and the ECT creator may have configured the authentication and authorization settings to allow you access. If, however, the business solution requires that each person who uses the external list have their own credentials, then you may be prompted for those credentials before you are able to view the external content in the external list.

To create an external list with the browser, use the following steps:

1. Open the site on which you want to create the external list. Click Site Actions, and then select More Options.

2. On the Create page, click external list, and then click Create. If you have a large number of list types, it's easier to find the external list option by clicking Data under All Categories.

3. On the New page, enter the name and description for the external list, and then select whether you want a link to this external list on the Quick Launch toolbar.

> **Note** An external list is just like any other list when you enter a name and description—that is, the name you type in the Name text box is used by SharePoint as both the URL for the list and the list title, which is sometimes referred to as the user-friendly name. The URL name is also of importance for the SharePoint Server search relevance algorithm, known as URL Matching. The text for the list title and the list description is used by search to measure content relevancy.
>
> You are able to change the list title later, but you are not able to change the URL. Therefore, do not use the characters \ / : * ? " < > | # { } % & <Tab> " !, do not use spaces as they get converted into the character %20, keep the name short and meaningful, and include terms that users will enter as keywords in their search queries if they want to find this list.
>
> Be consistent in your naming conventions. Some users create the list's URL name by concatenating two or more words. Each word is composed of two or more letters, with no spaces between the words. The first letter of each word is capitalized and the remaining letters are lowercase, such as AdventureWorksCustomers. This formatting is known as *camel case*. You might see the use of underscores (_) or hyphens (-) to separate words in a URL name, but hyphens are used as break points to wrap text on separate lines, so URLs that contain hyphens can cause problems similar to spaces with email and text editors. If you do not like camel case formatting, you can use underscores, so the list name would be Adventure_Works_Customers. Do take the time to consider the naming conventions you want to use for lists as well as other SharePoint components, such as sites, column names, and views.

4. To the right of the External Content Type text box, click the Select External Content Type icon, as shown in Figure 5-1.

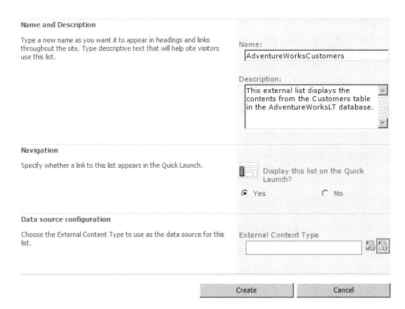

FIGURE 5-1 Select the ECT icon to display the list of ECTs.

The External Content Type Picker dialog box appears, as shown in Figure 5-2.

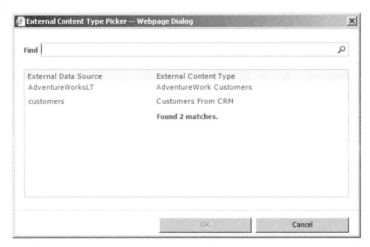

FIGURE 5-2 Use the External Content Type Picker dialog box to select an ECT.

The dialog box displays the name of the external system and the display name of the ECT. It is important that your ECT designers have created a meaningful display name for the ECT, so that end users can quickly identify the external content they want to work with. Once the external list is created, you cannot choose a different ECT. You would need to delete the external list and recreate it, choosing the correct ECT. The external list acts as a virtual container, displaying the contents from the external system; therefore, when you delete an external list or ECT, you are not deleting any content from the external system, just the virtual container and the definition of external content.

5. In the External Content Type Picker, select the ECT that defines the external content you want to display in your external list, such as AdventureWorks Customers, and then click OK to close the External Content Type Picker dialog box. The ECT that you have chosen is specified in the External Content Type text box.

6. Click Create. The external list displays, with content from the external system shown in the Read List view.

External lists have similar functionality to other SharePoint lists you are familiar with. The default view of the external list is based on a standard view, so you can use the individual column headers to sort or filter the external data. Similar to Microsoft Excel, filtering is enabled on the upper-right corner of every column, and a unique list of the values for each column is generated and presented in a drop-down list, as shown in Figure 5-3. If your external list contains a large number of unique values for the column you have chosen to use as a filter, then creating the drop-down list can put an excessive load on your browser.

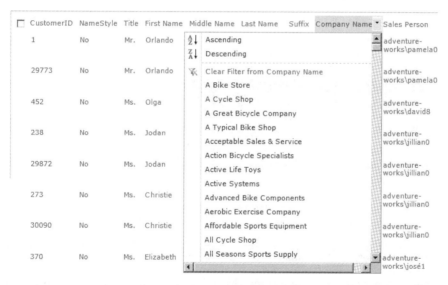

FIGURE 5-3 Use column headers to temporarily configure sorting and filtering of external data.

Filters are cumulative but are only set temporarily. That is, the next time a list view is selected, filter values are not remembered and have to be set again. If users want to filter the contents of an external list often, the list owner should create additional views where the filters and sorts are preconfigured.

Note You cannot associate RSS feeds to external lists, and you cannot create a view using the datasheet view or Access view.

Whenever you create a list, you should complete a number of other tasks, such as giving the list a user-friendly name, setting permissions, and creating additional views. Also, once you create an external list, you might find that no data from the external system is displayed. For example, if you create filters on the ECT Read List operation, then the default view will not display any data from the external system. You need to amend the view and configure the filter for the external data to be displayed.

As with other lists or libraries, each item within an external list is provided with a contextual drop-down list on the field defined in the ECT as the identity field, known as the list item menu (LIM). In Microsoft Windows SharePoint Services 3.0, this was known as the edit control block (ECB). The LIM provides functionality, including View Item, Edit Item, and Delete Item. You can add more actions to the LIM using SharePoint Designer.

Note You may want to remove the LIM from an external list when only the Read List and Read Item operations are defined—that is, when the data displayed in an external list is read-only. For information about how to hide the LIM, see *http://msdn.microsoft.com/en-us/library/cc768565.aspx*.

You may also find that in place of the data, an error message is displayed. For example, the default view of an external list might display the error message "Login failed for user 'NT AUTHORITY\ ANONYMOUS LOGON'," as shown in Figure 5-4.

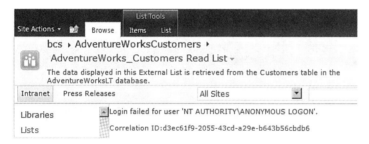

FIGURE 5-4 The external list does not show content from the external data source.

You may receive this message for a number of reasons:

- This message could indicate the double-hop issue if you are using the user's identity to authenticate with the external system, as explained in Chapter 2, "Introducing Business Connectivity Services."

- You do not have BDC permissions to execute the operations defined in the ECT.

- Your user ID does not have the correct access permissions in the external system.

Although you may have permissions to create the BDC model, ECT, and external lists, you may not be able to see the data in the external list or when a page that contains an external list XLV Web Part is displayed. You may need to contact your BDC application services administrator or the ECT creator before you can progress further with your solution.

See Also *See the section "Troubleshooting Connection Problems" in Chapter 3 for information on correlation IDs and how they can help you troubleshoot problems.*

Creating External Lists Using SharePoint Designer

In SharePoint Designer, you can create and manage external lists from the Lists and Libraries gallery, the Data Sources gallery, the ECT gallery, and the ECT settings page. To create an external list from the ECT gallery, follow these steps:

1. In the Navigation pane, click External Content Type. The ECT gallery is displayed.

2. Click the icon to the left of an ECT, such as AdventureWorks_Customers, and on the External Content Types ribbon tab, in the New group, click External List, as shown in Figure 5-5.

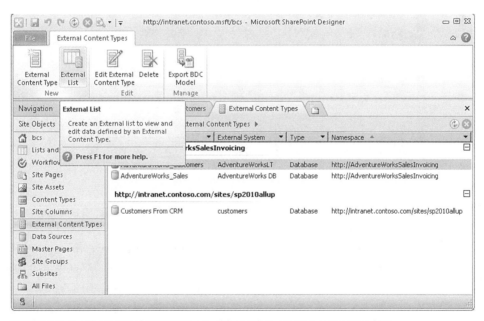

FIGURE 5-5 Use the External Content Types ribbon tab to create a new external list.

The Create External List dialog box opens.

3. In the Name text box, type AdventureWorksCustomers, and in the Description text box, type a description of the list contents. The text you enter in the Description text box will be used by the SharePoint search engine to identify content relevant to search queries. For example, type **The data displayed in this External List is retrieved from the Customers table in the AdventureWorksLT database.**, as shown in Figure 5-6.

 Note Similar to when you create an external list with the browser, the contents of the Name text box are used for the URL of the list as well as the title of the list. As noted in the previous section when you created an external list using the browser, you are able to change the list title later, but you are not able to change the URL, so type in the Name text box the URL that you would like to use for the external list. Also, you cannot have two lists with the same name, so the name you give the list must be unique within the site.

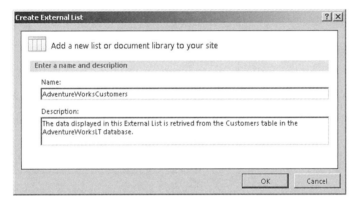

FIGURE 5-6 Enter the URL of the external list in the Name text box.

4. Click OK. The AdventureWorksCustomers list settings page displays in a new Workspace tab, as shown in Figure 5-7. In the Views area, one view is listed: AdventureWorks_Customers Read List. In the Forms area, three forms are listed: *DispForm.aspx*, *EditForm.aspx*, and *NewForm. aspx*. The view and the three forms use the XLV Web Part to display and update data on the external system.

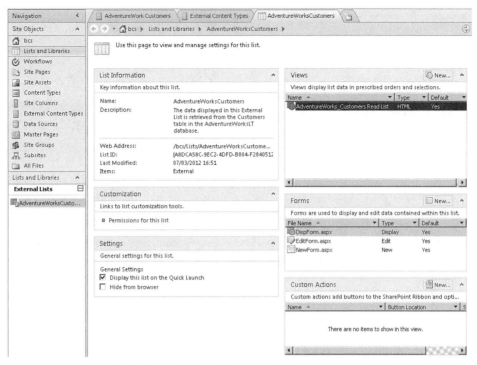

FIGURE 5-7 In SharePoint Designer, the list settings page displays a summary of information for the external list.

To create an external list from the ECT settings page using SharePoint Designer, follow these steps:

1. In the Navigation pane, click External Content Type and then click the ECT you want to be the basis for your external list. The ECT settings page appears.

2. On the External Content Types ribbon tab, in the Lists & Forms group, click Create Lists & Forms. The Create List and Form dialog box displays, as shown in Figure 5-8. If this is the first list created from the external list, then the Create New External List option is selected.

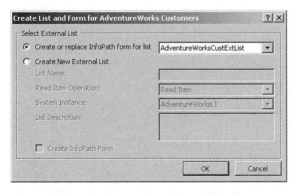

FIGURE 5-8 Use the Create List and Form dialog box to create an external list.

3. Select Create New External List and type the name of the external list and the Read Item operation the external list is to be based on. You can also select the Create InfoPath Form check box
to create the three form files as InfoPath forms.

Managing External List Views and Forms

When you create an external list, one or more views and up to three forms are created. A view is created for each Read List operation you created for the external content type (ECT). The view name is
created from the display name of the ECT Read List operation. The default view uses an XSLT List View
(XLV) Web Part to display the data returned when default ECT Read List operation is executed. Forms
are created when you define the ECT Create, Update, and Read Item operations.

The ECT Read List operation and any filters that you configure define the data that is transported
across the network from the external system to the SharePoint server. You can also configure the view
to limit the data transferred across the network from the SharePoint server to the user's computer,
where the user is displaying the view pages in a browser. You have two places to define the data that
you want to present on the page to the user: the ECT Read List operation and the view (see Figure
5-9).

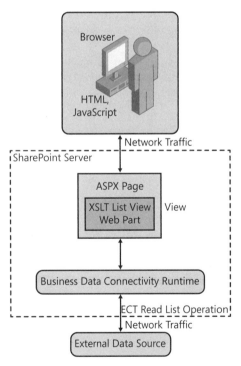

FIGURE 5-9 Define the data to present to the user either by configuring the ECT Read List operation or by configuring the view, or a combination of both.

If your external system uses a product designed for data manipulation, such as a database, it is better to configure the ECT operation to use the external system to filter and sort the external data than to place extra load on the SharePoint server to complete those activities.

When an end user can create external lists or create views on an external list, but the user cannot create or modify ECTs, then defining ECT filters allows the external list owner to control what is transferred from the external system to the SharePoint server. Thus, the creator of the external list or views can minimize the manipulation of the external data that a SharePoint server has to complete, which in turn improves the performance of the views. This is an important point to emphasize when training external list owners. The configuration of the Columns, Sort, and Filter sections on a view define the work that you want the SharePoint server to do. The SharePoint server saves in memory only the data in the columns you specified in the view, and sorts that data as per your view's configuration.

External Data and Throttling

The data retrieved by executing the ECT Read List operation is limited by the throttling settings for Business Connectivity Service (BCS) data. The throttling limit for external data is not the same as when the data is stored in SharePoint lists and libraries. The data presented in external list views bypasses the setting for lists and libraries and uses external system throttling rules, as described in Chapter 3. For example, the default maximum number of rows that can be obtained from a database is limited to 2,000 items. If more than 2,000 items are returned, the message in Figure 5-10 appears.

Unable to display this Web Part. To troubleshoot the problem, open this Web page in a Microsoft SharePoint Foundation-compatible HTML editor such as Microsoft SharePoint Designer. If the problem persists, contact your Web server administrator.

Correlation ID:c4ef21b3-d336-45ef-a43c-5c3a61a0f489

FIGURE 5-10 An error message appears when you try to display more than the number of items specified by the BCS throttle.

The error message displayed in the browser does not reflect that there is a throttling issue, but when your SharePoint farm administrator reviews the ULS logs for this problem, and your external system is a database, the message states: "Database response throttled. Maximum number of rows that can be read through the database system utility is 2000."

Note Only SharePoint farm administrators can modify the throttling limits using Windows PowerShell, as described in Chapter 3 and in the Microsoft Knowledge Base article at *http://technet.microsoft.com/en-us/library/ff607630.aspx*.

Creating Views Using the Browser

To create a new view for an external list using the browser, follow these steps:

1. On the List ribbon tab, in the Manage Views group, click Create View. The Create View page displays.

2. Under Choose a View Format, click Standard View.

3. In the Name section, type **ByCustomer**. In this section, you can also make this new view the default view.

4. In the Audience section, select to make this view either a personal view or a public view.

5. In the Columns section, select those columns you want to display in your view, as shown in Figure 5-11, and then in the Sort section, select the column that you want the data to be sorted by. For example, select the column CompanyName and select the option to show items in ascending order.

 Note If a filter limit has been applied to the Read List operation used for this view, then you will sort only the items returned to the SharePoint server from the external system, up to that filter limit.

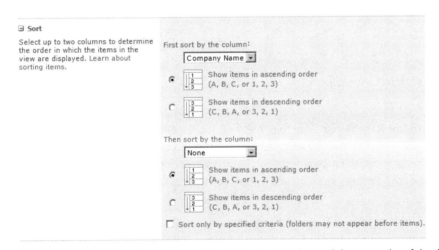

FIGURE 5-11 Select the columns you want to display in your view and the sort order of the data.

6. You then have two ways of filtering the data, as shown in Figure 5-12: the Data Source Filters section and the Filter section.

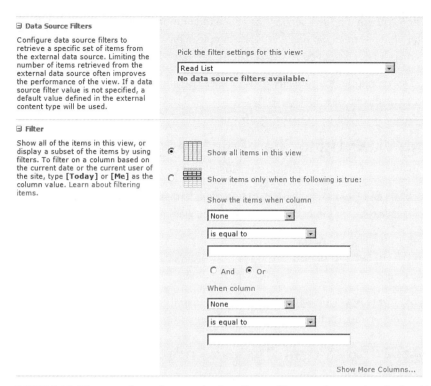

FIGURE 5-12 When creating a view, use the Data Source Filters section to select the Read List operation to use to obtain data from the external system.

When you first create a view, the Data Source Filters section lists the ECT Read List operations defined for the ECT. When you modify the view, you are able to set values for the filters, as shown in Figure 5-13, if you defined any filters on the ECT Read List operation.

⊟ **Data Source Filters**

Configure data source filters to retrieve a specific set of items from the external data source. Limiting the number of items retrieved from the external data source often improves the performance of the view. If a data source filter value is not specified, a default value defined in the external content type will be used.

Pick the filter settings for this view:

Filter Name	Filter Value
CustomerName	*
LimitFilter20Items	200

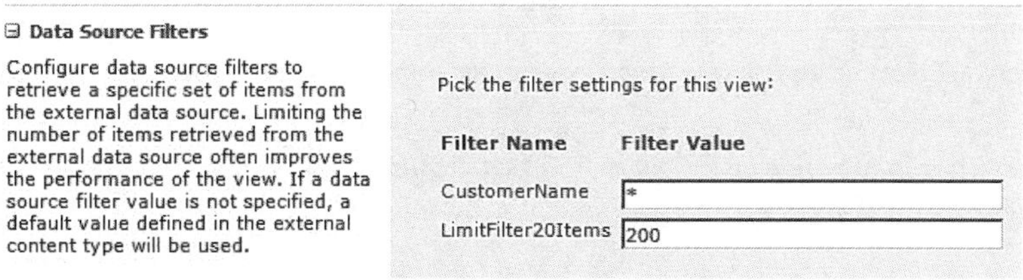

FIGURE 5-13 Modify the view to set the filters defined on the Read List operation.

To minimize network traffic between the external system and the SharePoint server, and to avoid exceeding the throttle limit, use the Data Source Filters section instead of the Filter section. When no filters are defined on the Read List operation, the Data Source Filters section contains the text "No data source filters available."

When you use the Filter section to reduce the number of items displayed in the view, and a filter limit has been defined with, for example, a limit of 200 on the ECT Read List operation, then your filter is applied to the 200 items provided by the external system.

7. You can configure the remaining options as with any other SharePoint list or library view. Click OK to save your view configurations.

Creating Views Using SharePoint Designer

To create new views for an external list using SharePoint Designer, follow these steps:

1. Click List and Libraries in the Navigation pane to display the List and Library gallery. Under External Lists, click the external list where you want to create a new view, such as Adventure-WorksCustomers.

2. On the List Settings ribbon tab, in the New group, click List View. The Create New View dialog box opens.

3. In the Name box, type **ByCustomer**, and then in the Finder list, select the ECT Read List operation that you want to create the view from, as shown in Figure 5-14.

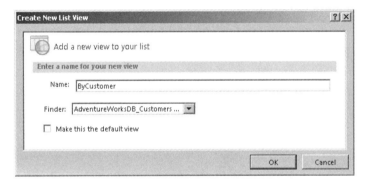

FIGURE 5-14 Create a new list view for an external list using SharePoint Designer.

4. Click OK. The Create New List View dialog box closes. In the Views area, ByCustomer appears, as shown in Figure 5-15.

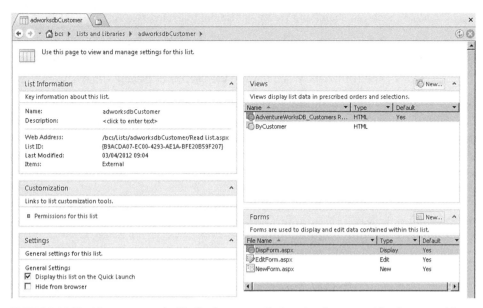

FIGURE 5-15 The Views area on the List Settings page displays the view created for the external list.

You can also navigate to the external list in SharePoint Designer by displaying the ECT Settings page. Then in the External Lists area, click the list where you want to create a new view, and on the External Content Types ribbon tab, in the Lists & Forms group, click Go to List, as shown in Figure 5-16.

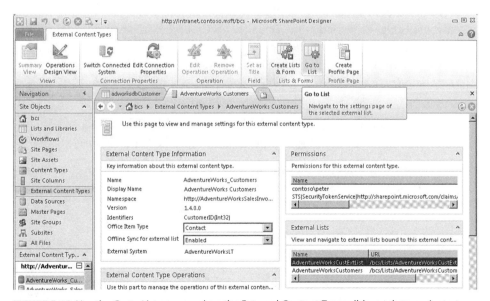

FIGURE 5-16 Use the Go to List command on the External Content Types ribbon tab to navigate to an external list created from the ECT.

To modify a view in SharePoint Designer, use the following steps:

1. Display the external list settings page in the SharePoint Designer workspace area, and then in the Views area, click the view you want to modify, such as ByCustomer. The *ByCustomer.aspx* page opens in edit mode, and the XLV Web Part is displayed within a blue rectangle named PlaceHolderMain.

2. In Design view, click CustomerID to display the List View Tools ribbon tab set, and then on the Options ribbon tab, click Sort & Group, as shown in Figure 5-17.

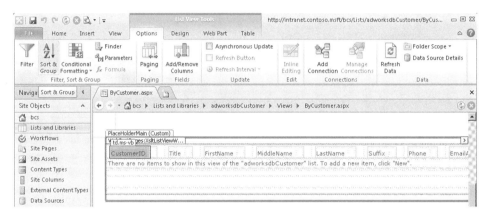

FIGURE 5-17 Use the tabs in the List View Tools ribbon tab set to configure the view.

Note When editing an XLV Web Part via the SharePoint Designer Options ribbon tab, the Finder command in the Filter, Sort & Group group is activated. When you click this command, the Configure Finder dialog box opens, allowing you to change the Read List operation associated with the Web Part and to configure the filters associated with the selected Read List operation.

3. In the Sort and Group dialog box, under Available Fields, click Company Name, and then click Add. Under Group Properties, select Show Group Header, as shown in Figure 5-18. Click OK.

   The Sort and Group dialog box closes, and the XsltListViewWebPart displays the contents from the AdventureWorks database sorted and grouped by company name, as shown in Figure 5-19.

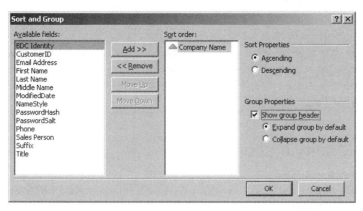

FIGURE 5-18 Use the Sort and Group dialog box to have the SharePoint server sort and group data from the external system.

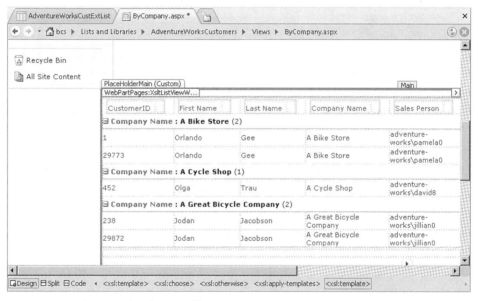

FIGURE 5-19 A view sorted and grouped by company name.

Note The XLV Web Part in SharePoint Designer shows only five items from the AdventureWorks database, even though there are more rows in the Customers table. When you use the browser to request *ByCustomer.aspx*, the rows are returned in sets of 30 items.

In SharePoint Designer, you can only create pages that display data from an external list using the XLV Web Part. With other SharePoint lists and libraries, and with external systems that are defined in SharePoint Designer as data sources, you can use the Data Form Web Part (DFWP) as well as the XLV Web Part to display data. When you try to create a DFWP by creating an empty data view, no external lists are displayed in the Data Source Picker dialog box. DFWP can only be used to create external list forms.

Creating and Modifying Forms

If you used the browser to create the external list, then by default the edit, new, and display forms are created as *.aspx* pages using the XSLT List Form (XLF) Web Part. You can modify this Web Part using the browser or SharePoint Designer.

Managing Forms Using the Browser

Modifying an external list form using the browser can be difficult because by default the forms are displayed as dialogs. On other lists, you can disable launching forms in a dialog by using the Advanced Settings page, which you can navigate to from the List Settings page. The Advanced Settings link is not available on the List Settings page for external lists.

> **Note** On external lists, you can disable displaying forms as dialogs by using Windows PowerShell or code.

The workaround is to first display the form as a dialog, and then right-click in the body of the form. On the browser menu, click Properties, as shown in Figure 5-20.

In the Properties dialog box, obtain the URL of the form by placing your cursor in the URL to the right of Address, pressing Ctrl+A, and then pressing Ctrl+C (see Figure 5-21).

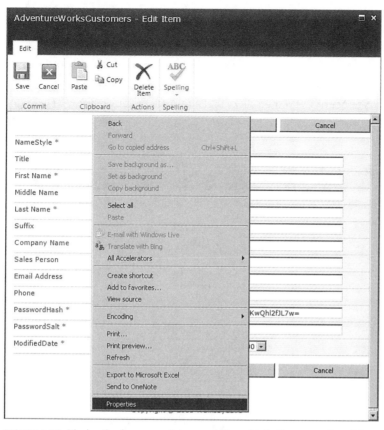

FIGURE 5-20 Display the form as a dialog, and then obtain the properties of the page.

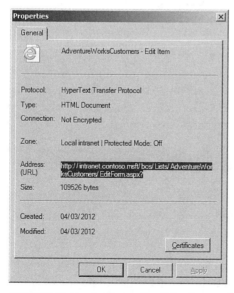

FIGURE 5-21 Use the Properties dialog box to obtain the URL of the form.

In the browser, paste the URL in the Address box, removing *&isDlg=1* from the end of the URL. Doing so displays the form with the Site Actions menu. For example, the URL of your external list NewForm should look similar to the following URL:

```
http://intranet/Lists/Customers/NewForm.aspx?RootFolder=%2Fbcs%2FLists%2FCustomers
```

To edit the form, click Site Actions, and then click Edit Page. Click the down arrow to the right of the Web Part title, and then click Edit Web Part, as shown in Figure 5-22, to display the Untitled Web Part tool pane.

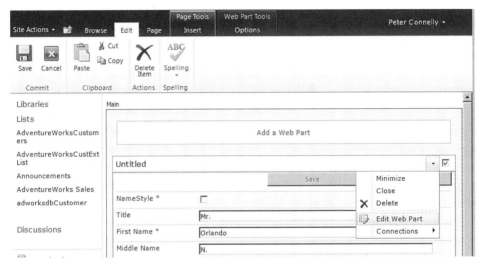

FIGURE 5-22 Use the Untitled Web Part tool pane to configure the XLF Web Part.

The XLF Web Part does not provide you with many options to customize the form or modify the fields to display on the form. You are dependent on the fields defined in the Create, Read Item, and Update ECT operations.

See Also *Web Part properties are discussed in Chapter 6.*

You can create new forms with the browser by using the Form Web Parts menu option on the List ribbon tab in the Custom List group, as shown in Figure 5-23. However, you are still limited to using the XLF Web Part and the fields defined in the ECT operations.

FIGURE 5-23 Use the Form Web Part menu to create new forms for an external list.

The alternative to using the XLF Web Part is to create forms using either InfoPath Designer to create an InfoPath form or SharePoint Designer to create an *.aspx* page that contains a DFWP. Both procedures allow you to build more complex forms and to choose which fields to display on the form.

If you alter the ECT to include additional fields, both forms will need to be amended. However, such amendments to the ECT may be so drastic that you would have to recreate the external list as well.

InfoPath forms can be displayed in the browser only if you are using the Enterprise edition of SharePoint Server and have configured InfoPath Services. With other lists, you can use the browser to create InfoPath forms for the three types of forms by clicking Form Settings on the List Settings page. This option is not available for all lists, including external lists—for example, it is not available for calendar, group calendar, circulations, phone call memo, resources, discussions, surveys, and libraries.

Creating Forms in SharePoint Designer

You can use SharePoint Designer on other lists to create *.aspx* forms by using the List Form command in the New group on the external list's List Settings ribbon tab or by using one of the three form commands in the New group on the Forms ribbon tab. However, if you try this option for an external list, a dialog box displays stating that SharePoint Designer could not save the list changes to the server as the list does not exist (see Figure 5-24).

FIGURE 5-24 When you use SharePoint Designer to create a new form using a command on the ribbon, a dialog box displays stating that the external list does not exist.

The workaround is to modify an existing form *.aspx* page or create a new *.aspx* or Web Part page in SharePoint Designer. On the Insert ribbon tab, depending on the type of form you want to create, in the Data Views & Forms group, click New Item Form, Edit Item Form, or Display Item Form, and then click Custom List From. The List or Document Library Form dialog box opens, from which you can select an external list. This creates a DFWP on the page.

You can use the DFWP in many business scenarios where traditionally a developer was needed to create a custom Web Part. Like other Web Parts, the DFWP and the XLV and XLF Web Parts follow these rules:

- They can be placed inside and outside EmbeddedFormField controls on wiki pages or Web Part zones on Web Part pages. That is, you can use both types of Web Part on pages other than external list view and form *.aspx* pages.

- They have the standard properties shared by all Web Parts, such as Title, Height, Width, and Frame State.

- Depending on the settings of the Web Part zone properties, they can be relocated to other Web Part zones by using the browser.

- Web Part properties can be accessed through the browser Web Part tool pane.

- When inside a Web Part zone, they support personal and shared views.

Table 5-1 describes the differences between the DFWP and the XLV and XLF Web Parts.

TABLE 5-1 Differences between the DFWP and the XLV and XLF Web Parts

DFWP	XLV and XLF Web Parts
Used to display to display and modify content stored in external lists and SharePoint lists and libraries. You can also use it to create views when external data is defined using the data source component within SharePoint Designer.	Used to display and modify content stored in external lists and SharePoint lists and libraries.
Can be added to a page using SharePoint Designer.	Can be added to a page using the browser or SharePoint Designer.
Cannot be easily configured in the browser. However, you can edit the XSL and the parameters passed to the XSL without needing to open the page in SharePoint Designer.	Can be easily modified in the browser.
Fields that the DFWP displays or modifies need to be added. You can then position the fields on the page as you wish.	XLF dynamically creates the all the fields defined in an ECT. You cannot position the fields within the Web Part.
Cannot be used to display multiple items from an external list. It can be used only to create forms.	XLV: Can position fields using either the browser or SharePoint Designer. XLF: Can use conditional formatting in SharePoint Designer to style, show, or hide external list items based on defined criteria.
Can connect to a Web Part on the same page as the DFWP or on other pages.	Can connect to other Web Parts displayed on the same page as the XLV/XLF Web Part.
Uses XSLT to format data.	Uses XSLT to format data.
Can easily format the XSLT using the SharePoint Designer Design and Code views. It includes additional XSLT formatting options such as XSLT filtering and an XPath editor.	Formatting XSLT is difficult. Using SharePoint Designer, a copy of the XSL files (vwstyles.xsl) that contain the XSLT for XLVs and XLFs can be modified and known in SharePoint Designer as customizing a file.

Using SharePoint Designer, you can also create InfoPath forms for external lists and other lists. You have two methods for creating InfoPath forms with SharePoint Designer:

- On the External Content Types ribbon tab, in the List & Forms group, use the Create Lists & Forms command to display the Create List and Form dialog box, as shown in Figure 5-8. This method allows you to create new forms, and edit and display forms. You used the Create List and Form dialog box earlier in this chapter to create an external list.

- Create and edit the form from the List Settings ribbon tab, in the Actions group, by using the Design Forms in InfoPath command as described in the following steps:

  1. Click Lists and Libraries in the Navigation pane to display the Lists and Library gallery. Under External Lists, click the external list where you want to create a new form.

  2. On the List Settings ribbon tab, in the Actions group, click Design Forms in InfoPath, as shown in Figure 5-25. InfoPath Designer 2010 opens.

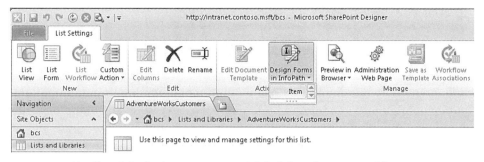

FIGURE 5-25 Use SharePoint Designer to create an InfoPath form for an external list.

3. Once you have completed your customizations, save the InfoPath file (*.xsn*). Publish it to the external list by clicking File to display the Microsoft Backstage view, and then click Publish Your Form. The default location to save the form is a folder named Item, below the external list.

Site Columns and External Data

You cannot create a site column that directly accesses data from an external system; however, you can create a site column where the type of information in the column looks up information from an external list. The external list should already be created on the site where the site column is created.

Manipulating Data in External Lists with Workflows

You cannot bind workflows to data that is not stored in SharePoint. Data presented in external lists is not stored in SharePoint, so SharePoint cannot trigger workflows on changes to the data that is made in the external system. However, using SharePoint Designer, you can create a site, list, library, or reusable workflow, and in those workflows you can look up, copy, delete, or modify data from one or more external lists.

Using External Data in Lists and Libraries

External data columns allow you to add external content to a standard SharePoint list or library. The external data column is similar to a lookup column, but in place of choosing values stored in another list or library, the data is retrieved from an external system. You create an external data column as you do any other column—that is, on the List tab, click Create Column. Then on the Create page, enter a column name, and then select External Data as the column type, as shown in Figure 5-26.

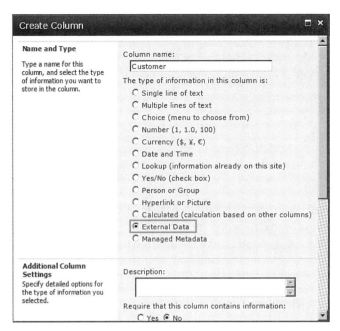

FIGURE 5-26 Choose External Data to create a column that looks up data from an external system.

In the Additional Column Settings section, to the right of the External Content Type text box are two icons: the Check external content type (ECT) icon, which you use when you know the name of the ECT, and the Select ECT icon, which when clicked opens the External Content Type Picker dialog box.

Once you select an ECT, the Additional Column Settings section contains a list of properties associated with the ECT, as shown in Figure 5-27. In the Select the Field to Be Shown on This Column drop-down list, select the column that your users usually associate with the external content. If the external content is a customer relationship management (CRM) system, then this column might be the customer name. You can then choose to add one or more fields from the ECT to become columns in your list or library, such as Email Address, First Name, or Last Name. You can also choose to add the fields to all content types, as well as adding them to the default view.

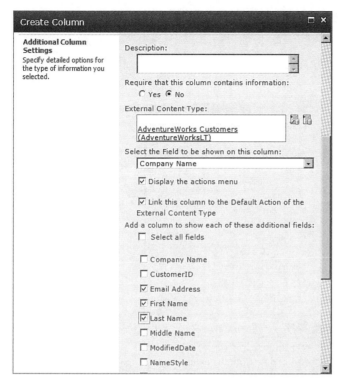

FIGURE 5-27 Select columns that you want to display external data in your list or library.

Only when you add a new list item or document and click the Select External Item(s) icon will the Business Data Connectivity (BDC) runtime connect to the external system to retrieve data to populate the Choose dialog box, as shown in Figure 5-28. The dialog box shows only those fields that had the external item picker check box selected when you configured the ECT Read List operations. When the external item picker check box is not selected for any field, all fields are displayed in the Choose dialog box.

The Choose dialog box is limited to the number of records returned from the external system. The person who created the ECT should have created filters, so that users can quickly find the data from the external system that they want to associate as metadata with the list item or document.

When the new list item or document is saved, the external data is stored in the SharePoint SQL content database, unlike when you use external lists, where the data is always retrieved from the external system and no external data is stored in the SQL database. To update the data in the external column, click the Refresh icon to the right of the external data column name, as shown in Figure 5-29.

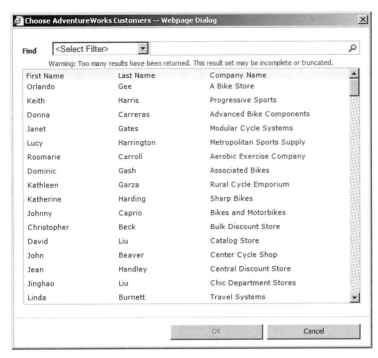

FIGURE 5-28 Use the Choose dialog box to select data from the external system that you want to save as meta-data for your list item or document.

FIGURE 5-29 Refresh the external content stored in external data columns.

A webpage is displayed, as shown in Figure 5-30, that warns you that this operation could take a long time. If you click OK, the BDC runtime connects to the external system. A copy of the updated external data is stored in the SQL database.

FIGURE 5-30 Refreshing external data in your list or library may take a long time.

When you copy external data into a list or library, the data inherits all list type operations, such as views, filters, and the ability to be used to trigger list workflows. When an external data column is added to a library, then the values in the external column can be made available as content controls in Microsoft Word 2010.

Using External Data Actions

When you create an external data column in a list or library, an icon appears on each list item to the left of the external content. This icon provides a drop-down list of links to pages that display information relevant to the external content type (ECT) item, such as the following:

- Displaying all the values for all the properties of the ECT item. This page is also known as the profile page, which you can create using the SharePoint 2010 Central Administration website or SharePoint Designer.

- Displaying a map of a location using the postal/zip code property of the ECT item.

These links are called actions, and a SharePoint farm administrator can create them with the SharePoint 2010 Central Administration website, using the following steps:

1. Navigate to the Business Data Connectivity (BDC) service application where the ECT is defined.

2. On the Edit tab of the Service Application Information page, in the View group, click External Content Types from the drop-down menu.

3. Click the ECT to display the External Content Type Information page.

4. On the Edit tab, in the Actions group, click Add, as shown in Figure 5-31.

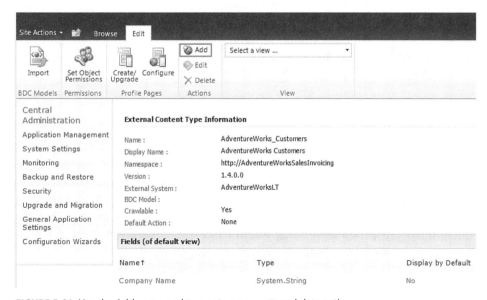

FIGURE 5-31 Use the Add command to create a new external data action.

5. On the Add Action page that appears (see Figure 5-32), type a name for the action, type the URL, specify whether to launch the action in a new browser window or not (default), add parameters to the URL if required, and then add the icon to display next to the action. You can choose from the Delete, Edit, or New icons, or you can choose your own image.

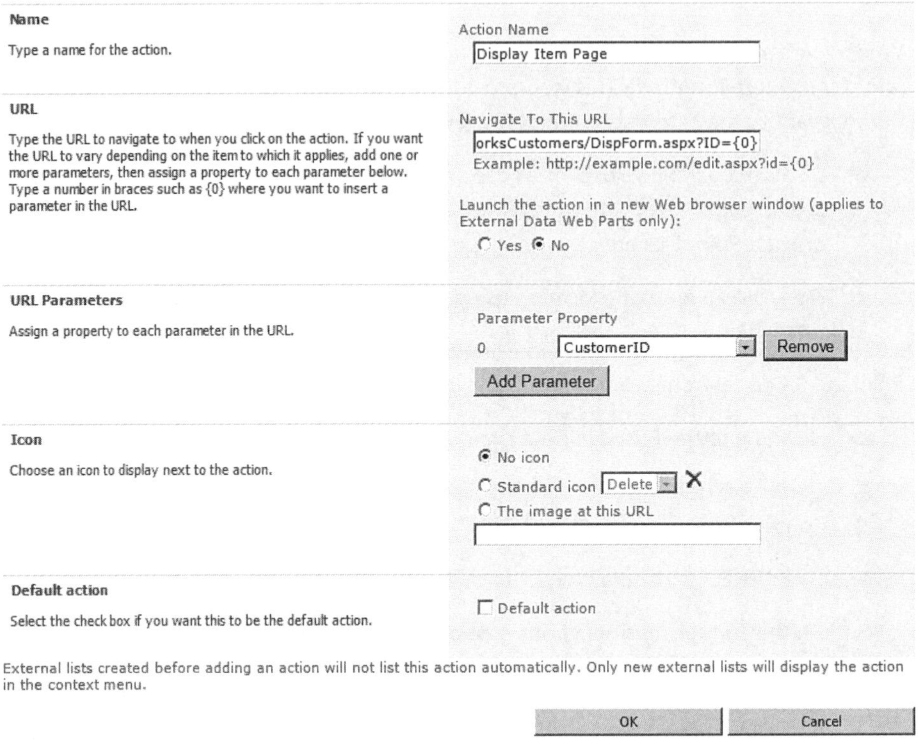

Name
Type a name for the action.

Action Name

Display Item Page

URL
Type the URL to navigate to when you click on the action. If you want the URL to vary depending on the item to which it applies, add one or more parameters, then assign a property to each parameter below. Type a number in braces such as {0} where you want to insert a parameter in the URL.

Navigate To This URL

orksCustomers/DispForm.aspx?ID={0}
Example: http://example.com/edit.aspx?id={0}

Launch the action in a new Web browser window (applies to External Data Web Parts only):
○ Yes ● No

URL Parameters
Assign a property to each parameter in the URL.

Parameter Property

0   CustomerID   ▼   Remove

Add Parameter

Icon
Choose an icon to display next to the action.

● No icon
○ Standard icon Delete ▼ ✕
○ The image at this URL

Default action
Select the check box if you want this to be the default action.

☐ Default action

External lists created before adding an action will not list this action automatically. Only new external lists will display the action in the context menu.

OK   Cancel

FIGURE 5-32 Specify the URL to navigate to when a user clicks the action and the parameters you want to pass to the URL so the URL varies depending on the items to which it applies.

Profile Page

If you are using the Enterprise edition of SharePoint Server, you can create a profile page automatically using either the SharePoint 2010 Central Administration website or SharePoint Designer, as explained in Chapters 3 and 4. The profile page created uses two Business Data Web Parts, Business Data Item Builder and Business Data Details, which are available only in the Enterprise edition of SharePoint Server 2010 and in the Office 365 E3 and E4 plans. At the same time that SharePoint creates the profile page, it also creates an external data action named View Profile.

See Also *For more information about the Business Data Web Parts, see Chapter 6.*

If you are not using the Enterprise edition of SharePoint Server or the Office 365 E3 or E4 plans, then you will need to create a profile page and external data action for each ECT to you create. This is easy to accomplish using external lists:

1. Create a single dedicated SharePoint site to host the profile pages for all your ECTs, as per Microsoft's recommendation. Ensure that the web application where the site is created is associated with the BCS service applications whose metadata store contains the ECT.

2. On the site, create an external list for each ECT you create. This will create at a minimum one view based on the Read List operation and a display form from the Read Item operation.

3. Give all users who will use the profile page at least read-only permissions to the external list. If you do not know who these users are, you should contact the BDC service application administrator, as they would have configured such users with similar access to the ECT object within the metadata store.

4. Ask the BDC service application administrator to create an external data action configured as follows:

   • Ensure the URL is the display form with one parameter—for example, *http://intranet/bcs/ AdventureWorksCustomers/DispForm.aspx?ID={0}*.

   • Add a parameter that maps parameter 0 to the identify field for the ECT.

   • Associate an icon with the action (optional). The standard icons provided on the Add Action page do not match the display form page, so you would need to create an image, save it to a library on the site, and configure permissions on the library so users who will use the action have Read permissions to the icon.

   • Set the action as the default action.

 Note When you delete ECTs, you need to delete the external list and the external action.

It is likely that this procedure will be completed by the BDC service application administrator or the creator of the ECT, although there is the option to create the display form as either an InfoPath form or by using a DFWP, as discussed earlier in this chapter. It is unlikely you will use an InfoPath form for the display form, as the reason for following the preceding procedure is that you are not using the Enterprise edition of SharePoint Server, and without that version of SharePoint Server, you cannot create InfoPath forms that can be displayed in webpages.

Summary

The preferred method of displaying data from external data sources is to use external lists. You create external lists using the browser, Microsoft SharePoint Designer, Windows PowerShell, or code. When you have created these lists, you will find that they have similar functionality to other SharePoint lists you are familiar with; however, you cannot associate RSS feeds to external lists. There is also no data-sheet view, and you cannot bind workflows to the data in an external list, because the data is not in SharePoint, so SharePoint cannot trigger workflows on data changes in an external system. However, using SharePoint Designer, you can create a site, list, or reusable workflow that accesses one or more external lists.

By default, the XSLT List View (XLV) Web Part is used on external list views, and the XSLT List Form (XLF) Web Part is used on external list forms. You can replace these Web Parts either by using the Data Form Web Part (DFWP) or Business Data Web Part or by using InfoPath forms.

CHAPTER 6

Building Business Data Dashboards

In this chapter, you will:

- Learn how business data dashboards can have a positive effect on your organization

- Discover how to build a dashboard within SharePoint 2010

- Explore the Business Data Web Parts, their uses, and how to configure them to present business data in an effective way

- Explore other Web Parts you can use to add the finishing touches to your business data dashboard

When you hear the word *dashboard*, you probably think of the everyday physical object in your car. To drive a car safely and to avoid mechanical breakdowns, you need the easily viewable information about the car's state and functioning that the dashboard provides. When you drive a car, you are constantly monitoring live data made available to you through the dashboard. Often the data is read-only, but it lets you know on an ongoing basis what is going on with the car: how much gas is in the gas tank so you know when to refuel, how fast the car is traveling so you can keep within the speed limits, and how many revolutions the engine is making per minute. In the past, many cars did not provide this much information, so perhaps it is not critical but nice to know. Important information from the dashboard includes warnings: the engine is overheating, the car is running out of gas, or a passenger is not wearing a seatbelt. This information is made visible to you through warning lights (and sometimes through sound) to grab your attention. Figure 6-1 shows an example of a car dashboard.

Imagine if your car didn't have a dashboard and you had to rely on monthly or weekly reports about the car instead. These reports might provide information like the car's average speed over the entire period or how many times the car ran out of gas. At least you would know if you had to schedule repairs for your car because it overheated on day 4 of the month. You might receive an attachment about the state of your car in a spreadsheet that you later find was duplicated, and you are not sure which is the correct version.

Many businesses rely on information provided to them in a weekly or monthly report. These reports are out of date the moment they are printed or sent via email, and by the time you receive them, it is too late to react constructively. It would be absurd to receive information about your car's operation in this way, but this is exactly how some business organizations operate. For instance, learning that you ran out of stock of your biggest-selling product three weeks ago isn't useful information.

But being warned that you will likely run out of stock of that product next week is useful, just as seeing that your car's fuel gauge is getting close to the 0 mark is useful in letting you know that the car will run out of fuel soon—you are able to react to the situation before it becomes a crisis.

FIGURE 6-1 Important information is made available to a driver through a car's dashboard.

It wouldn't be practical to email the dealership while you are driving your car and ask for an up-to-date status report every time you wanted to know the tire pressure or the engine's water level, yet this is what happens within businesses. Information workers are constantly being emailed for status updates, because the requestors may not understand how to obtain the information themselves. Perhaps they haven't had training on systems such as Microsoft Dynamics CRM, or they simply don't have time to look for the information and therefore delegate it to someone else in the organization.

Dashboards showing critical business information can be extremely powerful for an organization. They can help warn about cash-flow issues, stock levels, or targets not being met. Just like a dashboard in a car, you only need to glance at a business data dashboard to check the status of various types of business information.

Dashboards can also be used for a variety of other business reasons. Often in businesses, some roles or departments are not recognized as contributing to an organization's success. For example, the IT help desk responds to the needs of information workers, but because the IT help desk is not involved directly with selling or building something to sell, it is often considered a source of overhead expense. Using a dashboard, you can promote how well the IT help desk is performing and how much money the company has saved due to the efficiencies of the IT help desk. This dashboard could contain key performance indicators (KPIs) showing the number of calls successfully answered within the service-level agreement, how long the servers have been running without interruption, and how many employees considered their call to the help desk successful.

In this chapter, you will learn how to build Microsoft SharePoint dashboards and present external business data in a way that is useful to your business using the Business Data Web Parts, SharePoint Designer 2010 to customize those Web Parts, and other Web Parts such as the Microsoft Chart Web Part.

Building SharePoint 2010 Dashboards

In this section, you will learn how to build a SharePoint dashboard, what SharePoint provides for out-of-the-box functionality, and how can you use Business Connectivity Services (BCS) and the Business Data Web Parts to provide valuable information.

In its basic form, a dashboard in SharePoint is just a SharePoint page, whether you use a simple Web Part page stored within the Site Pages Library in a team site, a Web Part page created from a Reports Library, or a PerformancePoint dashboard. In any of these cases, the dashboard consists of Web Parts that display useful information that can be read easily. As dashboards consist of only Web Parts, you will usually create a Web Part page, rather than a wiki or a publishing page.

Designing a Dashboard

Before you create a dashboard, plan the layout first so you end up with a more effective dashboard. If you don't plan well first, you might run out of space, or the Web Parts won't quite fill the width of the Web Part zone. Before you create the dashboard, consider designing a *wireframe*, also known as a page schematic or blueprint, showing the layout of the dashboard, as shown in Figure 6-2. Using the wireframe, you can gather the business requirements and obtain approval for the dashboard from the business users who will be using it. You can also decide which Web Part Page template to use to create your dashboard page.

A wireframe consists of a drawing displaying the layout of the navigation, breadcrumbs, charts, Web Parts, and Web Part zones. You may want to provide the wireframe design to a designer capable of providing a custom layout within SharePoint, so that you can add Web Parts required by the business to the layout.

Creating a wireframe enables you to design a SharePoint Web Part page with Web Part zones that fit well with the Web Parts displaying the business-critical information. Microsoft Visio is a great tool to use to design the wireframe, as it provides a number of graphic stencils for wireframe creation. Other useful wireframe creation tools are available from websites such as *www.wireframe.com*.

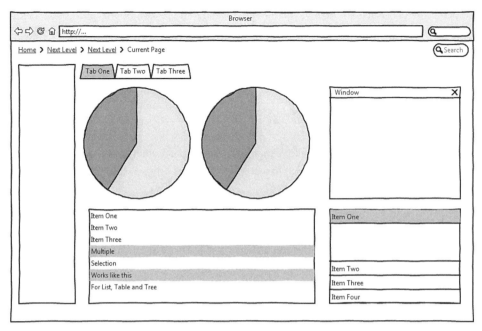

FIGURE 6-2 Before you create a dashboard, design a wireframe to show its layout.

PerformancePoint Dashboards

The Enterprise edition of SharePoint Server 2010 includes PerformancePoint Service (PPS), which allows you to analyze data in SharePoint through the use of dashboards, scorecards, reports, and key performance indicator Key Performance Indicators (KPIs). PPS is a service application that requires configuration.

See Also *For more information on service applications, see Chapter 3, "Creating and Maintaining Business Data Connectivity Service Applications."*

Once you have configured the PPS service application, you can create a Business Intelligence Center, a special type of SharePoint site containing libraries for storing dashboards, data connections, and content. You can configure connections to SharePoint lists, SQL Server Analysis Services, SQL tables, and Excel Services. Upon creating a Business Intelligence Center site, you can launch a client application called PerformancePoint Dashboard Designer from the Data Connection Library. Figure 6-3 shows how to create a new PerformancePoint data source connection, which will open the PerformancePoint Dashboard Designer.

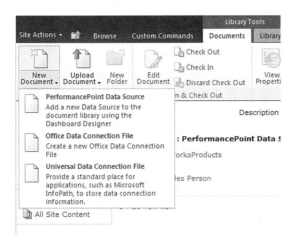

FIGURE 6-3 Use the PerformancePoint Dashboard Designer to create a new dashboard.

The PerformancePoint Dashboard Designer enables you to build very advanced dashboards. Although you can connect SQL tables as a data connection in a PerformancePoint dashboard, you cannot select an external content type (ECT) as a data source for your connection. It stands to reason that since you can create an external list from an ECT, and external lists act like SharePoint lists, that you can configure as data connections in PerformancePoint, you can configure an external list as a data connection in PerformancePoint. If you try this, however, you will receive an error message, since the data itself doesn't actually reside within SharePoint. Figure 6-4 shows that PerformancePoint can't be used to connect to external lists.

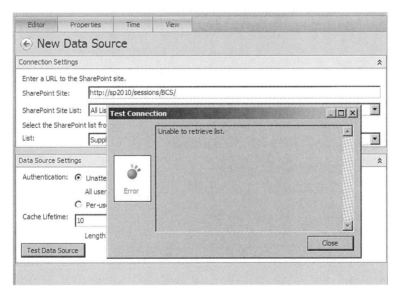

FIGURE 6-4 Attemping to connect to an external list through PerformancePoint Dashboard Designer doesn't work.

See Also *You can find more information about PerformancePoint at* http://technet.microsoft.com/en-us/library/ee661741.aspx.

Using PerformancePoint isn't the only way to create dashboards in SharePoint. Whether you use SharePoint Foundation 2010 or SharePoint Server 2010, you can easily create dashboards that display external data.

Using a Report Library to Create Dashboards

You can create a Web Part page using your browser or SharePoint Designer, and then add Web Parts to the page to create your dashboard. If you have the Enterprise edition of SharePoint Server, you can use a report library to create dashboards. Pages created in a report library already contain Excel Services Web Parts and KPI Web Parts, which you would otherwise need to add manually to a page. These Web Parts are useful on a dashboard, and many organizations use them on their webpages.

> **Note** The Reports Library template, Excel Services Web Parts, and KPI Web Parts are available only if you have the Enterprise edition of SharePoint Server 2010, and you have activated at the site level and site collection level the SharePoint Server Enterprise Site Features.

You can create a report library using the following steps:

1. Click Site Actions, and then click More Options to display the Create dialog box, where the list and library templates are displayed, as shown in Figure 6-5.

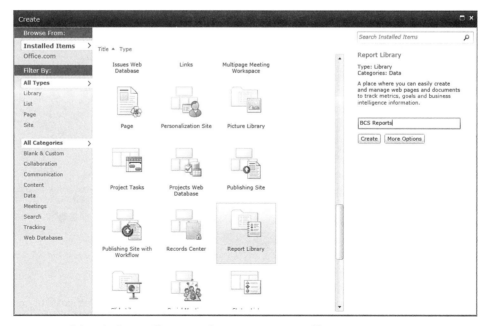

FIGURE 6-5 Select the Report Library template to create a report library.

2. In the middle section of the Create dialog box, select the Report Library template, and in the Report Library section, type a name for the library.

3. Click Create to create your library.

4. To create a dashboard, click the Documents tab on the ribbon, under Library Tools, and then in the New group, click New Document, and then click Web Part Page With Status List.

> **Note** The default content type associated with a report library is Report. When you click the New Document icon in the New group, you create a report that is an Excel spreadsheet. The default view of a report library is filtered to display only reports. To display both reports and dashboards on the Library tab, select All Reports and Dashboards or Dashboards.

5. In the Page Name section, type the name of the Web Part page—for example, **Sales Dashboard**—and a title and description.

6. Leave the default options selected on this page. Notice that the option selected in the Status Indicators section will create a status indicator list for you. Alternatively, you could select one of the other options and create the list manually at a later time. The name of the status list automatically created for you is *<Web Part page name>* Status Indicator Definitions.

7. Click OK to create the Web Part page. The newly created page will display in your browser, as shown in Figure 6-6.

FIGURE 6-6 A Web Part page with a status list displays in the browser.

The report dashboard consists of two Excel Web Access Web Parts, a List Web Part that displays the contents of the status list, an Apply Filters Button Web Part, a Related Information Summary Links Web Part, a Summary Web Part, and a Contact Details Web Part. Notice that no Business Data Web Parts are used to display data stored in external systems; this is the subject of the next section. The Excel Web Access Web Part and status list are explained later in this chapter.

Exploring the Business Data Web Parts

You can add any Web Part to your dashboard pages. In the Enterprise edition of SharePoint Server 2010, you can add Business Data Web Parts to simplify the creation of dashboards. If you have the Enterprise version of SharePoint Server 2010, and you want to build a good dashboard that presents external business data information, you will most likely use the Business Data Web Parts.

When you add a Web Part to your page, you will notice a Web Part category called Business Data. Not all the Web Parts listed within this category are directly related to Business Connectivity Services (BCS), but this section explains each of these Web Parts, starting with the Business Data List Web Part, because they are all useful when building a dashboard.

> **Note** The examples in this section use the Adventure Works database, which you can download from *http://sqlserversamples.codeplex.com*. To use the Business Data Web Parts, first create an external content type (ECT). The process to do so is detailed in Chapter 4, "Defining External System Connections Using SharePoint Designer."

Business Data List Web Part

You can use the Business Data List Web Part to display multiple rows of data from an external source, and you can easily configure it using the Web Parts properties. While you can further modify this Web Part within SharePoint Designer 2010, you can configure it using the browser to a stage where it displays data. Using the Edit View option within the Web Part, you can configure the order of the columns, filters, sorting, pagination, and item limits.

Upon adding the Business Data List Web Part to your page, click the down arrow to the far right of the Web Part title and then click Edit Web Part to open the Business Data List tool pane. You use the Business Data List tool pane to configure the Type property to select the external system where the data you want to present is stored. The Type property is referring to the ECT.

The lookup icon allows you to display the list of available ECTs. The list of ECTs is security trimmed, so it is possible that even though you can view external data within another Business Data List Web Part, you may not have permission to configure the same external data yourself.

Once you have configured the Type property, at the bottom of the tool pane, click Apply. The data within the Web Part itself displays. Notice that the title of the Web Part has changed to match the title of the ECT, as shown in Figure 6-7.

FIGURE 6-7 The Business Data List Web Part tool pane shows the ECT selected.

Other properties for Business Data List Web Part are explained later in this section. Figure 6-8 displays a Business Data List Web Part that is configured but not formatted.

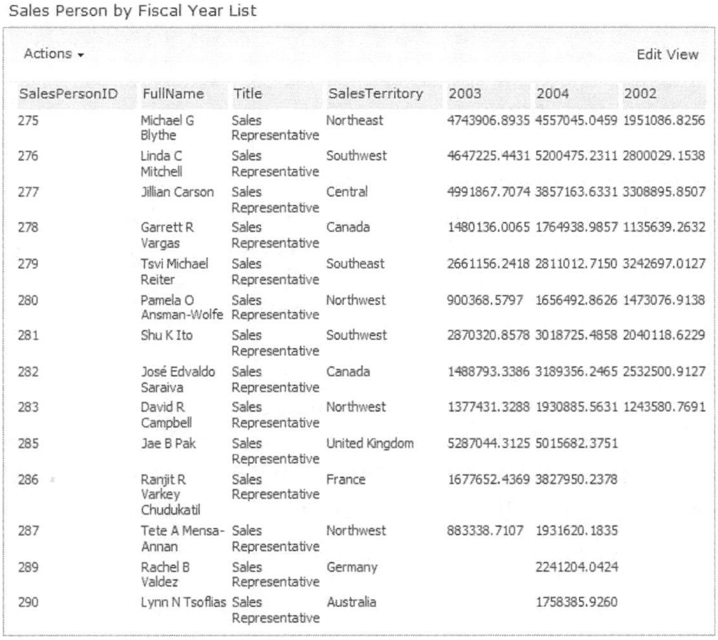

Sales Person by Fiscal Year List

Actions ▾						Edit View
SalesPersonID	FullName	Title	SalesTerritory	2003	2004	2002
275	Michael G Blythe	Sales Representative	Northeast	4743906.8935	4557045.0459	1951086.8256
276	Linda C Mitchell	Sales Representative	Southwest	4647225.4431	5200475.2311	2800029.1538
277	Jillian Carson	Sales Representative	Central	4991867.7074	3857163.6331	3308895.8507
278	Garrett R Vargas	Sales Representative	Canada	1480136.0065	1764938.9857	1135639.2632
279	Tsvi Michael Reiter	Sales Representative	Southeast	2661156.2418	2811012.7150	3242697.0127
280	Pamela O Ansman-Wolfe	Sales Representative	Northwest	900368.5797	1656492.8626	1473076.9138
281	Shu K Ito	Sales Representative	Southwest	2870320.8578	3018725.4858	2040118.6229
282	José Edvaldo Saraiva	Sales Representative	Canada	1488793.3386	3189356.2465	2532500.9127
283	David R Campbell	Sales Representative	Northwest	1377431.3288	1930885.5631	1243580.7691
285	Jae B Pak	Sales Representative	United Kingdom	5287044.3125	5015682.3751	
286	Ranjit R Varkey Chudukatil	Sales Representative	France	1677652.4369	3827950.2378	
287	Tete A Mensa-Annan	Sales Representative	Northwest	883338.7107	1931620.1835	
289	Rachel B Valdez	Sales Representative	Germany		2241204.0424	
290	Lynn N Tsoflias	Sales Representative	Australia		1758385.9260	

FIGURE 6-8 The Business Data List Web Part is configured to display the vSalesPersonSalesByFiscalYears view from the Adventure Works database.

Edit View

While the Web Part page is in Edit Page mode, the Business Data List Web Part contains an Edit View link in the top-right corner. Clicking Edit View allows you to configure some basic view options, such as sorting and filtering, as well as other options you cannot set through the browser. For example, the sales figures in Figure 6-8 are not displayed in currency format. In fact, it is strange that the sales figures are displayed to more than two decimal points. The Edit View option does not allow you to format values, but you can format values either when you create the ECT using Visual Studio or when you modify the view using SharePoint Designer.

The Edit View page is divided into six sections:

- **Items to Retrieve**   When you edit the view of your Business Data List Web Part in the browser, you will first notice that you can choose which items are displayed. This option is dependent upon creating filters when configuring the ECT. The default option is to retrieve all items from the external data source. However, when you create filter methods in the ECT, you can choose to allow the user to set the filter value or you can set a filter value yourself, which the user can modify if required. In Figure 6-9, these options are not available, since filter methods were not created in the ECT.

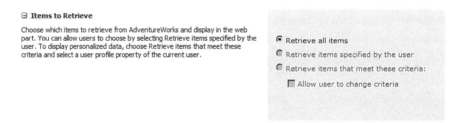

FIGURE 6-9 The Items to Retrieve options are unavailable within the Edit View page of a Business Data List Web Part if filter methods were not created in the ECT.

- **Item Limit**   When an external data source contains thousands of rows of data, you can use a filter method so that the ECT returns only a subset of the external data. You can also set the item limit for the ECT, which is especially useful when configuring a dashboard. For example, you may want to show only the top 10 performing sales representatives, instead of all 200 sales representatives.

- **Columns**   This section allows you to select which columns you want to display, set the order of the columns from left to right, and set one of the columns as the Title column. The Title column displays a drop-down list when you hover over it and allows actions to be triggered against the item selected. For example, an action could be a search for a salesperson within the SharePoint search center. Figure 6-10 shows how you can figure the view of the Business Data List Web Part within the browser.

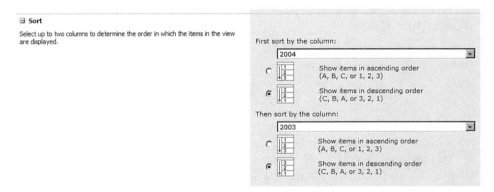

Columns

Select or clear the check box next to each column you want to show or hide in this view. To specify the order of the columns, select a number in the Position from the left box. The column you choose as the title column will contain the edit menu and will be linked to the profile page.

Display	Title	Column Name	Position from Left
☐	○	SalesPersonID	1 ▾
☑	○	FullName	2 ▾
☐	○	Title	3 ▾
☑	○	SalesTerritory	4 ▾
☑	○	2003	5 ▾
☑	○	2004	6 ▾
☐	○	2002	7 ▾

FIGURE 6-10 You can configure the columns to display and the column order within the Edit View options of a Business Data List Web Part.

- **Sort** This section allows you to sort by up to two columns in either ascending or descending order. For example, if you want to show the salesperson with the most overall sales for the past couple of years first, configure the view to show the most recent sales figures in descending order, and then sort by the previous year in descending order, as shown in Figure 6-11.

Sort

Select up to two columns to determine the order in which the items in the view are displayed.

First sort by the column:

2004

○ Show items in ascending order (A, B, C, or 1, 2, 3)

⦿ Show items in descending order (C, B, A, or 3, 2, 1)

Then sort by the column:

2003

○ Show items in ascending order (A, B, C, or 1, 2, 3)

⦿ Show items in descending order (C, B, A, or 3, 2, 1)

FIGURE 6-11 Set the Sort options within the Business Data List Web Part Edit View page.

- **Filter** Although you may have already configured filters when you created the ECT, it is possible to hard-code the filter values for the view of the Business Data List Web Part. When you set these filters, users cannot change them using the filter toolbar within the Business Data List Web Part.

- **Pages** The final section is for pagination. Here you can simply set the number of items you want to display on each page, as shown in Figure 6-12.

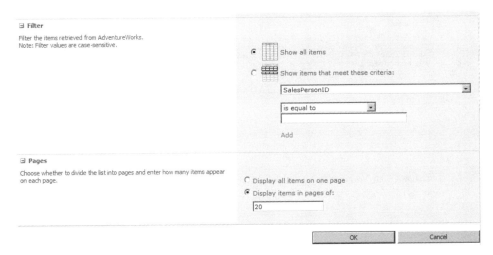

FIGURE 6-12 You can configure the filter and pagination options within the Edit View of the Business Data List Web Part.

Formatting Data

After you configure the view of the Web Part, the data is presented close to your requirements, but the lack of formatting may annoy users. You can address this issue by modifying the XSL of the Web Part.

 Note The Extensible Stylesheet Language (XSL) family of languages, including Extensible Stylesheet Language for Transformations (XSLT), is coding language for styling Extensible Markup Language (XML). XSLT provides similar results to that of a Cascading Style Sheet (CSS) file for HTML. You can use XSL within most SharePoint Web Parts to provide styling, branding, positioning, and general look-and-feel customizations to present the contents of the Web Part. You can also embed JavaScript in many cases within the XSL to provide custom functionality.

In the Business Data List Web Part tool pane, you can find the XSL Editor button in the Data View Properties section. When you click the button, a Text Editor – Webpage Dialog box appears, with the XSLT equivalent of the setting you configured in the Edit View page. The dialog box does not offer a good user experience for modifying XSL. However, you can copy and paste the XSL into SharePoint Designer 2010 or Visual Studio and use these tools to amend the code. It is certainly recommended that you back up the XSLT code before making any changes. Figure 6-13 shows the XSL editor built into the Web Part.

FIGURE 6-13 Modify the XSLT using the XSL Editor dialog box for the Business Data List Web Part.

If you used the Business Data List Web Part to display data from the Adventure Works database, then your currency column displays more than two decimal places. Using Visual Studio, locate the XSLT code that contains the column name. In the example for this book, the 2003 sales data has a column name of @_x0032x003, and the XSLT code is as follows:

```
<xsl:value-of select="@_x0032_003/>
```

To format the sales data to two decimal places, the code should be:

```
<xsl:value-of select="format-number(@_x0032_003, '$###0.00')" />
```

Copy the XSLT back into the Text Editor – Webpage Dialog box for the Business Data List Web Part, which results in the 2003 column being formatted as shown in Figure 6-14.

Sales Person by Fiscal Year List

Actions ▾			Edit View
FullName	SalesTerritory	2003	2004
Linda C Mitchell	Southwest	$4647225.44	5200475.2311
Jae B Pak	United Kingdom	$5287044.31	5015682.3751
Michael G Blythe	Northeast	$4743906.89	4557045.0459
Jillian Carson	Central	$4991867.71	3857163.6331
Ranjit R Varkey Chudukatil	France	$1677652.44	3827950.2378
José Edvaldo Saraiva	Canada	$1488793.34	3189356.2465
Shu K Ito	Southwest	$2870320.86	3018725.4858
Tsvi Michael Reiter	Southeast	$2661156.24	2811012.7150

FIGURE 6-14 You can format the column 2003 values as currency within the Business Data List Web Part using SharePoint Designer 2010.

If you are changing the XSLT, make sure to keep a copy of your modified XSLT. When you use the Edit View menu and make even subtle changes, the XSLT for the Web Part is regenerated and will wipe out any changes you made manually using the XSL Editor dialog box. If you add another column to the Web Part, such as the 2002 column, again you will lose the formatting on the 2003 column. It is good practice to store your XSLT in a separate file, upload that file to a document library, and then type the URL of the file in the XSL Link text box in the Miscellaneous section of the Business Data List Web Part tool pane.

Visual Studio does not provide a WYSIWYG experience when editing SharePoint data, so you need some understanding of XSL to format the business data. SharePoint Designer does have a WYSIWYG design view, though, so you can use SharePoint Designer to achieve some formatting changes without writing any XSL.

Using SharePoint Designer to Format Data

SharePoint Designer 2010 is an excellent tool for editing the Business Data Web Parts. You can use it to apply conditional formatting and implement KPIs. To modify the Web Part in SharePoint Designer 2010, follow these steps:

1. Click Site Actions and then click Edit in SharePoint Designer.

2. You can view all the files, reports, and dashboards stored in the report library by clicking All Files in the Navigation pane. When you select your dashboard, the Settings page appears.

3. In the Customization area, click Edit File to open the page in normal edit mode.

4. The Business Data List Web Part displays with sample data and the filter toolbar. From here, you can use the Common xsl:value-of Tasks dialog box to amend the number format, as shown in Figure 6-15.

In addition to formatting the columns, you can insert three images in place of the sales values for 2002. The images will be traffic light indicators—red, yellow, and green—which you will configure to display based upon conditional formatting.

Prior to formatting the page, upload the three traffic light images into a document library. In SharePoint 2010, a good place to upload images that represent data and are not uploaded by team members is the Site Assets Library, if you are on a team site. You can then use the Insert tab to insert the three traffic light images into a single row.

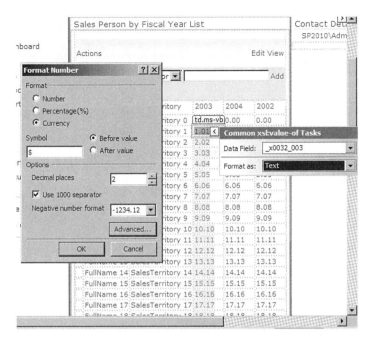

FIGURE 6-15 You can format the currency columns using SharePoint Designer 2010.

Alternatively, you can copy and paste the three traffic light images into a single row. SharePoint Designer then automatically displays a copy of the images in each row. Within a single row, click one of the traffic light images—for example, the green image—and then on the Options tab in the Data View Tools tab set, click Conditional Formatting, and then click Show Content. The Conditional Criteria dialog box appears, where you can set the conditional formatting to show the image only if a certain condition is met. For example, when the value in the 2004 sales column is greater than the value in the 2003 sales column, the green traffic light indicator displays. You can then repeat this procedure for the red image, and set the condition that when the 2004 sales column is less than 2003 sales, the red traffic light indicator displays. In addition to displaying images, you can apply formatting changes to the font or to the background color of each row. Figure 6-16 illustrates adding the images and applying conditional formatting to show the graphics.

You can implement many other formatting changes using SharePoint Designer. For example, you can display alternate rows with different background colors and change the page font to your organization's official font. SharePoint Designer is a great place to experiment, as long as you are in a development environment. If you do not have a development environment, then experiment in a separate site collection, and if that is not possible, create a separate page on the production site.

SharePoint ▸ All Files ▸ BCS Reports ▸ Sales Dashboard.aspx ▸ Editor
Pictures
Pictures
Sales Dashboard
Libraries
Site Pages
Shared Documents
BCS Reports
Lists
Calendar
Tasks
Sales Person by Fiscal Year List
Actions
Edit View
Filter name
Operator
Add
Retrieve Data
FullName
SalesTerritory
2003
2004
img
FullName 0
SalesTerritory 0
$0.00
$0.00
FullName 1
SalesTerritory 1
$1.01
$1.01
Condition Criteria
Specify criteria to determine when conditional formatting will be applied.
Field Name
Comparison
Value
And/Or
_x0032_004
Greater Than
@_x0032_003
And
And
Click here to add a new clause...
Group
Ungroup
Advanced...
OK
Cancel

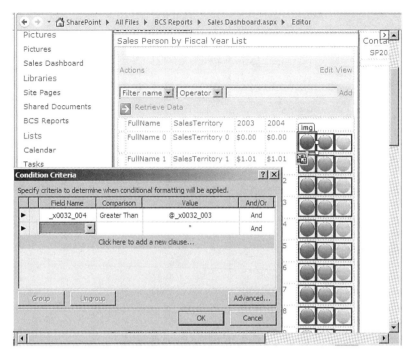

FIGURE 6-16 You can create KPIs using conditional formatting in SharePoint Designer 2010.

Figure 6-17 shows the Business Data List Web Part within the browser once you save the changes you made using SharePoint Designer.

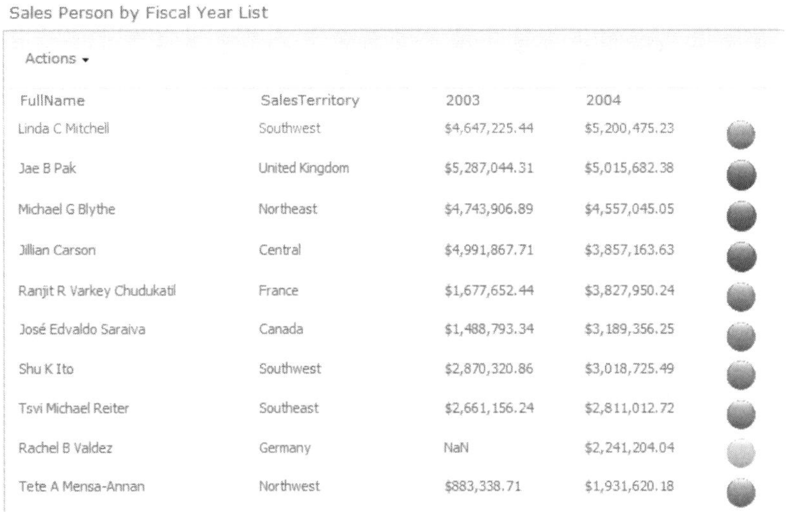

Sales Person by Fiscal Year List
Actions
FullName
SalesTerritory
2003
2004
Linda C Mitchell
Southwest
$4,647,225.44
$5,200,475.23
Jae B Pak
United Kingdom
$5,287,044.31
$5,015,682.38
Michael G Blythe
Northeast
$4,743,906.89
$4,557,045.05
Jillian Carson
Central
$4,991,867.71
$3,857,163.63
Ranjit R Varkey Chudukatil
France
$1,677,652.44
$3,827,950.24
José Edvaldo Saraiva
Canada
$1,488,793.34
$3,189,356.25
Shu K Ito
Southwest
$2,870,320.86
$3,018,725.49
Tsvi Michael Reiter
Southeast
$2,661,156.24
$2,811,012.72
Rachel B Valdez
Germany
NaN
$2,241,204.04
Tete A Mensa-Annan
Northwest
$883,338.71
$1,931,620.18

FIGURE 6-17 The completed Business Data List Web Part displays formatting and KPIs.

Now that this Web Part is on the dashboard page, users can modify the filters themselves to select the information they want to see. For example, a user may want to show only the salespeople within a specific region, as shown in Figure 6-18.

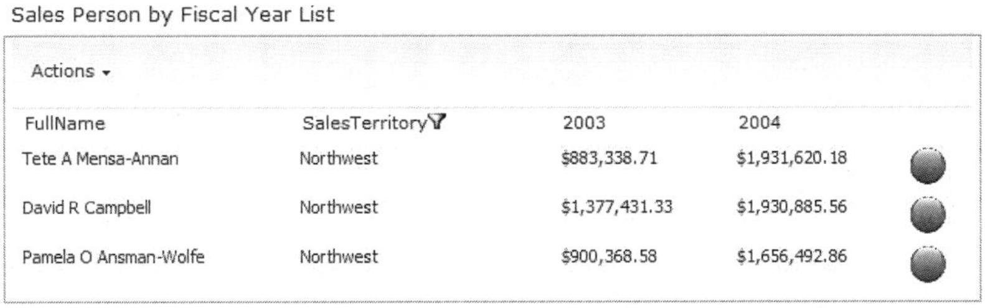

Sales Person by Fiscal Year List

Actions ▾				
FullName	SalesTerritory ▼	2003	2004	
Tete A Mensa-Annan	Northwest	$883,338.71	$1,931,620.18	
David R Campbell	Northwest	$1,377,431.33	$1,930,885.56	
Pamela O Ansman-Wolfe	Northwest	$900,368.58	$1,656,492.86	

FIGURE 6-18 Users can filter the completed Business Data List Web Part for a specific region.

The Business Data List Web Part is useful when you require a read-only view of the business data. It enables you to format, filter, and sort the data easily through either the Edit View option or Share-Point Designer customization.

Business Data Item and Business Data Item Builder Web Parts

The Business Data Item Web Part was designed to show read-only data. This Web Part, unlike the Business Data List Web Part, shows just one row at a time.

You can configure the Business Data Item Web Part to display a specific row in columnar format by providing it a unique value within a column marked as the identifier. For example, using the Adventure Works database, you may provide this Web Part a value of 11001, which is the identifier for Eugene Huang within the Sales.vIndividualCustomer table. You do not want to continue reconfiguring the Web Part each time you want to view a different customer's details, so you will likely use this Web Part to dynamically provide the row that you are looking for. The identifier value can be passed to the Business Data Item Web Part via a Web Part connection. You can connect the Business Data Item Web Part to a Business Data List Web Part, or from any other Business Data Web Part, including the Business Data Item Builder. The Business Data Item Builder Web Part takes a value from the URL parameter and passes it to the consuming Business Data Item Web Part, allowing you to open detailed information on another page, in the same way the profile page works for business data.

See Also *Chapters 4 and 5 describe the BCS profile page.*

The Business Data Item Web Part shows detailed information for one particular row. Displaying a number of rows, such as CustomerName, Address, Address2, Town, City, State, Zip, Phone, Fax, and Contact Name, in a Business Data List Web Part uses too much real estate on the page. To overcome the space limitations, you can display just CustomerName and City. Then when the user clicks CustomerName, the other columns appear within the Business Data Item Web Part, as shown in Figure 6-19, where the Business Data Item Web Part is connected to the Business Data List Web Part.

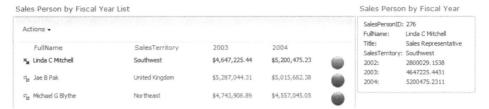

FIGURE 6-19 The Business Data Item Web Part can consume a connection from the Business Data List Web Part to show a specific row of data.

You can easily configure the properties for the Business Data Item Web Part. As with the Business Data List Web Part, you choose the ECT that you want to display. You can then optionally enter the identifier value for the item you want to display, as shown in Figure 6-20.

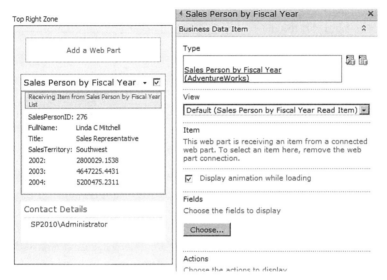

FIGURE 6-20 Enter the identifier value for the item you want to display in the property pane of the Business Data Item Web Part.

After you enter an ECT for the Business Data Item Web Part in the Type text box, click OK to close the tool pane. The page is now in edit mode, which allows you to configure the Business Data Item Web Part to consume a connection. You can set the connection either from the providing Web Part or from the consuming Web Part—the approach you choose doesn't make any difference. Figure 6-21 shows how to configure the Web Part connection from the providing Business Data List Web Part.

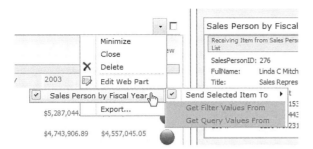

FIGURE 6-21 Configure the connection between the Business Data List Web Part and the Business Data Item Web Part to provide a summary and detailed view of the data.

You also use the Business Data Item Web Part on a profile page, which you create either in Share-Point Designer 2010 or within the SharePoint Central Administration website in the ECT settings. The profile page displays when you click the search result or when the action is clicked from one of the BDC Web Parts. Typically when you search for a document or list item, clicking the hyperlink associated with the item results in the item opening. This cannot happen with external data, so the summary information is shown in the search results, but when the hyperlink is clicked, the identifier for the returned item is passed via the URL to the profile page for that ECT. The profile pages look a bit basic, but you can modify them through XSL or SharePoint Designer 2010. Figure 6-22 shows a default profile page with the Business Data Item Web Part.

FIGURE 6-22 The profile page containing a Business Data Item Web Part is displayed.

If you edit a profile page, you will notice that the normally hidden Business Data Item Builder Web Part is displayed. The purpose of the Business Data Item Builder Web Part is to take the parameter from the URL passed via the custom action or the search results page, and pass it via a Web Part connection to the Business Data Item Web Part (as shown in Figure 6-23).

FIGURE 6-23 A profile page in edit mode shows the Business Data Item Builder Web Part.

You can also modify the Business Data Item Builder Web Part using XSL. Although you cannot modify the Web Part in SharePoint Designer 2010, you can modify the page itself.

Business Data Related List Web Part

The Business Data Related List Web Part is very similar to the Business Data List Web Part in that it displays multiple rows of data. However, it is designed to show data related to data displayed from another external content type (ECT). The ECT is related to the second ECT with an association, which you need to create when defining the ECT.

When you design a relational database, you will often join two or more tables using a primary key field in one table that points to a foreign key field in the second table. The table with the primary key is often referred to as the "one" side and the related table as the "many" side in a one-to-many relationship. An example of this type of relationship is that one customer can place many orders.

See Also *For more information on associations, see Chapter 4.*

Once an association exists, you can use the Business Data List Web Part to display the data from the one side of the relationship (the providing ECT). You can then configure the Business Data Related List Web Part to show the content from the many side (the receiving ECT).

Within the Web Part properties of the Business Data Related List Web Part, after choosing the correct type, select the relationship that you want to use. It is possible to have more than one relationship—for example, customers may be related to orders as well as contacts.

You can customize how you view the data in the same way as with the Business Data List Web Part. Figure 6-24 shows the configuration of the Business Data Related List Web Part.

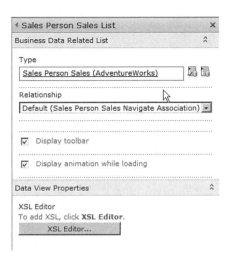

FIGURE 6-24 The properties of the Business Data Related List Web Part, with the Type and Relationship fields populated to display items from an ECT.

Once you set the Web Part properties and click OK, the Business Data Related List Web Part displays a message indicating that you must use Web Part connections to connect the two Web Parts. As with the Business Data Item Web Part, you can provide or consume the connection from either Web Part. Figure 6-25 shows the connected Business Data List and Related List Web Parts.

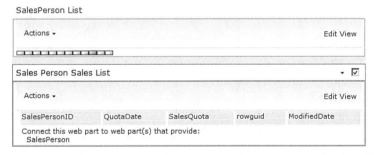

FIGURE 6-25 The Business Data List Web Part and Business Data Related List Web Part are about to be connected.

Once you've connected the Web Parts, an icon appears next to each row in the Business Data List Web Part. Clicking the icon fires the connection to the Related List Web Part, which in turn filters the results based on the provided value. Figure 6-26 shows how to configure the connection between the two Web Parts.

FIGURE 6-26 The Business Data Related Web Part consumes the connection from the Business Data List Web Part.

Once the connection has been created between the Business Data List and Business Data Related List Web Part, you are able to see the related items shown within the two Web Parts (see Figure 6-27).

SalesPerson List

Actions ▾   1 - 5 ▸

	SalesPersonID	TerritoryID	SalesQuota	Bonus	CommissionPct	SalesYTD	SalesLastYear
	268			0.0000	0.0000	677558.4653	0.0000
	275	2	300000.0000	4100.0000	0.0120	4557045.0459	1750406.4785
	276	4	250000.0000	2000.0000	0.0150	5200475.2313	1439156.0291
	277	3	250000.0000	2500.0000	0.0150	3857163.6332	1997186.2037
	278	6	250000.0000	500.0000	0.0100	1764938.9859	1620276.8966

Sales Person Sales List

Actions ▾

SalesPersonID	QuotaDate	SalesQuota
276	7/1/2001 12:00 AM	637000.0000
276	10/1/2001 12:00 AM	781000.0000
276	1/1/2002 12:00 AM	665000.0000
276	4/1/2002 12:00 AM	639000.0000
276	7/1/2002 12:00 AM	1355000.0000
276	10/1/2002 12:00 AM	1009000.0000
276	1/1/2003 12:00 AM	860000.0000
276	4/1/2003 12:00 AM	1021000.0000
276	7/1/2003 12:00 AM	1525000.0000
276	10/1/2003 12:00 AM	1276000.0000
276	1/1/2004 12:00 AM	894000.0000
276	4/1/2004 12:00 AM	1124000.0000

FIGURE 6-27 The Business Data List Web Part and the Related List Web Part are connected and displaying related data.

It is worth noting that you can achieve similar functionality using standard Web Part connections in SharePoint Designer between two Data View Web Parts or two Business Data List Web Parts. Building the connection within SharePoint Designer offers some advantages, such as the ability to join Web Parts across two pages within the same team site and also build connections to filter data based upon two columns that are not strictly primary and foreign keys. SharePoint Designer has some limitations when building associations between ECTs, mainly around a table that contains a composite key. A composite key is where a unique row is identified by two columns as a combination and not one unique column. SharePoint Designer requires that each table use a single column as the unique identifier to build an association.

Business Data Connectivity Filter Web Part

The Business Data Connectivity Filter Web Part is especially useful when you build a dashboard that displays data from an external source. You may already be familiar with some of the other out-of-the-box filter Web Parts, such as the Current User Filter Web Part. You can add the Current User Filter Web Part to a page, and then connect to a List or Content Query Web Part to filter the results based on the current user. For example, you can only display tasks where the assigned-to user is equal to the logged-on user.

The Business Data Connectivity Filter Web Part works in a similar way. The idea is that you add the Business Connectivity Filter Web to the Web Part page and map it to a specific ECT. You then choose a Value column, such as Period, that stores the year's quarter, such as Q1, Q2, Q3, or Q4. The value from the Period column is passed to other connected Business Data Connectivity Web Parts on the same page, allowing the user to select a period such as Q1 or Q2 and see all the data for the connected Web Parts for just that period. Using the Business Data Connectivity Filter Web Part becomes an easy way to filter all the data on the same Web Part page without requiring reconfiguration of the way the other Web Parts display the data. You select the value you want to pass to the connected Web Parts from a single dialog list that shows the data from the ECT.

You can set the Filter Name, which is a value that populates the Web Part Connections menu, and then select the ECT that contains the data you want to use as the filter. Figure 6-28 shows the Web Part with a view of Sales Person by Fiscal Year. The Value Column is the column that, when selected, contains the value sent to the connected Web Parts, where it will be used to filter their contents. You can also select a Description Column. For example, SalesPersonID contains only unique numbers, and a user visiting the page would not know who the salesperson was by looking at the number, which is the employee ID. The FullName column stores the name of the salesperson, so if you select the FullName column in the Description Column drop-down list, the FullName value displays instead of the SalesPersonID. A user will then know the name of the salesperson the user wants to see information about, and when the user selects the FullName of that salesperson, the data from the value column, the SalesPersonID, is sent to the consuming Web Part.

The purpose of configuring the Web Part is to provide dashboard readers the ability to initially see the performance of all salespeople as a default, but then to enable users to select a particular salesperson to see that salesperson's individual performance. The dashboard is then an interactive page, as the data is dynamically redisplayed depending on the interaction of a user with the page.

Now that you have configured the Web Part, check that you are able to select the required data before connecting the Web Part to other Web Parts on the page. Many of the Business Data Connectivity Filter Web Parts properties appear dimmed because they are unavailable to change once the Web Part is connected to others.

To test that the Search dialog box is returning data, click the Select External Item(s) icon (🔲) within the Business Data Connectivity Filter Web Part.

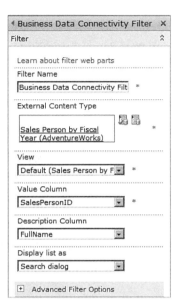

FIGURE 6-28 The Business Data Connectivity Filter Web Part properties are configured to pass the SalesPersonID to other consuming Web Parts on the same Web Part page.

The Search dialog box appears, and you are able to select a row. You should then see the Description Column displaying a value within the Business Data Connectivity Filter Web Part, as shown in Figure 6-29.

FIGURE 6-29 The Business Data Connectivity Filter Web Part search dialog box displays, allowing you to select items.

The final task is to connect the Business Data Connectivity Filter Web Part to other Web Parts on the same page. You can get strange results when configuring the connectivity from the Business Data Connectivity Web Part. A good practice is always to consume the connection from the Web Part that is to be filtered. That way, the behavior appears to be consistent.

To consume the connection, edit the Web Part page and click the shortcut menu of the consuming Web Part. In this example, you are consuming the connection from a Business Data List Web Part. Figure 6-30 shows how to configure the Web Part to consume the connection. You can do this for each Web Part to be filtered, including those that are also providing a connection.

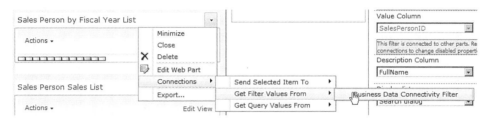

FIGURE 6-30 Configure the Business Data List Web Part to consume a connection from the Business Data Filter Web Part.

After configuring the connection, a dialog box appears that asks you to map the column that contains the filter value, such as SalesPersonID, which in turn matches the SalesPersonID value being sent from the Business Data Connectivity Filter Web Part, as shown in Figure 6-31.

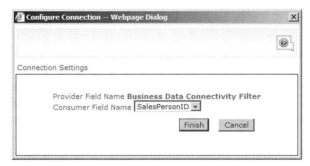

FIGURE 6-31 Set the Consumer Field value within the configuration of the Business Data Connectivity Filter Web Part connection.

The Business Data Connectivity Filter Web Part now filters the results within the connected Web Parts based upon the filter value selected.

Business Data Actions Web Part

Each ECT you create can have custom actions associated with it. The custom actions consist of a URL and a parameter, allowing an action to be run against a particular row. An example of an action is the View Profile link. If you create a profile page for an ECT, the View Profile link is automatically created as an action for the ECT. The profile page consists of a Business Data Item Web Part showing by default all the columns and values for a selected row. The row is selected when you trigger the custom action.

It is possible to create other custom actions. For example, consider a Customer ECT and how the user might get information they need about a customer, such as conducting an Internet search for more information about that customer. Opening a browser window, navigating to a search engine, and then typing the company name that you wish to search on is time-consuming. Using a custom action, you can search for the customer in a new browser window by configuring a custom action to pass through the Company Name column of the selected row of data. The user may search for the customer name using a website such as LinkedIn, Google, or Bing. These actions can be built using a URL. For example, the URL for a Bing search is similar to the following:

```
http://www.bing.com/search?q=Adventure+Works&qs=n&form=QBLH&filt=all&pq=adventure+works&sc=8-15&sp=-1&sk=
```

This example is specifically searching for "Adventure Works." But what if you don't know yet which company name will be searched? In that instance, you don't use specific words in the URL, but instead use parameters. The URL will look similar to the following:

```
www.bing.com/Search?{0}
```

The *{0}* is a placeholder for the column value. When you create the custom action, you choose the column value, such as CompanyName, that will replace the *{0}* at runtime against the selected item.

Actions can be triggered from most of the Business Data Web Parts. The Business Data List, Related List, and Business Data Item Web Parts contain an Actions drop-down list. You can also display the actions within the Business Data Actions Web Part, as shown in Figure 6-32, which displays two custom actions: View Profile and Search on Bing.

FIGURE 6-32 The configured Business Data Actions Web Part displays two actions: View Profile and Search on Bing.

See Also *To learn how to create a custom action, see Chapter 5.*

You can configure the Business Data Actions Web Part to show the actions for a specific ECT, and then a specific row via an identifier. However, you do not have to hardcode an identifier value for a specific row in the properties of the Web Part, as this will not be known to you at the time of configuring the Web Part. Again, you can use Web Part connections to join the Web Part to consume the custom actions for another Web Part to select the row. That way, when you click an item in a Web Part, such as a Business Data List Web Part, the custom actions are ready to run against the selected item.

In addition to being able to choose the style formatting for the display of your custom actions, you can customize which actions will display. For example, perhaps you don't want all actions to display, if they aren't appropriate. Figure 6-33 shows the configuration of the Business Data Actions Web Part.

FIGURE 6-33 Configure the Business Data Custom Actions Web Part to show the actions for an ECT.

The Business Data Custom Actions Web Part is a great addition to any business data dashboard, as it allows you to better arrange the dashboard. For example, you can hide the Actions menu from all other BDC Web Parts to obtain more real estate on the page and keep the actions neatly configured in one area.

Chart Web Part

As you probably realize from the name of this Web Part, it is not a BCS-specific Business Data Web Part, but you can use it with BCS. The Chart Web Part allows you to create most types of charts, including pie, bar, line, and column charts for many different data sources. The data sources include:

- Another Web Part on the page
- A SharePoint list
- An ECT
- Excel Services

A SharePoint dashboard is likely to present business data where the data source definitions are not limited to those stored in the BCS metadata store, but come from other data sources as well. A chart allows you to display the data in a manner that is sometimes more readable on a dashboard than displaying the raw data within a table or grid. In this section, you will learn how to configure the Chart Web Part for data source definitions stored in the BCS metadata store.

The Chart Web Part displays sample data in a 2D column chart when you first add it to the Web Part page. You configure the Web Part not through its tool pane like the other Web Parts described in this chapter, but through wizards triggered from the two links at the top of the Web Part, as shown in Figure 6-34.

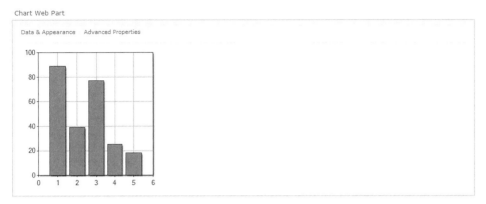

FIGURE 6-34 This Chart Web Part displays sample data.

To configure the Chart Web Part, follow these steps:

1. Click Data & Appearance to display the Data Connection & Chart Appearance Wizard page. This page contains two links:

   - Customize Your Chart

   - Connect Chart to Data

2. Click Connect Chart to Data to display step 1 of the wizard, Choose a Data Source.

3. To connect to an ECT, select Connect to Business Data Catalog, and then click Next. Step 2 of the wizard displays.

4. Select the ECT that contains the data you want to view within a chart. Figure 6-35 shows the selected ECT.

FIGURE 6-35 Choose the data source for the Chart Web Part.

5. Click Next to display step 3 of the wizard, as shown in Figure 6-36. On this page, you preview the data that will be used to display the chart. You may optionally expand the Filter Data section of the page to configure filter parameters, which allow the chart to be filtered using the out-of-the-box filter Web Parts.

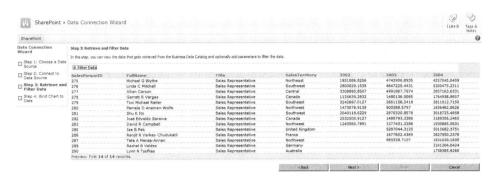

FIGURE 6-36 Preview the data within the Chart Web Part wizard.

6. Click Next to display step 4 of the wizard, where you can define the columns used to plot the chart. You can specify the column for the X axis and Y axis. As shown in Figure 6-37, the chart is also grouped by a column since it has multiple rows containing a region.

FIGURE 6-37 Configure the X axis and Y axis of the chart.

7. Click Finish to see the configured chart.

To change the chart's look and feel, click the Data & Appearance link at the top of the Web Part, as shown in Figure 6-38, to display the Data Connection & Chart Appearance Wizard page, where you click Customize Your Chart.

You can customize the look and feel of the chart, including changing the chart type, setting a title and legend, and configuring the size of the chart in pixels. The chart tends to be small by default. Changing the default size from 300 pixels to around 900 pixels wide makes a big difference in the readability of the chart. Figure 6-39 shows some of the chart types you can choose from.

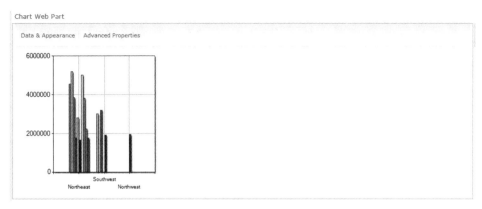

FIGURE 6-38 Display the configured Chart Web Part prior to changing the Data & Appearance settings to provide a better visual display.

FIGURE 6-39 Select the chart type in the Data & Appearance settings.

After you complete the wizard, you can plot the Adventure Works Sales by Fiscal Year data in a chart as well as set it to display as a Business Data List Web Part within the dashboard, as shown in Figure 6-40.

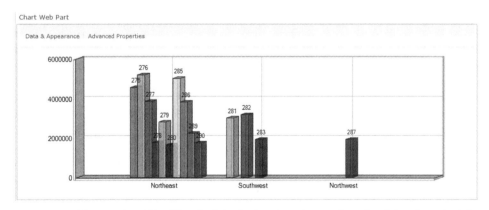

FIGURE 6-40 The completed Fiscal Year by Sales Region chart shows sales-related data from the Adventure Works database.

Other Business Data Web Parts

Other Web Parts useful for a dashboard are not related to Business Connectivity Services (BCS). A point of confusion is that these Web Parts are displayed within the Business Data category of Web Parts. Arguably, they are related to business data, just not Business Data Catalog (BDC) or BCS.

This section describes the other Web Parts, such as the Excel Web Access Web Part and Visio Web Part, and how you can use them within a business data dashboard.

Excel Web Access Web Part

Excel Web Access is an extremely powerful service within SharePoint Server 2010. Excel Web Access allows Excel workbooks to be published to a report library, which is essentially a special type of Share-Point document library. The report—an Excel workbook—can then be displayed using the browser, allowing information workers to view workbooks. The data in the workbooks can be changed by a user through the Excel Web Access Web Part by modifying certain parameters or values. Changing the values and parameters within the Web Part can provide updated calculations. For example, the Excel Web Access Web Part may display part of a workbook for mortgage calculations. Exposing the parameters for the borrowed amount or interest will affect the monthly payment.

The Excel Web Access Web Part allows you to display objects from a Microsoft Excel workbook stored within a report library. These objects could include a chart or data contained within a range or formatted as a table. An organization's business data is often stored within spreadsheets and not just in relational databases that can be consumed through BCS. The Excel Web Access Web Part therefore deserves a mention in this chapter, as it is likely to contribute to your business dashboards.

An Excel workbook is created either from within a report library or from the Excel client application and then published to the Reports Library. Using the Excel Web Access Web Part, you can select the workbook and the object you want to display within the Web Part.

Figure 6-41 shows a sample Excel workbook containing a table of sales-related data and an Excel chart. The workbook is stored within a report library.

You configure the Excel Web Access Web Part using its tool pane, which allows you to browse to the workbook and then type the name of the object you want to display. Figure 6-42 displays the properties of the Excel Web Access Web Part.

You can make many refinements to the Excel Web Access Web Part, including configuring the Web Part title, setting the type of toolbar, and choosing the options available on the toolbar. Figure 6-43 shows the configured Excel Web Access Web Part.

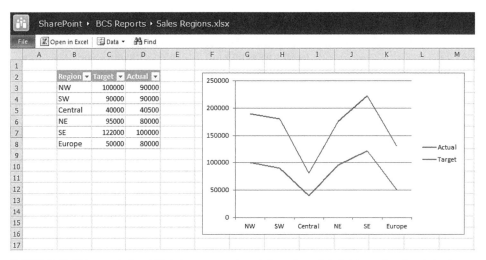

FIGURE 6-41 This sample Excel Web Access report contains sales-related data and an Excel chart.

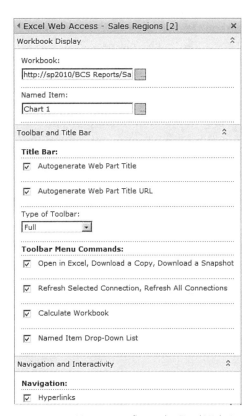

FIGURE 6-42 You can configure the Excel Web Access Web Part to display a chart from an Excel workbook.

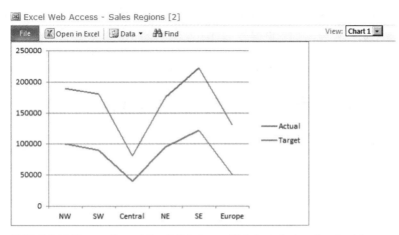

FIGURE 6-43 The configured Excel Web Access Web Part displays the chart from an Excel workbook.

The Excel Web Access Web Part can also consume filters from other Web Parts on the page, such as the Text Filter Web Part. This allows different objects to be displayed based upon the filter value.

Status List and Indicator Details

Most dashboards are likely to display key performance indicators (KPIs) of some sort that show how well different areas of the organization are performing. KPIs usually consist of a target and an actual value against a business goal, such as revenue per quarter. Traffic light indicators provide a visual cue of whether or not a particular goal was met. For example, assuming the revenue for the quarter was $50,000, but the target was $40,000, a green traffic light would display, indicating that the quarter revenue equaled or exceeded the target value.

SharePoint Server provides a Status List template that enables you to define your goals and targets within a SharePoint list. The Status List contains the definition and can dynamically obtain the actual value against a target from multiple data sources:

- SharePoint list

- Excel Web Access

- SQL Server Analysis Services

- Fixed-value indicator

Notice that BCS is not in the list of data sources. However, if your data resides in a Microsoft SQL Server database, then in place of using BCS, you could use SQL Server Analysis Services as a data source for your indicators.

A common misconception is that you can base a KPI on data from a BCS external list instead of using an external content type (ECT). Unfortunately, this is not achievable, as the data presented in an external list does not reside within SharePoint. Figure 6-44 displays the error message that appears if you try to create a new status indicator definition with an external list.

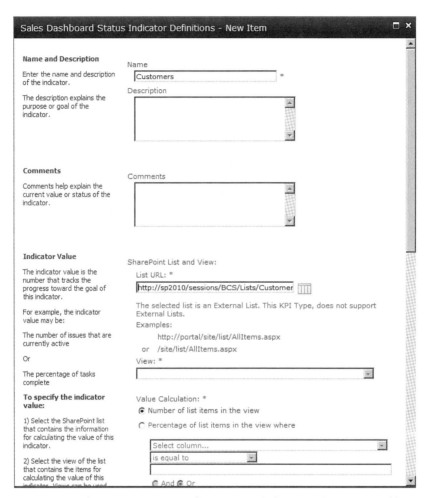

FIGURE 6-44 When you attempt to configure a status indicator against an external list, you'll get an error message letting you know this isn't possible.

If you do create a status indicator against one of the other data sources, once you have created the list item, you are able to display the KPI itself within the Status List Web Part. The Status List Web Part displays the description, goal, actual value, and status indicator, as shown in Figure 6-45.

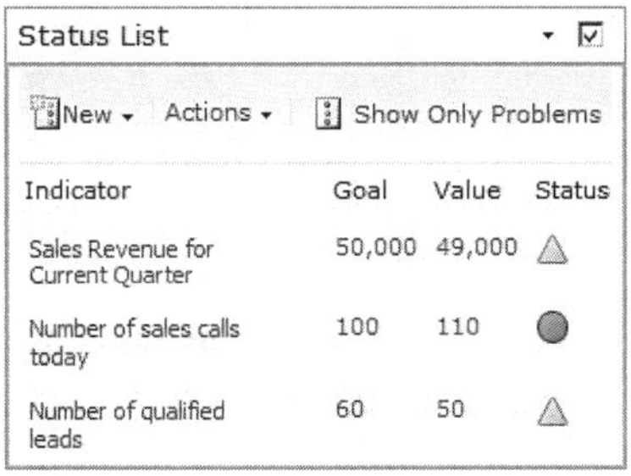

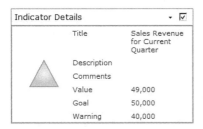

FIGURE 6-45 The configured Status Indicator List Web Part displays indicators against sales-related data.

The Status Indicator Details Web Part is virtually the same as the Status Indicator List Web Part, except that it focuses on just one of the indicators instead of providing a list of them. Within the tool pane of the Indicator Web Part, specify the location of the status list along with the indicator you want to display, as shown in Figure 6-46.

FIGURE 6-46 The configured Status Indicator Details Web Part displays a KPI in detail.

Because BCS is not one of the available data sources for the status indicators, you can use the Data View Web Part in SharePoint Designer or customize a Business Data List Web Part to show KPIs, as described earlier in this chapter.

Visio Web Access

The Visio Web Access Web Part is the last Web Part that appears in the business data category. The Visio Web Access Web Part is similar to Excel Web Access Web Part, in that you can display documents within the browser rather than in the client application. Visio drawings are another method of storing data diagrams and are therefore considered business data, albeit a type not associated with BCS.

Exploring Web Part Properties

This chapter described many of the Web Part properties that happen to be specific to each Web Part. However, other Web Part properties are common across many out-of-the-box Web Parts. Often these properties are ignored, but they are relevant and useful, especially when you're trying to design a pleasing SharePoint dashboard. Many of the Business Data Web Parts derive from the Data View Web Part and share some of the Data View Web Part properties. The Web Part tool pane contains four sections:

- **Miscellaneous** This section consists of four properties you can use while building the dashboard. Figure 6-47 shows the Miscellaneous section of a Business Data List Web Part.

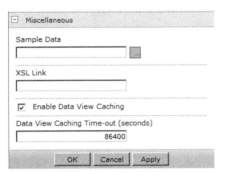

FIGURE 6-47 The Miscellaneous section of a Business Data List Web Part contains the Sample Data and Caching options.

- **Sample Data** The Sample Data property is useful when you modify the Web Part in an editor such as SharePoint Designer 2010. SharePoint Designer 2010 generates its own sample data when you modify the Web Part in SharePoint Designer instead of the browser. The sample data provides you with a realistic view of what the Web Part will look like within the browser once it has been configured. Occasionally, you might need to see more realistic data to test your calculations and formatting. The sample data can be pasted or typed into the Sample Data property as XML.

- **XSL Link** This property allows you to link to an XSLT file that may be stored within a library as a site resource or within the 14 folder on the SharePoint server. Linking to the XSL file allows you to continue modifying the XSL through an editor, such as Visual Studio or SharePoint Designer, so you don't have to modify the XSL without an editor in the XSL window of the Web Part, as described earlier in this chapter.

- **Enable Data View Caching** This property is checked by default. This setting allows the data to be cached for the period set in the Data View Caching Time-out (Seconds) property. The default is 86,400 seconds, which is equivalent to one day.

■ **Appearance** This section includes five properties, as shown in Figure 6-48.

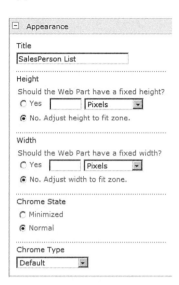

FIGURE 6-48 The Appearance section contains five properties.

- **Title** It is useful to change the Title property of the Web Part when using the Business Data Web Parts. The title automatically names itself after the ECT that the Web Part is configured to use. If the same ECT is used several times on a page, you will often see a number within parentheses next to the title, such as Customers (2). Renaming the Web Part allows the title to make more sense. When the Web Part is not a Business Data Web Part, the Title property is the name of the Web Part, and you should change it to indicate the purpose of the data it displays.

- **Height and Width** These properties can be useful for Web Parts, such as the Chart Web Part, when there is a graphic or a grid of information that needs to fit within a certain space. Often with these Web Parts, you end up with a lot of whitespace taking up valuable real estate on the dashboard.

- **Chrome** This property is the surrounding border of the Web Part. You can specify to show the Default option, None, Title and Border, Title, or Border only. Often in a dashboard, a title may not be required at all. In the Chart Web Part, for instance, you can place a title within the chart itself.

- **Layout** This section contains four properties, as displayed in Figure 6-49.

FIGURE 6-49 The Layout section contains four properties.

- **Direction** This property controls the direction of the text. You can set it left to right or right to left, which is useful within some language packs.

- **Zone and Zone Index** You can set these two properties by dragging and dropping the Web Part between Web Part zones. You may also set the zone and the Web Part order by setting the properties within the Layout category. The Zone Index is the order from top to bottom within the Web Part zone.

- **Hidden** Other Web Parts you have learned about include the Filter Web Parts. Such Web Parts are hidden by default, but you can unhide them. Unhiding a Web Part is useful when you're trying to troubleshoot or while you're building the dashboard. It might be that you aren't getting expected results when linking to a hidden Web Part, and you want a better understanding of the values stored in the hidden Web Part.

- **Advanced** This section contains the many of the properties that configure whether a user can modify the personal properties of a Web Part. As the designer of the page, you can enable users without design permissions to perform only certain operations, such as Allow Minimize, Allow Close, Allow Hide, Allow Zone Change, and Allow Connections. Figure 6-50 displays the Advanced properties.

- **Export Mode** When a developer creates a Web Part property, the designer can specify whether the property can be marked as sensitive. When you export a Web Part, those Web Part properties that are flagged as sensitive will not be exported. For example, a data source connection string could include a password to an SQL server. If a Web Part property was created to store a data source connection string, then it would be a security risk to allow users of the Web Part to export all of the properties the Web Part property that included the data source connection string values. Therefore, a password field or connection string field can be marked as sensitive. As the person who configures Web Part properties, you may prevent anything marked as sensitive from being exported.

FIGURE 6-50 The Advanced section of a Web Part shows numerous properties.

- **Title URL** This property enables you to type a URL in a text box and configure the Web Part title as a hyperlink pointing to that URL. This property is used widely in SharePoint with List View Web Parts, where you click the Web Part title and are redirected to the default view of the list.

- **Description** The text within this text box is displayed as a tooltip when a user hovers the mouse over the Web Part title. Within a dashboard, you can use this description property to include a description of the data returned from BCS.

- **Help URL** This property allows you to reference a help page. The referenced help page then opens instead of the standard help pages provided by SharePoint.

- **Help Mode** This property describes how the help window will be displayed.

- **Catalog Icon Image URL** and **Title Icons Image URL** Use these text boxes to define the URL of a descriptive custom icon. The image size must be 16 pixels by 16 pixels. The Catalog image is used when listing a Web Part, such as within the Web Part pane that appears when you add a Web Part to a page. The Title image is used in the Web Part title bar and can add visual impact to your dashboard.

- **Import Error Message** Use this property to define a custom error message displayed when an attempt to add the Web Part onto the page is not successful.

- **Audience Targeting** This property allows you to show a Web Part to current users whose profile positions them into an audience. For example, if a user enters the **Sales Team** domain group in the Audience Targeting text box, and the user is not a member of the Sales Team domain group, SharePoint automatically hides the Web Part from the user.

Summary

Microsoft SharePoint business data dashboards are a powerful way to display data throughout your organization in an easy-to-read and understandable manner. Without these kinds of dashboards, businesses may rely on emailed attachments of reports, or information workers may need to obtain the required data for themselves.

In its basic form, a dashboard in SharePoint is just a SharePoint page that contains more than one Web Part displaying related business data. These pages tend to be interactive, so a user can select data in one Web Part, thereby affecting the data displayed in another Web Part. To create an effective dashboard, you should plan the layout of your page using a wireframe or page schematic.

As dashboard pages tend to contain only Web Parts, it is customary to create Web Part pages as dashboard pages. You can add any Web Part to your dashboard pages, but the Enterprise edition of SharePoint Server 2010 provides additional Web Parts that are categorized as Business Data Web Parts, which simplify the creation of dashboards.

Using the Business Data Web Parts, you can easily create dashboards that bring together data from different Excel workbooks and Business Connectivity Services (BCS) applications, and display the data within views or charts. Key performance indicators (KPIs) provide a clear vision of the performance within your company, and you can create these on your business data through either the status list or customization of the Business Data List Web Parts.

CHAPTER 7

Using External Data with Office Client Applications

In this chapter, you will:

- Learn how to use external data within Microsoft InfoPath forms

- Discover how to modify external list forms with InfoPath 2010

- Learn how to make external data available in Microsoft Word, Microsoft Outlook, Microsoft SharePoint Workspace, and Microsoft Access

- Establish how to troubleshoot Business Connectivity Services on the client

Business Connectivity Services (BCS) is often misunderstood as being just a read-only view of data displayed via Microsoft SharePoint Web Parts, but BCS has many other services to offer. Potential users of BCS sometimes develop their own Web Parts to display external data, or even consider purchasing third-party products, without realizing the many capabilities of BCS. One of the most powerful services BCS can provide is the ability to use external data offline within Microsoft Office client applications, such as Microsoft Word and Microsoft Outlook.

Information workers often duplicate data unnecessarily. Users sometimes copy and paste external data into Word documents, such as customer address details into an invoice. They may type or copy and paste email addresses into Outlook when sending an email, or create calendar entries manually when an appointment is already recorded within an external data system. It is also very typical for users to print external data when going offline so they have the data available when traveling. With BCS, users can look up and select external data using the Microsoft Office client applications, and they can also access this data in these programs while offline.

For example, when using Word to create an invoice for a customer, you may need to enter the customer billing address details and also look up products and enter the price of each product. Rather than typing or pasting these values from external systems, you can look up the values using BCS, such as contact data made available within Outlook. Since many Outlook users make use of Microsoft ActiveSync, contacts can be made available to their mobile devices.

Note ActiveSync, originally released in 1996, is a mobile data synchronization technology and protocol developed by Microsoft. The latest release, ActiveSync 4.5, is supported on Windows XP and can be downloaded from Microsoft's download site at *www.microsoft. com/downloads*. For Windows Vista and Windows 7, when a mobile device is connected to a computer, it triggers an automatic download and install of Windows Mobile Device Center (WMDC), which can then be used to sync contacts stored in Microsoft Exchange. If you do not use Exchange, see the following webpage for details about how to sync contacts into Outlook: *http://rhizohm.net/irhetoric/post/2010/11/16/Missing-ActiveSync-How-To-Sync-and-Import-Contacts-Into-Windows-Phone-7-From-Outlook-Using-Windows-Live-Hotmail-As-A-Bridge.aspx*. See the following webpage for information about Exchange ActiveSync considerations when using Windows Phone 7 clients: *http://social.technet.microsoft.com/wiki/contents/articles/exchange-activesync-considerations-when-using-windows-phone-7-clients.aspx*.

A new application introduced in Microsoft Office 2010 is Microsoft SharePoint Workspace 2010. SharePoint Workspace is not BCS specific, but it allows you to take any SharePoint list or library offline, including external lists, so that external data is available even when you are in a disconnected environment. BCS is also available through Microsoft InfoPath 2010 and Microsoft Access 2010.

BCS is divided into server services and client services. The client services include a client runtime and cache of the external data, making it available within Microsoft Office applications. Figure 7-1 shows the BCS Business Data Connector, which provides a client-side connection to the external data. The external data is cached locally within an in-memory Microsoft SQL Compact Edition database, so that it can be made available to the Office application.

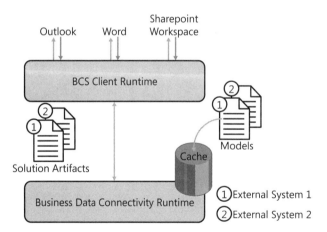

FIGURE 7-1 The architecture of the BCS Client Runtime.

In this chapter, you will first examine how to make external business data available to Microsoft Word. Then you will learn how to configure Microsoft InfoPath 2010 to use business data and explore SharePoint Workspace, Microsoft Outlook, and Microsoft Visio. Finally, you will find out how to troubleshoot client-side connections to BCS.

Surfacing External Data in Word 2010

SharePoint users have by now familiarized themselves with the concept of document metadata. One issue with metadata is that the information you get out is only as good as the information you enter. So if users do not enter data in a consistent manner, trying to filter or create views on that data can be challenging. To answer this challenge, Business Connectivity Services (BCS) offers the *external data column*, which allows users to select metadata for a column within a list or library from an external data source. Once configured, the external data can be selected from the browser when setting the list item or document properties.

To configure the external data column, you enable the SharePoint Server Enterprise Site Collection features. You can then create a new external data column within a list or a library. You are able to choose an external content type (ECT) and the column from the ECT that you would like to store. As well as selecting the column value that you would like to store as a property value, you can select other column values from the external data source to display. Figure 7-2 shows the configuration of the external data column within a document library.

See Also *The capability to create external data columns is not available in SharePoint Foundation 2010. For more information about using external data in lists and libraries, see Chapter 5, "Creating External Lists and Using External Data in Lists and Libraries."*

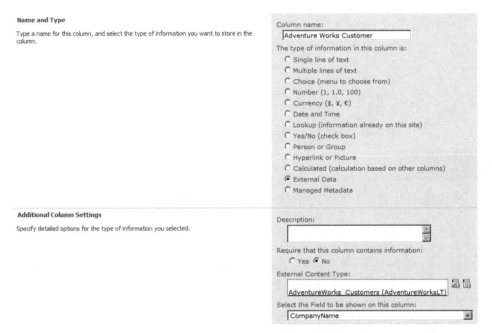

FIGURE 7-2 You can configure an external data column within a SharePoint library.

Once the column is configured, it is ready to be used within the browser. You can set the column value by editing the properties of an uploaded document and then choosing the metadata from the external data source. The dialog box for the external data column can show only 200 items at a time, so you may see a red error message indicating that results have been truncated. The only way to overcome this limitation is to create a filter on your read list method when creating the ECT in Share-Point Designer.

See Also *For more information about creating an ECT, see Chapter 4,"Defining External System Connections Using SharePoint Designer."*

The filter allows you to set the returned results to fewer than 200. For example, you could create a Wildcard filter so that the first few values can be entered in the filter box to return fewer than 200 results. Figure 7-3 shows the dialog box where you can select an external data value to store as metadata.

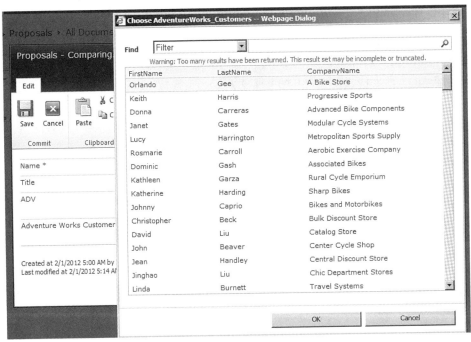

FIGURE 7-3 The BCS External Data Picker dialog box shows an error when too many items are returned.

In addition to using external data as metadata on a document or list item, you can use external data within the Word document itself. In the Enterprise edition of Microsoft Office SharePoint Server 2007, you could achieve a similar result, but you had to write the code yourself using Visual Studio Tools for Office (VSTO). In Word 2010, you can insert a Quick Part into a document, which allows you to embed BCS data. You first select the external data column's display name—for example, Adventure Works Customer, as shown in Figure 7-4. You can then insert the document properties into the page, which is automatically populated when a value is selected.

Note The Quick Parts menu option is on the Insert ribbon tab, in the Text group.

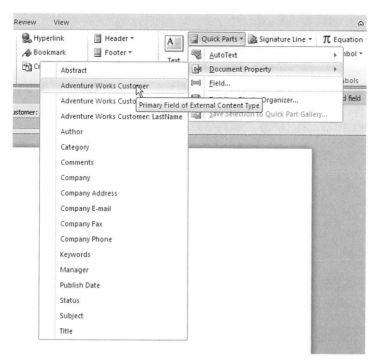

FIGURE 7-4 Inserting a BCS Quick Part into a Word document provides external data lookups from within the document.

You can create the contents of the document in the same way you create a document with a mail merge. You can see in Figure 7-5 that the customer has the ability to enter a value or look up a value to be inserted into the Adventure Works Customer Quick Part.

FIGURE 7-5 The Adventure Works Customer Quick Part is added to the page to provide external data lookups.

In Word, you can select external data in a similar way to how you select external data within the browser. You can browse to the external list item you would like to select, or you can search for a value using the search box provided (as shown in Figure 7-6).

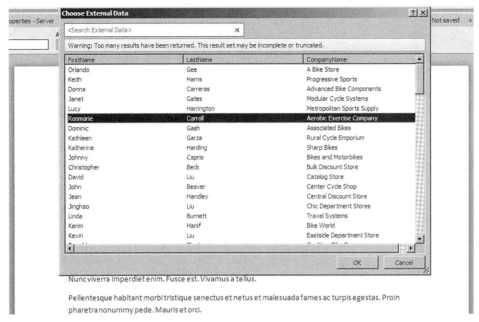

FIGURE 7-6 The BCS picker within Microsoft Word provides external data to be selected.

Once you select an external list item and click OK, the other display columns are populated with relevant values from the same row of data. Figure 7-7 displays the completed Word document.

Aerobic Exercise Company

Dear Rosmarie,

Lorem ipsum dolor sit amet, consectetuer adipiscing elit. Maecenas porttitor congue massa. Fusce posuere, magna sed pulvinar ultricies, purus lectus malesuada libero, sit amet commodo magna eros quis urna.

Nunc viverra imperdiet enim. Fusce est. Vivamus a tellus.

Pellentesque habitant morbi tristique senectus et netus et malesuada fames ac turpis egestas. Proin pharetra nonummy pede. Mauris et orci.

FIGURE 7-7 The completed Quick Part is populated with values from BCS within a Word document.

Notice that by setting document properties using a Quick Part, not only are the column values displayed within the document, but also your document properties are populated in the Document Information Panel (DIP) within Word, as shown in Figure 7-8. This in turn allows the metadata to be set and improves your ability to search and find the documents.

FIGURE 7-8 The Document Information Panel metadata tags are populated through Quick Parts.

Using External Data in InfoPath Forms

InfoPath is still a relatively new addition to the Office product suite compared with Office products such as Word or Excel. Introduced in Microsoft Office 2003, InfoPath provides you with a great tool for collating electronic information in electronic form format. Prior to that (and even today, in some cases), Word or Excel was used to collect information from vendors, customers, and employees for all types of reasons. Trying to complete an electronic form in Word is simply frustrating, especially when underscores are used to indicate the area where you are to type your details. Any data entry ends up destroying the original page formatting.

For forms such as purchase requisition forms, purchase orders, or time-off requests, using InfoPath makes a lot of sense. As a nascent product, InfoPath's adoption has been slow, mainly due to the lack of some required features. Dealing with date calculations was an issue, and until the Enterprise edition of SharePoint Server 2007, you needed an installation of InfoPath to enter data into the forms. This meant that InfoPath couldn't be relied upon outside of an organization, as you couldn't guarantee that your vendors or customers had adopted InfoPath. The Enterprise edition of SharePoint Server 2007 introduced integrated forms services, allowing data to be entered into forms using the browser. InfoPath 2010 is divided into two clients: InfoPath Designer 2010 and InfoPath Form Filler 2010. InfoPath Designer is required to design forms, but only InfoPath Form Filler is needed to complete forms that have already been designed.

InfoPath 2010 is now very well integrated with SharePoint 2010, not just through InfoPath Form Services, but also through the InfoPath Forms Web Part, which enables you to create InfoPath and SharePoint solutions. Information workers can complete forms using the InfoPath form embedded onto a SharePoint Web Part page. Having the InfoPath form embedded on the page creates an environment that is very efficient for filling in business information. The completed form can then be saved to a form library, allowing the information to be stored, analyzed, and consumed, perhaps as part of a workflow.

InfoPath has always (including the 2003 version) been able to write back to SQL databases or even look up information from SQL databases. As you learned in previous chapters, BCS can connect to all kinds of external data throughout your organization, not just Microsoft SQL. To bring all of that business information together in an InfoPath Form, InfoPath 2010 has now adopted BCS.

Using External Data as Lookup Data

One of the problems with collecting manually typed-in information is that it often contains abbreviations or typing mistakes, which can result in difficulties while analyzing the data or during a workflow run on the data. For example, a user may enter a vendor name as Adventure Works, Adventure Works Cycles, Adventure Works LLC, or even AW Cycles. As the form designer, you can create a lookup column with values already entered, but this requires a lot of maintenance to ensure that new vendors are added to the form design, plus the information already resides in the external data source. To provide consistency and accuracy, you can add a lookup field to the form that looks up data using an ECT. The lookup provides much more than just a list of company names, for example. You have the ability to show multiple columns, filter the values, and search the values using the lookup dialog box.

One of the controls in the InfoPath Designer toolbox is the External Item Picker, shown in Figure 7-9. You can bind the External Item Picker to a field within your form, allowing the looked-up data to be stored. Before you use the External Item Picker, it is recommended that you do a bit of homework. You will need to know certain information, which you can find in two places: in SharePoint Designer on the ECT settings page, or on the SharePoint 2010 Central Administration website in the BCS application. The information you need is:

- ECT Namespace

- ECT Name

- System Instance Name

- Finder Name

FIGURE 7-9 The External Item Picker appears in the InfoPath 2010 controls.

You can easily identify the ECT Name and ECT Namespace values in the External Content Type Information area in SharePoint Designer. The System Instance Name that InfoPath requires is listed as the external system in SharePoint Designer. The Finder Name is the ECT operation (method) that returns the list of information from the external data source. If you used SharePoint Designer to create your ECT, you will usually find that the operation is called Read List. Figure 7-10 shows the External Content Type Operations in SharePoint Designer, where you can gather the information InfoPath requests.

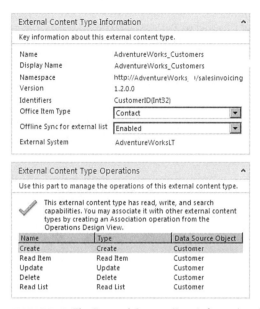

FIGURE 7-10 The External Content Type Information shown in SharePoint Designer provides information such as the namespace required by InfoPath.

Upon adding the External Item Picker control to your InfoPath form, select the External Item Picker Properties menu item from the context menu of the External Item Picker control, as shown in Figure 7-11.

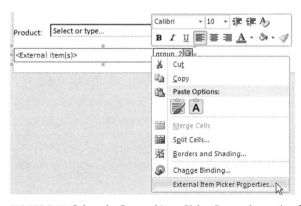

FIGURE 7-11 Select the External Item Picker Properties option from the External Item Picker control.

A large dialog box appears that allows you to name the control. The name you enter should reflect the type of information that you will be displaying from the external source—for example, **Customer_ Name**.

Select the General tab (second tab) of the dialog box to enter the required ECT information you gathered in advance from SharePoint Designer. Figure 7-12 shows the information obtained from SharePoint Designer, now entered into the InfoPath External Item Picker control properties.

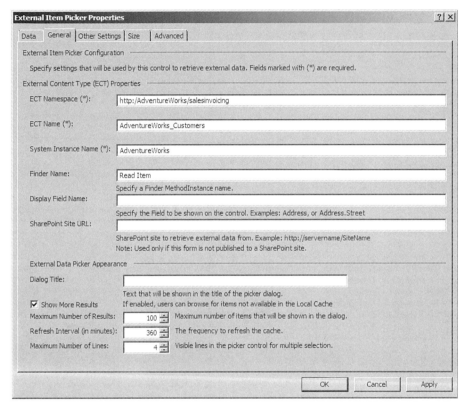

FIGURE 7-12 The External Item Picker control properties can be configured to retrieve external data from an ECT.

Another property that you may need to enter is the SharePoint Site URL. When you plan to publish the form to a form library within a SharePoint site, you should specify the SharePoint Site URL. If you do not set this property, the dialog box on the form will display empty results.

You can make other refinements using the dialog box that are not required but are useful, such as entering the Dialog Title information. Rather than displaying the text "Choose AdventureWorks_ Customers," a more appropriate title is "Select a customer."

Setting the maximum number of results is also useful. You may have over 1,000 customers—too many to display in the form's dialog box. As long as you created a filter when you created the ECT, you will be able to filter the results. For example, you can display customers perhaps by region, or even by the first few letters of the company name, if a Wildcard filter was defined. Setting a filter also improves client performance.

The Other Settings tab has a field that may determine if your External Item Picker control works successfully or not. You can set the Picker Mode to obtain cached data from the client or live data from the SharePoint server. In some cases, the data may not have been cached to the client, meaning that the dialog box displays empty results.

Depending on the complexity of the external data that you are using for lookup, you may have created an association between two ECTs to provide the information you would like to see. For example, Customer Name may be in a Customers table, while Customer Address is stored within a Contact Address table. Therefore, you will need to create an association between the two ECTs mapped to the two tables. In this instance, you set the Association Name, which you can also find in SharePoint Designer under the ECT properties. You set the Identifiers that are used to map the two ECTs. Figure 7-13 displays the Other Settings tab of the External Item Picker Properties dialog box and shows how you can set the Picker Mode at the bottom of the dialog box.

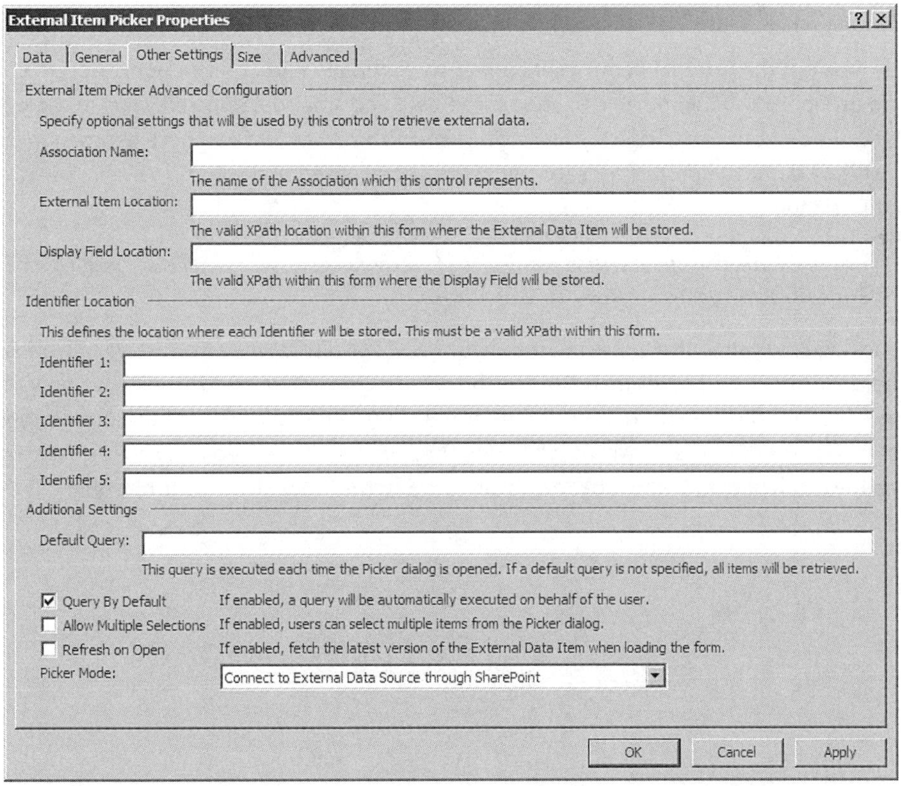

FIGURE 7-13 The External Item Picker Properties dialog box shows the contents of the Other Settings tab fields, such as Association Name.

The External Item Picker control provides you with a text box and two icons, enabling you to type and then verify your entry using the icon with the green check mark, the first icon to the right of the text box, as shown in Figure 7-14. Alternatively, you can display the lookup dialog box using the second icon to the right of the text box. Figure 7-14 displays the External Item Picker control on the InfoPath form, illustrating how the data can be looked up.

FIGURE 7-14 The External Item Picker on the InfoPath form is configured and ready to use.

You can now test the External Item Picker control by clicking Preview on the Home ribbon tab, in the Form group. You should be able to choose the data and store the selected value in the picker control. If results do not appear, check your settings and also review that you have permission to view the external data. The permissions for the ECT can be viewed and set using the ECT settings in SharePoint Designer.

See Also *For more information about setting permissions for external data, see Chapter 3, "Creating and Maintaining Business Data Connectivity Service Applications."*

A red message indicating that there are too many results to display may also appear. There is little that can be done about this, other than filtering the results. Users often need training on how the filters work to reduce the number of items to fewer than 200. Filtering on a column, such as Region, or the first few letters of a column will usually bring the number of returned items below 200. Figure 7-15 shows the external data being looked up from the External Item Picker control within a browser.

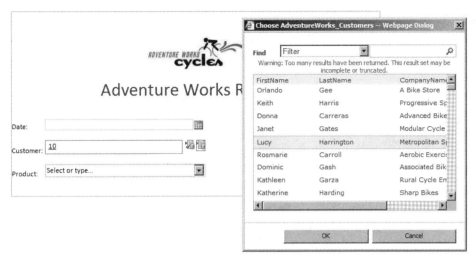

FIGURE 7-15 You can look up external data using the External Item Picker in InfoPath 2010.

Implications of Web Forms vs. Client Forms

InfoPath allows forms to be completed using a client application or the Office Web Application (Form Services). In InfoPath 2007, there were many limitations when using the browser as compared with using the InfoPath client. The limitations include the use of some controls, such as Combo Box controls and Repeating List controls. The list of unsupported features in InfoPath 2010 is much shorter. Combo Box controls and other controls work the same in the browser as they do in the client application. Many more browser types are supported, and you are not limited if a browser lacks ActiveX control support. The good news is that the External Item Picker control is supported in the browser. Most forms will behave similarly whether you use the InfoPath client or the browser to complete the form, but some visual differences will be apparent.

You can use Design Checker when designing a form for use in the browser. Using Design Checker is a good practice if you are designing a form for the client application and as a web form displayed in the browser. However, if you are designing a form specifically for use in the browser, you should set the Form Type in the Form Options dialog box, which opens when you click Form Options in the Microsoft Office Backstage view of InfoPath. You can switch to the Backstage view by clicking the File tab on the ribbon. Select the Compatibility category to select Web Browser Form to ensure that you will be able to use only Web Browser controls on your form. Figure 7-16 shows where to find the compatibility settings when designing a form for use within the browser.

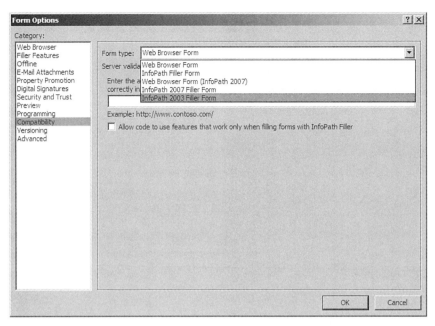

FIGURE 7-16 The Form Options dialog box shows the compatibility settings of the InfoPath 2010 form, and specifically, how the Form type can be changed.

InfoPath Data Connections

InfoPath data connections provide a mechanism to receive data or submit data to an external data source, including BCS external lists. InfoPath data connections can therefore contribute to an external data/SharePoint business solution. An InfoPath data connection allows you to submit data to and receive data from the following:

- SOAP web service

- REST web service

- SharePoint library or list

- Database (Microsoft SQL only)

- XML document

As well as collecting data within an InfoPath form and saving the form to a form library, you may want to store the collected data into an external data source. You can use a purchase order, for example, to store the purchase order information into a customer relationship management (CRM) system when an order is placed. External data can also be received from an external data source and displayed on the form.

You can store the file that contains the data connection definitions in a Data Connection Library in SharePoint, so that the data connection definitions can be reused time and again. Storing the data connection file also means that if ever the database is moved between servers, you have only one place to make a change. Files are stored in the library as Office Data Connection (ODC) files or Universal Data Connection (UDC) files. InfoPath uses a version of UDC called UDCX.

To create a Data Connection Library, navigate to the SharePoint site where you would like to create it. You can then create the new library by clicking Create on the View All Site Content page, and then use the Data Connection Library template, as shown in Figure 7-17. It doesn't matter what name you give to the library since the URL to the Data Connection Library will be copied and pasted.

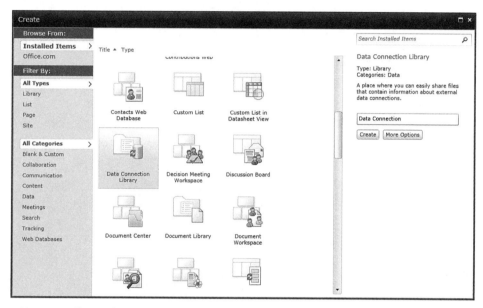

FIGURE 7-17 Choose the Data Connection Library template to create a Data Connection Library.

Once you have created the Data Connection Library, you can create a new blank form in InfoPath Designer 2010. In InfoPath Designer 2010, on the Data ribbon tab, in the External Data group, click Data Connections. You can then select to create a data connection to send (submit) data to or receive data from an external data source, as shown in Figure 7-18.

If you select Receive Data and then click Next, you can select the type of data source you want to create. If you select SharePoint List or Library and then click Next, the next page of the wizard allows you to provide the URL to a site containing an external list, as shown in Figure 7-19, where the URL is set to the Adventure Works BCS site.

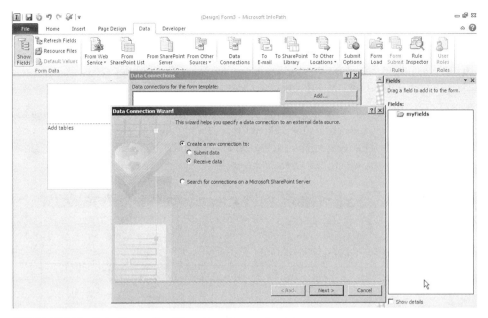

FIGURE 7-18 The Data Connection Wizard is set to receive data.

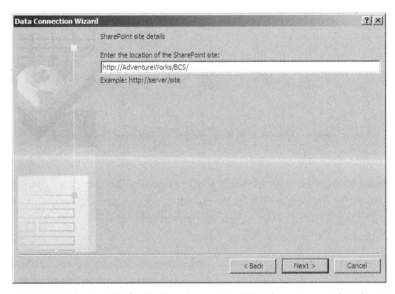

FIGURE 7-19 Set the URL for the Data Connection Wizard so you can select the external list.

When you click Next, the SharePoint site will be contacted and the lists and libraries on that site will be displayed. You can then choose your external list, as shown in Figure 7-20. Having the external list as an external data source option is unusual in Microsoft Office, as InfoPath is the only client where an external list can be a valid data source using the Data Connection Wizard.

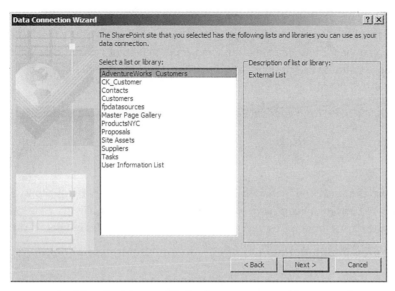

FIGURE 7-20 Select the AdventureWorks_Customers external list as your data source.

You can then select the columns from the external list that you would like to display within your InfoPath form. At this point, think carefully about the field you want to make available, to save working through the Data Connection Wizard again from the start. You should select any fields needed for your form, including any that you would like users to be able to update on the external data source. Figure 7-21 shows the Data Connection Wizard providing a list of external list columns for selection.

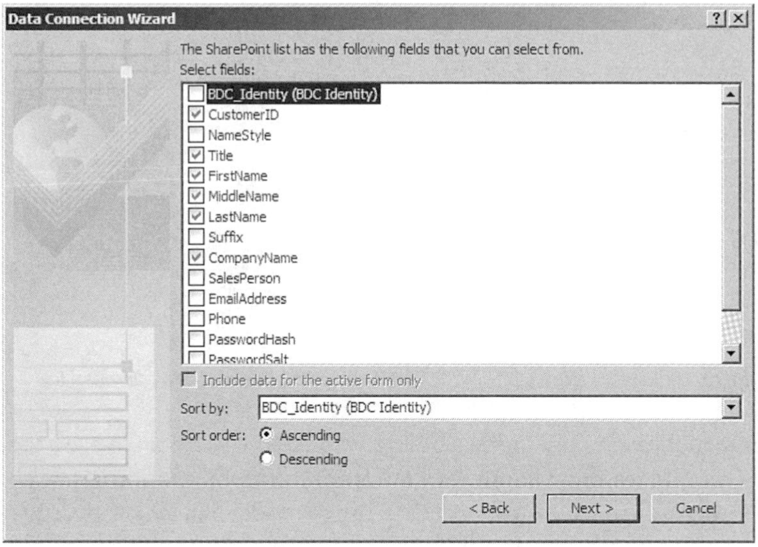

FIGURE 7-21 The Data Connection Wizard allows you to select columns from the external list.

The data from the data source can also be stored within the form template so that it can be made available offline for the first use of the form. Making the data available on the first use means that there is no delay in opening the form while data is obtained. From that point onward, data will be synchronized. You are advised not to do this if the data is sensitive. However, do note that it will improve performance upon first use of the form.

When you click Finish, the fields from your data source will be available in two groups:

- Query Fields

- Data Fields

You can drag and drop the fields from either group onto the form. The Query Fields allow you to enter a value into a field to perform a query, whereas the Data Fields automatically show the data in a repeating section on the form. Figure 7-22 shows the InfoPath 2010 form in design mode, with the external data columns placed on the form with their labels.

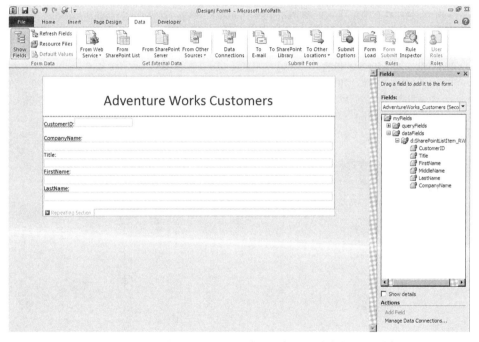

FIGURE 7-22 You can design the Adventure Works InfoPath form with fields added from an external list.

When you first preview your form to test the changes, you are asked if you want to allow the connection to take place for security reasons. Choose Yes if this is not a concern, and you will be able to view the external data. Figure 7-23 shows the external data displayed within the InfoPath 2010 client.

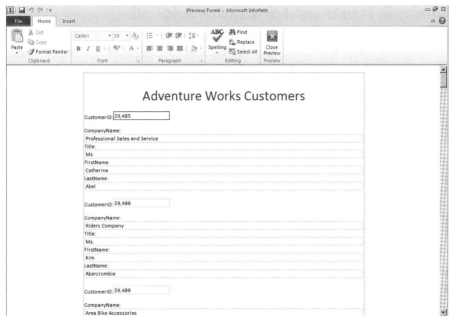

FIGURE 7-23 The external list data is displayed within an InfoPath 2010 client form.

To submit data to an external list, add a Submit button to your page, and then configure the Submit action using the stored data connection file in the Data Connection Library. You may then reuse the connection file when you create an InfoPath form. Figure 7-24 shows the Submit button being configured.

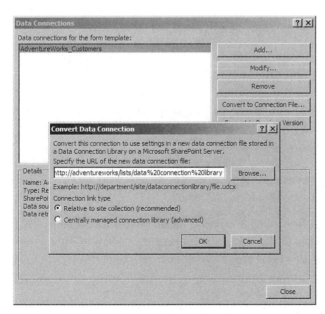

FIGURE 7-24 You can configure a Submit button to use a stored external data connection.

Customizing External List Forms with InfoPath

InfoPath Designer 2010 is also the tool to customize external list forms. It is a common belief that you cannot customize external list forms in the same way you can customize other SharePoint lists. Throughout SharePoint, within SharePoint standard lists, you will find a Customize Form with InfoPath icon on the list ribbon. There is also a link within the list settings named Form Settings. Figure 7-25 shows the InfoPath 2010 Customize Form command on the List ribbon tab, in the Customize List group.

FIGURE 7-25 The Customize Form button within a SharePoint task list.

 Note You cannot create InfoPath forms to display or amend content stored in SharePoint libraries.

In an external list, the Customize Form command is unavailable, and if you choose the option to customize the form from the list settings within an external list, you will get a message indicating that the external list forms cannot be edited in InfoPath. Figure 7-26 displays the error message that appears if you try to modify an external list form with InfoPath 2010 via the List Settings page.

FIGURE 7-26 This error message appears when you try to modify an external list form.

The way to modify an external list form is to use SharePoint Designer 2010 as a stepping stone to InfoPath 2010. Open your SharePoint site within SharePoint Designer by clicking Site Actions, and then click Edit in SharePoint Designer. Open the external list within SharePoint Designer, so you see the List Settings page displayed in the workspace. The Design Forms in InfoPath command is now available on the List Settings ribbon tab, in the Actions group, as shown in Figure 7-27. Click the Design Forms in InfoPath command to open the form in InfoPath.

Using InfoPath, you can apply logic such as input masks or validation rules to the fields within your form. You can use conditional formatting to highlight values such as low stock, and you can change fonts and colors as well as make other cosmetic changes. When you have completed your modifications, click the File tab, and then in the Backstage view, click Quick Publish, which publishes your form back to the external list. Figure 7-28 shows the external list form being modified in InfoPath 2010.

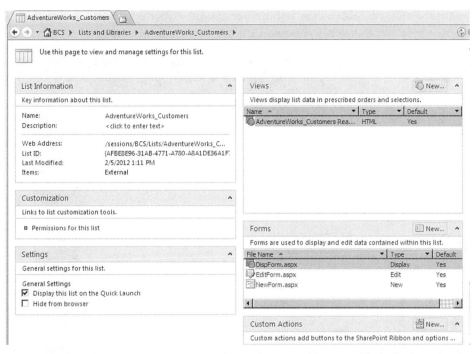

FIGURE 7-27 Use SharePoint Designer 2010 and open the external list to modify the list forms in InfoPath 2010.

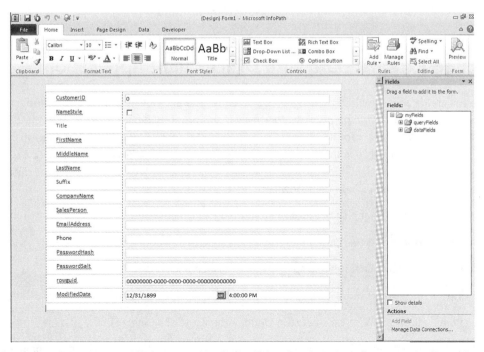

FIGURE 7-28 You can modify the external list form within InfoPath 2010 to allow customizations to it, such as formatting or validation.

Once the form is published, you can test the changes within your external list. Some obvious changes have been made, as shown in Figure 7-29.

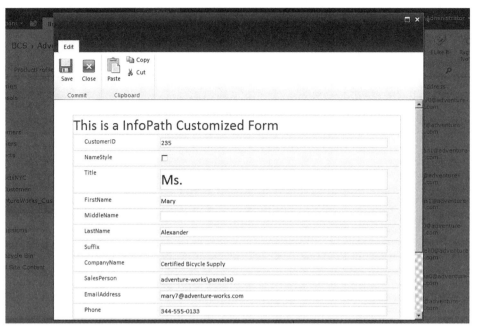

FIGURE 7-29 The changes to the external list form are complete.

Connecting External Data with Office Client Applications

When you create an External Content Type (ECT) in either SharePoint Designer or Visual Studio, you can set the Office Item Type property for the ECT. This property determines the way your data is treated when you connect to the external data source in Microsoft Outlook 2010. While you are configuring the ECT, you can map each of the columns using the Office Property control for a specific Office item type. Setting the Office property is important so that Outlook 2010 displays the data as desired. The Office types include the following:

- **Generic List**   Default choice; doesn't determine an Office type

- **Appointment**   Allows Outlook to display the data as an appointment

- **Contact**   Allows Outlook to display the data as a contact

- **Task**   Allows tasks to be created in Outlook

- **Post**   Allows a post to be created in Outlook (similar to Ctrl+Shift+S)

Figure 7-30 displays the ECT configuration wizard in SharePoint Designer 2010, where the mapping between external data columns and Office property columns is made.

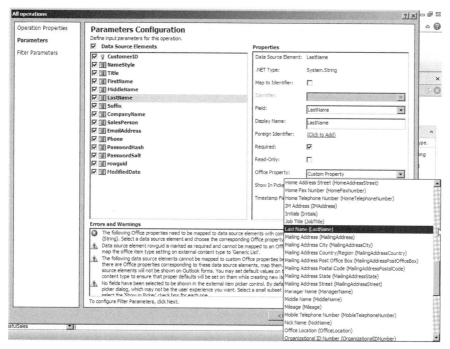

FIGURE 7-30 Configure the mapping in SharePoint Designer between external data columns and Office property columns to provide mapping to the Microsoft Outlook Business Card.

Once the Office type is set for the ECT and the Office properties are mapped, you can connect the external data to Outlook. Each user can make the data available in Outlook by clicking the Connect to Outlook button on the List ribbon tab in the List Tools tab set of an external list. Figure 7-31 shows an external list with Adventure Works customers being connected to Outlook as contacts.

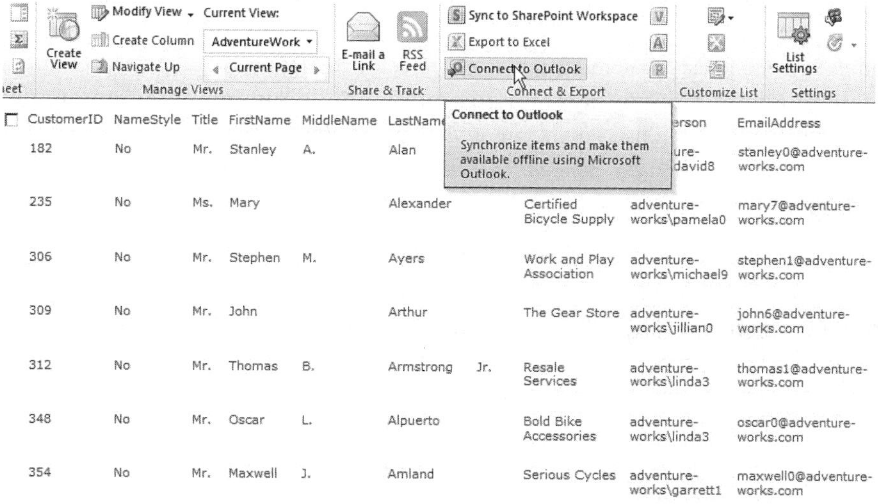

CustomerID	NameStyle	Title	FirstName	MiddleName	LastName			EmailAddress
182	No	Mr.	Stanley	A.	Alan		ure-david8	stanley0@adventure-works.com
235	No	Ms.	Mary		Alexander	Certified Bicycle Supply	adventure-works\pamela0	mary7@adventure-works.com
306	No	Mr.	Stephen	M.	Ayers	Work and Play Association	adventure-works\michael9	stephen1@adventure-works.com
309	No	Mr.	John		Arthur	The Gear Store	adventure-works\jillian0	john6@adventure-works.com
312	No	Mr.	Thomas	B.	Armstrong	Jr. Resale Services	adventure-works\linda3	thomas1@adventure-works.com
348	No	Mr.	Oscar	L.	Alpuerto	Bold Bike Accessories	adventure-works\linda3	oscar0@adventure-works.com
354	No	Mr.	Maxwell	J.	Amland	Serious Cycles	adventure-works\garrett1	maxwell0@adventure-works.com

FIGURE 7-31 You can connect an external list to Outlook to provide external data to the Outlook client application offline.

After you click the Connect to Outlook button and verify that you want to continue, the Outlook client opens and you can see a folder created under SharePoint external lists within your Outlook data file. The contacts will be synchronized, and you can use them as you do any Outlook contact. Modifying a contact also modifies the contact in the external list (if you have permission to do so), which in turn makes the modification in the external data source. Figure 7-32 shows the Adventure Works data residing in Outlook as a contacts list.

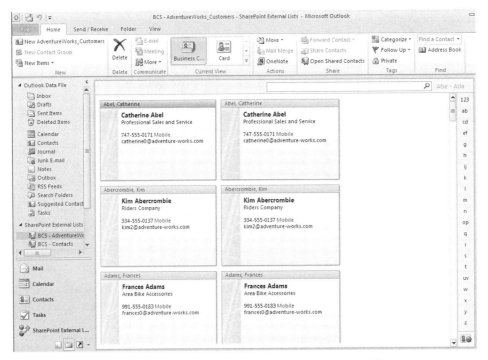

FIGURE 7-32 You can show external data as Outlook contacts from an external list.

Unlike other SharePoint lists or libraries that are connected to Outlook, the synchronization settings of connected external lists are not controlled by the Send/Receive settings. External lists are synchronized by default every six hours. When you right-click an external list in Outlook, you can find the Synchronization status and when the data was last refreshed from the external system. You can then force synchronization.

If you have the Enterprise edition of SharePoint Server, and the ECT is configured to allow Offline Sync for External Lists, you can view and edit cached copies of the SharePoint content, but your modifications are not synchronized with the external data source. To synchronize the content, you must go online.

SharePoint Workspace 2010

SharePoint Workspace is a new Microsoft Office product (formerly known as Groove) that allows you to take some SharePoint list or library offline within a client application and keep the data synchronized with the list or library on the server. Some lists or libraries cannot be taken offline, including publishing libraries, page libraries, calendars, and wiki pages.

You can view, modify, and delete external data from SharePoint Workspace while you are disconnected—for example, perhaps you are traveling without an Internet connection. The Sync ribbon within SharePoint Workspace allows you to force synchronization between the client and the server. External list data is made available to SharePoint Workspace in the same way that external list data is made available to Outlook. When you have an external list open, you can click the Sync to SharePoint Workspace button on the list ribbon. Figure 7-33 shows the external data synchronized within SharePoint Workspace.

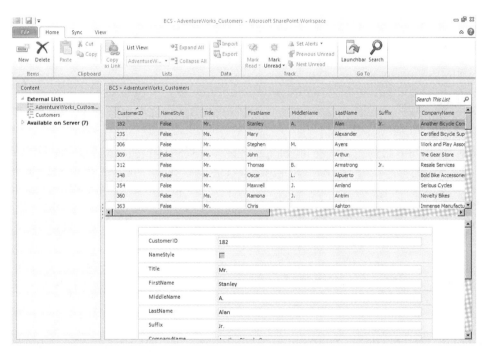

FIGURE 7-33 SharePoint Workspace is providing an external list offline, making external data available to view and modify, even in a disconnected environment.

The external list functionality in SharePoint Workspace allows you to sort, filter, and search the external data. Double-clicking an item enables you to edit the item, and you can select the New and Delete options from the ribbon.

External Data and Access 2010

For a long time, you have been able to create linked tables from an external data source in Microsoft Access. A *linked table* means that the data does not actually reside within the Access database, but is linked to instead, and the Access database stores the schema for the external data source that it is connected to.

Within Access 2010, you can connect to the following external data sources:

- Excel
- ODBC database
- Text file
- XML file
- SharePoint list
- Data services
- HTML document
- Outlook folder
- dBase file

These options provide you with plenty of opportunities to connect to most external data sources to create a linked table. Once you have a linked table in Access, the business solution opportunities are vast. You have the ability to create mashups of data from external sources and Access data within queries, build simple forms, and report on external data. You cannot connect to an external list as you would any other SharePoint list or library; rather, you need to use the external data source type Data Services.

 Note *Mashup* is a term used in web development. It refers to a page, dashboard, or application that combines data from two or more sources.

One of the types of external data sources you can connect to is Data Services, which allows you to connect to a BCS definition file, also known as the BDC model. First create a BDC model—that is, in SharePoint Designer, right-click the ECT that defines your external data source and select Export BDC Model, as shown in Figure 7-34.

FIGURE 7-34 Export the ECT as a BDC model definition file so it can be imported into Access.

In the Export BDC Model dialog box, type the name of the BDC model and select Client from the Settings list. Save the file with an *.xml* extension to a location on your hard drive or desktop, and then open Access. Within Access, create a new blank database. On the External Data ribbon tab, in the Import & Link group, click More, and then click Data Services, as shown in Figure 7-35. A Create Link to Data Services dialog box opens that allows you to connect to your business data through BCS.

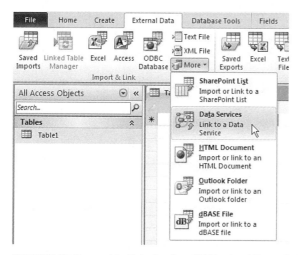

FIGURE 7-35 Connect to Data Services (BCS) using Microsoft Access 2010 to provide the ability to query and report on external data.

At the bottom-left of the Create Link to Data Services dialog box, click Install New Connection. The Select a Connection Definition File dialog box opens, where you can browse to the saved BDC definition file that you exported from SharePoint Designer 2010. When you open the definition file in Access, you can view the properties of the ECT and optionally provide a filter value to return a subset of the data, as shown in Figure 7-36. The filter must be configured already in the ECT.

At the bottom-right of the Create Link to Data Services dialog box, click Create Linked Table. You can open the linked table within Access to view the external data. Figure 7-37 displays the finished result: a linked table in Microsoft Access showing data accessed via BCS.

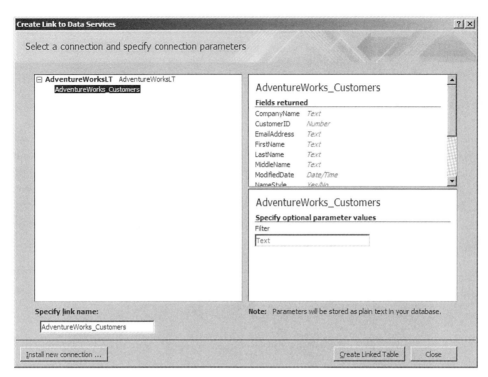

FIGURE 7-36 Use the Create Link to Data Services dialog box in Access 2010 to connect to an ECT.

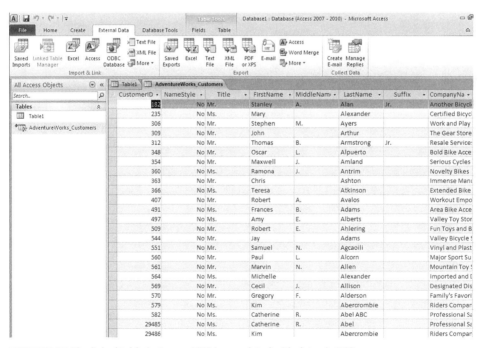

FIGURE 7-37 The linked table in Access 2010 is populated with data via BCS.

Using the linked table, you can now use Access to create queries, forms, and reports. You do not need to be connected via a SharePoint server—Access will connect directly with the external data source.

Data Visualization in Excel and Visio

Microsoft Excel does not provide any integration with Business Connectivity Services (BCS). However, both Excel and Visio 2010 tools offer great data visualization. *Data visualization* is an interesting and effective way to display data. Data displayed in this way is easier to read than lists of data. Excel 2010 has improved on the way that external data can be displayed. Notice that in Excel 2010, you can connect to Microsoft SQL Server databases and Microsoft SQL Server Analysis Services (SSAS), among many other choices. Once you are connected to the data, you can create pivot tables and charts, and use conditional formatting to display the data in an appealing way. Although connecting to BCS is not an out-of-the-box option for Excel 2010, you can write server-side code to provide the connectivity to Excel from an external list. Connecting to Excel using server-side code is covered in Chapter 12, "Building Server-Side BCS Solutions." Figure 7-38 shows the external data connection choices in Excel 2010.

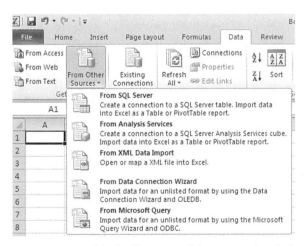

FIGURE 7-38 Excel 2010 offers external data connection choices.

A new feature of Excel 2010 allows cell-embedded shading, charts, and icons to show the compared values within a table. These options are created by conditional formatting. Sparklines also add data visualization to a table of external data—these are the small line-graphs that compare values within a column, as you can see in Figure 7-39.

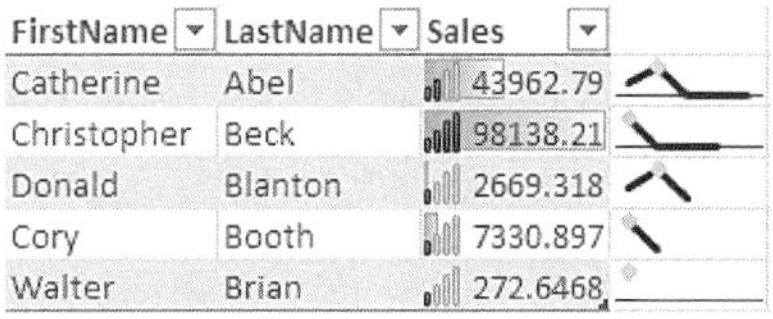

FirstName	LastName	Sales	
Catherine	Abel	43962.79	
Christopher	Beck	98138.21	
Donald	Blanton	2669.318	
Cory	Booth	7330.897	
Walter	Brian	272.6468	

FIGURE 7-39 The data visualization features in Excel 2010 offer easy ways to view data.

Visio 2010 also provides the ability to display data visualization diagrams, but it doesn't currently connect directly to BCS. You can connect to an external data source using the Link Data to Shapes button on the Data ribbon tab, as shown in Figure 7-40.

FIGURE 7-40 Click Link Data to Shapes to create data visualization in Visio 2010.

On the Data tab, in the External Data group, click Link Data to Shapes to open a dialog box with connection choices, as shown in Figure 7-41. If you select the option Microsoft SharePoint Foundation List, you cannot connect to a BCS external list as you can in InfoPath Designer, but you can still connect directly to an SQL database or any other SharePoint list.

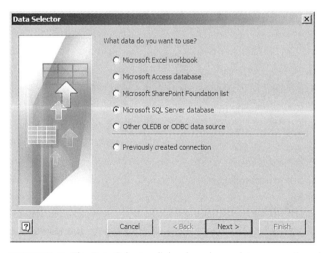

FIGURE 7-41 The Data Selector dialog box shows data connection choices in Visio 2010.

Once you have completed the connection wizard and connected to your external data source, you can drag rows of data from a table onto the page to insert a data shape. On the Data ribbon tab, in the Display Data group, click Data Graphics to refine the shape. Figure 7-42 shows the external data from SQL being mapped using shapes within a Visio diagram.

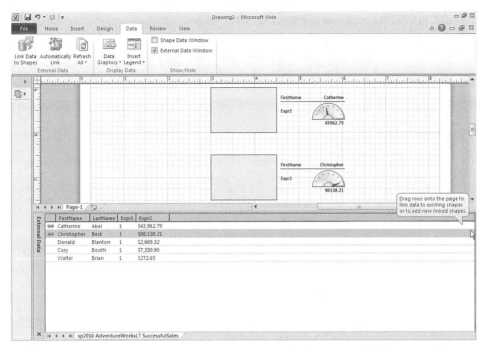

FIGURE 7-42 External data from the Adventure Works SQL database mapped within a Visio diagram provides diagrams with live data.

Troubleshooting BCS Solutions on the Client

Typically, any issues that arise in Business Connectivity Services (BCS) are related to the logged-on user having insufficient permissions to view or write back to the external data source. You can, however, create a trace to monitor BCS on the server and the client using Performance Monitor, and then view the events using Event Viewer.

To set up Performance Monitor to monitor BCS, follow these steps:

1. Click Start, and then type **Perfmon** in the Search Program and Files text box.

2. In Performance Monitor, expand Data Collector Sets.

3. To display the Create New Data Collector Set dialog box, right-click User Defined, point to New, and then select Data Collector Set, as shown in Figure 7-43.

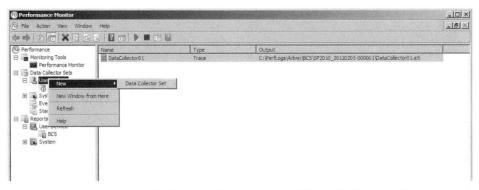

FIGURE 7-43 You can configure Performance Monitor to trace BCS troubleshooting information on the client.

4. In the Name text box, type a name for your Data Collector Set and select Create Manually (Advanced).

5. Click Next to display the What Type of Data Do You Want to Include page.

6. Select Performance Counter and Event Trace Data. Then click Next to display the Which Performance Counters Would You Like to Log page.

7. For the Performance Counter, add a BDC Metadata Cache Hits Per Second counter and then click Next to display the Which Event Trace Providers Would You Like to Enable page.

8. For the provider, add Microsoft SharePoint Products–Business Connectivity Services, as shown in Figure 7-44.

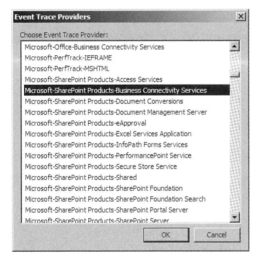

FIGURE 7-44 The BCS provider selected for performance monitoring within the Event Trace Providers window.

9. Click Finish.

Follow these steps to open Windows Event Viewer:

10. Click the Start button, select Administrative Tools from the Start menu, and then select Event Viewer.

11. Right-click Saved Logs and choose Open Saved Log.

12. In the Open Saved Log dialog box, navigate to the Saved log you created in Performance Monitor.

13. Perform some offline activities such as view, edit, and delete.

14. View your event log.

See Also *For more information about monitoring and diagnostic logging in BCS, go to* http://technet.microsoft.com/en-us/library/ff463594.aspx.

Optimizing Back-End Synchronization

You have a few options to consider when coding a BCS connection with Visual Studio that will have an impact on the performance of your data retrieval. When using SharePoint Designer to create the connection, one of the main methods of increasing back-end synchronization is to create filters—the less data to synchronize to the client, the better. Using SharePoint Designer 2010, when you create an ECT, you can create a filter on your data.

The filters supported by the synchronization framework that you can use to reduce the number of items downloaded are Wildcard, Comparison, and Limit filters. You can use a Wildcard filter to synchronize all customers whose company name starts with *A* as the filter value, for example. Or you can select all customers whose zip code is equal to "34216" by using a Comparison filter. You can use a Limit filter to limit the number of returned items. Since external lists can provide a maximum of only 5,000 items, you will be forced to display fewer items than you actually have within your external data source. If you sort your customers as an example by country, it may mean that if you have 5,500 customers, the last 500 of those in the United Kingdom or United States are not shown. You can therefore create better filters, such as a view for United Kingdom customers only, and create your own filter, such as 500 if you only had around 300–400 customers. These filters are also useful for limiting the items below 200, which is beneficial for the item picker dialog box, which can display a maximum of 200 items. Figure 7-45 shows the Filter Configuration dialog box within the SharePoint Designer ECT configuration wizard.

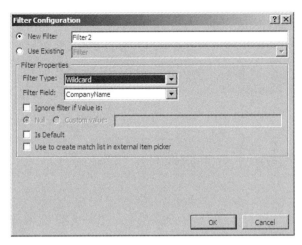

FIGURE 7-45 The Filter Configuration dialog box in SharePoint Designer with a Wildcard filter set.

Summary

In this chapter, you explored how you can use Business Connectivity Services (BCS) within client applications. You examined using SharePoint Designer when setting the Office type, which controls the behavior of the data when it is connected to in Outlook. You also looked at how to use SharePoint Workspace to take data offline, along with Microsoft Access, Microsoft Word, and Microsoft InfoPath. You learned that you can now use Microsoft Access to create a linked table to BCS, and how you can use InfoPath and Word to look up external data.

CHAPTER 8

Finding Information from External Systems

In this chapter, you will:

- Discover how organizations can search external data using SharePoint

- Learn how SharePoint Search and Business Connectivity Services work together

- Learn how to create content sources to crawl external systems

- Establish how to customize the search results pages

Information workers today often spend more time than they should unsuccessfully searching for business data. When they don't find the data they're looking for, they spend more time recreating or duplicating it. Duplicate data or content leads to inconsistencies and mistakes being made within an organization, and ultimately costs the organization a lot of money. According to a Butler Group survey ("Enterprise Search and Retrieval: Unlocking the Organization's Potential," October 2006), around 10 percent of a company's salary costs are wasted due to time spent searching for content. To put that into perspective, if you take an organization employing 500 information workers who each earn $30,000 per year, around $1,500,000 is spent on searching for data. If you can save just 1 percent of that time in your organization, you will save $150,000 per year.

See Also *You can read more about the Butler Group survey here:* www.networkworld.com/news/2006/102006-search-cuts-productivity.html.

Millions of people use Internet search engines such as Bing and Google every day to find information. The search procedure is simple and intuitive, and through an engine's clever indexing and crawling, you can find relevant information within seconds from billions of webpages.

Microsoft SharePoint provides the ability to search information in a similar way to Internet search engines, providing search results from your SharePoint content and any other data that is relevant to your organization. Instead of your organization's users spending hours trying to find information, you can increase their search efficiency by cleverly configuring the SharePoint search functionality to find information quickly and provide a better return on your SharePoint investment. Depending on the SharePoint license you have, such as SharePoint Foundation, SharePoint Server 2010 Standard, or SharePoint Server 2010 Enterprise, you can search for content from documents, lists, other intranet sites, Internet sites, shared folders, and external data sources.

Within an external data source such as a customer relationship management (CRM) system, it is not unusual to find duplicate data, such as duplicate contact or company information. The cause of the duplication is usually that someone didn't find the information during a search and then inserted a new record, not realizing that the same information was already in the system. If it was easy to find the required record in the first place, the instances of duplication would be greatly reduced. Therefore, investing some time into configuring Standard search to search Business Connectivity Services (BCS) external data can be beneficial to the organization, reducing duplication of information and increasing users' efficiency (thus decreasing salary overhead).

Microsoft SharePoint Foundation 2010 provides a simple site search that allows you to search SharePoint content such as documents and list items. Microsoft SharePoint Server 2010 provides a choice of search: Standard or Enterprise. You can also opt to install Microsoft FAST Search Server 2010 for SharePoint, which provides even more search capabilities. Standard search includes the SharePoint Server Search Connector Framework, which enables you to search external content, such as external sources that you can connect to using BCS. These search options enable users to search for all relevant business data, be it SharePoint content or data outside of SharePoint.

When an overwhelming number of search results is returned, Standard search allows you to reduce the number of items returned to show more relevant results through search scopes, recently authored content, best bets, and relevancy tuning.

Enterprise search in SharePoint also provides contextual search (searches based on the profile of the user), similar results, thumbnails and previews, and much more. Many small to medium-sized organizations tend not to be able to justify the additional cost of the Enterprise edition of SharePoint Server or FAST Search Server, but for large organizations, it is often a good financial investment.

In this chapter, you will examine the benefits of configuring SharePoint to search external data. You will also learn how to configure SharePoint to crawl external data to help provide a central search location for all data and content of use to your organization.

How SharePoint Search and BCS Work Together

SharePoint Server provides a search center that is internal to your organization but is comparable to an Internet search site. You'll find a simple page with a single search box like you find on the Bing or Google site. The Enterprise Search Center provides two tabs by default: an All Sites tab and a People tab. The All Sites tab provides search across all content sources, including SharePoint lists, documents, external data, and people, while the People search tab returns results from the people search scope only, allowing you to search across user profiles without having to decipher people from other results. For example, say that within your organization you have a requirement for an employee to have .NET development skills. If a SharePoint user has listed .NET development as a skill within their user profile, you can easily find that information through a people search and not make the costly error of hiring a new employee or consultant unnecessarily. Using the People tab within the search center narrows the results to just people instead of returning other content that contains ".NET development" keywords. You can create additional tabs to limit the results for other search scopes, including creating tabs for a specific external data source, such as a CRM database.

Figure 8-1 illustrates search results using the All Sites tab, which returned results from a mixture of content sources, including All Sites and an external data content source. Notice that the search returned a Microsoft Word document containing the word *bike* as well as results from the Adventure Works database.

> **Note** The BCS results display a folder icon with a four-digit number as the link. This number will be replaced with a URL once you create the profile page for the external content type (ECT).

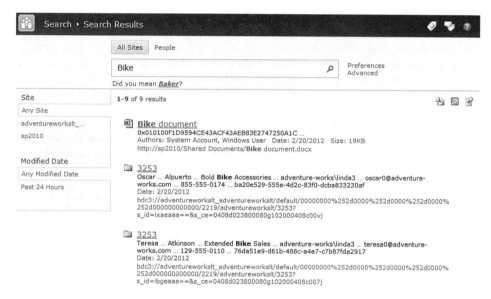

FIGURE 8-1 Search results display from the Adventure Works SQL database within the SharePoint Enterprise Search Center.

You can customize the search center to show additional tabs beyond All Sites and People. Creating a search page and a custom tab specific to an external data source allows users to limit the results returned in the same way that the People tab works. Notice in Figure 8-2 that the Word document containing the keyword *bike* is no longer returned, but data from the Adventure Works database containing the word *bike* is returned. To achieve search results from an external data source, you create a content source and a search scope prior to creating a search results page. Then you customize the search results Web Parts on the search results page. You will learn how to do so in this chapter.

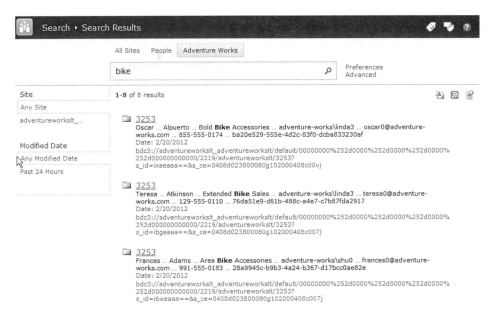

FIGURE 8-2 This custom search page shows search results focused on a particular search scope.

When you click the hyperlink for a search result, such as a document or list item, you are taken to that content. For example, the document will open or you will view the list item. With a BCS search result, you will be taken to a profile page showing a page with a Business Data Item Web Part. If you haven't created a profile page for that particular ECT, you receive an error message. You can create a profile page in Microsoft SharePoint Designer 2010 after creating your ECT or in the SharePoint 2010 Central Administration website under the Business Data Connectivity (BDC) service application settings. The process for creating the profile page is discussed in detail in Chapter 3, "Creating and Maintaining Business Data Connectivity Service Applications," and Chapter 4, "Defining External System Connections Using SharePoint Designer." Figure 8-3 shows an example of a BCS profile page.

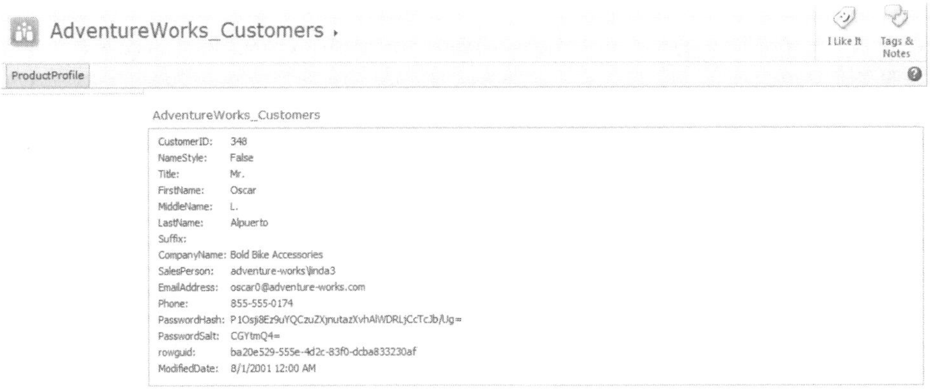

FIGURE 8-3 A BCS profile page allows you to see all columns of data from a specific row in the database when you click a search result.

The profile page is made up of two Web Parts: the Business Data Item Web Part and the Business Data Item Builder Web Part. The Business Data Item Builder Web Part is visible only when modifying the profile page. These Web Parts are discussed in Chapter 6, "Building Business Data Dashboards." Once you have created a profile page for your ECT, notice that the search results look a lot cleaner without the folder icon and four-digit code, as shown in Figure 8-4.

FIGURE 8-4 The search results look cleaner after the creation of the profile page.

Creating Content Sources to Crawl External Systems

To successfully configure SharePoint to search your external content, follow the steps outlined in this section. Some of these steps are required, while others are recommended to provide a good end-user experience and to refine the search results:

- Create the External Content Type with a Read List operation (required)

- Create a profile page for the ECT (required to avoid an error when the search result is clicked)

- Create a line-of-business (LoB) data content source (required)

- Run a full crawl on your content source (required)

- Create a search scope (optional; allows you to refine the search results)

- Configure crawl settings and managed properties (optional; allows additional metadata to be filtered)

- Customize the search center (optional; provides a more refined search)

If you configured a LoB data crawl in the Enterprise edition of Microsoft Office SharePoint Server 2007 Business Data Catalog, you will probably remember having to create an IDEnumerator method for the content crawling to work successfully. The IDEnumerator method simply returned the Unique Identifier column for an entity, which was the previous name for an ECT. The IDEnumerator method was used for enumerating each row of data for the crawl. The IDEnumerator method is no longer required, but it is still supported if you are upgrading from BDC to BCS. The Read List operation is a multipurpose method that is used for the content source crawl. The SharePoint crawl uses the operation to create an index, allowing it to enumerate each row from the data source. Figure 8-5 shows the Read List operation being created within SharePoint Designer. Chapter 4 discusses using SharePoint Designer to create the ECT and the Read List operation.

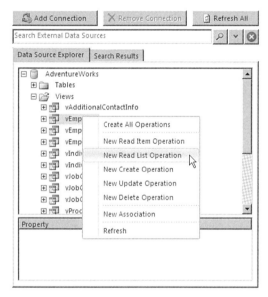

FIGURE 8-5 Use SharePoint Designer to create the Read List operation.

Once you have created the ECT with the required Read List operation, you can configure the content source within the SharePoint 2010 Central Administration website, or you can use Windows PowerShell commands. The content source tells SharePoint where to go to crawl content. A content source can be created to crawl SharePoint sites, websites, file shares, Microsoft Exchange public folders, LoB data (BCS), and custom repositories. A default content source, All Sites, will already exist for SharePoint sites. Creating a content source to crawl websites can be useful to allow information workers to search your company website as well as perhaps some of your largest customers' and competitors' websites. Those websites and other sites linked to from those pages will also be crawled, so crawl external sites with caution, as you could end up crawling more content than you planned. Business information also exists within file shares and Exchange public folders, so creating a content source for those resources can be beneficial.

This chapter focuses on using LoB data content sources. A LoB data content source enables you to search the content even if the content lives in external data sources. You can configure the content source to allow crawling of an external data source such as Adventure Works and any ECT within that external data source or all external data sources. You may want to target individual external data sources, allowing different priorities and crawl schedules to be created depending upon the importance of the data that will be searched. To create a content source, follow these steps:

1. Open the SharePoint 2010 Central Administration website by either navigating to the URL or clicking the Start button, selecting All Programs from the Start menu, choosing Microsoft SharePoint 2010 Products, and then selecting SharePoint 2010 Central Administration.

2. Click General Application Settings on the Quick Launch toolbar.

3. On the General Application Setting page, under Search, click Farm Search Administration to display the Farm Search Administration page.

4. Under Search Service Applications, click your Search Service Application to display the Search Administration page.

5. Under Crawling, click Content Sources on the Quick Launch toolbar. The Manage Content Sources page displays, where you can see a list of your content sources.

6. Click New Content Source to display the Add Content Source page.

Note You may not have permission to use the SharePoint 2010 Central Administration website. If this is the case, request help from a SharePoint farm administrator.

Figure 8-6 shows the Add Content Source page, where a content source is being created for the Adventure Works external data source.

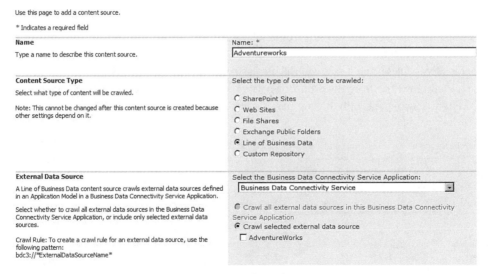

FIGURE 8-6 You can create a content source to crawl LoB data.

Toward the bottom of the Add Content Source page is a Crawl Schedules section, where you can create a schedule, such as daily or weekly, for external data to be crawled. You may specify the time for a full crawl as well as an incremental crawl. When you have multiple content sources, you can control the priority of each content source, ensuring the highest-priority content source is always crawled first.

After you have configured the content source, click OK to return to the Manage Content Sources page. From here, you can start a full crawl using the drop-down list, as shown in Figure 8-7. A full crawl of your external data must be completed successfully before you see any search results through the search center.

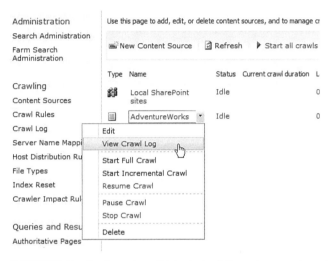

FIGURE 8-7 Use the drop-down list to start a full crawl on an external data content source.

You will need to refresh the Manage Content Sources page periodically during the crawl to see when it has finished. If the crawl takes a while to finish and doesn't fail immediately, you should consider it successful, since if it fails you will be alerted quickly. You can investigate any problems by choosing View Crawl Log from the drop-down list on the content source. Figure 8-8 shows the Crawl Log – Content Source page with the number of items returned for each content source.

SharePoint 2010 Central Administration ▸ Search Service Application: Crawl Log - Content Source

I Like It   Tags & Notes

Administration
Search Administration
Farm Search Administration

| Content Source | Host Name | URL | Crawl History | Error Message |

Use this page to view a summary of items crawled per content source.

Crawling
Content Sources
Crawl Rules
Crawl Log

Content Source	Successes	Warnings	Errors	Top Level Errors	Deletes
AdventureWorks	110	0	0	0	0
Local SharePoint sites	1,422	2	4	3	3

FIGURE 8-8 The Content Source page shows the items returned during a content source crawl.

From the Crawl Log – Content Source page, you can drill further into the crawl log for a specific content source by clicking the Content Source hyperlink to display the Crawl Log – Crawl History page. This page shows each crawl and its status, along with any error messages, which you can then use to troubleshoot errors. Figure 8-9 shows an example of crawl logs for a specific content source.

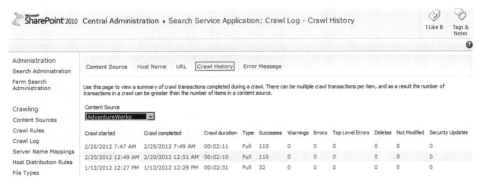

FIGURE 8-9 Viewing the crawl logs of an external content source allows you to see if the crawl was successful.

If the crawl completed successfully without errors, you should test the search using the All Sites tab within your search center. Typically, if the crawl is unsuccessful, it fails due to the permissions granted to the ECT, which you can investigate in the BDC service pages. There are two types of error that may be seen in the crawl logs: an Error and a Top Level Error. An Error can be raised if one record from the ECT fails to be crawled, but a Top Level Error implies the whole content source/start address could not be crawled.

See Also *For more information on BCS security options and how to configure them, see Chapters 3 and 4.*

Creating a Search Scope and Scope Rules

Once you have created the content source, you are able to return search results from your ECT. However, before you can create a custom search results page that allows you to show more relevant results, you need to create a search scope. You can create search scopes using the SharePoint 2010 Central Administration website on the Search Administration page for your search service application.

To create a new search scope:

1. Under Queries and Results, click Scopes on the Quick Launch toolbar.

2. On the View Scopes page, click New Scope to display the Create Scope page.

In the Target Results Page section, you are asked to provide a name for the results page. You should have in mind the name of the search results page that you want to create. For example, if you are going to create a custom search results page for all items returned from Adventure Works, you could name the search results page *adventureworks.aspx*, or if you are returning just products from Adventure Works, you could name the page *adventureworks_products_results.aspx*. Creating the search scope will not create the page for you. You need to create the results page within the search center, so it is important to make a note of the URL. Figure 8-10 shows the settings when creating a custom search scope.

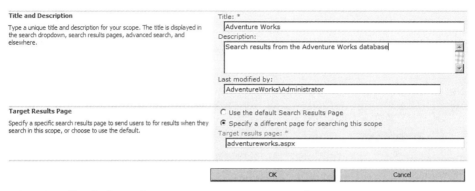

FIGURE 8-10 Use the Create Scope page to create a custom search scope.

When you click OK, you return to the View Scopes page, where you see the two default search scopes along with your newly created search scope. The newly created search scope currently does not have any rules associated with it, as denoted by the Add Rules hyperlink (see Figure 8-11). You must add a rule to specify the content source used for this search scope.

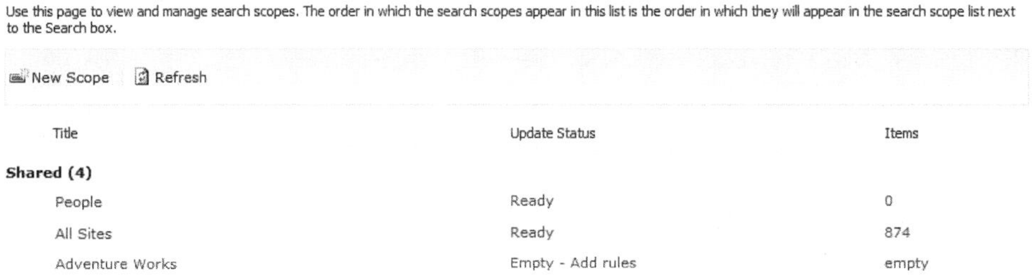

Use this page to view and manage search scopes. The order in which the search scopes appear in this list is the order in which they will appear in the search scope list next to the Search box.

🖼 New Scope   🖪 Refresh

Title	Update Status	Items
Shared (4)		
People	Ready	0
All Sites	Ready	874
Adventure Works	Empty - Add rules	empty

FIGURE 8-11 The search scopes page prior to a scope rule being created shows the existing and newly created search scopes.

Click Add Rule to display the Add Scope Rule page, where you can define rules to display the search results specific to your ECT that will appear on your custom search page. You can create different types of scopes for different reasons. For example, it is possible to create a scope returning SharePoint list items created with a specific content type or with a specific column value. You can then use this scope with the Core Search Results Web Part to provide a great way to "roll up" SharePoint list content from across multiple site collections. In this case, you will use the scope to map your ECT content source with a custom Core Search Results Web Part on your custom search page.

On the Add Scope Rule page, in the Scope Rule Type section, select Content Source. Then in the Content Source section, select your content source, such as Adventure Works, from the Content Source drop-down list. Figure 8-12 shows the configured scope rule mapping the content source to the search scope.

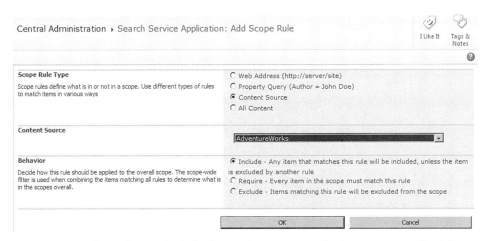

FIGURE 8-12 Configure the search rule for the search scope to map the content source and search scope together.

Configuring Crawled and Managed Properties

Managed properties provide a method of refining a search. SharePoint search provides many out-of-the-box managed properties. These managed properties allow you to refine a search on SharePoint content or people. You can reduce the number of search results by specifying managed properties such as Author: Brett, for example, which would limit the results to those documents authored by Brett (and possibly reduce 50 results down to just a few). Managed properties also allow you to refine searches. For example, say you perform a search using a specific keyword, such as *giant*. Performing a search on this keyword may return all kinds of content that contains the word *giant*. Because *giant* is a common word as well as the brand name for a bicycle, performing a search on the brand name for a bicycle part is likely to also bring back other non-Giant products. Specifying the managed property Product Brand Name: Giant would provide very refined results.

Crawled properties are columns and metadata properties that SharePoint has crawled that can be mapped to managed properties, allowing them to be used within an advanced search. From the Search Administration page for your search service application, under Queries and Results, click Metadata Properties on the Quick Launch toolbar to display the Metadata Property Mapping page, as shown in Figure 8-13.

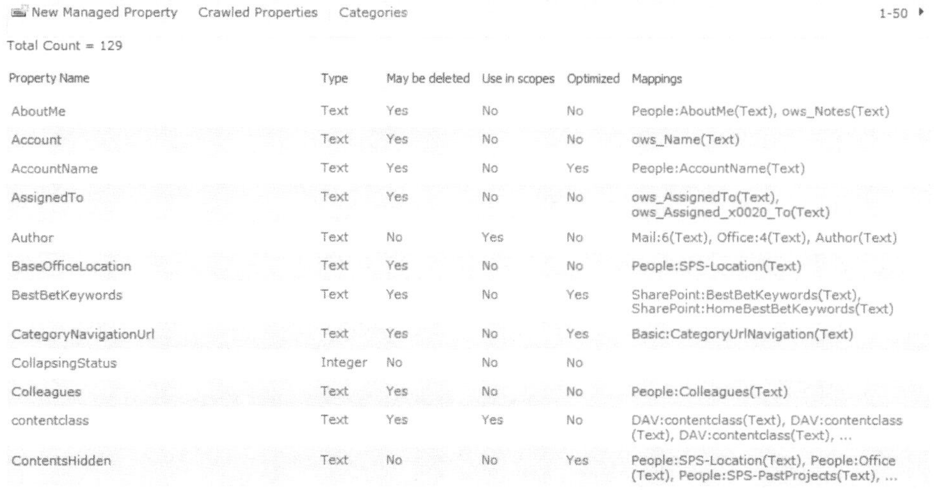

Total Count = 129

Property Name	Type	May be deleted	Use in scopes	Optimized	Mappings
AboutMe	Text	Yes	No	No	People:AboutMe(Text), ows_Notes(Text)
Account	Text	Yes	No	No	ows_Name(Text)
AccountName	Text	Yes	No	Yes	People:AccountName(Text)
AssignedTo	Text	Yes	No	No	ows_AssignedTo(Text), ows_Assigned_x0020_To(Text)
Author	Text	No	Yes	No	Mail:6(Text), Office:4(Text), Author(Text)
BaseOfficeLocation	Text	Yes	No	No	People:SPS-Location(Text)
BestBetKeywords	Text	Yes	No	Yes	SharePoint:BestBetKeywords(Text), SharePoint:HomeBestBetKeywords(Text)
CategoryNavigationUrl	Text	Yes	No	Yes	Basic:CategoryUrlNavigation(Text)
CollapsingStatus	Integer	No	No	No	
Colleagues	Text	Yes	No	No	People:Colleagues(Text)
contentclass	Text	Yes	Yes	No	DAV:contentclass(Text), DAV:contentclass(Text), DAV:contentclass(Text), ...
ContentsHidden	Text	No	No	Yes	People:SPS-Location(Text), People:Office(Text), People:SPS-PastProjects(Text), ...

FIGURE 8-13 Managed properties are displayed on the Metadata Property Mapping page within the Search Administration pages for your search service application.

FirstName is a good example of a managed property. When you click FirstName to display the Edit Managed Property page, you can see that it is mapped to two crawled properties, People:FirstName and People: SPS_PhoneticFirstName, as shown in Figure 8-14.

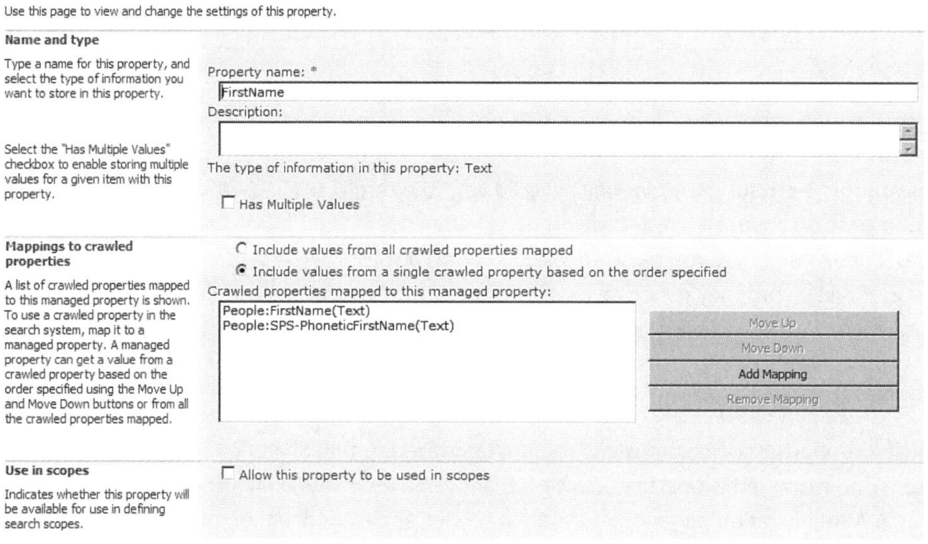

Use this page to view and change the settings of this property.

Name and type

Type a name for this property, and select the type of information you want to store in this property.

Property name: *
[FirstName]

Description:
[   ]

Select the "Has Multiple Values" checkbox to enable storing multiple values for a given item with this property.

The type of information in this property: Text

☐ Has Multiple Values

Mappings to crawled properties

A list of crawled properties mapped to this managed property is shown. To use a crawled property in the search system, map it to a managed property. A managed property can get a value from a crawled property based on the order specified using the Move Up and Move Down buttons or from all the crawled properties mapped.

○ Include values from all crawled properties mapped
● Include values from a single crawled property based on the order specified

Crawled properties mapped to this managed property:
```
People:FirstName(Text)
People:SPS-PhoneticFirstName(Text)
```

Move Up
Move Down
Add Mapping
Remove Mapping

Use in scopes

Indicates whether this property will be available for use in defining search scopes.

☐ Allow this property to be used in scopes

FIGURE 8-14 A FirstName managed metadata property is created on the Managed Metadata Property page.

Within a SharePoint search, you are able to perform a People search by specifying **FirstName: Scott**. Doing so prevents the search from returning people whose first name is not Scott. Clicking Search Options on a people search page also displays some managed properties through the People search box, as shown in Figure 8-15.

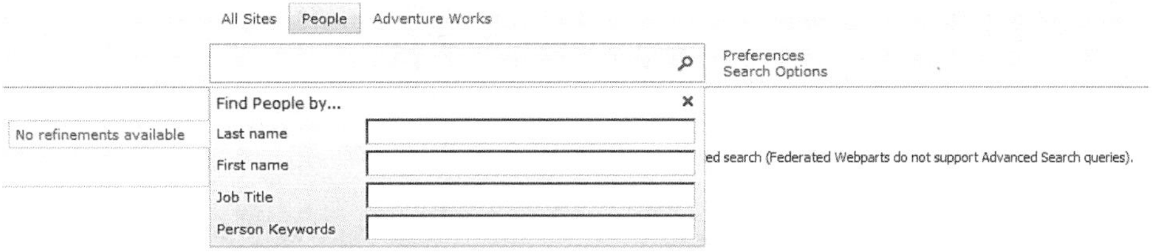

FIGURE 8-15 The Search Options page on a people search allows you to refine the results.

You can create a similar configuration for BCS crawled properties. The AdventureWorks_Customer ECT that you created in Chapter 4 contains columns such as Customer Name, Address, City, State, and Zip. These columns are crawled properties that you can map to a custom managed property. You can map multiple columns to a managed property—for example, you can map Contact Last Name and Employee Last Name to the LastName managed property. Mapping in this way allows you to refine your search using an advanced search based upon the LastName. Configuring the Advanced Search box, including exposing managed properties, is covered toward the end of this chapter.

To create a custom managed property, on the Metadata Property Mappings page, click New Managed Property to display the New Managed Property page. In the Name and Type section, provide a managed property name and description, along with the type of data, such as Text. In the Mappings to Crawled Properties section, click Add Mapping to display the Crawled Property Selection modal dialog box, where you can choose from a large number of crawled properties. All of the crawled properties are categorized, so using the Select a Category drop-down list, you can select Business Data, as shown in Figure 8-16. Note that the crawled properties will include Read Item as well as Read List properties.

Click OK once you have selected the crawled property. On the New Managed Property page, in the Use in Scopes section, you may also select the Allow This Property to Be Used in Scopes box to make this managed property available to search scopes. This means that you can create search pages with a scope that will provide users with the ability to show very refined searches that perhaps allow only product names to be searched. Figure 8-17 displays the configured Productname managed property.

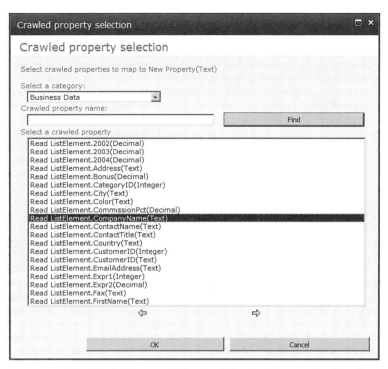

FIGURE 8-16 The Crawled Property Selection dialog box shows a selection of properties to be mapped to.

FIGURE 8-17 This configured managed property can now be used to refine searches.

Now that you have created a managed property, you can use the property within your searches—for example, **Productname: Road Frame HL**. You can also create an Advanced Search page that allows the managed property to be selected.

In the next section of this chapter, you will learn how to create the search pages and the Advanced Search pages. You will also examine how to configure the search Web Parts.

Customizing the Search Center

At the start of this chapter, you explored the desired results of customizing the search center, including creating custom search results pages and tabs, and allowing refined results to be shown from the ECT. In this section, you will look at the Web Parts that make up those search pages, learn how to configure them, and learn how to create the pages themselves.

To begin, you will create a new search results page that already contains the Web Parts you are going to configure. You create the search results page as you do any other Web Part page. After you navigate to the search center, click Site Actions, and then click New Page. You are prompted to specify the name of your page, as shown in Figure 8-18. Remember from earlier in this chapter that the name you provide must match the name defined on the Create Scope page.

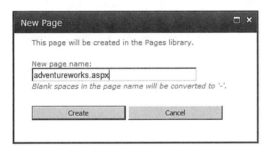

FIGURE 8-18 Create a custom search results page that will be mapped to the search scope created earlier in this chapter.

When you click Create, a new page is created that will be stored within the Pages Library of the search center. You can navigate to the Pages Library by clicking Site Actions and then View All Site Content. You may need to access the Pages Library to check in and check out your page when customizing it, but you can also do this by using the Page ribbon tab. To display the Page ribbon tab, click Site Actions and then click Edit Page. You may also need to navigate to the Pages Library when you want to modify a search page, a search results page, or an advanced search page.

Note When you first navigate to the search center, a default page, *default.aspx*, displays. This page has no search results and contains two tabs, All Sites and People. When you click the People tab, another page, *people.aspx*, displays that contains no results. When you type a keyword in the search text box and press Enter, a page displays that contains the results of the search. This is known as a search results page. For an All Sites search, the results page is *results.aspx*. This is not the same page displayed when you navigate to the search center. For a People search, the results page is *peopleresults.aspx*. A third set of pages can be used when you click the Advanced Options link. Out of the box in SharePoint, only one Advanced Search page is provided, *advanced.aspx*, which is configured to be used when the Advanced link is clicked on any search or search results page.

Creating Search Tabs

Before you configure the Web Parts, it is a good idea to create the custom tab. You will now have three results pages within your search center: All Sites, People, and Adventure Works. You will need to create the Adventure Works tab on all three results pages to provide navigation. First, navigate back to the results page in the search center so that you have the All Sites tab selected. Click Site Actions and then click Edit Page to edit the *results.aspx* page. Click Add New Tab to create a new tab within the search center. You will need to specify a tab name, such as Adventure Works, as well as the search page to be opened upon clicking the tab. The search page will be the same URL as the page that you created in the previous section, and it will be specified within your search scope. To make the tab display on the People page and your Adventure Works page, repeat the process of adding the tab for each page. Figure 8-19 shows the creation of the Adventure Works tab.

FIGURE 8-19 Create the Adventure Works tab in the search center. This tab will map to the new custom search results page.

After you have created the tab on each search results page, make sure that you save your changes and check the page in so that other users may modify it.

Note To add tabs on search result pages, add list items in the Tabs in Search Results list in the search center. Using this list is an alternative method of creating, modifying, or deleting tabs. Search pages have their own set of tabs, which are stored in the Tabs in Search Pages list. The tabs are rendered on the pages by the ListBoundTabStrip SharePoint control.

Introducing the Search Web Parts

You will include a number of search Web Parts on your search page:

- Search Box
- Search Summary
- Refinement Panel
- Related Queries
- People Matches
- Search Statistics
- Search Action Links
- Search Core Results
- Search Best Bets
- Top Federated Results
- Search Paging

You are initially concerned with just two of the Web Parts that are on the search results page by default: the Search Box Web Part and the Search Core Results Web Part.

Search Box Web Part

The Search Box Web Part provides users with the text box in which to enter search keywords. It also provides Preferences and Advanced links to the right of the search text box, which you need to configure. Figure 8-20 shows the Search Box Web Part when the search page is in Edit mode.

FIGURE 8-20 The Search Box Web Part in Edit page mode allows you to configure properties.

The tool pane of the Search Box Web Part contains some good refinement options as well as some properties that you should set. The Scopes Dropdown section, shown in Figure 8-21, provides three properties: Dropdown Mode, Dropdown Label, and the Fixed Dropdown Width. If you have multiple scopes, setting the Dropdown Mode to provide a choice of scopes allows users to specify which scope they would like to search. There are no required properties that should be changed in the Scopes Dropdown category.

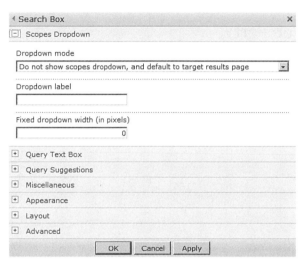

FIGURE 8-21 Set the Dropdown Mode property within the Search Box Web Part.

The Query Text Box section allows further refinements, such as Query Text Box Label and Query Text Box Width, as shown in Figure 8-22. The Query Text Box label allows you to add text as a prefix to the search text box. The Additional Query Terms property enables you to append text to the search, which can be used to filter the search automatically to perhaps a specific year or even a division within the organization. If you do append text to the search, then you should enter text in the Additional Query Description Label text box. This description appears immediately below the search box and lets users know what you have configured.

The Query Suggestions section, shown in Figure 8-23, provides search suggestions as you type your query. You can choose to turn this feature on or off, and you can also set properties such as the Minimum Prefix Length, Suggestion Delay, and Number of Suggestions to Display.

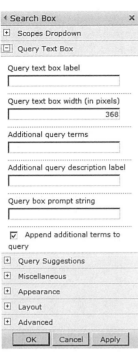

FIGURE 8-22 The numerous Query Text Box properties of the Search Box Web Part.

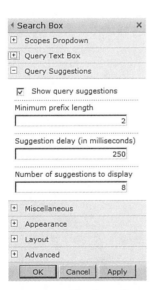

FIGURE 8-23 The Query Suggestions section of the Search Box Web Part contains default values.

The Miscellaneous section of the Search Box Web Part, shown in Figure 8-24, contains the most useful properties, some of which you should set if you are creating a custom search results page. Many of the properties are self-explanatory, such as Search Button Image URL, should you wish to display an image for the Search button.

A useful property is the ability to turn off the Advanced Search link. If you do not want to build an Advanced Search page, turning off this setting will avoid confusion when users click the Advanced Search link and receive an error message because the page does not exist. If you do want to build an Advanced Search page, you may set the URL to an Advanced Search page within the Pages Library in the search center.

The default URL for the Target Search Results Page URL is *results.aspx*. This property displays the *results.aspx* page, which is the same page the All Sites tab uses. So when users perform a search, even though the Web Part is configured to use the correct scope, the results are displayed on the incorrect page. Change this page to *AdventureWorks.aspx* for this example or to your custom search results page.

FIGURE 8-24 The Miscellaneous properties of the Search Box Web Part allow you to refine the behavior and configure the Web Part to display the results on the correct search page.

Search Core Results Web Part

The Search Core Results Web Part is where the results of your search are actually displayed. This Web Part displays a title that is the hyperlink to the ECT profile page, an icon showing the type of result, a summary description with highlighted keywords, and the full URL to the item.

As previously explained, the profile page consists of two Web Parts: the Business Data Item Builder Web Part and the Business Data Item Web Part. The Business Data Item Builder Web Part uses the URL of the search result and takes the parameter (in this case, the customer ID) and stores it temporarily within the hidden Web Part. The Business Data Item Builder Web Part contains a Web Part connection to the Business Data Item, allowing the Business Data Item to display a specific row of data.

Along with the results, you will see text showing the number of items returned in the top-left corner, providing you with an estimate of how many results to page through or refine. In the top-right corner is a link to the RSS feed for the search results, an alert notification icon, and an icon allowing you to search the same location again using Windows Explorer. Configuring an alert of the search results will send an email notification when the search results change. For instance, if you were searching products for a red-framed mountain bike, and suddenly a new red-framed mountain bike was added to your product catalog, the next time your external content was crawled, you would receive an email notifying you of the addition. The alert functionality does not work within claims-based authenticated web applications. The RSS feed is also a suitable way to keep track of the results changing through an RSS viewer, such as the one built into Microsoft Outlook. The icon at the far right allows you to perform the search again through Windows Explorer. When you click the icon for the first time, you are prompted to download and install a *Search.odx* file. Figure 8-25 shows the dialog box prompting you to add this search connector to Windows.

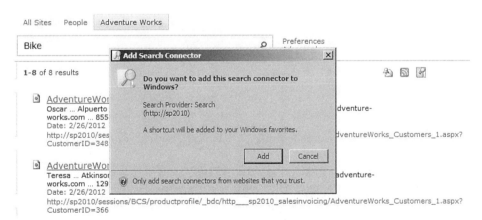

FIGURE 8-25 Add the search connector to Windows to allow searches to be performed from Windows Explorer.

Once the control has been added, through your Favorites within Windows Explorer, you are able to search the search scope again without having to open your browser and navigate to the SharePoint search center. Double-clicking one of the search results opens the browser window and displays the profile page for the row that was double-clicked. Figure 8-26 displays the results of a BCS search on the keyword *mountain* using Windows Explorer.

FIGURE 8-26 Results from a BCS search using Windows Explorer.

If you click the Alert Me option, you are taken to a page where you can configure the alert for new additions or changes to the search results. Note that you can configure the alert for other users besides yourself either by email or by SMS. Figure 8-27 shows the New Alert configuration page.

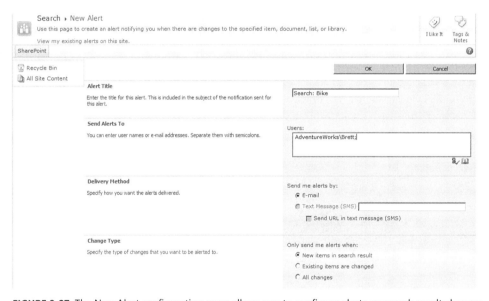

FIGURE 8-27 The New Alert configuration page allows you to configure alerts on search result changes.

Clicking the RSS Feed icon immediately displays an RSS feed view of the search results. Using the RSS feed is a useful way to redisplay the results within another part of SharePoint or in an external application such as Microsoft Outlook. The Data View Web Part (DVWP) within SharePoint Designer allows you to display and reconfigure the RSS results, providing a Web Part of BCS search results that can be displayed on another SharePoint webpage. Figure 8-28 shows the RSS view of a BCS search.

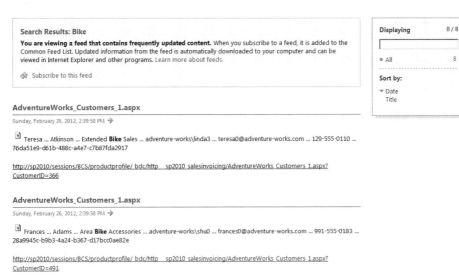

Search Results: Bike

You are viewing a feed that contains frequently updated content. When you subscribe to a feed, it is added to the Common Feed List. Updated information from the feed is automatically downloaded to your computer and can be viewed in Internet Explorer and other programs. Learn more about feeds.

Subscribe to this feed

Displaying 8 / 8

All 8

Sort by:
Date
Title

AdventureWorks_Customers_1.aspx

Sunday, February 26, 2012, 2:39:58 PM

Teresa ... Atkinson ... Extended **Bike** Sales ... adventure-works\linda3 ... teresa0@adventure-works.com ... 129-555-0110 ... 76da51e9-d61b-488c-a4e7-c7b87fda2917

http://sp2010/sessions/BCS/productprofile/ bdc/http___sp2010_salesinvoicing/AdventureWorks_Customers_1.aspx?CustomerID=366

AdventureWorks_Customers_1.aspx

Sunday, February 26, 2012, 2:39:58 PM

Frances ... Adams ... Area **Bike** Accessories ... adventure-works\shu0 ... frances0@adventure-works.com ... 991-555-0183 ... 28a9945c-b9b3-4a24-b367-d17bcc0ae82e

http://sp2010/sessions/BCS/productprofile/ bdc/http___sp2010_salesinvoicing/AdventureWorks_Customers_1.aspx?CustomerID=491

FIGURE 8-28 An RSS view of the BCS search results allows you to view search results through an RSS viewer.

You can configure the Search Core Results Web Part to show the results from a specific search scope. You may also customize it to improve the display of the search results using Extensible Stylesheet Language Transformations (XSLT).

One of the first properties you should set to enable the Web Part to display the correct results is the Search Scope property. Set this property to the name of the search scope you configured in the SharePoint 2010 Central Administration website. The Search Scope property resides in the Location Properties section of the Search Core Results Web Part property pane, as shown in Figure 8-29. The location choices include Internet Search Results, Internet Search Suggestions, Local Search Results, Local People Search Results, and Local FAST Search Results, which are federated connectors defined within the service application.

FIGURE 8-29 The Location Properties section of the Search Core Results Web Part, showing federated connectors.

The Display Properties section provides property settings that will affect the sorting of the results, the number of items returned on a search results page, the number of characters to show within the summary description of the search results, and the number of characters within the URL. You can also make modifications to the Fetched Properties, allowing other managed metadata properties to be displayed. An XSL editor allows properties such as sorting, conditional formatting, and branding of the search results. Branding the search results is especially useful within an Internet-facing SharePoint site, where you want the results to match that of the company brand within the website. Click the XSL Editor button to display a dialog box showing the XSLT within the browser. The XSLT from the Share-Point XSLT editor is unclear, without any structured formatting. Use SharePoint Designer or Visual Studio to more easily make modifications to the XSLT prior to copying and pasting the modified XSLT back into the XSL editor. Figure 8-30 shows the Display Properties within the Search Core Results Web Part.

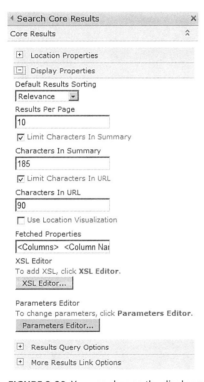

FIGURE 8-30 You can change the display properties of the Search Core Results Web Part.

The Results Query Options section provides the locale settings and Cross-Web Part Query ID. Sometimes it is possible to have multiple Search Box Web Parts and Search Core Results Web Parts on the same page. Setting the query ID allows each query to be mapped to the correct Search Core Results Web Part.

You can check options to set the removal of Duplicate Results, Enable Search Stemming, or Ignore Noise Words within the search.

Occasionally, you will find the Search Core Results Web Part providing a slightly different function than is intended. You can use the Search Core Results Web Part as an alternative to the Content Query Web Part, to enable you to aggregate content anywhere within the farm. You can provide a permanent search term in the Fixed Keyword Query and Append Text to Query boxes for this purpose. Figure 8-31 displays the Results Query Options of the Search Core Results Web Part.

FIGURE 8-31 The Results Query Options section of the Search Core Results Web Part.

In the More Results Link Options section, select the Show More Results Link to provide a link to show more results than the maximum per page. You can also type your own word for the more results link in the More Results Link Text Label text box.

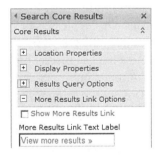

FIGURE 8-32 The More Results Link section of the Search Core Results Web Part.

The Search Core Results Web Part is an Ajax Web Part, just like many other Web Parts available within SharePoint 2010. You will find that the Ajax options allow you to specify in seconds how often the Web Part should refresh its results without performing a page postback.

See Also *You can find more information about the Ajax options in Chapter 6.*

The Miscellaneous section, shown in Figure 8-33, contains a number of properties, including Highest Result Page, Display Discovered Definition (which displays the keyword you search for), Show Search Results, Show Action Links, and Show Messages. Beyond those properties, notice that you can specify whether to show sample data, which helps you customize the look and feel of the Web Part's XSLT.

FIGURE 8-33 The Miscellaneous properties of the Search Core Results Web Part.

Note You can modify the search results page only within the browser and not with SharePoint Designer because it is a publishing page based on a page layout. Pages in the search center use the following four page layouts: Advanced Search, People Search Results, Search Box, and Search Results. When you create a new page in the search center, by default it will use the Search Results page layout. SharePoint Designer can modify only wiki pages, Web Part pages, HTML pages, and plain ASPX pages. Attempting to modify a publishing page with SharePoint Designer will cause SharePoint Designer to prompt you to modify the Search Results page layout. A search site created from the Basic Search Center site template does not contain publishing pages, nor does it contain tabs. Pages in a Basic Search Center site are Web Part pages and can be modified using SharePoint Designer.

Amending the Search XSLT

You may amend the XLST of the Search Core Results Web Part for several reasons:

- You want to display custom Cascading Style Sheets (CSS) classes to allow modifications to the formatting of the results to be applied.

- You want to make changes to the results layout by modifying the XSLT templates to include a managed property that you have defined.

- You want to conditionally change a search result based on a specific keyword.

Before you begin to modify the XSLT within the Search Core Results Web Part, it is recommended that you copy the default XSLT and paste and save it into a Notepad file so you can reset the XSLT to the default should you need to. Changing the XSLT is not straightforward, and it is possible to break the results page, so having a backup will at least allow you to reset it to begin working again.

To amend the XSLT, copy the existing XSLT and paste it into a XSLT editor such as Microsoft Visual Studio or XML Notepad 2007. An XSLT editor will provide you with search, tree views, edit and redo operations, IntelliSense, and scheme validation, which the Search Core Results Web Part XSL Editor pane cannot do.

To modify the contents, edit the Search Core Results Web Part, expand the Display Properties category, and click XSL Editor to display the XSLT, as shown in Figure 8-34.

 Note If the XSL Editor button is not active, clear the Use Location Visualization check box.

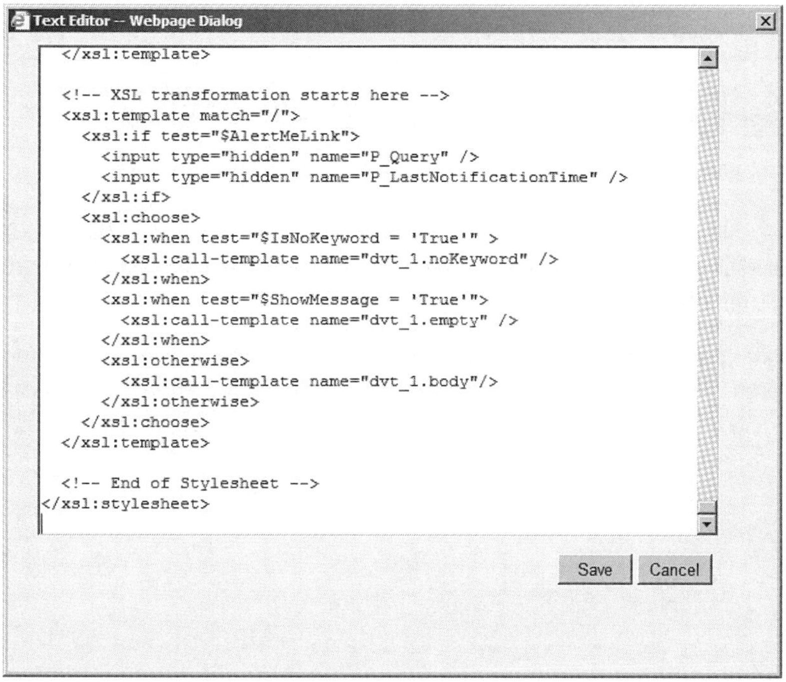

```
Text Editor -- Webpage Dialog                              x

  </xsl:template>

  <!-- XSL transformation starts here -->
  <xsl:template match="/">
    <xsl:if test="$AlertMeLink">
      <input type="hidden" name="P_Query" />
      <input type="hidden" name="P_LastNotificationTime" />
    </xsl:if>
    <xsl:choose>
      <xsl:when test="$IsNoKeyword = 'True'" >
        <xsl:call-template name="dvt_1.noKeyword" />
      </xsl:when>
      <xsl:when test="$ShowMessage = 'True'">
        <xsl:call-template name="dvt_1.empty" />
      </xsl:when>
      <xsl:otherwise>
        <xsl:call-template name="dvt_1.body"/>
      </xsl:otherwise>
    </xsl:choose>
  </xsl:template>

  <!-- End of Stylesheet -->
</xsl:stylesheet>

                                    Save    Cancel
```

FIGURE 8-34 It is recommended that you use an editor other than the XSL Editor of the Search Core Results Web Part to make changes to the XSLT.

Highlight the entire XSLT and copy it into your editor. Figure 8-35 shows the XSLT in Visual Studio. Notice that you can collapse the XSLT to provide better navigation using the shortcut key combination Ctrl+M+L.

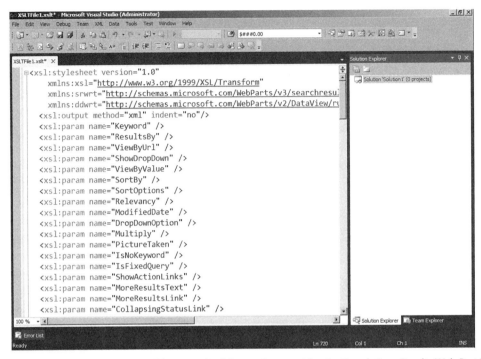

FIGURE 8-35 Visual Studio provides a good editing environment for the Search Core Results Web Part XSLT.

The first part of the XSLT defines parameters, which are values that will be used within the XSLT. Then you will find the XSL templates, which you can liken to subroutines that are units of XSL. You pass control to the XSL templates by using the *xsl:call-template* tag.

Most of the templates provide transformations of the XSLT; however, the root template determines which template is chosen based upon conditions. If a keyword isn't provided within your search (so effectively, you are doing an empty search), you will see a message indicating that nothing was found, as shown in Figure 8-36.

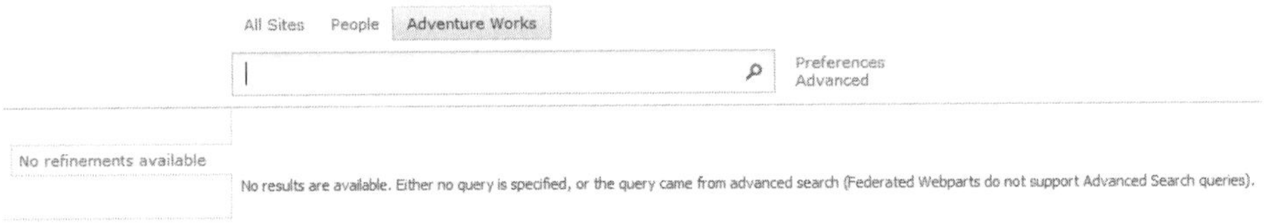

All Sites   People   Adventure Works

Preferences
Advanced

No refinements available

No results are available. Either no query is specified, or the query came from advanced search (Federated Webparts do not support Advanced Search queries).

FIGURE 8-36 These results are from an empty search.

When a keyword is provided, the XSLT acts accordingly and continues to run. The contents of the root element are as follows:

```
<xsl:template match="/">
  <xsl:variable name="Rows" select="/All_Results/Result" />
  <xsl:variable name="RowCount" select="count($Rows)" />
  <xsl:variable name="IsEmpty" select="$RowCount = 0" />
  <xsl:if test="$AlertMeLink">
    <input type="hidden" name="P_Query" />
    <input type="hidden" name="P_LastNotificationTime" />
  </xsl:if>
  <xsl:choose>
    <xsl:when test="$IsNoKeyword = 'True'" >
      <xsl:call-template name="dvt_1.noKeyword" />
    </xsl:when>
    <xsl:when test="$IsEmpty">
      <xsl:call-template name="dvt_1.empty" />
    </xsl:when>
    <xsl:otherwise>
      <xsl:call-template name="dvt_1.body"/>
    </xsl:otherwise>
  </xsl:choose>
</xsl:template>
```

Displaying a collapsed view of the XSLT within Visual Studio is useful, as you can easily see where each of the templates starts and finishes. If no keyword was entered, the dvt_1.nokeyword template is applied and returns the message shown in Figure 8-37.

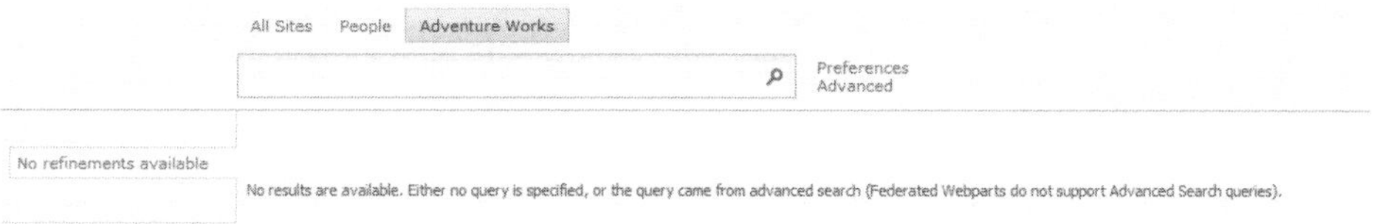

FIGURE 8-37 This message appears when no results are returned because a keyword wasn't provided.

If a successful search was executed but no results are returned, the dvt_1.empty template is given control. It returns a message indicating that no results matching your search were found, as shown in Figure 8-38.

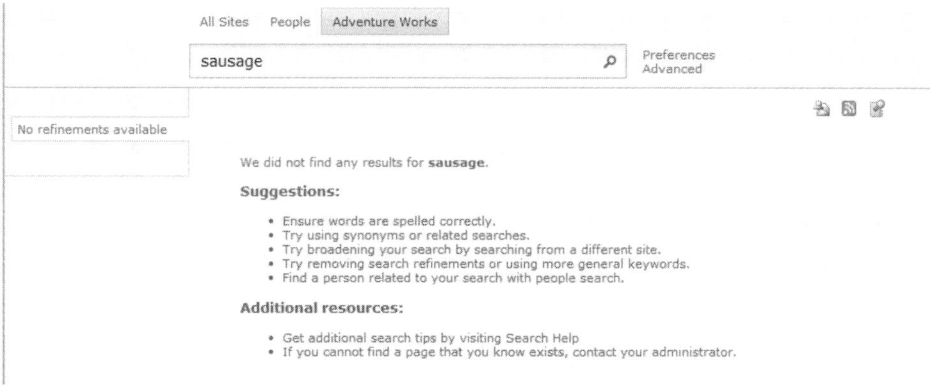

FIGURE 8-38 This message appears when no results are available because the keyword wasn't found.

If search results are returned, one of the first templates to be called is dvt_1.body, which displays a summary such as "1-8 of 8 Results." Then the Result template is called, which displays an icon, title, description, and metadata, as shown in Figure 8-39.

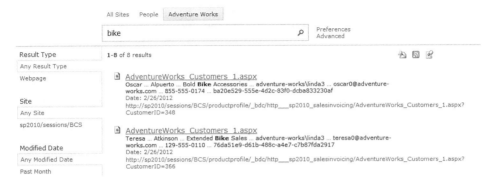

FIGURE 8-39 A successful search showing results with image, title, description, and metadata returned.

Within the Results template, three more templates are called:

- **HitHighlighting** This template is responsible for applying highlighting to keywords. Within the HitHighlighting template, you can make changes to the first, second, third, and so on highlighted keyword. C0 is the first, C1 is the second, C2 is the third, and so on. You can change the style for each keyword. Figure 8-40 shows the template C0 modified to change the highlighting color.

```
<xsl:template match="ddd">...</xsl:template>
<xsl:template match="c0">
  <strong>
    <b style="color: #990066">
    <xsl:value-of select="."/>
  </strong>
</xsl:template>
<xsl:template match="c1">
  <strong>
    <xsl:value-of select="."/>
  </strong>
</xsl:template>
```

FIGURE 8-40 Applying color to the first returned keyword found within the search results.

- **DisplaySize** This template determines the size of the results.

- **DisplayString** This template determines the string for the results, such as the Author and Last Modified date.

Once you complete your modifications to the XSLT, make sure that you copy and paste the results back into the XSLT editor of the Search Core Results Web Part.

Creating Advanced Search Properties

If users perform a search and find that they receive too many search results, they can refine the results using an advanced search. If you created a custom search page, the Search Box Web Part on the custom search page contains a link to the Advanced Search page. However, the link to the Advanced Search page is likely to be broken, unless you already provided the name of a page within the Search Box Web Part property Advanced Search Page URL.

To provide a custom Advanced Search page, first create a page within the search center, and then on your custom search page, map the Advanced link in the Search Box Web Part to the URL of your custom Advanced Search page. Return to your custom Advanced Search page, where you can either change the page layout to Advanced Search using the Page Layout command on the Page ribbon tab or add an Advanced Search Box Web Part.

The Advanced Search Box Web Part provides refinements by property, and these properties are categorized by the type of document, language, and other managed properties. Just as with the Search Box Web Part, you set the scope and the URL of the page to display the results. Figure 8-41 shows the Advanced Search Box Web Part added to the custom Advanced Search page.

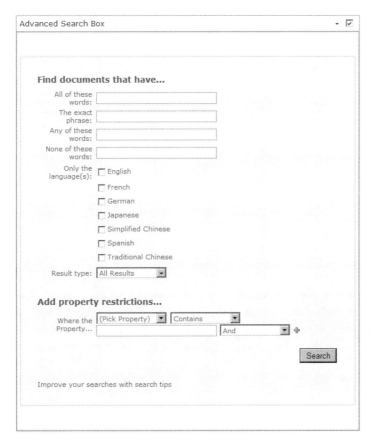

FIGURE 8-41 You can add the Advanced Search Box to the custom Advanced Search Web Part page.

You can set the search scope can in the Scopes section of the Advanced Search Box toolbar. The Properties section contains the Properties text box, as shown in Figure 8-42. If you click in the Properties text box, and then click the ellipses to the right of the box, a Text Editor dialog box opens where you will see the properties. Back up the properties by copying the properties in the dialog box and saving them to a *.txt* file. Once you have performed a backup, highlight the full contents, and then copy and paste the contents into your XML editor.

FIGURE 8-42 The Scopes and Properties sections of the Advanced Search Box Web Part.

With the XML now within an XML editor, notice that each property consists of a *PropertyDef* tag and a *PropertyRef* tag. The *PropertyDef* tag registers the managed property and the *PropertyRef* tag as a child of the *ResultType* tag, which is used for the visualization. Figure 8-43 displays the XML within Visual Studio .NET and shows the default *PropertyDefs* and *PropertyRefs* prior to adding a custom managed property.

See Also *Managed properties were discussed at the beginning of this chapter.*

```
XSLTFile1.xslt*  X
      </Languages>
      <PropertyDefs>
        <PropertyDef Name="Path" DataType="text" DisplayName="URL"/>
        <PropertyDef Name="Size" DataType="integer" DisplayName="Size (by
        <PropertyDef Name="Write" DataType="datetime" DisplayName="Last N
        <PropertyDef Name="FileName" DataType="text" DisplayName="Name"/>
        <PropertyDef Name="Description" DataType="text" DisplayName="Desc
        <PropertyDef Name="Title" DataType="text" DisplayName="Title"/>
        <PropertyDef Name="Author" DataType="text" DisplayName="Author"/>
        <PropertyDef Name="DocSubject" DataType="text" DisplayName="Subje
        <PropertyDef Name="DocKeywords" DataType="text" DisplayName="Keyw
        <PropertyDef Name="DocComments" DataType="text" DisplayName="Comm
        <PropertyDef Name="CreatedBy" DataType="text" DisplayName="Create
        <PropertyDef Name="ModifiedBy" DataType="text" DisplayName="Last
      </PropertyDefs>
      <ResultTypes>
        <ResultType DisplayName="All Results" Name="default">
          <KeywordQuery/>
          <PropertyRef Name="Author" />
          <PropertyRef Name="Description" />
          <PropertyRef Name="FileName" />
          <PropertyRef Name="Size" />
          <PropertyRef Name="Path" />
100 %
```

FIGURE 8-43 The default *PropertyDefs* and *PropertyRefs* before adding the custom managed property to the XSLT.

The managed property that you created earlier in this chapter is called Productname. To add Productname to the Advanced Search, create a *PropertyDef* element setting the DataType to "text" and the DisplayName to "Product Name". Then add a *PropertyRef* element to the All Results *ResultType*, so the property is available in the drop-down list on the Advanced Search page. Figure 8-44 displays the completed XML.

After you copy and paste the XML back into the Properties field of the Advanced Search Box Web Part, you can select and provide a value for your managed property. Figure 8-45 shows the completed Advanced Search Box Web Part.

```
    <PropertyDef Name="Title" DataType="text" DisplayName="Title"/>
    <PropertyDef Name="Author" DataType="text" DisplayName="Author"/>
    <PropertyDef Name="DocSubject" DataType="text" DisplayName="Subject"/>
    <PropertyDef Name="DocKeywords" DataType="text" DisplayName="Keywords"/>
    <PropertyDef Name="DocComments" DataType="text" DisplayName="Comments"/>
    <PropertyDef Name="CreatedBy" DataType="text" DisplayName="Created By"/>
    <PropertyDef Name="ModifiedBy" DataType="text" DisplayName="Last Modified
    <PropertyDef Name="Productname" DataType="text" DisplayName="Title"/>
  </PropertyDefs>
  <ResultTypes>
    <ResultType DisplayName="All Results" Name="default">
      <KeywordQuery/>
      <PropertyRef Name="Author" />
      <PropertyRef Name="Productname" />
      <PropertyRef Name="Description" />
      <PropertyRef Name="FileName" />
      <PropertyRef Name="Size" />
      <PropertyRef Name="Path" />
      <PropertyRef Name="Write" />
      <PropertyRef Name="CreatedBy" />
      <PropertyRef Name="ModifiedBy" />
```

FIGURE 8-44 The completed modified XML to add a managed property allowing searches to be refined.

FIGURE 8-45 The completed Advanced Search Box Web Part after the XSLT changes were made.

This chapter mainly covered SharePoint Server Search 2010, which provides you with the ability to connect to external data via BCS. FAST search provides many other performance and feature improvements, such as Deeper Refinements and Thumbnail Previews. The Indexer offers other external database connectors, such as the Lotus Notes database connector and database connector. FAST also provides a JDBC connector, allowing other structured external databases to be crawled directly.

See Also *You can find more information about FAST Search Server 2010 connectors on the TechNet website at* http://technet.microsoft.com/en-us/library/ee781286.aspx.

Summary

In this chapter, you explored how correctly configuring the default search in Microsoft SharePoint can save organizations valuable time and money. You learned how to index search results and provide refined search capabilities through content sources and search scopes. You also examined how to build a custom search page, configure search tabs, and set the Search Web Part properties to return results in a more refined manner. Finally, you modified the XSLT of the Search Core Results Web Part and the XML of the Advanced Search Web Part to display a configured managed metadata property.

CHAPTER 9

Using External Data in User Profiles

In this chapter, you will:

- Explore User Profile service applications

- Learn how to import user profile properties from external systems

- Use external data and My Sites together

- Understand Duet Enterprise for Microsoft SharePoint and SAP

Users of SharePoint today are likely familiar with social networking sites such as LinkedIn, Facebook, and Twitter. If you apply the same social networking technologies within a private organization, the result can be an extremely powerful way to share information among users throughout the business. User profile information in Microsoft SharePoint Server 2010 enables users to find others easily through SharePoint Server 2010 people searches, SharePoint content can be targeted to audiences, and users can discover other users through My Sites.

User profile information can be populated by users within SharePoint via their My Sites. When you first create your My Site, you have the opportunity to complete your profile and provide information such as the skills you have, who you report to, your colleagues, and which office you are based out of. Even without having a My Site, a user profile can be created. By having complete user profile information, you are able to easily discover useful business information from your colleagues. For example, you may have a need to hire an employee with a specific skill, such as copywriting ability. Using a people search, you may be able to discover existing employees who have that skill or appropriate accreditation.

In addition to easily discovering other users, as a user yourself with a complete user profile, you will find that the information you view throughout SharePoint becomes more relevant to you. You can configure audience targeting to create audiences of users with commonalities among parts of their profiles. For example, you may have a New York audience for users based at your New York office, and perhaps a Developers audience for users with development skills. With audience-enabled lists, when you create a list item, you can target that item to a particular audience. All users with appropriate permissions will be able to view the content, even if it is targeted to an audience that they are not a member of. However, when you aggregate that content using a tool such as the Content Query

Web Part (CQWP), you are able to target the rolled-up items to the logged-on user, meaning different content will be rolled up for each user, as user profiles differ.

You can also use audience targeting with Web Parts, allowing you to show entire Web Parts only to specific audiences. Consider a Business Data List Web Part configured to display data specific to the New York office. Users based in the London office may not find the information valuable at all and therefore don't need to see the Web Part. You may choose to display the Web Part only to users who are a member of the New York audience. Users who set their user profile location field to New York become members of the New York audience.

As with many things in SharePoint, if users don't adopt the technology and don't complete their user profiles, the solution becomes less useful. That said, much of the user profile information may already exist elsewhere within your organization. Some of it may be stored in Active Directory (AD), but other external data sources, such as human resource (HR) databases or enterprise relationship programs (ERP) such as SAP, may contain more authoritative and up-to-date user profile data. You can connect to this external data using Business Connectivity Services (BCS), allowing user profiles to be populated from the external data source.

In this chapter, you will first learn about the benefits of using SharePoint 2010 features such as people search and audience targeting. You will then learn how to configure the User Profile service application both for AD and an external data source. Finally, you will look at a specific example of obtaining user profile information from a SAP human resources data source.

Audience Targeting

Audience targeting in SharePoint Server 2010 is often confused with SharePoint permissions. Permissions in SharePoint can be set for a user or a group, granting a certain level of permission for an object such as a list item. If you do not have permission to read the list item, you will not be able to view it while logged into SharePoint with your own credentials. Audience targeting is different—it is about providing content that is of relevance to you based upon your user profile. If you have an interest in car racing, rugby, and fine foods, information about these topics will likely be of interest to you, whereas information about bicycles may not. If you apply that analogy to a business, you can see how beneficial it can be to provide users with information targeted to their interests. Perhaps you don't have time to read announcements from every department or team site within your SharePoint environment on a daily basis, as not every announcement is relevant to you. There is nothing preventing you from reading all announcements if you choose to navigate to every announcements list, but a rollup tool such as the Content Query Web Part (CQWP) enables you to view just the announcements targeted to an audience that you are a member of, saving you time and energy.

You configure audiences in SharePoint using the User Profile service application settings available through the SharePoint 2010 Central Administration website, as shown in Figure 9-1. Within the People category is the Manage Audiences link, which provides you with the options necessary to configure your audiences.

FIGURE 9-1 You can configure audiences in the User Profile service application settings within the SharePoint Central Administration website.

Click Manage Audiences in the People section to see a list of your compiled audiences and the option to create a new audience. You create audiences with a rule that determines how each user becomes a member. The rule can be based upon a domain group that the user is a member of or one or more properties that are set in the user's profile. A default audience exists that includes every user and is listed as All Site Users.

After you click New Audience, you are able to set a name for the new audience, a description of the audience, the audience's owner, and the rules option. With the rules option, you have two choices: the user has to satisfy either all of the defined rules or any of them. For example, you could populate users in an audience based on their being a member of a Developers domain group or having .NET development skills. Selecting the Satisfy Any of the Rules option allows this to be the case, as this option is essentially an AND or an OR statement. Figure 9-2 shows the creation of a SharePoint Developers audience.

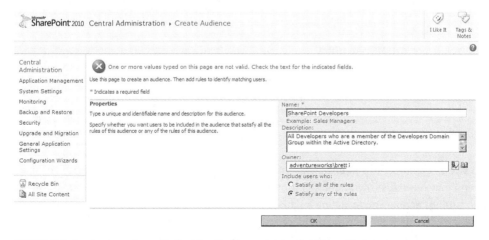

FIGURE 9-2 Create an audience in the User Profile service application settings.

When you click OK, you are taken to the Add Audience Rule page for your audience. Rules are based on the user, such as being a member of a Windows security group, or based on a property, such as a field within the user profile. Figure 9-3 shows the option to configure the user membership based on the user reporting to another user or being a member of a security group.

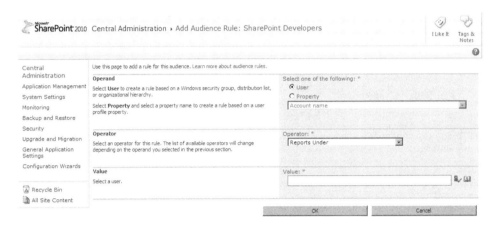

FIGURE 9-3 You can configure the audience rule based on user membership.

You may also configure the membership based on a user profile property. Figure 9-4 shows how the audience can be configured for users who have a particular skill listed in their profiles.

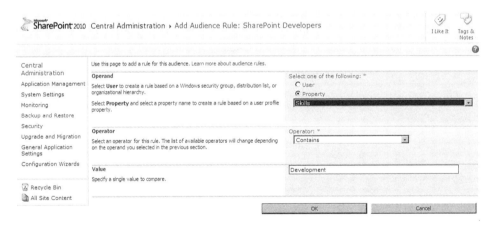

FIGURE 9-4 You can also configure audience membership based on a property.

Once you've created an audience, you'll need to compile it. Compiling the audience ensures that users who match the rule(s) you defined for the audience become members of the audience. Compilation settings enable you to define a schedule when new the compilation will run again. Because users may modify their profiles regularly to ensure that they become members of appropriate audiences, you should regularly run compilations.

Now that you have defined your audience, you can enable SharePoint lists or libraries to allow audience targeting. Enabling audience targeting creates another column in the list, allowing the audience to be targeted. You can enable audience targeting by navigating to each list, choosing List Settings from the ribbon, and then selecting the Enable Audience Targeting check box, as shown in Figure 9-5.

FIGURE 9-5 Select the Enable Audience Targeting check box in the List Settings section.

Once you have enabled this setting, as a user, you may target the list item to a specific audience or audiences. All users with permissions to the list will see the list item within the list, but when aggregating the list item using the CQWP, the list item may show up only if a user is a member of the particular audience. Figure 9-6 displays the Target Audiences field in a new announcement.

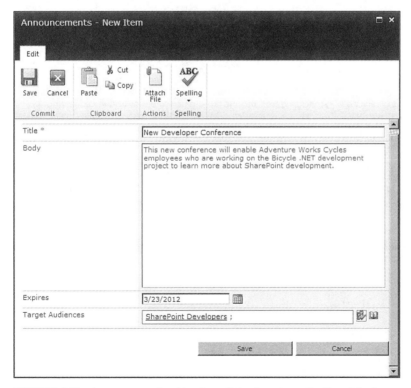

FIGURE 9-6 The Announcements – New Item dialog box shows the Target Audiences column.

The CQWP can roll up SharePoint list items or documents from sites within the current site collection. Items can be filtered based on a content type, Site Column value, or audience. To show aggregated content that is relevant to the logged-on user, you can configure the Web Part to roll up list items and then apply audience filtering. You do not need to specify which audience you would like to apply—you simply apply audience filtering. The logged-on user's profile will be cross-checked against the audiences listed in the aggregated results. Figure 9-7 shows a CQWP configured to roll up announcements from the current site collection and apply audience filtering.

FIGURE 9-7 The Content Query Web Part aggregates announcements and applies audience filtering.

Aggregated content can be audience targeted, as can entire Web Parts. The Advanced section of SharePoint Web Parts contains an Audience Targeting field. In the Target Audiences section, you can list all of the audiences that should be able to view the entire Web Part. All other users will not see the Web Part on the page. Figure 9-8 shows a Web Part configured to display only to the SharePoint Developers audience.

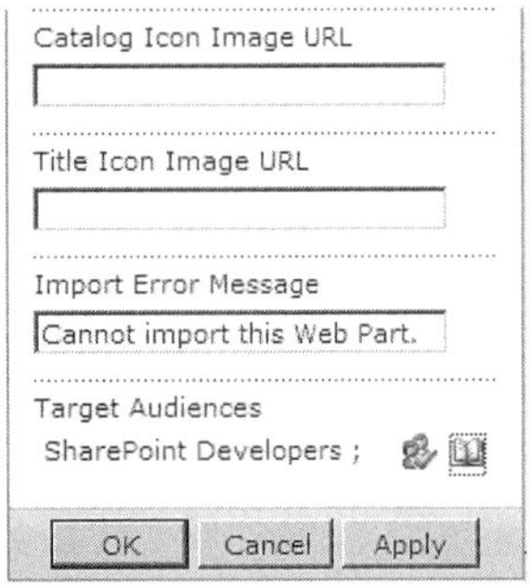

FIGURE 9-8 This Web Part is configured to appear only to the SharePoint Developers audience.

People Search

If the user profiles in your organization are populated, you're able to search for other users using keywords that match information stored in their SharePoint user profiles. Often, you'll want to search for users by a skill or interest documented in their profiles, rather than by first or last name. This type of search is successful only if users have taken the time to complete their user profile information. To perform a search, you can either navigate to your search center or search from within your own My Site. Figure 9-9 shows how to perform a search within My Site.

FIGURE 9-9 Using the people search within My Site.

The Enterprise search center by default contains a People tab as well as an All Sites tab. The People tab returns only users, whereas the All Sites tab returns content, including people from all content sources. Figure 9-10 displays the People search in a search center.

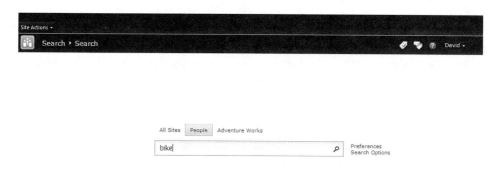

FIGURE 9-10 Use the People tab to perform a People search in a search center.

See Also *Content sources are discussed in detail in Chapter 8, "Finding Information from External Systems."*

The search results for a person returns their profile picture, About Me property, and Ask Me About property. The keyword that you searched on is highlighted, as shown in Figure 9-11.

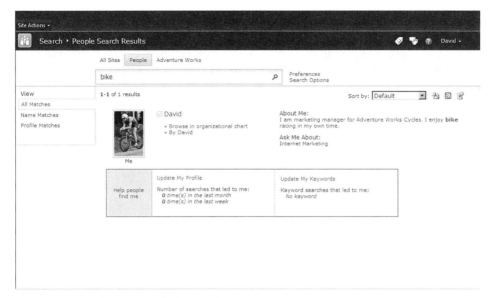

FIGURE 9-11 People search results in a search center.

People searches can be refined by Name Matches or Profile Matches, enabling you to reduce the number of people profiles returned by your search keyword. If you perform a search on yourself, you will see the Help People Find Me section, which allows you to view how many times you have been searched in the last week or month. It also shows the keywords used to find you, which is helpful information for improving your profile so that it may be found more easily.

Populating your user profile in SharePoint and keeping it up to date is a time-consuming process that is often not carried out. However, if you do take the time to populate your user profile, you will be able to see better results and receive targeted information when navigating SharePoint. You can create user profile properties in addition to the default ones for employees to complete, or you can import them from an external data source. The next section discusses how to configure the user profile import.

Introducing User Profile Service Applications

Service applications are new to SharePoint 2010 and provide a way of sharing services across web applications or farms. Each service application can provide a set of services to SharePoint packaged as a service application. This model allows for an improved SharePoint architecture, as services can be configured to run on the appropriate server within the farm.

See Also *Service applications are discussed in Chapter 3, "Creating and Maintaining Business Data Connectivity Service Applications."*

A service application can be configured to run on the most appropriate server within the farm. A processor-intensive service, such as Search, for example, may be configured to run on its own server within a large organization. The Business Data Connectivity Service and the User Profile Service can also be configured to be shared across farms.

The User Profile service application is not available in Microsoft SharePoint Foundation 2010, but it is available in Microsoft SharePoint Server 2010 Standard and Enterprise. The User Profile service application is responsible for My Sites, profile pages, social tagging, and audience targeting. You can start the User Profile Service by clicking the Manage Services on Server link. You then select the server on which you would like to start the service.

Active Directory (AD) contains user profile information that can be supplemented by an external data source, such as a human resources application. To configure an external data user profile synchronization connection, you must first have a successfully configured AD profile import.

See Also *Configuring the User Profile service application is a big task that is sometimes not performed correctly. TechNet provides a good step-by-step article on configuring the User Profile service application at* http://technet. microsoft.com/en-us/library/ee721050.aspx *as does many of the blog posts on Spence Harber's website,* www. harbar.net.

The Manage User Profile Service page on the SharePoint 2010 Central Administration website enables you to configure the connections to AD and external data sources as well as configure user properties, user profiles, organization profiles, audiences, and much more. You configure a connection to AD by clicking Configure Synchronization Connections. You can configure the Synchronization timer job to run periodically to synchronize the SharePoint user profile with AD and external data user profiles. Figure 9-1 displays the User Profile Service Application settings page.

Once you have configured the AD user profile import correctly and the import was successful, you can configure the import from Business Connectivity Services (BCS). Follow these steps to import user profile information using BCS:

1. Configure an external content type (ECT) for your user profile information from the external data source.

   See Also *For more information about configuring an ECT, see Chapter 4, "Defining External System Connections Using SharePoint Designer."*

2. Create a profile page for the ECT.

   See Also *For more information about creating a profile page, see Chapter 4.*

3. Create a Managed User Property field that maps the AD account information with the user profile information in your external data source.

4. Create a Business Data Connectivity (BDC) synchronization connection in the User Profile service application.

5. Create other managed user properties for any other column that you want to import.

6. Run a full synchronization on your external data synchronization connection.

Mapping External Data to User Profile Properties

You must create a managed user property so that the AD user profile can be related to the BDC user profile information. You may have within your ECT a column that is already related to each AD user profile, such as Employee ID or Social Security Number. However, if this is not the case, you can create either an attribute in AD or a new column in your database table. Often, applications such as Microsoft Dynamix CRM cannot be modified at the table level without compromising the product support agreement or risk of breaking product functionality. If this is the case, it may be easier to create an attribute in AD that will relate the data. In the Adventure Works HumanResources.Employee table, you will find a LoginID column that can be mapped to the sAMAccountName property in AD. For this mapping to work successfully, you will need to make sure that the LoginID column is marked as an identifier in your ECT.

> **Note** Any column in an ECT that you want to use to map to AD should be of the same type. The sAMAccountName property is of type string.

To create a new managed property, follow these steps:

1. On the SharePoint 2010 Central Administration website, click Manage Service Applications.

2. Click the link to open the User Profile service application.

3. Click Manage User Properties.

4. Click New Property to create a new managed user property.

5. Type a name such as **MyAWLoginID**.

6. Type a display name such as **Adventure Works Login ID**, as shown in Figure 9-12.

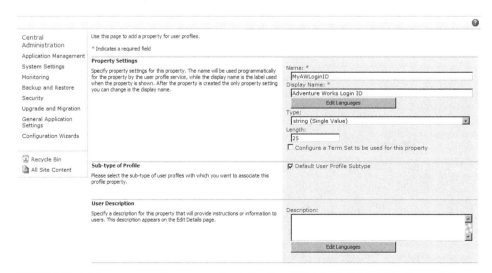

FIGURE 9-12 Adding a managed user property via the SharePoint Central Administration website.

7. Set the Source Data Connection to the Active Directory synchronization connection (Adventure Works Domain, in this example).

8. Select sAMAccountName as the Attribute.

9. Click Add to add the new mapping.

10. Click OK to complete the mapping, as shown in Figure 9-13.

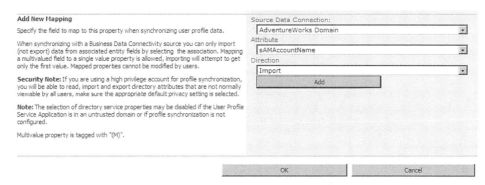

FIGURE 9-13 Completing the mapping of the managed user property.

You have now created a new user profile property called MyAWLoginID and set it to be populated by the user sAMAccountName from AD. You can map multiple properties from the ECT. Before you can do so, however, you need to configure the BDC synchronization connection so that you can select the columns from the ECT to map.

Business Data Connectivity Synchronization Connection

The BDC synchronization connection provides the User Profile service application with the connection settings it requires to import the user profile information from the external data source. By now, you have created an ECT that maps to the database table containing your user profile information. To create the BDC synchronization connection, follow these steps:

1. On the SharePoint 2010 Central Administration website, click Manage Service Applications.

2. Click the link to open the User Profile service application.

3. Click Configure Synchronization Connections.

4. Click Create New Connection.

5. Type a Connection Name, such as **Adventure Works User Information**.

6. In the Type section, select Business Data Connectivity.

7. Select an ECT using the lookup icon next to the Business Data Connectivity Entity field.

8. In the Return Item Property select MyAWLoginID, as shown in Figure 9-14.

9. Click OK.

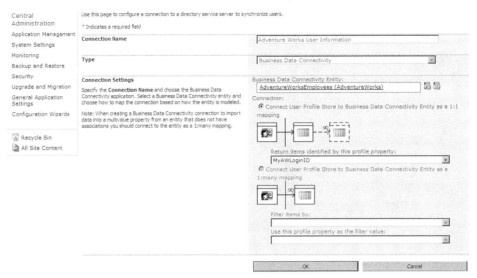

FIGURE 9-14 Create the BDC synchronization connection.

You can repeat this process for each property that you want to map to the user profile. For example, the Adventure Works Employees table contains a column (National ID) that contains an identification number similar to a Social Security number. The National ID would be a useful addition to the user profile information within SharePoint. You can create a new managed user profile property as shown in Figure 9-15.

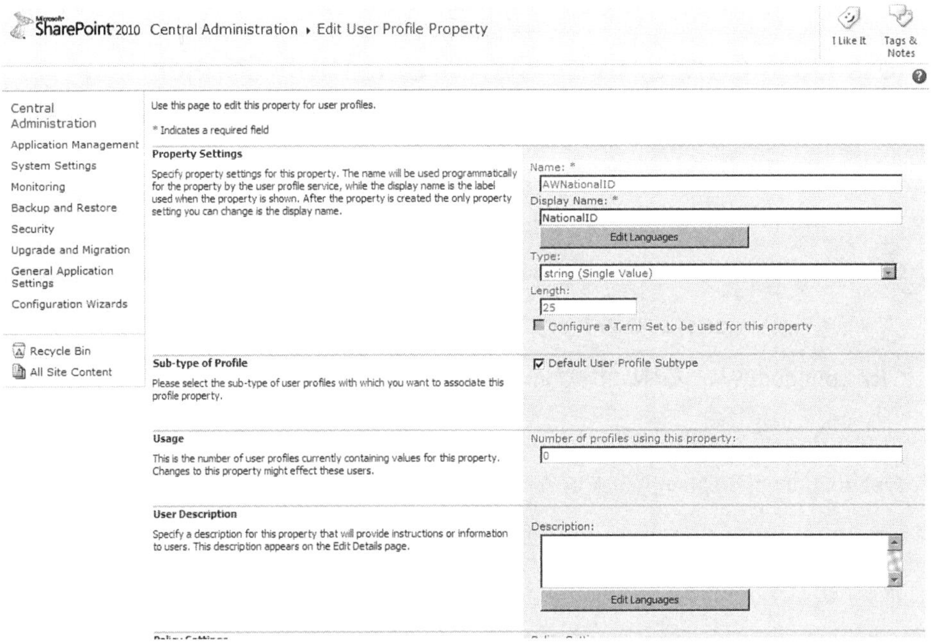

FIGURE 9-15 Create a new managed user property to map additional columns from the ECT.

Once you have provided a name, display name, and type for your new managed user property, you can refine the property by setting options such as whether the user is allowed to edit the property and whether the property will show on the Edit Details page. Finally, set the mapping to the BDC connection and the NationalIDNumber attribute. Repeat these steps for each column you want to import. Figure 9-16 shows the user property mapping to an ECT.

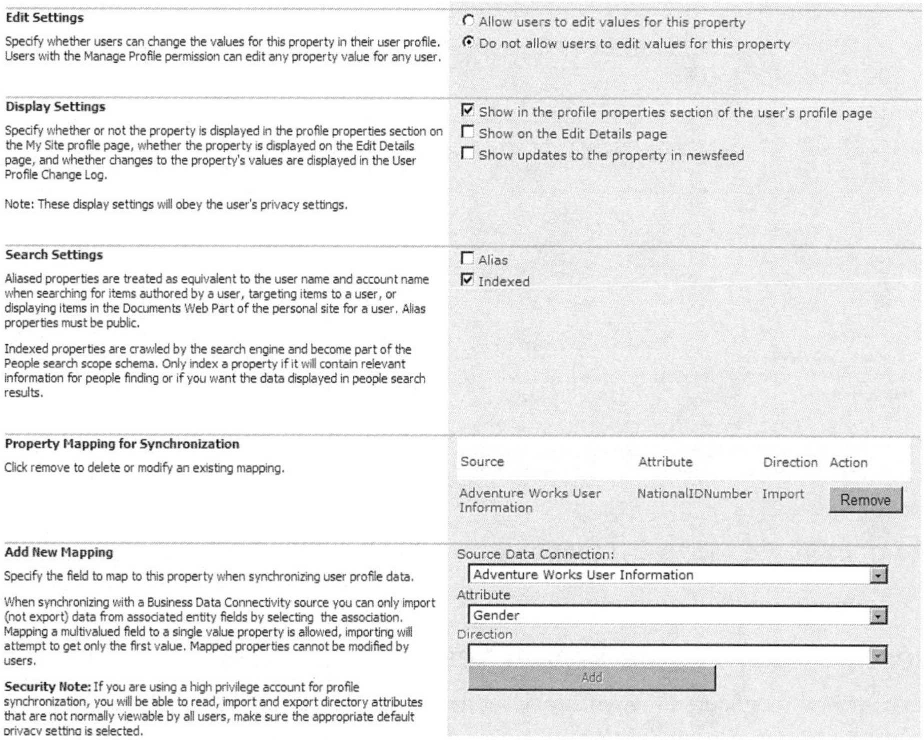

Edit Settings	
Specify whether users can change the values for this property in their user profile. Users with the Manage Profile permission can edit any property value for any user.	○ Allow users to edit values for this property ◉ Do not allow users to edit values for this property
Display Settings	
Specify whether or not the property is displayed in the profile properties section on the My Site profile page, whether the property is displayed on the Edit Details page, and whether changes to the property's values are displayed in the User Profile Change Log. Note: These display settings will obey the user's privacy settings.	☑ Show in the profile properties section of the user's profile page ☐ Show on the Edit Details page ☐ Show updates to the property in newsfeed
Search Settings	
Aliased properties are treated as equivalent to the user name and account name when searching for items authored by a user, targeting items to a user, or displaying items in the Documents Web Part of the personal site for a user. Alias properties must be public. Indexed properties are crawled by the search engine and become part of the People search scope schema. Only index a property if it will contain relevant information for people finding or if you want the data displayed in people search results.	☐ Alias ☑ Indexed
Property Mapping for Synchronization	
Click remove to delete or modify an existing mapping.	Source Attribute Direction Action Adventure Works User NationalIDNumber Import [Remove] Information
Add New Mapping	

Specify the field to map to this property when synchronizing user profile data.
 	
When synchronizing with a Business Data Connectivity source you can only import (not export) data from associated entity fields by selecting the association. Mapping a multivalued field to a single value property is allowed, importing will attempt to get only the first value. Mapped properties cannot be modified by users.
 	
Security Note: If you are using a high privilege account for profile synchronization, you will be able to read, import and export directory attributes that are not normally viewable by all users, make sure the appropriate default privacy setting is selected.
	Source Data Connection:
	`Adventure Works User Information ▼`
	Attribute
	`Gender ▼`
	Direction
	`▼`
	[Add]

FIGURE 9-16 Map additional properties for the user profile import.

You can check that the managed user property was created successfully by navigating to the Manage User Profiles link in the User Profile service application settings and conducting a user profile search, as shown in Figure 9-17.

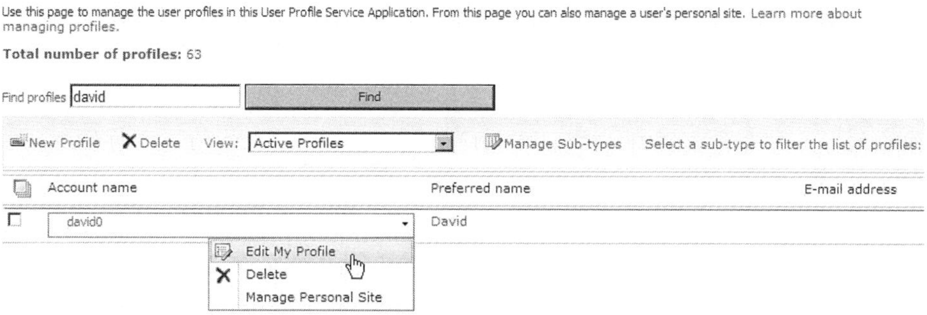

Use this page to manage the user profiles in this User Profile Service Application. From this page you can also manage a user's personal site. Learn more about managing profiles.

Total number of profiles: 63

Find profiles `david`   [Find]

📧 New Profile   ✖ Delete   View: `Active Profiles ▼`   🗇 Manage Sub-types   Select a sub-type to filter the list of profiles:

☐	Account name	Preferred name	E-mail address
☐	david0 ▼	David	

📝 Edit My Profile
✖ Delete
    Manage Personal Site

FIGURE 9-17 Searching user profile properties.

Perform a search for a user, such as David, from the Adventure Works database. From the search results, click the drop-down menu for the user, and then click Edit My Profile (shown in Figure 9-17). You will be able to see the NationalID managed user property, as shown in Figure 9-18.

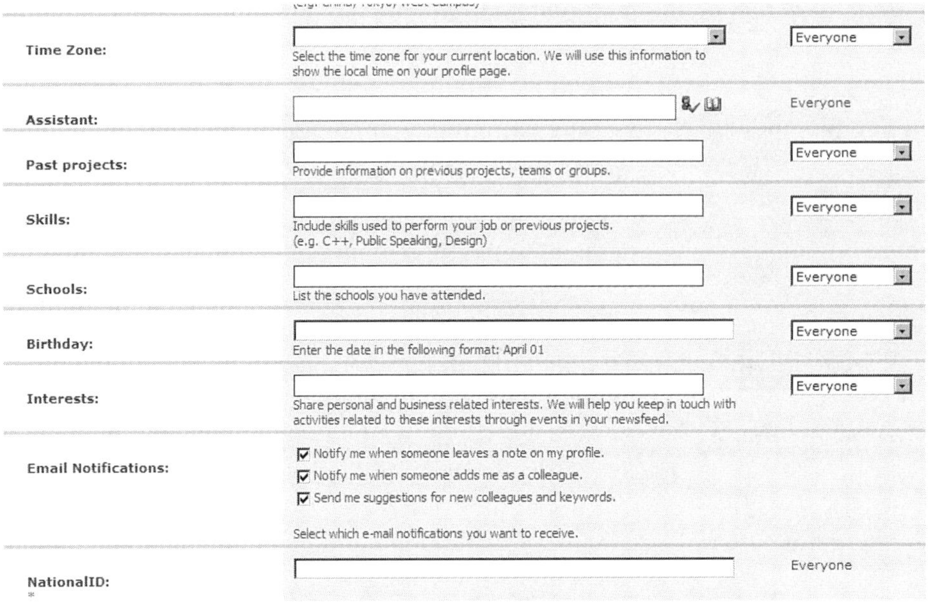

FIGURE 9-18 The newly created NationalID managed user property displays in the user profile.

Importing User Profile Properties from External Systems

Now that you have configured the synchronization connection and the managed user properties, you can import the user profile information. It is worth noting that you can include or exclude BCS connections through the Configure Synchronization Settings page in the User Profile service application, as shown in Figure 9-19.

To start the import of the data, click the Start Profile Synchronization link. You are prompted to choose between an Incremental synchronization and a Full synchronization, as shown in Figure 9-20. The Incremental synchronization will usually suffice, unless you are performing the operation for the first time or you want to reset the data store.

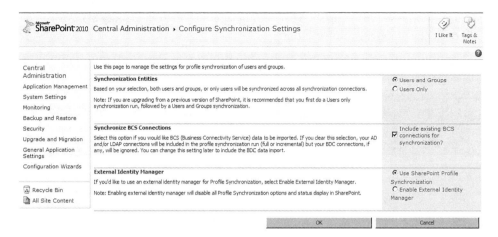

Use this page to manage the settings for profile synchronization of users and groups.

Synchronization Entities

Based on your selection, both users and groups, or only users will be synchronized across all synchronization connections.

Note: If you are upgrading from a previous version of SharePoint, it is recommended that you first do a Users only synchronization run, followed by a Users and Groups synchronization.

◉ Users and Groups
○ Users Only

Synchronize BCS Connections

Select this option if you would like BCS (Business Connectivity Service) data to be imported. If you clear this selection, your AD and/or LDAP connections will be included in the profile synchronization run (full or incremental) but your BDC connections, if any, will be ignored. You can change this setting later to include the BDC data import.

☑ Include existing BCS connections for synchronization?

External Identity Manager

If you'd like to use an external identity manager for Profile Synchronization, select Enable External Identity Manager.

Note: Enabling external identity manager will disable all Profile Synchronization options and status display in SharePoint.

◉ Use SharePoint Profile Synchronization
○ Enable External Identity Manager

[OK]   [Cancel]

Central Administration

Application Management

System Settings

Monitoring

Backup and Restore

Security

Upgrade and Migration

General Application Settings

Configuration Wizards

🗑 Recycle Bin
📄 All Site Content

FIGURE 9-19 The Configure Synchronization Settings BCS connection options.

Use this page to start a full or incremental Synchronization.

Start Profile Synchronization

Select Incremental Synchronization to start an incremental synchronization now. Only data that has changed in connected sources and User Profile will be synchronized.

Not recommended: In most case, Incremental sync should be sufficient. Selecting Full Synchronization is time and compute intensive and is not recommended unless absolutely required to reset data store in User Profile.

◉ Start Incremental Synchronization
○ Start Full Synchronization

[OK]   [Cancel]

FIGURE 9-20 Select a synchronization option: Incremental or Full.

When you click OK, the synchronization starts. It may take several minutes for the synchronization to complete. Once it has completed, you should find that the profiles have been populated with the information from the external system described by your ECT.

The synchronization itself doesn't provide great detail as to whether or not the synchronization was successful. For more detailed synchronization information, you can use Synchronization Service Manager 2010, which is part of Microsoft Forefront Identity Manager 2010, available from *www. microsoft.com/en-us/server-cloud/forefront/identity-manager.aspx*.

Important Making changes to the Forefront configuration using the Forefront Identity Manager (FIM) is completely unsupported and may actually break the relationship between SharePoint and FIM.

Figure 9-21 shows the Synchronization Service Manager of Forefront Identity Manager monitoring the synchronization of the user profile imports.

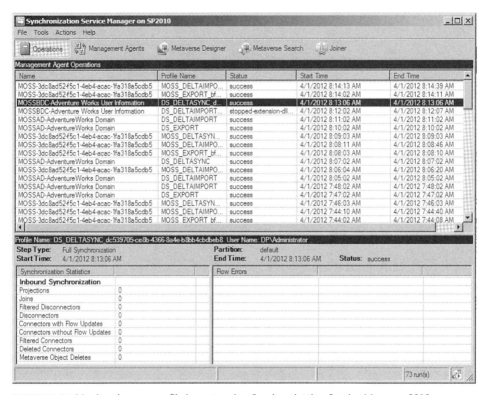

FIGURE 9-21 Monitor the user profile imports using Synchronization Service Manager 2010.

Using Duet Enterprise for Microsoft SharePoint and SAP

Business Connectivity Services (BCS) can connect to just about any external data source, whether you are connecting directly using providers for SQL, Oracle, ODBC, or web services. Often, some external data sources such as SAP require much work to provide the connectivity that may include authoring web services or custom connectors.

SAP is an enterprise resource planning application designed for enterprise organizations. It is broken into modules such as Customer Relationship Management, Materials Management, and Sales & Distribution. SAP is developed in a language called Advanced Business Application Programming (ABAP), which is similar to COBOL.

As SAP was among one of the most difficult data sources to connect to, Microsoft and SAP joined forces to develop Duet Enterprise. If you have the Enterprise edition of SharePoint Server 2010 and SAP NetWeaver 7.02 or higher, you can use Duet Enterprise to connect with SAP. Figure 9-22 displays a diagram of the services provided by Duet Enterprise.

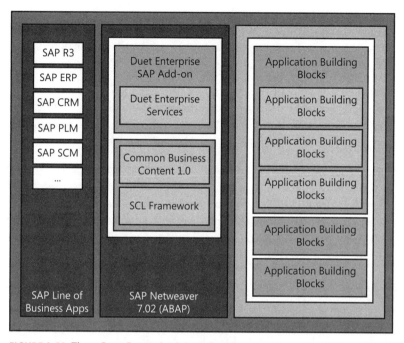

FIGURE 9-22 These Duet Enterprise 3.0 services are available within SAP and SharePoint 2010.

Connecting to SAP manually via BCS requires a lot of hard work. SAP provides a communication interface called Remote Function Call (RFC), which can be accessed via web services. The web services need to call the RFC to expose the SAP data via web methods that BCS can use. With Duet Enterprise, however, organizations that use SAP and the Enterprise edition of SharePoint Server 2010 can interact with SharePoint through SAP and SAP through SharePoint. The following tools are available with Duet Enterprise:

- Collaboration workspaces

- Contextual workflows

- Duet Enterprise sites

- Duet Enterprise Profile

- Duet Enterprise Reporting

Collaboration workspaces are templates allowing SharePoint Server 2010 users to create a SharePoint workspace around a particular topic such as an employee. Information about that employee can be accessed via connected Business Data Web Parts. Social information such as user profiles can be shown, and documents can be managed through document libraries.

Contextual workflows provide SharePoint Server 2010 and Office 2010 users with the ability to interact with SAP data via SharePoint workflows. Through Microsoft Outlook 2010 or SharePoint Server 2010, you are able to access rich contextual information, and approve workflows via email or SharePoint tasks. SAP workflows may also be extended through Microsoft SharePoint Designer 2010.

Duet Enterprise sites provide site templates including Customer, Employee, Product, Customer Quote, and Customer Inquiry. These templates are perhaps the most useful feature of Duet Enterprise. Security trimming through roles allows the content available to you as a user to be made available through external lists and libraries within a SharePoint site.

Duet Enterprise Profile enables you to extend the SharePoint Server user profile with SAP Enterprise Resource Planning (ERP) Human Capital Management (HCM) modules. Alerts on SAP data can be delivered through SharePoint, while SAP Person provides Education, Geography, Tenure, and Employment. My Timesheets is an example of an HCM module. Such information can be made available to SharePoint My Sites using the Duet Enterprise Profile service. Figure 9-23 shows a sample SAP ERP HCM Timesheet module.

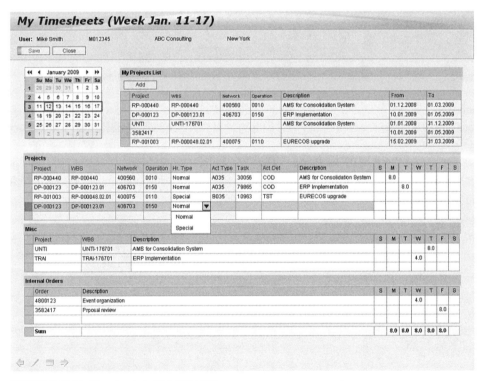

FIGURE 9-23 My Timesheets in SAP ERP HCM.

Duet Enterprise Reporting provides SharePoint users with the ability to schedule and personalize SAP reports. The reports are provided by SAP ERP but scheduled and delivered through SharePoint libraries. The reports can be taken offline through Microsoft SharePoint Workspace.

It is worth noting that Duet Enterprise does not just make SAP data available to SharePoint Server 2010 and Office 2010. Duet Enterprise also provides SharePoint functionality within SAP.

Displaying HR Information from SAP Applications in My Site

Earlier in this chapter, you learned how to create managed user profile properties when connecting to an external data source to provide an extended user profile. The extended user profile provides additional columns that can be made available through the user's My Site. The user can then view, search, and discover other users' profiles as well as modify their own profile. The SAP Employee module contains some columns that we recommend you map to the user profile managed properties. Table 9-1 lists these column mappings.

TABLE 9-1 User profile managed properties

SharePoint user property column name	SAP attribute	Description
SAP Employee ID	EmployeeIDDesp	Unique ID for the employee
SAP Position ID	IwemporgpositionCode	Position ID for the employee
SAP Position Description	IwemporgpositionCodeText	Employee's position or title
Hire Date	IwemporgstartDate	Employee's date of hire
Birth Date	IwempbasbirthDate	Employee's date of birth

See Also *To learn more about Duet Enterprise, visit* www.microsoft.com/duet, *where you can watch videos and obtain purchase information.*

Summary

In this chapter, you learned the benefits of using user profile information within SharePoint Server 2010. You initially explored audience targeting and how to configure this feature in the User Profile service application. You then examined the people search and how you can search on user profile properties beyond a user's first and last name.

This chapter's focus was configuring managed user properties and using the Business Data Connectivity (BDC) synchronization settings. You create managed user properties as a mapping between the Active Directory (AD) user profile and the external data user profile.

Finally, you explored how you can connect to SAP as an external data source using Duet Enterprise and how you can configure SAP to populate SharePoint Server user profiles.

CHAPTER 10

Exploring Office 365 and Connecting to External Data

In this chapter, you will:

- Learn about Microsoft Office 365

- Explore Business Connectivity Services functionality in Microsoft SharePoint Online

- Learn the differences between Business Connectivity Services in Office 365 and in on-premises SharePoint 2010 installations

- Build Business Connectivity Services solutions in SharePoint Online

In Chapter 8, "Finding Information from External Systems," you learned how to connect Microsoft Office 365 to external systems when using the Microsoft cloud platform. In this chapter, you will take a look at Microsoft SharePoint Online to get an understanding of how it compares to and contrasts with working with the on-premises version of SharePoint with regard to Business Connectivity Services (BCS). You will then work through an example of building a SharePoint Online solution.

Introducing Office 365

As previously stated, Office 365 is Microsoft's solution for communicating and collaborating in the cloud. Office 365 currently allows users to host SharePoint, Exchange, and Lync online. These cloud services enable businesses to change the way they think about their IT infrastructure and allow organizations to relieve the burden of requiring on-premises hardware and technical expertise. There are pros and cons for both options—running your own hardware and using services in the cloud. If you choose to run your own hardware, you have greater control of your environment, and this may be the only option for some secure environments. The downside is the cost of the hardware and the infrastructure to support it. However, Office 365 offers a compelling, useful solution if you want to use SharePoint without purchasing the hardware to support it and you can scale the solution as the demand requires, but you will be sacrificing some control.

SharePoint Online comes in two flavors: Standard and Dedicated. SharePoint Online Standard is the multitenant environment in which you are sharing hardware with other users. SharePoint Online Dedicated is where you get dedicated hosting and hardware to run your SharePoint environment in the cloud. There are a few differences between these options with regard to how much control you have over the environment and the degree to which you can customize it. Table 10-1 outlines some of the differences between hosting SharePoint Online Standard and Dedicated.

TABLE 10-1 Differences between hosting SharePoint Online Standard and SharePoint Online Dedicated

Feature	SharePoint Online Standard	SharePoint Online Dedicated
Tenancy	Multitenant	Dedicated
Hardware	Shared	Dedicated
Location	Microsoft datacenters	Microsoft datacenters
Code support	Partial trust	Full and partial
Customization	SharePoint Designer	SharePoint Designer and Visual Studio
Target audience	Any company size	Companies with 20,000+ seats
Custom solutions (Full-trust code)	No	Yes
Sandboxed solutions (Partial-trust code)	Yes	Yes
Silverlight Web Part (.*xap* files)	Yes	Yes
BCS (back-end LoB integration)	Yes	No
SharePoint Designer 2010	Yes	Yes
Client Object Model	Yes	Yes
Web services	Yes	Yes
OOB browser configuration (Web Parts, themes)	Yes	Yes
Visual Studio 2010 (SharePoint Tools)	Sandbox only	Farm and sandbox
InfoPath forms	Sandbox only	Admin and sandbox
Workflows	Declarative only	Custom and declarative

Exploring BCS Functionality in SharePoint Online

SharePoint Online provides much of the same functionality that is available when working with the on-premises version of SharePoint. You get access to the following:

- External lists

- External data columns

- Business Data Web Parts

- Secure Store

- Client Object Model

You can provide the same level of collaboration with your external system line-of-business (LoB) data as with the on-premises version of SharePoint.

Let's take a look at the available options with SharePoint Online. In the Administration Center, you can find a Manage Business Data Connectivity section, as shown in Figure 10-1.

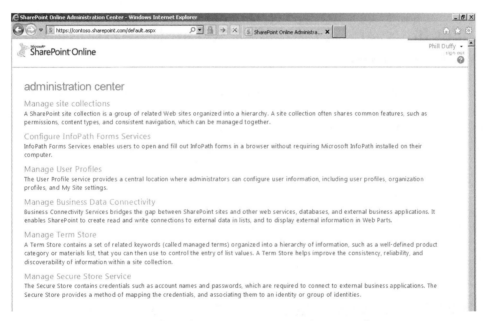

FIGURE 10-1 The SharePoint Online Administration Center provides options for managing SharePoint.

Take a look at the options available for Managing Business Data Connectivity. You will see many of the same options when you work with BCS on-premises. You can see any external content types (ECTs) that have been deployed, and you are able to perform actions such as importing models, creating profile pages, and setting permissions on the model, as shown in Figure 10-2.

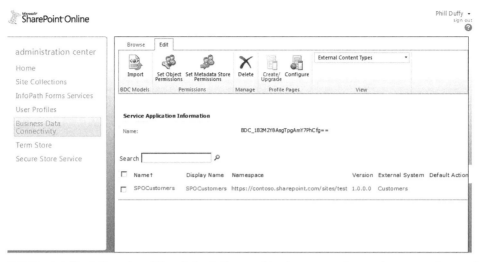

FIGURE 10-2 The BCS section of SharePoint Online provides the same options as the on-premises version of SharePoint.

Differences Between BCS in Office 365 and On-Premises SharePoint 2010 Installations

With Office 365 multitenant, you are able to connect only to Windows Communication Foundation (WCF) services. Direct connections to databases and connections to SQL Azure are only supported in Office 365 Dedicated. The fact that you are unable to deploy a DLL to SharePoint Online means that creating a .NET Assembly Connector is not an option. A WCF web service can still call any external system that you can with the .NET Framework, and there are even some new features available that allow you to still work with on-premises data while hosting SharePoint and your WCF service in the cloud.

You won't be deploying the BDC models using WSP packages with Office 365. Instead, the tool to use is SharePoint Designer, where you are able to build and save the ECTs directly to your Office 365 multitenant environment.

Building BCS Solutions in SharePoint Online

The simplest way to create a BCS solution for SharePoint Online is to use SharePoint Designer. Because SharePoint Online is only able to connect to WCF services, you need to have a WCF web service to connect to in order to surface your data.

When building your BCS solution for SharePoint Online, make sure that you are connecting to a compatible WCF web service that is surfacing its data in a way that is compatible with BCS. In this section, you will learn how to build a cloud-based BCS solution.

Different SharePoint Online Scenarios

This section presents several different scenarios for connecting to external data. In the first scenario, the external system is also in the cloud, such as SQL Azure (see Figure 10-3).

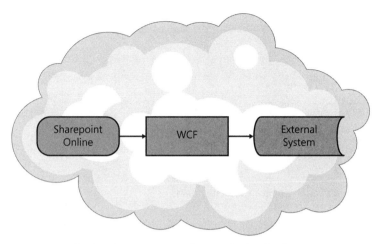

FIGURE 10-3 Connecting to an external system in the cloud.

Another scenario is when you are connecting to an external system that is public-facing but could be hosted anywhere, such as servers inside an organization (see Figure 10-4).

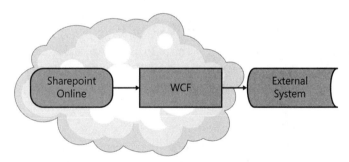

FIGURE 10-4 Connecting to an external system that is public-facing.

If you want to have data on-premises but still make it available through SharePoint Online, there is a third scenario, which is to use the service bus that allows BCS to work with data behind a corporate firewall (see Figure 10-5).

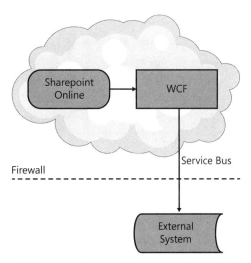

FIGURE 10-5 Allowing BCS to work with data behind a corporate firewall.

The Windows Azure Service Bus provides a convenient way to access your LoB system inside your own firewall from SharePoint Online. The service bus acts as a messenger between your on-premises data and the cloud. The benefit of this setup is that it allows you to host SharePoint online but still retain control over your data systems. Due to the nature of what the service bus is achieving, you need to take a few steps to make it work.

Connecting to SQL Azure with SharePoint Online

If you want to connect to SQL Azure using SharePoint, you will need to use an Azure web service. The following sections walk you through the steps required to create the SQL Azure database, create the Azure web service, and then build the model using SharePoint Designer.

Creating the SQL Azure Database

To begin, you need a Windows Azure account. If you don't have an account yet, you can obtain a trial by visiting *www.microsoft.com/windowsazure/free-trial/*. Once you have an account, head over to *https://windows.azure.com/default.aspx* and log in with your credentials.

In the bottom-left of the Azure homepage, click the Database button, as shown in Figure 10-6.

You will see a few options in the main panel. When you click Create a New SQL Azure Database, you are prompted for a subscription to use. On the next screen, you choose the name, edition, and size of the database. Table 10-2 lists the database settings.

FIGURE 10-6 Click the Database button to create a SQL Azure database.

TABLE 10-2 Database settings

Setting	Value
Database Name	AdventureWorksOnline
Edition	Web
Maximum Size	1 GB

Click Finish to create the database. The next step is to add your machine to be able to connect to the remote database using Microsoft SQL Server Management Studio. By default, the firewall will block access and require that the IP address be added. Figure 10-7 shows the error that displays if the IP address is not enabled.

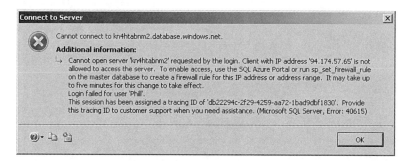

FIGURE 10-7 This error appears when the IP address has not been configured on the Azure firewall.

To enable the IP address, click the server from your chosen subscription and add a new rule for the IP address being used. When you connect again, you should be successful. You can find the server address by clicking the server name under the Windows Azure subscription. It will appear in the Properties pane with the label Fully Qualified DNS Name.

Once you have connected to the SQL Azure database using SQL Server Management Studio, you can create a new table. In this example, you will create a very simple Customer table using the following SQL script:

```
CREATE TABLE [Customer](
    [CustomerID] [int] IDENTITY(1,1)NOT NULL PRIMARY KEY CLUSTERED,
    [Title] [nvarchar](8)NULL,
    [FirstName] [nvarchar](50)NOT NULL,
    [LastName] [nvarchar](50)NOT NULL,
)
```

Once you execute this script, the table is created, as shown in Figure 10-8.

FIGURE 10-8 The Customer table in SQL Azure.

Next, use the following script to populate the table with some sample data, so there is something to see when you call the table from BCS:

```
INSERT INTO [Customer]
    ([Title],[FirstName],[LastName])
VALUES
    ('Dr', 'Julia', 'Ilyina'),
    ('Mr', 'Tom', 'Perham'),
    ('Ms', 'Timm', 'Linda'),
    ('Mrs', 'Roxanne','Kenison'),
    ('Mr', 'Justin','Thorp' ),
    ('Mr', 'Mohammad','Chami' ),
    ('Mr', 'Peter','Fischer'),
    ('Mr', 'Manjinder','Kaur'),
    ('Mr', 'Shmuel', 'Yair'),
    ('Mrs', 'Karen', 'Berg'),
    ('Ms','Isabel', 'Martins')
```

You can test that the rows were added by performing a simple select query on the data, as shown in Figure 10-9.

```
SELECT [CustomerID]
     ,[Title]
     ,[FirstName]
     ,[LastName]
  FROM [AdventureWorksOnline].[dbo].[Customer]
GO
```

	CustomerID	Title	FirstName	LastName
1	1	Dr	Julia	Ilyina
2	2	Mr	Tom	Perham
3	3	Ms	Timm	Linda
4	4	Mrs	Roxanne	Kenison
5	5	Mr	Justin	Thorp
6	6	Mr	Mohammad	Chami
7	7	Mr	Peter	Fischer
8	8	Mr	Manjinder	Kaur
9	9	Mr	Shmuel	Yair
10	10	Mrs	Karen	Berg
11	11	Ms	Isabel	Martins

FIGURE 10-9 Select newly added customers in SQL Azure.

So far, you have created the data for the external system in SQL Azure. Only a connection to a WCF service is supported by SharePoint Online, so the next step is to create a WCF service that exposes this data in a format that BCS can consume.

Creating the Windows Azure WCF Web Service

You can create a WCF web service using Microsoft Visual Studio 2010. First, install the Azure SDK, which you can download from *www.windowsazure.com/en-us/develop/downloads*. After you install the SDK, access the Windows Azure Project in Visual Studio, as shown in Figure 10-10.

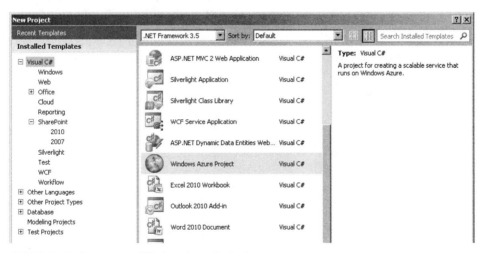

FIGURE 10-10 Create a new Windows Azure Project.

Create a new project in Visual Studio and name it **AzureExternalSystemProject**. On the next screen, you are prompted for the role to use. Click WCF Service Web Role, click the right arrow to add it, and rename the role as SPO_ExternalSystem, as shown in Figure 10-11.

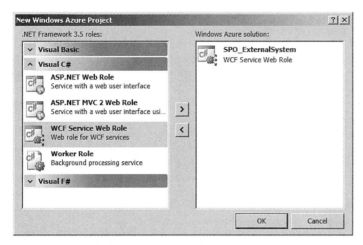

FIGURE 10-11 Add a WCF service web role to the project.

When you click OK, Visual Studio will add a service project along with the Azure project.

The next step is to add a way for the WCF service to interact with the data from SQL Azure. One way to achieve this is to use the Entity Data Framework (EDF). The EDF requires a data source to connect to—in this case, the SQL Azure database. In Visual Studio, click the Data menu bar, click Add New Data Source, click Database, and then click Entity Data Model. Another wizard page appears, asking how you want to create the Entity Data Model. Click Generate from Database, as shown in Figure 10-12, as you will use the Tables structure to build the EDF model.

You are then asked for the connection details to the database. You can enter the server information as you did when connecting. Using SQL Server Management Studio, you can test the connection to make sure you entered the correct details.

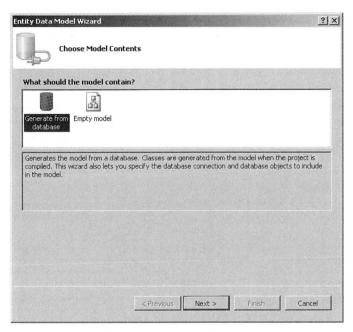

FIGURE 10-12 Choosing to create a model from an existing database in the Entity Data Model wizard.

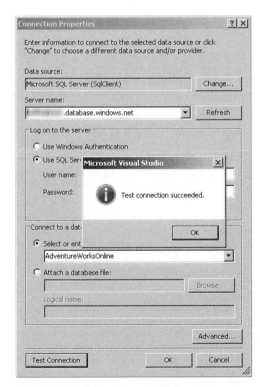

FIGURE 10-13 Connecting to SQL Azure.

You can choose whether to store the connection details in *web.config* or obfuscate them in your application code. For simplicity in this case, the connection details will be stored in *web.config*, but the decision of where to store the connection information will require careful consideration for production code, just as you would treat any sensitive connection string. When you click Next, the wizard connects to the SQL database and returns a list of tables available to you. Expand the Tables node and select the Customer table (the one you created earlier). Leave the other default values and click Finish. The EDF model is added to your project. To ensure this model gets compiled and copied without issues, select the *Model1.edmx* file from the Solution Explorer and make sure the two properties are set as listed in Table 10-3.

TABLE 10-3 Entity Data Framework properties

Property	Value
Build Action	EntityDeploy
Copy to Output Directory	Copy Always

Next, you'll add a code representation of your Customer table, so you'll add a strongly typed class. Right-click the SPO_ExternalSystem project, click Add, and then click New Item. From the C# node, select Class, and name the new file **AzureCustomer.cs**. In this class, you want to add the corresponding properties to match the fields in your database table. Edit the class so it contains the following code:

```
namespace SPO_ExternalSystem
{
    public class AzureCustomer
    {
        public int CustomerId { get; set; }
        public string Title { get; set; }
        public string FirstName { get; set; }
        public string LastName { get; set; }
    }
}
```

This is the object that will be returned by the WCF web service. The next step is to define the WCF interface that provides a contract of the service methods. Open the *IService1.cs* file. Clear out the existing code such that you are left with the following:

```
using System.ServiceModel;
namespace SPO_ExternalSystem
{
    [ServiceContract]
    public interface IService1
    {

    }
}
```

Now you can add interface signature methods. Only provide a Finder and a SpecificFinder method, which will return all records and just a single record, respectively. The method signatures are fairly simple. The Finder method will return an array of AzureCustomers, and the SpecificFinder method will be passed in a CustomerId and return the matching AzureCustomer. Update the code so that you now have the two methods added:

```
using System.ServiceModel;
namespace SPO_ExternalSystem
{
    [ServiceContract]
    public interface IService1
    {
        // Finder Method
        [OperationContract]
        AzureCustomer[] GetCustomers();

        // Specific Finder Method
        [OperationContract]
        AzureCustomer GetCustomer(int customerId);
    }
}
```

Now you need to implement the methods defined in the interface. The *Service1.svc* has some code-behind inheriting from the *IService.cs* interface, so you'll need to go in here and implement the methods. Open the *Service1.svc.cs* class and remove the existing two methods so that you are left with the following:

```
namespace SPO_ExternalSystem
{
    public class Service1 : IService1
    {

    }
}
```

It is time to add the methods that will retrieve the data from SQL Azure via the Entity Data Framework. Start with the Finder method, which means you need to add a method signature that matches the interface's signature for the Finder method:

```
public AzureCustomer[] GetCustomers()
{
    // Get Connection to External System through Entity Data Framework
    using (var db = new AdventureWorksOnlineEntities())
    {
        // Return records as strongly typed Azure Customer
        return db.Customers.Select(customer => new AzureCustomer
                                        {
                                            CustomerId = customer.CustomerID,
                                            Title = customer.Title,
                                            FirstName = customer.FirstName,
                                            LastName = customer.LastName
                                        }).ToArray();
    }
}
```

With the Finder method completed and returning an array of the strongly typed AzureCustomer class for each record in the external system, you can move on to the SpecificFinder method. Add the following method just below the Finder method:

```
public AzureCustomer GetCustomer(int customerId)
{
    // Get Connection to External System through Entity Data Framework
    using (var db = new AdventureWorksOnlineEntities())
    {
        // Get single record matching the Customer ID
        var matchedCustomer = db.Customers.Single(c => c.CustomerID == customerId);

        // Return AzureCustomer with the details of the matched customer
        return new AzureCustomer
            {
                CustomerId = matchedCustomer.CustomerID,
                Title = matchedCustomer.Title,
                FirstName = matchedCustomer.FirstName,
                LastName = matchedCustomer.LastName
            };
    }
}
```

You can now deploy your solution to Windows Azure in a couple of ways. Read this article to see how it can be achieved: *http://msdn.microsoft.com/en-us/library/windowsazure/ff683672.aspx*.

Once the service has been achieved, you can find the path by going to the Hosted Services, Storage Accounts & CDN section of Windows Azure, locating your project, and then viewing the DNS name, as shown in Figure 10-14.

FIGURE 10-14 Obtain the address for the web service in the Hosted Services, Storage Accounts & CDN section of Windows Azure.

Navigate to the URL and append *Service1.svc* to get to your service, such as *http://XXXXXXX.cloud-app.net/Service1.svc*. You will see a screen similar to the one shown in Figure 10-15.

You now have a web service running in Windows Azure that is referencing the data in SQL Azure. The final step is to configure a BDC model using SharePoint Designer to consume the web service.

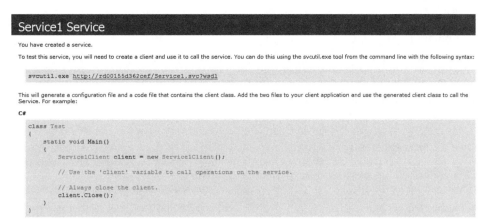

```
Service1 Service

You have created a service.

To test this service, you will need to create a client and use it to call the service. You can do this using the svcutil.exe tool from the command line with the following syntax:

    svcutil.exe http://rd00155d362cef/Service1.svc?wsdl

This will generate a configuration file and a code file that contains the client class. Add the two files to your client application and use the generated client class to call the
Service. For example:

C#

class Test
{
    static void Main()
    {
        Service1Client client = new Service1Client();

        // Use the 'client' variable to call operations on the service.

        // Always close the client.
        client.Close();
    }
}
```

FIGURE 10-15 Viewing the service running on Windows Azure.

Connecting to the Windows Azure Web Service Using SharePoint Designer

You connect to a Windows Azure web service in the same way you connect to any other web service, but this time you will connect to it from SharePoint Online.

Open SharePoint Designer and click Open Site. Enter the URL of your SharePoint Online account. You will be prompted for your Office 365 credentials (see Figure 10-16).

```
X https://login.microsoftonline.com                                    X

        Microsoft
        Office 365

        User ID:
        phill@adventureworks.com

        Password:
        ••••••••••

        Forgot your password?

        ☑ Remember me
        ☑ Keep me signed in

        [ Sign in ]

        Don't have a user ID assigned by your organization?
        Use a Hotmail account to sign in

        Show saved user IDs


        ©2012 Microsoft Corporation  |  Privacy  |  Legal
```

FIGURE 10-16 Log into SharePoint Online in SharePoint Designer.

Once you have connected, on the External Content Types ribbon tab, in the New group, click External Content Type.

Change the Name of the ECT to **SPOCustomers**, and then click the Click Here to Discover External Data Sources and Define Operations link. On this page, you can add the connection to your WCF web service. Click the Add Connection button and choose WCF Service. Table 10-4 lists some example credentials to enter in the next dialog box.

TABLE 10-4 Example credentials

Property	Value
Service Metadata URL	http://YOURSERVICE.cloudapp.net/Service1.svc?wsdl
Service Endpoint URL	http://YOURSERVICE.cloudapp.net/Service1.svc
Name	Customers

Once you have connected to the web service, you will see your methods appear in the Data Source Explorer, as shown in Figure 10-17.

FIGURE 10-17 View the web service methods in the Data Source Explorer.

You now want to use these methods as your BCS methods. Right-click GetCustomers (Finder method), and from the new method menu click New Read List Operation, as shown in Figure 10-18. Doing so adds the method as a Finder method.

FIGURE 10-18 Add the GetCustomers WCF method to retrieve all customers from the External System.

Once you have selected the method type, a wizard will appear where you can configure some properties and behaviors for the model. You don't need to do anything on the Operations Properties page or the next page, Input Parameters Configuration. On the Return Parameter page, define the field that is the identifier—in this case, CustomerId. Select the field in the Data Source Elements pane and then choose Map to Identifier from the Properties pane. Click Finish to complete adding the Finder method.

You add the SpecificFinder method GetCustomer in a similar fashion, although this time you are adding a new Read Item operation, and you need to configure the Input parameter, too. Add the

Read Item method, and on the second page select CustomerId and choose Map to Identifier. Click Next. Again, you will need to specify in the Return parameter for the method which field is the identifier, just like you did for the Finder method. Click the CustomerId field, and then choose Map to Identifier from the Properties pane. Click Finish.

It is time now to save the ECT and test it out on SharePoint Online. Navigate to a SharePoint page and add a Business Data List (see Figure 10-19).

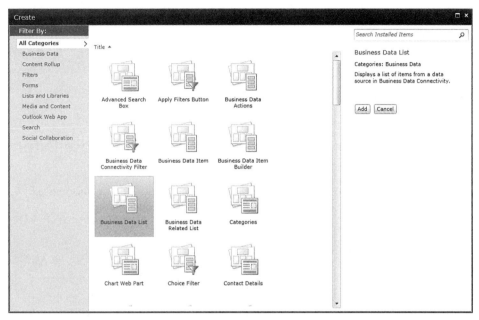

FIGURE 10-19 Add a Business Data List to test the ECT.

Once you have added the Business Data List, you can configure it to use the ECT you just created, as shown in Figure 10-20.

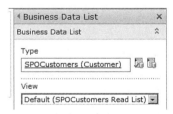

FIGURE 10-20 Select the new Customers ECT.

Once you have configured the Web Part, you are able to see your SQL Azure data in SharePoint Online, as shown in Figure 10-21.

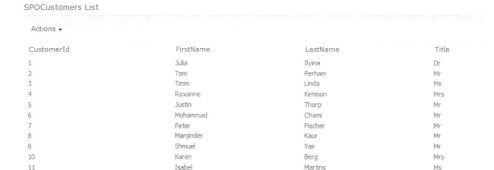

SPOCustomers List

Actions ▾

CustomerId	FirstName	LastName	Title
1	Julia	Ilyina	Dr
2	Tom	Perham	Mr
3	Timm	Linda	Ms
4	Roxanne	Kenison	Mrs
5	Justin	Thorp	Mr
6	Mohammad	Chami	Mr
7	Peter	Fischer	Mr
8	Manjinder	Kaur	Mr
9	Shmuel	Yair	Mr
10	Karen	Berg	Mrs
11	Isabel	Martins	Ms

FIGURE 10-21 The SQL Azure data is now in SharePoint Online.

Using a Data Source in SharePoint Designer to Expose External Data

You can expose external data in other ways to SharePoint Online without needing to use BCS. SharePoint Designer provides a way to add a data source, as shown in Figure 10-22.

FIGURE 10-22 Add a source to expose external data.

As you can see, SharePoint Designer offers connections to numerous sources:

- Linked Data Source

- Database Connection

- SOAP Service Connection

- REST Service Connection

- XML File Connection

These methods of connecting to data sources provide a way to connect to external systems using SharePoint Online if you do not want to make use of the complete BCS functionality and just want to display data on a SharePoint page.

See Also *For more information about SharePoint Designer data sources, see* http://office.microsoft.com/en-us/sharepoint-designer-help/CH010373541.aspx.

Summary

The example in this chapter showed you how to use data stored in SQL Azure and surface it to SharePoint Online by making use of a Windows Azure WCF service. This scenario works well if you want to store your data in SQL Azure and you want to be able to scale as the data and demand for the data grows. You can make use of the Azure platform to scale with you. SQL Azure is not the only external system that you can connect to with Windows Azure—you can also easily connect to any other system supported by the .NET Framework.

PART III

Extending the Out-of-the-Box BCS Functionality

CHAPTER 11

Using Client-Side Code and External Data

In this chapter, you will:

- Create web-based solutions using external data

- Understand the SharePoint 2010 Client Object Model

- Build external data solutions using jQuery

- Create client application solutions

- Create Visual Studio Tools for Office add-ins

- Use the Business Connectivity Services Artifact Generator

- Learn how to package client-side solutions

In previous chapters, you learned how to build a Business Connectivity Services (BCS) model and how the data from an external system can be displayed through the various out-of-the-box Web Parts, search, and Office client applications. You have many options for working with your line-of-business (LoB) data, but what happens when you want to create your own application or web-based solution that makes use of the external data? In this chapter, you will learn how to leverage client-side code to create solutions, and in Chapter 12, "Building Server-Side BCS Solutions," you will examine what you can achieve using server-side code.

Many applications have been created to read and write data to a LoB system. The new external list functionality in Microsoft SharePoint 2010 handles many of the basic chores associated with creating such applications. With the user interface (UI) creation being taken care of by SharePoint, you can easily add functionality to create, read, update, and delete (CRUD) data in a data source. The ability to edit the Microsoft InfoPath 2010 forms makes adding business logic and branding customizations much easier and quicker than if you were creating your own application with forms to interact with your business data.

For example, if you have a database that contains a list of customers, and you want to keep that list updated through SharePoint, you simply create an external content type (ECT) for the Customers table with the CRUD methods (also known as operations) defined, and it is uploaded into SharePoint and an external list is created using the ECT.

Previously, when you required a solution for working with LoB data, you needed to develop the application around a technology that supported the external system. For example, a developer would need to know how to code against the Oracle database to be able to write an application with Oracle as its back-end data store. The same was true if a developer coded against Microsoft SQL Server, a web service, or even an Open Database Connectivity (ODBC) system such as MySQL, AS400, or DB2. With the use of these separate systems, it took time and knowledge to build and maintain the business solution.

With SharePoint and the BCS architecture, you now simply need to create the Business Data Connectivity (BDC) model, which includes the ECT and the CRUD methods, and it is deployed to the SharePoint environment with the ECTs available. Then any solutions that you want to work with the external data can do so through the SharePoint Object Model.

The BDC model is the "translator," as it were, between the different types of connections supported by BCS, enabling development to be done against the SharePoint Object Model without concern to what the external system is. In the real world, this means that your developers just need to program against the ECT, and that will perform the required functions on the external data without the developers needing to know exactly how to program against each individual external system. Having a single object model makes it easier to develop solutions, and SharePoint offers a great framework for working with ECTs.

In this chapter, you will work with external data using client-side code rather than server-side code. You will learn how and why to do this, and you will see some examples that show that by leveraging client-side applications, you can greatly extend how users work with your LoB data.

Creating Web-Based Solutions Using External Data

With most users' experience of using SharePoint being in the browser, the most obvious solutions to build are web based and typically consist of a Web Part on a Web Part page or an Application page, but these aren't the only ways to work with external data. Developers have the option to choose where the code is executed, depending on different requirements; they can write code that executes either on the client or on the server. Next, you'll look at the differences between and uses of server-side and client-side code.

Server-Side vs. Client-Side Code

The two different coding options both have advantages and uses when working with ECTs.

Server-side operations are concerned with processing the external data on the SharePoint server, as the name suggests. If a page requires any more information—for example, when a user chooses a category to see the products in it—then the page needs to perform a *postback*, where information is sent back to the server, and the server performs the new operation before sending the new content back to the browser to display on the page. Typically, server-side code is written in either C# or Visual Basic, and the SharePoint server itself executes the code and performs the required functionality. With the SharePoint server doing the main work, it is possible for developers to have more control of the ECT and its behavior. In Chapter 12, you will learn how to leverage server-side code to great effect.

Client-side code offloads most of the work to the client—that is, to the user's computer—so that the load can be lessened on the server. The SharePoint server is still used to retrieve the data, but its role is changed to being the data provider rather than being in charge of displaying the data. In SharePoint 2010, you can use an extra Client Object Model, which allows you to create solutions that don't need to be located on the server. You have different sorts of clients to consider when thinking about client-side versus server-side code with SharePoint—the client could be a browser, an Office application, or another standalone .NET application.

Client-side code is often used when presenting the data to an end user in a Web Part, application page, or desktop application, whereas server-side code can be used in workflows—for example, where a decision is made based on values in an external system. Essentially, server-side code does most of its processing on the SharePoint server, and client-side code performs its duties in a client, whatever that client may be.

Now that you know the differences between client-side and server-side code, you can start investigating working with external data on the client side. Next, you will look at how you can use the Client Object Model to create a web-based solution.

SharePoint 2010 Client Object Model

As mentioned previously, SharePoint 2010 offers developers a new programming object model to use when working with SharePoint: the Client Object Model. You can now create solutions that use only SharePoint to provide data, rather than being limited to server-side solutions. While it was possible to write client-side solutions in SharePoint 2007 by calling the exposed web services, it did not offer as much flexibility or functionality as in SharePoint 2010. It's worth remembering that even though you are using the Client Object Model, some actions are still performed by the server.

Three flavors of the Client Object Model are available:

- **ECMAScript Client Object Model**   ECMAScript is a scripting language (such as JavaScript and JScript). The JavaScript Object Model (JSOM) is designed for working with SharePoint in an asynchronous manner and is extremely useful when you want to work with the data once it has been loaded to the client in a browser, for example. JSOM is a collection of JavaScript libraries that provide the necessary functionality to work with SharePoint objects.

- **Silverlight Client Object Model**   As its name suggests, this model is for writing solutions in Microsoft Silverlight that have access to SharePoint. With the user experience capabilities Silverlight offers, it is possible to create rich interactions within your SharePoint environment.

- **.NET Managed Client Object Model**   This option allows developers to work with SharePoint in a "managed" code language, such as C# or Visual Basic. It is possible to create desktop applications, web solutions, or Microsoft Office add-ins using the .NET Managed Client Object Model. When you are working with the Client Object Model, you have a limited set of functionality compared to working with the full SharePoint Object Model. One of the great advantages of working with the Client Object Model is that calls are executed in batches, resulting in fewer trips to and from the server to get data.

The following list describes a few scenarios for each of the Client Object Models:

- **.NET managed applications**   Custom .NET applications in your organization can now use the Client Object Model to interact with the SharePoint Object Model directly. This approach allows for synchronous interactions with SharePoint.

- **Silverlight applications**   Silverlight applications give you the chance to work with the Share-Point Object Model with a rich UI, which can run in the browser or outside of the browser for a desktop-type experience. Silverlight applications can run synchronously or asynchronously, depending on your requirements.

- **ECMAScript (JavaScript)**   ECMAScript provides a way for developers to work with the SharePoint Object Model using JavaScript, allowing applications to run entirely within a browser. By using the Client Object Model, these applications can interact with the SharePoint data asynchronously. This is particularly useful if you want to create solutions that run in the browser, but you don't want the page to refresh when you display new data, as you can implement AJAX functionality.

The three platforms have been designed so their usage is very similar. They closely resemble the Server Object Model, providing a consistent, familiar means of developing against the different models.

The Client Object Model makes use of a SharePoint web service called *Client.svc*, which takes a request from the client, gets the requested information or performs the desired action on the server, and then returns the result. Figure 11-1 shows the information flow between the client and the server.

As shown in Figure 11-1, an XML request is built by the Client Object Model and passed to the *Client.svc* web service, which then performs the action using the SharePoint Server Object Model and returns a JavaScript Object Notation (JSON) object back to the client.

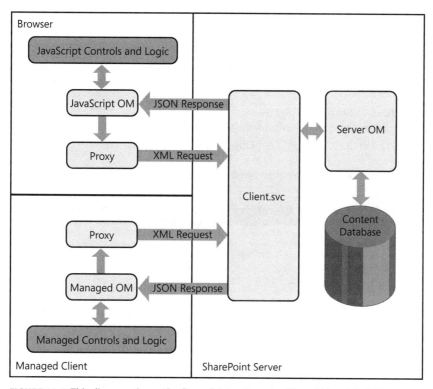

FIGURE 11-1 This diagram shows the flow of data when the Client Object Model interacts with SharePoint.

Client Object Model and Business Data Connectivity

You have a few limitations when working with external data and the Client Object Model. This section explores some of these limitations and how you can use the Client Object Model to work with external data.

The Client Object Model cannot perform any actions directly on an ECT, so any actions on external data must be performed via an external list (see Chapter 5, "Creating External Lists and Using External Data in Lists and Libraries"). When you use an external list, be aware of the following .NET types, which you are not able to use and are omitted from the list:

- System.GUID
- System.Object
- System.URI

- System.UInt64

- System.Int64

You can, however, use these fields with the BDC Object Model.

When using one of the Client Object Models, developers are able to write code against an external list as if it was a standard SharePoint list. There is no way to page or get chunks of data from the external list. It is not possible to run bulk operations, such as reading 25 instances simultaneously. Also, it is not possible to stream binary large objects (BLOBs), and complex associations cannot be used.

The following example demonstrates how you can use the Client Object Model to provide an alternate way of displaying products from the product list. Figure 11-2 shows the standard list, and Figure 11-3 shows how it looks with a little bit of Client Object Model coding in a Web Part.

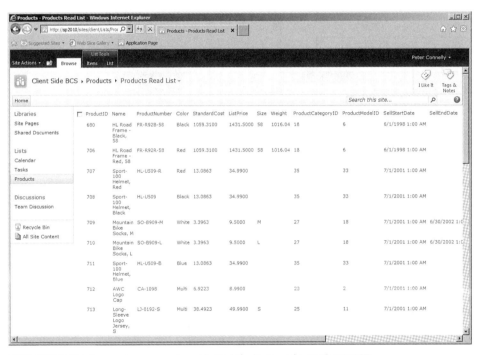

FIGURE 11-2 This image shows an external list's default view of a product's ECT.

The Client Object Model is useful when retrieving data from SharePoint, but if you want to create an alternate way of interacting with the data, a framework such as jQuery makes this task a lot easier. In the next section, you will learn some of the functionality that can enhance the user's experience of working with external data in the browser.

FIGURE 11-3 You can present the same product data in various ways.

Building External Data Solutions Using jQuery

This section's example demonstrates how you can use jQuery to create a rich UI for working with external data from within SharePoint. jQuery is a JavaScript library that simplifies HTML coding tasks and provides a great partner to the Client Object Model.

Figure 11-4 shows an interactive page of business data, in which end users are allowed to drag and drop products from the list to a shopping cart, where the total cost for the order is displayed. You can easily implement drag-and-drop operations and other such features using jQuery.

You can also use jQuery widgets to help display your business data in a rich UI. For example, you could use the Accordion widget, which is part of the jQuery UI plug-in, to split products into their product categories to allow users to easily find products by expanding the relevant accordion menu (see Figure 11-5).

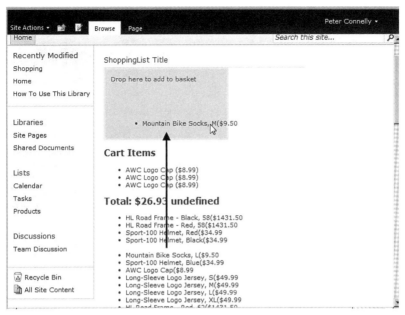

FIGURE 11-4 This simple jQuery-based shopping cart example shows how external data can drive client-side applications.

FIGURE 11-5 An accordion widget is being used to split products into categories, making it easier for end users to find the information they want.

When working with external lists, you are not restricted to just reading the information. As long as you created the methods on the ECT, it is also possible to update, add, and delete. Figure 11-6 shows an example of how an end user could use a custom UI to update the list price of some items.

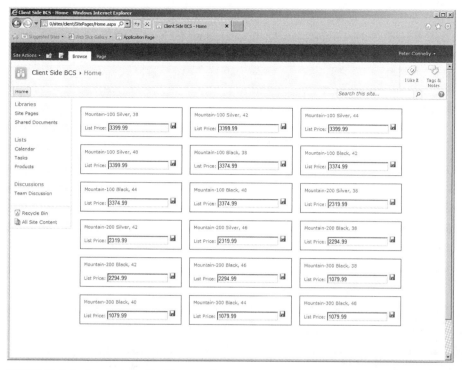

FIGURE 11-6 As demonstrated in this example, you can create your own UIs to update external systems.

Editing a value and clicking the save icon reflects the changes back in the external system. For example, the first item, Mountain-100 Silver, 38, has a price of $3,399.99. Entering **2500** in the List Price box and clicking the save icon updates the LoB system with the new value of $2,500. Figure 11-7 shows the updated value in SQL Server.

FIGURE 11-7 The cost has been updated here from the custom updating UI.

Other Example Scenarios

There are many other ways you can use the Client Object Model in the browser to make business data accessible. The following are just a few examples of different ways to present your LoB data:

- **KPI Web Part**   Allow users to easily filter items depending on the status of the indicator.

- **Reorder Page**   Show a list of items that are nearing their minimum stock levels. Because you cannot use workflows on an external list, you can simply show a list of items needing reordering, allow users to specify a new order, and then update the changes.

- **BI Dashboard**   Show business intelligence in various formats, and allow users to see how information is related by making use of BCS associations.

Creating Client Application Solutions

The previous examples showed how to use various Client Object Model calls. Another way to work with information from your external system is to use the BCS Client Runtime.

Client Object Model vs. BCS Client Runtime

When creating a solution using the Client Object Model, whether it is using the JavaScript, Silverlight, or .NET Client Object Model, you are using the Client Object Model method to connect to your external system and you are working via SharePoint. The BCS Client Runtime allows for solutions that work directly with the external system, bypassing SharePoint, as shown in Figure 11-8.

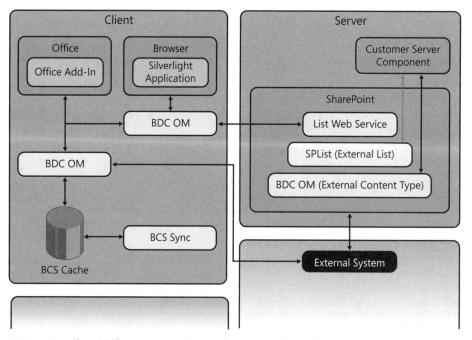

FIGURE 11-8 The BCS Client Runtime allows a client application to directly connect to external systems.

You can use a couple of additional features in the BCS Client Runtime: BCS Cache and BCS Sync.

BCS Cache

The BCS Cache allows for an offline experience and helps client applications perform more efficiently by working with a local copy of the data rather than calling the external system each time. A great way to think of this is that if information workers who are out in the field still want work with the business data, then they can—provided that the information has been copied to the cache first. The cache is a SQL Compact Edition (CE) database created in the profile for the logged-on user in Windows when the BCS Sync service first synchronizes. When using the cache offline, a user can create, read, update, and delete business information and then synchronize it with the external system when the user comes back online.

The SQL CE database is secured initially by the fact that the database is tied to the user. For added security, you can use a data-protection feature such as BitLocker to encrypt the drive and database.

Because the cache is stored for the individual user in the user's profile, the same cache could be used in any Office application or other application that makes use of the BCS Client Runtime. This way, the data needs to be duplicated only once from the external system to the user's cache, rather than needing a cache for each application accessing the data.

Earlier in the chapter when looking at the Client Object Model for web-based solutions, you saw how solutions can work with external data by communicating through SharePoint. The same is true when working with either the .NET Managed Client Object Model or the Silverlight Client Object Model. Both need to be given a SharePoint context in which to run, and the solution can execute in that context.

BCS Sync

The BCS Sync service is responsible for automatically refreshing the cache and for synchronizing that data between the local machine and the external system. It runs as a service on the client's machine and is installed only as part of the Office 2010 suite.

Using the BCS Client Runtime in an Excel Add-In

Using Microsoft Visual Studio 2010, you can create add-ins for most of the Microsoft Office client applications, as shown in Figure 11-9.

Visual Studio provides these out-of-the-box project templates:

- Microsoft Excel 2010

- Microsoft InfoPath 2010

- Microsoft Outlook 2010

- Microsoft PowerPoint 2010

- Microsoft Project 2010

- Microsoft Visio 2010

- Microsoft Word 2010

In all these Office client applications, you can combine the power of these applications with data from an external system by using the BDC Client Runtime Object Model.

There are many different scenarios in which you can use the client runtime. For example, you can pull through data for a report in a Word document, analyze information in an Excel workbook, or graph the latest business data in a PowerPoint presentation.

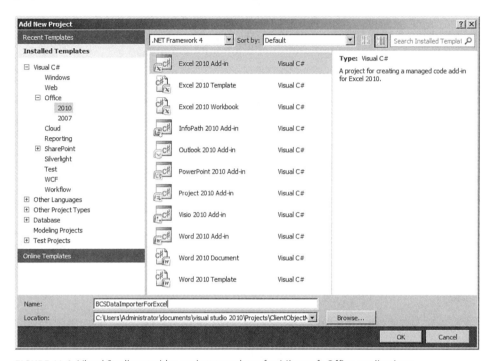

FIGURE 11-9 Visual Studio provides project templates for Microsoft Office applications.

Creating VSTO Add-Ins

Creating a Visual Studio Tools for Office (VSTO) ClickOnce package is now much easier in Visual Studio 2010 than in previous versions with the VSTO Project types, which have all of the necessary files to add custom ribbon elements and begin to build the solution. In the example in this section, you will read and write data from an Excel document. The example solution makes use of the ribbon in Excel, but it could use a tool pane if that was required.

The example solution also makes use of the BCS Cache. As you learned in Chapter 7, "Using External Data with Office Client Applications," it is possible to cache data from an external system for processing offline on a user's computer and then have it synced back to the external system once the user is back online. SharePoint 2010 makes use of Microsoft SharePoint Workspace 2010 to synchronize the data. When you display an external list in the browser, on the Lists ribbon tab, in the Connect & Export group, click Sync to SharePoint Workspace, as shown in Figure 11-10. This command makes the list and the external data available to SharePoint Workspace, as well as to add-ins using the BDC Client Runtime.

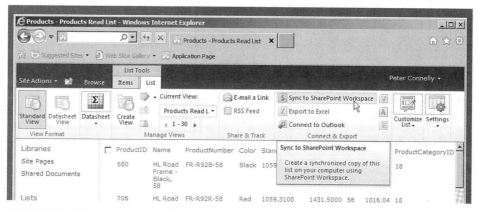

FIGURE 11-10 You can take data offline using SharePoint Workspace.

When you click Sync to SharePoint Workspace, the dialog box shown in Figure 11-11 appears, warning you of the implications of synchronizing data on your computer.

FIGURE 11-11 A warning dialog box explains the issues with syncing to SharePoint Workspace.

When you click OK, the dialog box shown in Figure 11-12 opens, asking whether you want to install a package. The package contains the BDC model, and once you install it, the BCS Client Runtime directly connects with the external system.

With the deployment completed, you should see the list appear in SharePoint Workspace, as shown in Figure 11-13.

FIGURE 11-12 The VSTO that has been created gets installed on the local machine.

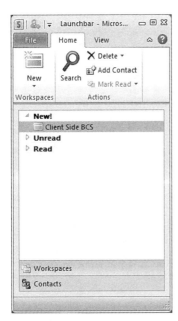

FIGURE 11-13 Once installed, the external list displays in SharePoint Workspace.

As mentioned previously, this example uses an Excel add-in to populate an Excel worksheet. In the following screenshot, you can see the new elements added to the ribbon. On the Data ribbon tab, there is a command in the BCS group to select the ECT, as shown in Figure 11-14. Once you select the ECT, click Get BCS Data to execute the ECT Finder method (operation).

FIGURE 11-14 You can find BCS-related commands in Excel on the Data ribbon tab.

The only ECTs available are those that you have made available. When writing against the BCS Object Model, it is possible to choose these methods of working with the ECT data:

- Get the data from the external system directly

- Work with the cached version

- Do a mixture of both, where the code will get the latest version from the external system if available, or it will use the cached version if not

To recap, the ECT Finder method is the method that returns all data from the external system. If a filter is being used, then you can add extra UI functionality to allow the user to enter one or more values, and those values would limit the amount of data returned. In this example, however, no filters have been defined, so all data is returned.

After you click Get BCS Data, the Finder method executes and populates the Excel worksheet with all of the information stored in the cache, as shown in Figure 11-15. Bringing the data into Excel enables you to easily analyze it.

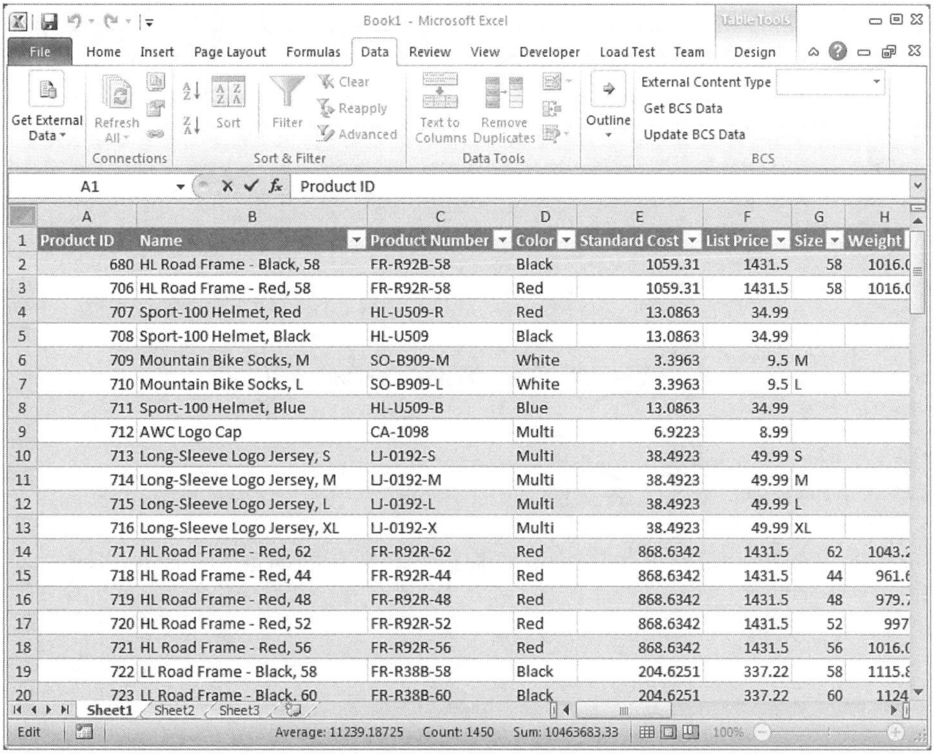

	Product ID	Name	Product Number	Color	Standard Cost	List Price	Size	Weight
1	Product ID	Name	Product Number	Color	Standard Cost	List Price	Size	Weight
2	680	HL Road Frame - Black, 58	FR-R92B-58	Black	1059.31	1431.5	58	1016.0
3	706	HL Road Frame - Red, 58	FR-R92R-58	Red	1059.31	1431.5	58	1016.0
4	707	Sport-100 Helmet, Red	HL-U509-R	Red	13.0863	34.99		
5	708	Sport-100 Helmet, Black	HL-U509	Black	13.0863	34.99		
6	709	Mountain Bike Socks, M	SO-B909-M	White	3.3963	9.5	M	
7	710	Mountain Bike Socks, L	SO-B909-L	White	3.3963	9.5	L	
8	711	Sport-100 Helmet, Blue	HL-U509-B	Blue	13.0863	34.99		
9	712	AWC Logo Cap	CA-1098	Multi	6.9223	8.99		
10	713	Long-Sleeve Logo Jersey, S	LJ-0192-S	Multi	38.4923	49.99	S	
11	714	Long-Sleeve Logo Jersey, M	LJ-0192-M	Multi	38.4923	49.99	M	
12	715	Long-Sleeve Logo Jersey, L	LJ-0192-L	Multi	38.4923	49.99	L	
13	716	Long-Sleeve Logo Jersey, XL	LJ-0192-X	Multi	38.4923	49.99	XL	
14	717	HL Road Frame - Red, 62	FR-R92R-62	Red	868.6342	1431.5	62	1043.2
15	718	HL Road Frame - Red, 44	FR-R92R-44	Red	868.6342	1431.5	44	961.6
16	719	HL Road Frame - Red, 48	FR-R92R-48	Red	868.6342	1431.5	48	979.7
17	720	HL Road Frame - Red, 52	FR-R92R-52	Red	868.6342	1431.5	52	997
18	721	HL Road Frame - Red, 56	FR-R92R-56	Red	868.6342	1431.5	56	1016.0
19	722	LL Road Frame - Black, 58	FR-R38B-58	Black	204.6251	337.22	58	1115.8
20	723	LL Road Frame - Black, 60	FR-R38B-60	Black	204.6251	337.22	60	1124

Average: 11239.18725   Count: 1450   Sum: 10463683.33   100%

FIGURE 11-15 This Excel spreadsheet is populated with data from the external system.

If you want to edit the data as a whole, Excel provides you with helpful features, such as data sheet view and the ability to update items in bulk. With this solution, you can use Excel to manipulate the data, and then using a combination of your own business logic and the BDC Object Model, you can easily update the information to your external system by clicking the Update BCS Data command on the Data ribbon tab, in the BCS group (see Figure 11-16). You can then write the information back to your external system.

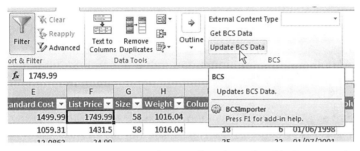

FIGURE 11-16 Modifications made in Excel can be updated in the external system.

Declarative Outlook Solutions

BCS enables information workers to surface ECTs, such as Customer, Employee, or Order, within Microsoft Outlook 2010 as a native Outlook item type, such as a Contact, Task, Post, or Appointment. You don't need to write any code to do this—it can all be done declaratively. To do so, configure the ECT to map columns to the Office item columns, so that Outlook can parse the data when an external list is connected to it. In Microsoft SharePoint Designer 2010, on the Summary View of the ECT, in the External Content Type Information area, select an Office item type, as shown in Figure 11-17.

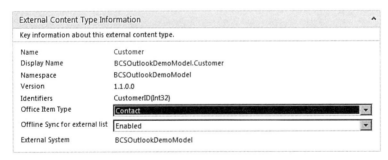

FIGURE 11-17 In SharePoint Designer, you can define the Office item type.

See Also *For more information on Office item types, see Chapter 4, "Defining External System Connections Using SharePoint Designer."*

The fields of the SpecificFinder are the fields used by the consuming Office application. When you first create the method, you receive a number of warnings to set up some minimum mappings for the Office item mapping to work. For example, when the Office item type is Contact, you must map a column to either the LastName or FullName Office property, as shown in Figure 11-18.

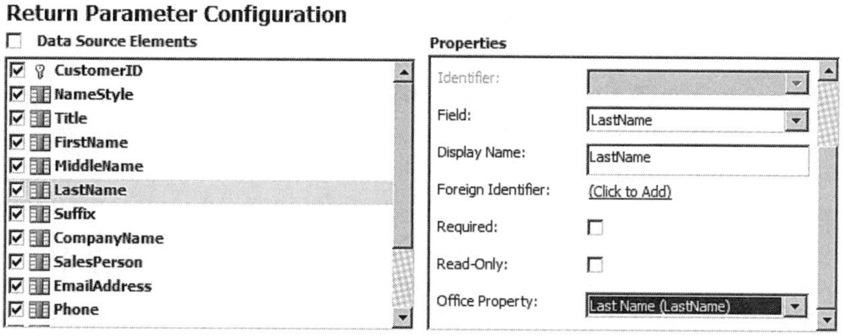

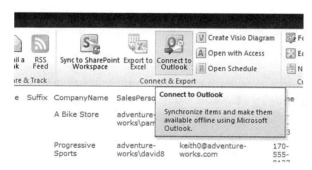

Return Parameter Configuration

☐ Data Source Elements

☑ 🔑 CustomerID
☑ NameStyle
☑ Title
☑ FirstName
☑ MiddleName
☑ LastName
☑ Suffix
☑ CompanyName
☑ SalesPerson
☑ EmailAddress
☑ Phone

Properties

Identifier: ▼
Field: LastName ▼
Display Name: LastName
Foreign Identifier: (Click to Add)
Required: ☐
Read-Only: ☐
Office Property: Last Name (LastName) ▼

FIGURE 11-18 For a Contact Office item type, map a return parameter to the LastName Office property.

Once you have configured all the columns and the ECT has been deployed, you can then use the ECT in Outlook via an external list by clicking Connect to Outlook on the List ribbon tab, as shown in Figure 11-19.

FIGURE 11-19 Click Connect to Outlook to use the ECT in Outlook via an external list.

A VSTO package is created, and it installs the required files into Outlook, making the contacts available. If the full CRUD methods have been created, you can read to and write from Outlook to the external system. As the tooltip shown in Figure 11-19 states, this data will be available through caching even when the user is offline. In Figure 11-20, the contacts are shown as if you had created a normal contacts list in Outlook.

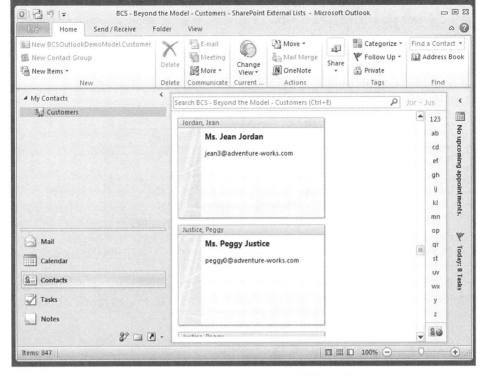

FIGURE 11-20 Contact details stored in an external system are displayed in Outlook.

This method of pulling data from an external system into Outlook is known as a *simple Outlook solution*, where just the flat data is pulled through. But what happens if you want to be able to see all of a customer's orders alongside their contact information, to save your users from changing systems to view this information? This is possible by progressing to an *intermediate declarative Outlook solution*. A couple more steps are required for the intermediate version, and some tools are available to help you out. Alternatively, you can write the necessary files to get the results you want. The following are two tools you will use in this example:

- **BCS Artifact Generator** Creates the necessary files to tell Outlook how to subscribe to the external system. The Artifact Generator gets fed in a BDC model and then generates the necessary files. The BCS Artifact Generator is available from the MSDN Archive at *http://archive.msdn.microsoft.com/odcsps14bcsgnrtrtool*.

- **BCS Packager** Takes the files generated from the Artifact Generator to build a VSTO package that enables you to deploy the solution to Outlook. The BCS Packager is available at *https://archive.msdn.microsoft.com/odcsps14bcspkgtool*.

Creating a Declarative Outlook Solution for BCS

In this walk-through, you will see the different components required to create an intermediate declarative Outlook solution. First up is the BCS Artifact Generator. You can create the files generated manually, but for most situations, using the BCS Artifact Generator will meet your requirements or at least get you most of the way to a complete solution. As mentioned previously, this tool requires a BDC model that is used by the solution to work with your external system. In this scenario, you are pulling customer contact details and the customer order history. To create a master-detail scenario of customers and orders, create a BDC model using either SharePoint Designer or Visual Studio, with the two ECTs with an association method on the Orders ECT, which will get the orders for a particular customer.

See Also *For more information on creating associations, see Chapter 4.*

Figure 11-21 shows that the ECT for the orders has the association defined.

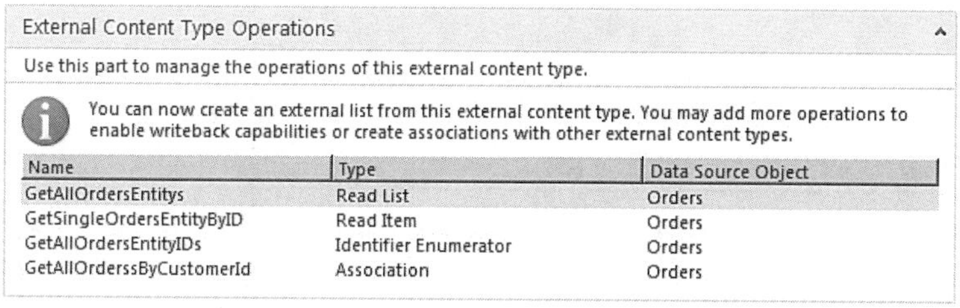

External Content Type Operations			^
Use this part to manage the operations of this external content type.			
(i) You can now create an external list from this external content type. You may add more operations to enable writeback capabilities or create associations with other external content types.			
Name	**Type**	**Data Source Object**	
GetAllOrdersEntitys	Read List	Orders	
GetSingleOrdersEntityByID	Read Item	Orders	
GetAllOrdersEntityIDs	Identifier Enumerator	Orders	
GetAllOrderssByCustomerId	Association	Orders	

FIGURE 11-21 You can define an association between customers and orders in SharePoint Designer.

The second ECT is the one used in the previous example, where the Customer ECT has its Office item type set to Contact. With the two ECTs configured, you need to export them so that they are both contained in one BDC model, and the BCS Artifact Generator tool can work with associations. From the External Content Types gallery in SharePoint Designer, select both ECTs by holding down the Shift or Ctrl key. Right-click and then select Export BDC Model, as shown in Figure 11-22.

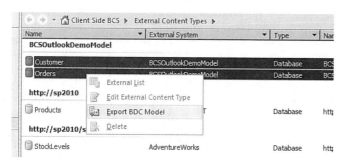

FIGURE 11-22 Export the two ECTs in a BDC model using SharePoint Designer.

Both ECTs are saved in one BDC model file. This file is required for the next step, when you use the BCS Artifact Generator.

Run the BCS Artifact Generator tool. You are presented with a simple form, where you enter the location of the exported BDC model file and provide a name for the solution. The application will validate the model and display any error or warning messages in the Status text box, as shown in Figure 11-23, where a warning is shown. These errors are due to the fact that both the Order and the Customer ECTs used in this example have no filters defined. You'll address this issue later.

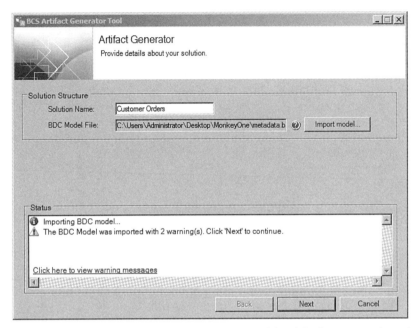

FIGURE 11-23 Artifact Generator validates the BDC model and displays error and warning messages.

Click Next to show all the ECTs defined in the BDC model and some information about them. To see the associated orders for a customer, you customize the imported BDC model and "declaratively" tell Outlook to generate a task pane to contain the information.

The customization process starts a wizard that takes you through up to three pages. Click Customize to the right of the Customers ECT to start the wizard and display the Item Details page, where you can configure the Display Name and Icon settings. Click Next.

When an association is defined in the BDC model, the BCS Artifact Generator displays the Taskpane page so it can create a form automatically for you to show the data from the associated ECT, which in this example is Orders, as shown in Figure 11-24. However, you can also create your own form using InfoPath to display the information to suit your business requirements and choose the region in which the information is displayed. In that case, select Display Related Item Details in InfoPath Form, and then specify the location of the InfoPath form.

Note The easiest way to create an InfoPath form is to create an external list from the associated ECT – Orders. Create the InfoPath form on that list and then export the *.xsn* form using SharePoint Designer.

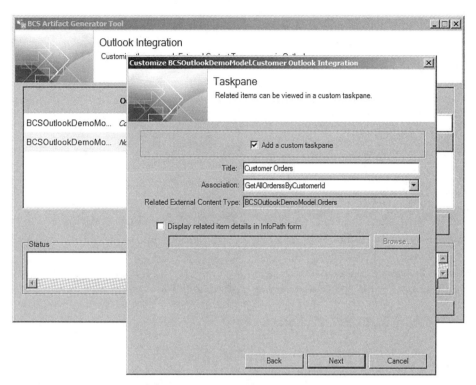

FIGURE 11-24 You can use Artifact Generator to create a custom task pane.

Once you have selected Add a Custom Taskpane, accept the default, and then click Next to display the Action page. You can add actions and ribbons to Outlook to enhance the way in which the ECT can be used; for this example, however, you are interested only in showing the related data. When the wizard is completed, you are returned to the overview page, where you confirm that the settings are updated, as shown in Figure 11-25. Notice that Customers is an Outlook Contact type, the custom region will be autogenerated, and there will be a task pane.

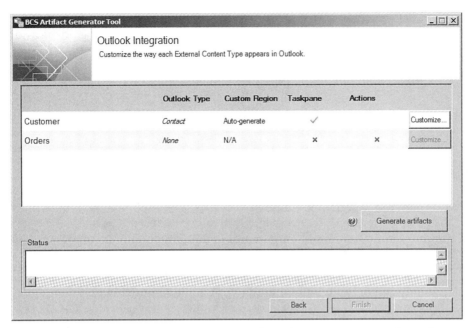

FIGURE 11-25 The artifact for the Customer ECT is configured to autogenerate a region and to create a task pane.

Click Generate Artifacts to create the files, as shown in Figure 11-26. These artifacts include subscription files, an OIR file, the BDC model file, and a relationship file.

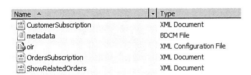

FIGURE 11-26 Without the Artifact Generator tool, you would need to write these files manually. You can edit them if you need further customization.

Subscription Files

There are the two subscription files: one for customers and one for orders. A subscription file contains the following information:

- **Queries** These are the Finder queries that must be executed to get the entity instances into the cache. These queries can take filters, if provided in the BCS model, to limit the information being subscribed to.

- **Associations** These are related entity instances from the external data source. You should add associations to the subscription file only if you need to use them; otherwise, they represent an unnecessary overhead to the BCS Client Object Model.

- **Explicit identities**   These are explicit requested items from your external system, even though they may not be returned by the queries. For example, if you're returning customers and filtering them by their state, but you want to make sure a few other people from another state are included, you can do so by explicitly stating those customers' identifiers.

The file also contains information about how long to cache the information or whether it should be cached at all.

OIR File

The OIR file is a solution manifest file that contains the details Outlook uses to create the UI, behavior, and business logic associated with the ECTs in the solution. As well as mapping the ECT to the Outlook type and properties, the file also adds the various UI elements, such as declaratively adding ribbons, buttons, or even actions to Outlook. An action, for example, could be to show the task pane associated with the solution.

When you configure the ECT using the BCS Artifact Generator and you choose to customize it, the OIR file gets updated. If you want to configure the file further than is possible to do with the Artifact Generator tool, then you can make changes such as presenting the data in an InfoPath form, creating regions, or adding Outlook folders.

BDCM File

The BDCM file is the BDC model. You need to rename this file *metadata.xml* for the BCS Solution Packaging tool to be able to use it. The BCS Artifact Generator will name it correctly for you.

Relationship File

The relationship file contains information about the association between the two ECTs.

Packaging the Outlook Declarative Solution

To package the files generated by the BCS Artifact Generator, use the BCS Solution Packaging tool. The Packaging tool takes the artifacts and generates a ClickOnce package to allow you to deploy the intermediate declarative Outlook solution.

The BCS Solution Packaging tool, as shown in Figure 11-27, allows you to name the solution, provide a version number, select a solution type such as Outlook Intermediate Declarative Solution, point the source folder path to where the artifact files are located, and then choose a path where you want the packaged files to be created.

Note   You can use the BCS Solution Packaging tool to create other solutions, such as an Outlook advanced code-based solution or a data solution for Office add-in. These solutions are covered later in the chapter.

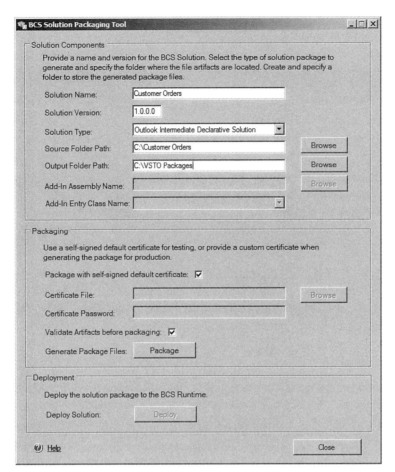

FIGURE 11-27 Use the BCS Solution Packaging tool to package the artifact files created by the BCS Artifact Generator tool.

You are able to sign the file; doing so removes the security warning when the package is used. It also indicates to end users that this solution comes from a trusted source.

In the Packaging section, click the Package button to create the necessary files to deploy the solution. You can then either take a look at the generated files or deploy them to your current environment to test them out immediately. Once you have created a package, the Deploy button in the Deployment section of the tool becomes active. Clicking Deploy installs and opens Outlook, where you can see the Customer Orders solution alongside the standard Outlook items, as shown in Figure 11-28.

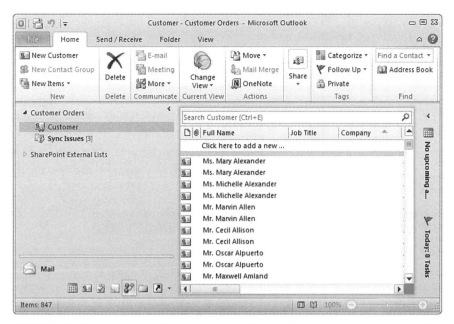

FIGURE 11-28 You can see here that the Customer Orders solution has been deployed to Outlook.

Currently, you have the same level of functionality as you had earlier when you clicked the Connect to Outlook button on the Lists ribbon tab for an external list. However, if you double-click a contact, in the detail view you can see a pane that shows the contact's orders (as shown in Figure 11-29).

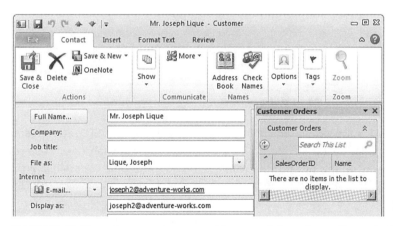

FIGURE 11-29 The custom pane is now providing more information on the contact form.

It is very useful to be able to supplement Outlook with business data using a declarative solution that doesn't require you to write any code, yet can make good use of your business data. If you want more control, you can write an add-in and further tailor your end-user experience, or you can add custom business logic and still have your end users using the familiar Outlook interface.

To make this solution available to your SharePoint users, simply put the files and folder in the same format in which they were created by the tool into a document library, as shown in Figure 11-30.

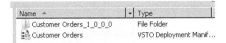

FIGURE 11-30 These files are required to install the VSTO you want to make available in SharePoint.

The easiest way to add the files is to use the multiple upload functionality of a document library, as shown in Figure 11-31. This allows the files to be dragged from Windows Explorer onto the dialog box.

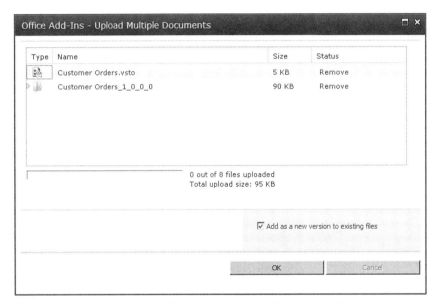

FIGURE 11-31 Use the document library multiple upload function to add the package.

After you've uploaded the files in a document library, provide a link to the VSTO file in an email or on a page. A user can then click the link to install the package. Usually, though, developers add a command button on the ribbon that points to a link to the package, providing users with a similar experience to the Connect to Outlook command. Once the user clicks the link, the Microsoft Office Customization Installer dialog box opens and asks the user to confirm the installation, as shown in Figure 11-32.

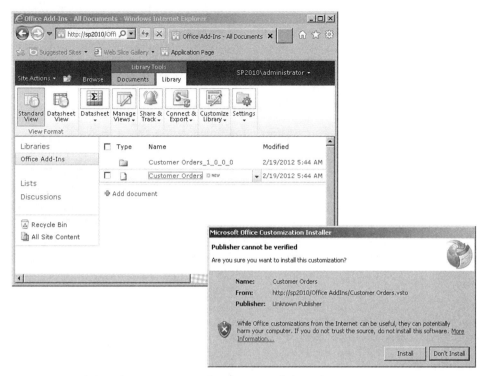

FIGURE 11-32 Clicking the VSTO prompts the user to install the package.

Outlook Advanced Code-Based Solutions

In addition to creating intermediate declarative Outlook solutions, you can also create advanced solutions, which allow you to use code for greater control and enable further customization of the user experience using BCS with Outlook. The types of solutions you can create include code-based actions that allow for greater meshing between the data and Outlook. For example, you can create an Outlook task to follow up with a customer or add information to the Outlook Calendar. Another possibility is to create data parts, which give you the opportunity to create a user control element in which to interact with the data in ways above and beyond what you are able to do declaratively.

Data Solution for Office Add-In

BCS supports VSTO add-in projects for any Office Professional Plus 2010 application, which can access external data from either an external data source directly or the BCS Rich Client Cache through runtime APIs. For a data solution for an Office add-in type, a developer can create two different types of solutions.

The first solution is an Office add-in: a standard VSTO Office Add-In Project. Within the project, runtime APIs are invoked to access external data. The solution should be implemented to ensure that the data solution is functioning before invoking the runtime APIs.

The second is a data solution for Office add-in. This is a special solution component that does not provide any UI in the Office application. The sole purpose of this solution component is to manage the lifecycle of the BDC metadata and the BCS Rich Client Cache population.

Client-Side Authentication Considerations

When creating solutions that make use of client-side code, it is important to understand how you plan to authenticate with the external system. If you are creating a declarative solution, then the solution will use the authentication method defined in the BCS model. If the model is using Windows or claims-based authentication, then it will be able to use those credentials to connect to the external system. In a scenario where credentials other than the identity of the logged-on user are required, then the authentication can be achieved using credentials stored in the Credential Manager tool in Windows. BDC models that use either the Secure Store Service or an application pool ID will require a different authentication mode, as these are unavailable to a solution that bypasses SharePoint. In such cases, the user is prompted to provide the credentials to be used to authenticate with the external system.

See Also *For more information on authentication and authorization security options, see Chapter 3, "Creating and Maintaining Business Data Connectivity Service Applications."*

Client-Side Caching Considerations

When working with the metadata cache, you should take several things into consideration, such as how often the cache is updated, what happens when the connection to the external system is unavailable, and so on. It is worth noting that SharePoint doesn't ever cache BCS data on the server; only Office clients have this functionality. SharePoint caches only the BDC model on servers that are configured in the web role.

When the VSTO package is installed, the installation stores the files from the VSTO package into the user's AppData folder: C:\Users\{UserName }\AppData\Local\Microsoft\BCS. This is also the location of the SQL CE database, which is where the cached data is stored. For each entity, a table is created in the database. The database should not be edited in any way, as this is an unsupported activity; however, you can use the Cache Object Model to access information in the cache to complete activities such as refreshing the data.

See Also *You can find information on coding against the client cache at* http://msdn.microsoft.com/en-us/library/ie/ee558772.aspx.

The *BCSSync.exe* service is responsible for providing automatic cache refresh and data synchronization. This service processes the subscription files and is used to populate the metadata cache using the Finder method, SpecificFinder method, and associations, depending on the queries in the subscription files. This service ensures that data stored in the cache is kept up to date according to the settings in the subscription. As mentioned previously, each element of the subscription file contains information on how long to persist the data using the *RefreshInterval* attribute. Also, garbage collection is part of the synchronization process. During garbage collection, data that is no longer required in the cache—that is, information that is no longer in the external system—is removed. This process keeps the cache file size down. If the *BCSSync.exe* process is no longer running, data synchronization will not happen, but the Office solution will still continue to work with the cached data.

Operations on the data are not performed directly against the external data. Rather, they are put in an operation queue, which is a location in the cache, to be performed one by one when the external data source is available.

Summary

The client side of Business Connectivity Services (BCS) gives an organization the ability to express its data and make it accessible to those who require it. Applications that used to take a long time for developers to write because they had to learn the ins and outs of a particular line-of-business (LoB) system can now be developed in a fraction of the time.

The other benefit of BCS is that because SharePoint can talk to any of the external systems in a uniform manner, a front end to the data—whether that is a web-based solution using the Client Object Model, a jQuery solution, an Office add-in, or a declarative solution—can be written without any regard to what the back-end system is.

Microsoft Office provides a rich, familiar user interface to information workers. As a result, there are benefits associated with providing your users with the information they need in the applications they use to perform most of their duties.

CHAPTER 12

Building Server-Side BCS Solutions

In this chapter, you will learn to:

- Use Microsoft Visual Studio to build Microsoft SharePoint solutions

- Create Business Connectivity Services connectors

- Import Business Data Connectivity models into Visual Studio

- Build solutions using the Business Connectivity Services application programing interface

- Build workflows with external data

- Amend the SharePoint user interface to support your Business Connectivity Services solutions

- Package and deploy solutions

In this chapter, you will learn how to build and use server-side solutions for working with your external data through Microsoft SharePoint Business Connectivity Services (BCS). As discussed in the previous chapter, and as the title of this chapter suggests, the solutions you will learn about execute the code on the server itself rather than on a user's client. You will look at how Microsoft Visual Studio 2010 gives you the ability to build SharePoint solutions for BCS and also how to make use of the Business Data Connectivity Model project in Visual Studio to create and deploy a model.

Using Visual Studio 2010 to Create SharePoint Solutions

Microsoft has made some major investments in the SharePoint tools for Visual Studio 2010 Pro and above, which means creating solutions is now much easier than was possible in previous versions. The first major improvement is including a rich set of Visual Studio project templates to give developers a start for their solutions. Figure 12-1 shows the different project types available.

In addition to creating SharePoint projects in Visual Studio, you can create an empty SharePoint project and add various SharePoint project items to it or to other project types, as shown in Figure 12-2.

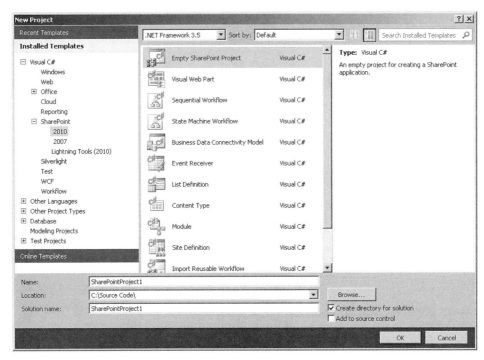

FIGURE 12-1 Many SharePoint 2010 project templates are available in Visual Studio 2010.

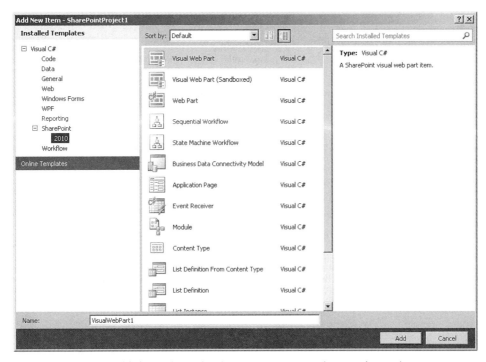

FIGURE 12-2 You can add SharePoint project items to an empty project or other project type.

The next much appreciated improvement is the automatic packaging of solutions based off the Visual Studio SharePoint projects. Developers can now concentrate on writing the code for their solutions and adding the required artifacts to the Visual Studio project, and when they want to test or deploy the solution, Visual Studio will package the necessary files into a *.wsp* package. So after developers have fully tested and debugged their solutions, they can provide a *.wsp* package for their SharePoint administrators to deploy and test in the staging environment (see Figure 12-3). The developers can configure the feature and solution manifests using wizards, rather than editing the XML manually, as was previously required.

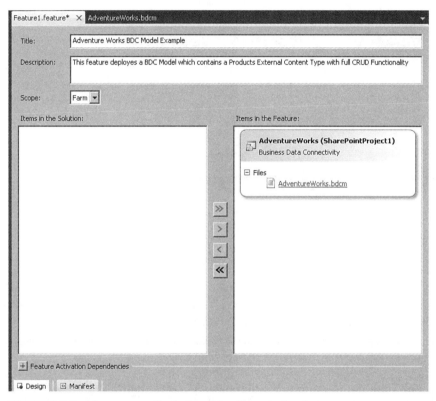

FIGURE 12-3 Developers can edit a feature using the new wizard.

The final improvement we will examine is the improved ability to debug the solutions that developers are writing. Instead of manually packaging and attaching hooks to the necessary processes to see what the code is doing, developers can use the F5 deployment functionality, which will build the code and package and deploy the *.wsp* file to SharePoint.

More Info If you are using Microsoft SharePoint Foundation, you need to take additional steps to add an event receiver. You can read more at *http://archive.msdn.microsoft.com/ BDCSPFoundation*.

If required, once the solution is deployed using F5, developers can step through their code as it is being executed by SharePoint (see Figure 12-4). Once a solution has been debugged, Visual Studio can retract the *.wsp* file to clean up after itself. The steps executed when developers deploy the solution can again be configured to meet their requirements.

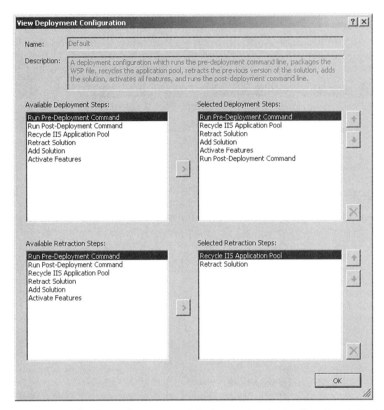

FIGURE 12-4 Configure the automated deployment and retraction steps in the View Deployment Configuration dialog box.

Visual Studio 2010 has made it easier to develop and work with SharePoint solutions. Next, you will take a look at the tools included to work with BCS. You may have noticed that there is a Business Data Connectivity Model project type available in Visual Studio. You will learn in the next section how to use this project type to create a BDC model, and why you would want to use this approach rather than simply using SharePoint Designer.

Creating BCS Connectors

Before diving into how to create a BCS connector in Visual Studio, let's first take a step back to determine when you would and wouldn't want to create one.

The first thing to note is that creating a BDC model in Visual Studio can be a lengthy process if you are unsure of how a BDC model is structured. You need to understand elements such as In and Return parameters, and the different method types and the code signatures required can lead to some confusion initially. Once you have written a handful of models, the process becomes easier, but understanding the principles first will help in the long run.

You shouldn't need to create a BCS connector if all you want to do is perform simple CRUD functionality against a connection supported by SharePoint Designer. If you want to read and write data to a SQL table, for example, and you don't need to transform or run any further business logic on the data, then it doesn't make sense to write the code to do this when SharePoint Designer will generate the SQL scripts for you. SharePoint can connect with an external system through the SQL script in a model without the need to read and use a BCS connector DLL, which can help improve performance.

If, however, you want to create an external content type (ECT) based on multiple sources of data, and you want to transform the data before making it visible to SharePoint, add custom permission management, or even add in some custom business logic when a user updates or deletes a record, then a BCS connector is the way to add these custom requirements. A BCS connector also allows developers to get the context in which the ECT is being called, such as reading any properties from the BCS model and seeing the current user calling the ECT. Creating a BCS connector gives you a way to connect to a data source not supported by SharePoint Designer, such as Oracle or non-BCS-compatible web services. For the web services, you need to write a wrapper, and for any other data sources, you can connect in any way supported by the .NET Framework.

Stepping Through a BCS Connector Example

For this chapter's example, you will use the Adventure Works Products SQL table and business logic to show the ProductId, Name, and list price for three different currencies—U.S. dollar ($), pound sterling (£), and yen (¥)—calculating the list price based on the latest exchange rate. The table shows the list price in U.S. dollars, so you will need to add custom type descriptors for the other two currencies dynamically—that is, the data will not come from the SQL table. You will create only read methods in this scenario, so the methods you create will be a Finder and a SpecificFinder.

First, open Visual Studio 2010 and create a new Business Data Connectivity Model project called ProductExchangeModel, as shown in Figure 12-5.

The next dialog box asks if you want to deploy as a sandboxed or a farm solution. Because the BCS connector DLL gets deployed to the global assembly cache (GAC), the farm solution is the only option available. The URL is the site that will be opened when the solution is deployed using F5. The F5 deployment is useful, as it allows you to configure a Web Part (for example, to use the ECT), and it will open to that page each time to let you test that you're getting the results you expect. Click Finish to close the dialog box and load the project.

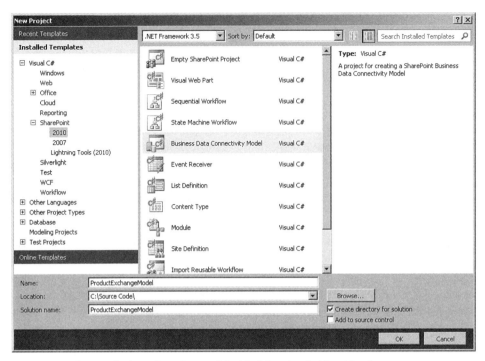

FIGURE 12-5 Create a Business Data Connectivity Model project in Visual Studio.

When the project first loads, you will see that an ECT is already created on the design surface. The default entity is similar to the "Hello World" application that a developer might write to show that the most basic functionality is working. If you were to press F5 now, you would have an ECT that shows "Hello World" for the Finder and SpecificFinder methods.

Understanding the User Interface with the "Hello World" Example

Now you'll take some time to explore the user interface (UI) to understand the different components you use to configure the BDC model. You won't make any changes to the default "Hello World" model you have at the moment, to make things easier to understand. The first item to look at is the visual representation of the ECT on the design surface, as shown in Figure 12-6.

FIGURE 12-6 The Entity1 ECT is shown on the design surface.

The design surface with the ECT that you can see in Visual Studio is the *BdcModel1.bdcm* file. To view any BDC models in your solution, simply double-click the **.bdcm* file to open it in this designer view.

> **Note** If you have ever seen a SharePoint 2007 application definition file (ADF), it is interesting to know that this *.bdcm* file type is essentially the same file (with some changes). If you were to open the file in XML view, you would see the structure of the model is almost identical to what used to be created in SharePoint 2007. Fortunately, you now have a nice UI in which to work with the model.

Taking a look at the Entity1 ECT, notice that it has an identifier defined called Identifier1 and it has two methods: ReadList and ReadItem. As you know by now, the identifier is the type descriptor that uniquely identifies a row of data in your external data and must be returned by each method. The names of the two methods give you a clue as to their method type: ReadList is the Finder method, and ReadItem is the SpecificFinder method. To confirm the method types, use the BDC Method Details tool pane at the bottom of the design surface (you may need to click its tab to display it). If you do not see the tool pane, go to the Visual Studio Menu toolbar at the top of the application and navigate to Views, click Other Windows, and then click BDC Method Details. The tool pane that displays looks similar to the one shown in Figure 12-7. Make sure the ECT is selected on the design surface.

FIGURE 12-7 View method details for the Entity1 ECT in the BDC Method Details tool pane.

In this view, you can see the two methods, ReadList and ReadItem, and for each method you can see the parameters, instances, and filter descriptors. For now, you are only interested in instances; you will look at the rest later. Click the ReadList line under Instances (not the one at the top; rather, the one six lines down from there). When you click this method instance, you can see its properties in the Properties tool pane, as shown in Figure 12-8. If the tool pane doesn't appear, press F4 to display it or find it under the Views menu.

FIGURE 12-8 View the method instance type in the Properties tool pane.

If you click the identifier on the ECT, you will see that its properties also display in the Properties tool pane. You can see both the identifier name and its data type, System.String. This is where you will configure various properties of the model later on.

So far, you have seen what the ECT looks like on the design surface and the information it offers. You have also viewed some of the properties of the model. The last thing to look at before writing your own ECT is the BDC Explorer tool pane. The BDC Explorer provides an overall view of the structure of the ECT and a means of working with the type descriptors of the model. When you work with a table as a data source, there is usually a simple mapping of one column to one type descriptor; however, as you will learn, you can add your own independent type descriptors to add more data to the ECT. You can access the BDC Explorer through its tab to the right of the Solution Explorer. If you do not see the BDC Explorer tab there, you can locate it through the Views menu. Figure 12-9 shows the BDC Explorer displaying the "Hello World" model.

FIGURE 12-9 The BDC Explorer shows the "Hello World" model.

You can click the various nodes in the BDC Explorer to easily access the properties of the BDC model.

You should now have a good sense of the BDC connector environment before diving into the code. There is a tight correlation between the code and the model, so it is important to understand where properties are configured.

Creating Your First External Content Type

Go ahead and delete the Entity1 ECT—it's had its time in the spotlight. Now it's time to create one with code. You should now have a blank design surface. Before you can move ahead, you'll need to complete some housekeeping tasks. In the Solution Explorer, you'll find two *.cs files to delete (see Figure 12-10). These are the C# code files that were used by the ECT that you just deleted.

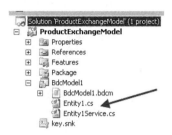

FIGURE 12-10 Delete these redundant C# files.

After you delete the two .cs files, you should rename the model to something more appropriate than *BdcModel1*. Change to the BDC Explorer view and click the first node, BdcModel1. In the Properties pane, update the name to **BdcConnectorProductModel**, and also update the rest of the nodes to match Figure 12-11. These changes will help you identify the model and ECTs when using them inside of SharePoint.

FIGURE 12-11 The BDC Explorer shows the current model structure.

Now it's time to create an ECT. Right-click the design surface, click Add, and then click Entity. You can also drag an Entity toolbox item from the Toolbox.

Because this ECT will be used for product exchange rates, name it **ProductExchangeRates**. You can set the display name separately to make it easier for end users to read, but for the sake of the code, the name shouldn't contain any spaces. To set the display name, click the ECT and change the Default Display Name in the Properties tool pane. If you look at the Solution Explorer, you should see that a file called *ProductExchangeRatesService.cs* has been automatically generated, as shown in Figure 12-12.

FIGURE 12-12 The *ProductExchangeRatesService.cs* file has been automatically generated.

This service class is the class used as the data access layer to the external system. As methods and some changes are added to the BDC model, this file also gets updated. Visual Studio is writing the signature for the method for you to just enter the code logic to return the required data. If you look into the file now, you will see that it is just an empty C# class.

When you deleted the files from the Entity1 ECT earlier, you may recall that there were two files: a service class, like you have now, and another file. The second file is a class that defines the data you are getting from your external system. Essentially, you are building a strongly typed class that defines an ECT. To put this into simple terms, you need to think about the data you want to display in SharePoint. For this scenario, you want to return products with different exchange rates, so you will create a C# class that defines what a "product" in this context looks like.

In Solution Explorer, right-click the BdcModel1 folder, click Add, and click New Item. From the Code node, click Class, name it **Product.cs**, and click Add. Now you have an empty C# class to which you can add the necessary code to define what a product is. Because some of the data is coming from SQL Server, navigate to the SQL table using SQL Server Management Studio and have a look at the column types of the columns you are interested in. Figure 12-13 shows the view in SQL Server Management Studio.

FIGURE 12-13 View the column setup for the Product table.

The columns you are interested are ProductID, which is the primary key and has a type of Integer (int), Name (nvarchar(50)), and ListPrice (money). To add these properties to your C# code, you need to understand what their .NET equivalents are. A useful table available on MSDN presents the conversions: *http://msdn.microsoft.com/en-us/library/ms131092.aspx*. Some of the .NET types have Nullable<*Type*>, which is used when the standard .NET type expects to have a type. Usually it causes an error if, for example, a property of type Int (a number) is set to a null value (that is, no value). Using Nullable allows it to have no value. This is useful when you may not have all the values completed in your table—for example, say you have a database that contains people data, and one of the fields is Age, an optional field. If users have opted not to provide their age, then the value is null; it doesn't exist. If you don't use Nullable in this example, and SharePoint tries to set the Age property to null, it will throw an exception, whereas if you do use Nullable, SharePoint will allow the Age property to contain no value.

Converting the columns gives you the properties in Table 12-1, which you will add to the C# class.

TABLE 12-1 C# class properties

Property	SQL type	.NET type
ProductId	int	Int
Name	nvarchar(50)	String
ListPrice	money	Decimal
ListPriceSterling	*	Decimal
ListPriceYen	*	Decimal

*Not in SQL; these extra properties exist only in code.

The following code for the C# file shows that *Product.cs* was added:

```
using System;
using System.Collections.Generic;
using System.Linq;
using System.Text;
namespace ProductExchangeModel.BdcModel1
{
    public class Product
    {
        public int ProductId { get; set; }
        public string Name { get; set; }
        public decimal Price { get; set; }
        public decimal PriceInPoundSterling { get; set; }
        public decimal PriceInYen { get; set; }
    }
}
```

When you write the names of these properties, they do not need to match the names of the columns in the SQL table. You should remember that the data used to populate this object that you are calling a "product" could come from anywhere and could include as many or as few properties as needed. An external system could be just code or a hybrid such as this one, with a SQL table and code. Although these property names don't have to match the source's name, they do need to match the type descriptors in the BCS model. Naming the type descriptors is often where issues arise when building BCS models, and it is simply a case of a type descriptor not matching a property name perfectly (spelling, casing, and so on).

Now that you have defined what a Product ECT will look like in code, you can configure the BCS model to match by adding an identifier, a Finder method, and a SpecificFinder method. The identifier (the type descriptor that uniquely identifies a row) is the ProductId. You can add this identifier to the ECT by right-clicking it, clicking Add, and then clicking Identifier. By default, the identifier is called Identifier1 and its type is System.String, as shown in Figure 12-14.

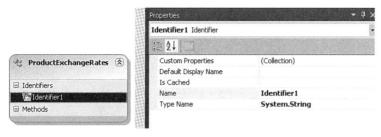

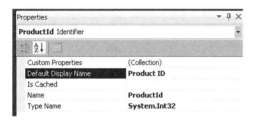

FIGURE 12-14 The identifier properties can be viewed in the Properties tool pane.

This doesn't match up with the identifier you want defined in the code: ProductId, with the type name System.Int32. Update the Properties pane to reflect your Product class, as shown in Figure 12-15. Don't forget to check that the name matches the actual property's name and ensure that the type is identical as well. Also set the Display Name to make it easier to understand what the column represents when it is used in SharePoint.

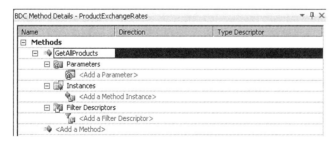

FIGURE 12-15 Updated properties for the identifier.

Next, you'll add your first method to the model. Right-click the ECT again, and this time click Add, and then click Method. Call the new method **GetAllProducts**, as this will be the Finder method that gets all of the products.

You can edit the properties of the method to add a default display name, so your end users know what's going to happen when they call this method. Entering **Get All Products** will suffice.

If you take a look at the BDC Method Details pane for the new method, you will see it is empty, as shown in Figure 12-16.

FIGURE 12-16 The newly created method before configuration.

Now you'll add some more properties to the method to describe its behavior. First, you'll look at the parameters. When creating a basic Finder method, the only parameter required is a Return parameter. The majority of the time, a method has either an In and a Return parameter or just a Return parameter. An In parameter defines in the model that a value is going to be passed into your query. For example, if you have a filter, then you will be passed in the value to filter by. The SpecificFinder, as you will see later, gets passed in the identifier of the item to get from your external system. The Return parameter defines what data SharePoint can expect to be returned from your code, such as a Finder method returning a collection of items from your external system or a SpecificFinder returning just a single item from your external system.

Click the <Add a Parameter> text, and then click Create Parameter to create an In parameter (helpfully called "parameter" by default). You will want to change its name and also change the type to Return. Open the Properties tool pane and amend it to match Figure 12-17.

FIGURE 12-17 The parameter has been configured.

With a Return parameter defined, you now need to define what is being returned. The easiest way to do this is using a combination of the BDC Explorer and the Properties tool pane. If you take a look at the BDC Explorer pane now, you will see the parameter that you have just added (see Figure 12-18).

FIGURE 12-18 The BDC Explorer displays ReturnParameter.

A type descriptor has been created for you, but you will need to do some work to make it fit with your requirements. As mentioned previously, type descriptors define the structure of the data that is going to be returned by your code, and this is where you define what that structure looks like. A Finder method typically returns a collection of objects (a Product), which have properties (Name, Cost, and so on). You will need to configure your type descriptors to reflect this detail, and its structure will look something like the following:

I am going to be returning a list of Products

This is a Product

This is a property of a Product

The default type descriptor created for you is defined to say that when the method is called, a single item—a string—will be returned, as shown in Figure 12-19.

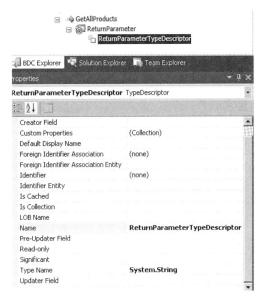

FIGURE 12-19 The default Return parameter type descriptor with a string type.

Rename the parameter to **ProductsList**, as you want to return a list of products. Click the Type Name, and then click the little arrow on the right to open a dialog box where you can select the type of data being returned. In this dialog box, you will set the outer level of data you are returning to be a collection of products. Not just any products, though—a collection of our C# code definition of products. As shown in Figure 12-20, select the Is Enumerable check box to return enumerable data (a collection that can be iterated over) and select the Product class.

FIGURE 12-20 Select the custom Product class as an enumerable type descriptor.

Once the outer type descriptor has been created, you'll add a type descriptor to the ProductsList type descriptor to define what each of the items is inside of the collection. Right-click ProductsList in the BDC Explorer and click Add Type Descriptor to add a sub–type descriptor. This time call it **Product**, and set its Type to just Product, without selecting the Is Enumerable check box.

You'll now add the properties of a Product to the product definition. At the moment, the model doesn't contain a definition of a Product, so you need to define it. Right-click Product and choose Add Type Descriptor. Do this four more times, making sure you're adding the type descriptor to Product each time (see Figure 12-21).

FIGURE 12-21 The Product with five type descriptors defined.

You added five type descriptors to define each property in your C# class, as shown in Table 12-2. For each type descriptor, you should edit the properties so the name exactly matches the name in the C# class, and also set the Type to match.

TABLE 12-2 Type descriptors

Name	Type
ProductId	System.Int
Name	System.String
Price	System.Decimal
PriceInPoundSterling	System.Decimal
PriceInYen	System.Decimal

Once you have set the values, the BDC Explorer should look like Figure 12-22.

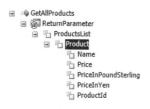

FIGURE 12-22 Configure the type descriptor names to match the property names in the C# class.

The final step is to let SharePoint know that this method is returning the identifier. To do so, select the ProductId type descriptor, and in the Properties pane, set Identifier to ProductId, as shown in Figure 12-23.

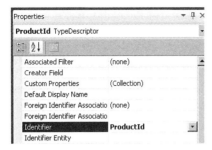

FIGURE 12-23 Setting the identifier for the ProductId type descriptor.

Adding Filters

As mentioned previously in this book, you should always consider working with the smallest subset of data you can when working with BCS. There is no point pulling superfluous data across your network and taking up both resources and bandwidth. You have seen how to add filters using SharePoint Designer; in this section, you will look at how to add filters when building a BDC model in Visual Studio.

In this scenario, you will add a Limit filter and a Wildcard filter. The Limit filter will limit the number of items returned from the external system that match the Product Name specified by the Wildcard filter. To configure the method with a Limit filter, you need to add a filter descriptor and In parameter for the Limit and Wildcard filters.

Open the BDC Method Details tool pane for the GetAllProducts method and click the <Add a Filter Descriptor> text. Click Create Filter Descriptor to add a new filter descriptor called FilterDescriptor. You will want to configure the properties shown in Table 12-3.

TABLE 12-3 Property values for a new filter descriptor

Property	Value	Description
Default Display Name	Limit	The name you'll see when configuring the Limit filter inside SharePoint
Filter Field	ProductId	The field to which the filter applies
Name	LimitFilter	The internal name of the filter
Type	Limit	The filter type

With the Limit filter descriptor added, you will add the Wildcard filter in the same way, this time using the property values listed in Table 12-4.

TABLE 12-4 Property values for another new filter descriptor

Property	Value
Default Display Name	Product Name
Filter Field	Name
Name	ProductName
Type	Wildcard

Now you'll add the two In parameters. The value for the Limit filter will have a default value assigned to it, but you will be able to configure it inside SharePoint. The Wildcard filter will get its value set by the end user, or you could configure it with a static value inside SharePoint.

Back in the Parameters section of the BDC Method Details pane, add a new parameter called **Limit-Parameter** and set its direction to In. Add a new parameter for the Wildcard filter, called **Wildcard-Parameter**, and again set its direction to In.

It is now time to configure the type descriptors that let SharePoint know the data that is going to be passed into this method. Navigate to the BDC Explorer and locate LimitParameter under the GetAll-Products method node. Table 12-5 lists the properties to configure for the type descriptor.

TABLE 12-5 Properties for the type descriptor

Property	Value
Name	limit
Type Name	System.Int32
Associated Filter	LimitFilter

The Limit filter will take a number of items to return, so set its Type to Int32. The Associated Filter tells SharePoint where it should use the value that is passed in to this parameter. Next, configure the Wildcard parameter as shown in Table 12-6.

TABLE 12-6 Property values for the Wildcard parameter

Property	Value
Name	wildcard
Type Name	System.String
Associated Filter	ProductName

The final step is to add the method instance. Here you are defining in the model the type of the method, whether it is the default method, the parameter that is being returned, and its display name. In the BDC Method Details pane, click <Add a Method Instance>, and then click Create Finder Instance. Set the properties for the method instance to values listed in Table 12-7, leaving the rest the same.

TABLE 12-7 Property values for the method instance

Property	Value
Default	True
Type	Finder
Return Parameter Name	ReturnParameter

You are specifying the Return parameter to the first parameter you created; this is the one that returns the collection of Products and defines what a single property consists of.

The Finder method has now been configured with regard to the model. Next, you will add the SpecificFinder method, which allows the end user to select a single record. If you want to be able to use your ECT with an external list, make sure you have these two methods at a minimum.

Adding a SpecificFinder Method

There are quite a few steps involved in creating the SpecificFinder method. Some of the tasks are easier, because you have already done some of the legwork. Add a new method to the Product-ExchangeRates ECT, and call this new method **GetSingleProduct**. Your ECT should now look like Figure 12-24.

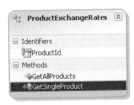

FIGURE 12-24 Add a new GetSingleProduct method to the ECT.

For a SpecificFinder method to function, it needs to receive the identifier that uniquely defines a record, so the first thing you will need to do is add an In parameter. As before, select the method and open the BDC Method Details pane. Make sure you find the correct GetSingleProduct method, as this pane now shows both the Finder method and the newly created method. You can minimize the method you're not interested in by clicking the hyphen (-) next to the method name of the Finder method. Add a new parameter with the property configuration shown in Table 12-8.

TABLE 12-8 Property configuration for the new parameter

Property	Value
Name	InParameter
Parameter Direction	In

By making these simple changes, you can add the Return parameter to the new parameter. This time, however, the parameter will define a single object that your method will return, which is a Product (see Table 12-9).

TABLE 12-9 Parameter for the Product object

Property	Value
Name	ReturnParameter
Parameter Direction	Return

The parameters are added for both accepting data into and returning data from the method. Next, you will define the type descriptors to use. Go to the BDC Explorer and expand all of the method, parameter, and type descriptor nodes, as shown in Figure 12-25.

FIGURE 12-25 Showing the parameters for the methods so far.

The first node to tackle is InParameterTypeDescriptor. This type descriptor must match the identifier defined in our code, both the name and the type. As this value is also the identifier, you must set it, too (see Table 12-10).

TABLE 12-10 Setting the identifier

Property	Value
Identifier	ProductId
Name	ProductId
Type Name	System.Int32

This is all that is required. It is worth noting that a SpecificFinder does not use a filter descriptor to get the single item; it just uses an In parameter.

Now you will configure the ReturnParameter. Last time, you needed to add the outer type descriptor that defined the collection, and under that, you defined the Product. With the SpecificFinder returning only a single item, you don't need to add the outer level. A neat feature in Visual Studio is that you don't need to create the Product structure again, since you can just copy it from the Finder method's type descriptor. Right-click Product under the ProductsList type descriptor and click Copy, as shown in Figure 12-26.

FIGURE 12-26 Copying the type descriptors.

With the type descriptors now on the clipboard, you can right-click the ReturnParameter of the SpecificFinder method and paste the type descriptors (see Figure 12-27). You will get a warning that you will replace the existing one. Click Yes.

FIGURE 12-27 The type descriptors have been copied.

This is all you need to do for the type descriptors. You have defined the In parameter type as the identifier, and you have also defined the single object that is being returned by the method. You can now move on to add the method instance using the BDC Method Details pane. In the Instances section, add a new method instance and update its properties, as shown in Table 12-11.

TABLE 12-11 Properties for a new method instance

Property	Value
Default	True
Type	SpecificFinder
Return Parameter Name	ReturnParameter

That's it—the BDC model is now configured to support both a Finder and a SpecificFinder method. Before you can use the model in SharePoint, you need to write the code to retrieve the data.

Writing C# Code for the BDC Model

While you have been configuring the BDC model, Visual Studio has been maintaining the file called *ProductExchangeRatesService.cs* in the Solution Explorer with the method signatures required by the BDC model. The automatic signature generation makes writing the code a good deal easier, as it is easy to see the parameters being passed into the method as well as the return type. The code generated for the model should look like the following:

```
using System;
using System.Collections.Generic;
using System.Linq;
using System.Text;
namespace ProductExchangeModel.BdcModel1
{
    public partial class ProductExchangeRatesService
    {
        public static IEnumerable<Product> GetAllProducts(int LimitParameter, string
WildcardParameter)
        {
            throw new System.NotImplementedException();
        }        public static Product GetSingleProduct(int InParameter)
        {
            throw new System.NotImplementedException();
        }
    }
}
```

We have two methods in the code that match the methods that were created in the model. The first method, GetAllProducts, is the Finder method. It has two parameters, one for the Limit filter and another for the Wildcard filter value. You can also see that the method is returning a collection of Products, just as we specified. The SpecificFinder method has a parameter for the ID, and this time it will return just a single Product.

It is worth reiterating at this point that the model and the code are completely independent from any external system. All you have done is configured a model that defines the concept of a Product-ExchangeRate ECT. If you want to make this ECT get its data from any single external system, or even pull data from numerous systems, this is all possible in the code. If the .NET Framework can get the data, then you can use it here. For now, though, you will continue with the scenario of getting some of the data from SQL and enhancing it with some exchange-rate calculated data.

 More Info Various technologies are available to connect to a Microsoft SQL database, such as LINQ to SQL (*http://msdn.microsoft.com/en-us/library/bb425822.aspx*) and the ADO.NET Entity Framework (*http://msdn.microsoft.com/en-us/library/bb399572(v=vs.90).aspx*).

For the sake of brevity, you will use a generic method to get your data to help demonstrate how this data could come from anywhere. The code also uses a method called GetExchangeRate, which could perform any functionality you want to on your data before presenting it to SharePoint.

The following code is an example you can use for the Finder method:

```
/// <summary>
/// Finder Method
/// </summary>
/// <param name="LimitParameter">Limit Filter</param>
/// <param name="WildcardParameter">Wildcard</param>
/// <returns>Collection of Products matching filters</returns>
public static IEnumerable<Product> GetAllProducts(int LimitParameter, string
WildcardParameter)
    {
        // Get the items from the External System(s)
        IEnumerable<DataAccessLayer.ExternalSytemProduct> externalSystemProducts =
            DataAccessLayer.GetProductsFromExternalSystem(LimitParameter,WildcardParameter);

        // Get Exchange rate for pound sterling
        decimal poundSterlingExchangeRate =
CurrencyHelper.GetExchangeRate(Currency.PoundSterling);

        // Get the Exchange rate for Yen
        decimal yenExchangeRate = CurrencyHelper.GetExchangeRate(Currency.Yen);

        // Return collection of Products created from External Data and own values
        return externalSystemProducts.Select(
            externalSystemProduct => new Product
                                    {
                                        ProductId = externalSystemProduct.ProductID,
                                        Name = externalSystemProduct.Name,
                                        Price = externalSystemProduct.ListPrice,
                                        PriceInPoundSterling =
externalSystemProduct.ListPrice * poundSterlingExchangeRate,
                                        PriceInYen = externalSystemProduct.ListPrice *
yenExchangeRate
                                    }
            );
    }
```

The code is passing the filters to a custom method that will call the external system and retrieve the matching data. The code also has methods that call another method to get the exchange rates you are interested in. The final step is to iterate through each item returned from the external system and to create a Product object that we have defined in your own *Product.cs* class and is also the object that the BDC model has been configured to expect.

For the SpecificFinder method, the code is fairly simple. You are passing in the identifier to get one item that you then convert to a Product and set its properties.

```
/// <summary>
/// Specific Finder Method
/// </summary>
/// <param name="InParameter">Identifier</param>
/// <returns>Single record with matching Identifier</returns>
```

```
public static Product GetSingleProduct(int InParameter)
{
    // Get the items from the External System(s)
    DataAccessLayer.ExternalSytemProduct externalSystemProduct =
        DataAccessLayer.GetSingleProductFromExternalSystem(InParameter);

    // Get Exchange rate for pound sterling
    decimal poundSterlingExchangeRate =
CurrencyHelper.GetExchangeRate(Currency.PoundSterling);

    // Get the Exchange rate for Yen
    decimal yenExchangeRate = CurrencyHelper.GetExchangeRate(Currency.Yen);

    // Return collection of Products created from External Data and own values
    return new Product
    {
        ProductId = externalSystemProduct.ProductID,
        Name = externalSystemProduct.Name,
        Price = externalSystemProduct.ListPrice,
        PriceInPoundSterling = externalSystemProduct.ListPrice *
poundSterlingExchangeRate,
        PriceInYen = externalSystemProduct.ListPrice * yenExchangeRate
    };
}
```

This is the final piece of the puzzle, provided that you have written the code. In the accompanying source code to this book, you will find an example that has the blanks filled in.

To use this ECT, simply press F5 in Visual Studio to deploy the model. Once the model has been deployed, you can use the ECT on a Business Data Web Part, just as you would use any other ECTs you have deployed. In Figure 12-28, you can see all five columns from the Product object, including the two different exchange rates. The Wildcard filter is applied to show the products with *Sport* in their name.

Product Exchange Rates List

Actions ▾

| Product Name ▾ | contains ▾ | Sport | Add |

⊡ Retrieve Data

Name	ProductId	Price	PriceInYen	PriceInPoundSterling
Sport-100 Helmet - Red	707	34.99	2903.1203	21.924734
Sport-100 Helmet - Black	708	30.25	2509.8425	18.954650

FIGURE 12-28 Viewing the BCS connector ECT on a business data list.

Using Custom Connectors

Custom connectors offer even more flexibility than is possible with the sort of .NET connector you created in the previous example. Customer connectors offer the ability to create models and code that can be dynamically updated without the need to rewrite the code. The custom connector code can inherit numerous methods that allow it to reflect on the model to change its behavior and a lot more. When creating a custom connector, you are required to make some manual changes to the model and code that are not currently supported by the Visual Studio UI.

See Also *For more information about custom connectors, see* http://msdn.microsoft.com/en-us/library/ ff953161.aspx.

Connecting to Non-Microsoft SQL External Data Sources

In the BCS connector walk-through, you learned that there are two distinct parts of the creation process. The first part is defining the model and the ECTs, and the second part is writing the code methods that return the data in the same format as described by the model. This two-part procedure makes it easy to connect to any data source supported by the .NET Framework. The model itself doesn't contain information about where the data is coming from, and it just needs to have a strongly typed object that it can use with SharePoint. For example, if you want to connect to Oracle, you can look at the Oracle table manually and work out which fields you want to use, their type, and which field is the primary key/identifier. Once you have this information, you can create a strongly typed class in a BDC model project to represent the data object, and the object would contain all of the fields you are returning from the Oracle table. The next step would be to configure an ECT with the identifier and the methods you want to have, and then add the necessary parameters and type descriptors to match your C# object. Once the model is defined, you are free to connect to your Oracle external system using any method supported by .NET in your service class.

In this section, you will learn how to take models that have been created using SharePoint Designer and scale them up to a Visual Studio solution.

Importing BDC Models into Visual Studio

It is possible to import a BDC model that was previously created in SharePoint Designer to allow you to manage its deployment through a *.wsp* package. This section outlines this simple process.

First, to export a BDC model from SharePoint Designer, from the navigation tab locate the ECT you want to use. If several ECTs make up a model, you can select multiple items. Then right-click and choose Export BDC Model, as shown in Figure 12-29.

FIGURE 12-29 You can export ECTs from SharePoint Designer.

Provide a name for the file you're exporting, and leave the remaining settings at their defaults. Click OK. In the next dialog box, choose a location to save the *.bdcm* file, so you can find it later.

The next step is to import the model into Visual Studio. With Visual Studio open, create a new empty SharePoint project from the list of projects available. Choose to deploy it as a Sandboxed Solution and click Finish. Once the project has been created, right-click the project name, click Add, and then click Existing Item. Navigate to the *.bdcm* file you exported earlier. If the model does not contain a .NET assembly, Visual Studio will ask if you want to create one, as shown in Figure 12-30.

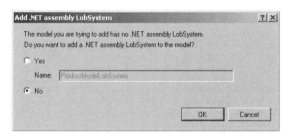

FIGURE 12-30 Choose if you want to add a .NET assembly to the imported model.

You will not be able to use the UI to manipulate the model the same way you could if you created the model from scratch, but you will be able to deploy the packaged *.wsp* file.

Using Fully Trusted vs. Sandbox Solutions

When creating a .NET Connectivity Assembly for use with a BCS model, it is important to understand that the DLL will be placed into the GAC. This means that if you want to be able to use a BDC model and Office 365, you will not be able to use a .NET assembly as access to the file system, as this is not permitted. If you want to use SharePoint Online and BCS, you will need to create a WCF model type.

Building Solutions Using the BCS Application Programming Interface

For developers, the ability to write code against the SharePoint Object Model provides a great way to create solutions without needing to understand the nuances of specific external systems. The code a developer could write for a Microsoft SQL Server external system will be the same for Oracle or even a web service.

Note The SharePoint Object Model provides an extensive application programming interface (API) for working with BCS. In addition to enabling you to work with ECTs through the object model, the API allows you to administer BCS to perform tasks such as creating and modifying BDC models programmatically. You can read more at *http://code.msdn.microsoft.com/windowsdesktop/Creating-SharePoint-2010-ad694d17.*

Using the SharePoint Object Model, developers can create solutions that the out-of-the-box Web Parts don't offer. Writing a BCS solution for a dashboard can really help support a business by providing data from multiple external systems through BCS. Working with the BCS programmatically also opens up the possibility of making decisions based on business data, which we will look at shortly.

Let's take a look at some code that connects to an ECT, iterates through product category items, and returns products from an associated product category:

```
private void GetProductAndProductCategortyData()
    {
        using (new SPServiceContextScope(SPServiceContext.GetContext(SPContext.Current.
Site)))
        {
            // Get the BDC service and metadata catalog.
            var service = SPFarm.Local.Services.GetValue<BdcService>(String.Empty);
            IMetadataCatalog catalog = service.GetDatabaseBackedMetadataCatalog(SPService
Context.Current);
            // Get the entity by using the specified name and namespace.
            IEntity entity = catalog.GetEntity("AdventureWorksModel", "ProductCategory");
            ILobSystemInstance lobSysteminstance = entity.GetLobSystem().
GetLobSystemInstances()[0].Value;

            IFilterCollection defaultFilter = entity.GetDefaultFinderFilters();

            IEntityInstanceEnumerator entityInstanceEnumerator = entity.FindFiltered(default
Filter,lobSysteminstance);

            KeyValuePair<string, IAssociation> keyValuePair =
entity.GetSourceAssociations()[0];

            IAssociation association = keyValuePair.Value;

            // Iterate through each Product Category
            while (entityInstanceEnumerator.MoveNext())
            {
                IEntityInstance currentProductCategory = entityInstanceEnumerator.Current;
                if (currentProductCategory != null)
                {
                    // Get Name of the Product Category
                    var productCategoryName = currentProductCategory.GetFormatted("Name");

                    // Get Enumerator for the Association
                    IEntityInstanceEnumerator associationEnumerator =
currentProductCategory.GetAssociatedInstances(association);
```

```
                         // Get Data Table contain Association data
                         var dataTable =
         entity.Catalog.Helper.CreateDataTable(associationEnumerator);
                }
            }
        }
```

Building Workflows with External Data

Workflows are an excellent example of using external data to drive your organizational business processes. When you consider what BCS offers in terms of providing access to data residing in external systems and making use of that data within SharePoint, it enables scenarios that would have traditionally required human interaction.

For example, consider a simple holiday request form. Say that employee information is stored in an external system—it doesn't matter what this system is. This external system contains information about the number of paid holidays employees are entitled to. With an ECT already configured with the CRUD methods, it is possible to create the following workflow. A Holiday Request custom list could be created within SharePoint with columns for the employees' requested days off. When an employee submits a holiday request, a workflow can read the creating user's details, look up the employee's current holiday entitlement; and either reject the request or automatically accept it if the employee has a certain job title, or escalate the request to the employee's manager if it requires further approval. Once a manager accepts the holiday, the workflow can automatically deduct the remaining days from the employee's record and email a confirmation to the employee. All of this can be achieved without human interaction. If you consider the traditional approach of an employee emailing the personnel team with requested holiday dates, and then personnel team needing to log on, look up a user, work out the user's entitlement, respond to the user, and then log the holiday in the external system, you can see how building a workflow such as this can really simplify a business process.

Customer order processing is another good candidate for a workflow. If you imagine an InfoPath form library with a Customer external data column, you can see how BCS can benefit this process further. The first benefit of BCS here is that you are assured the customer details associated with the document are correct, because the user who added the document was required to select a customer from the external system rather than enter the information manually, which is error-prone. Once an order has been created and the workflow initiated, it is possible to read the order details from the InfoPath form and check if the items are in stock by looking them up from another ECT. If the items are in stock, the order can continue; if not, the workflow can create a task to notify the customer and create an order to restock the products.

You can write a workflow for use with BCS in several different ways. One way is to create a BCS action, which is a reusable component that you can write in Visual Studio and then use within SharePoint Designer, as shown in Figure 12-31. Creating this type of action provides a way to easily make business decisions in various scenarios based on your existing data.

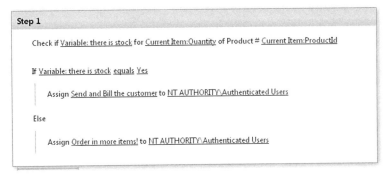

FIGURE 12-31 A custom BCS workflow action in SharePoint Designer.

It is also possible to create more complete Sequential and State Machine workflows using Visual Studio and use the BCS Object Model to interact with your external data.

Deploying BDC Models

As mentioned previously, Visual Studio packages the BCS model and, if you're using a .NET connectivity assembly, the necessary DLLs when you build the project. There is also an option in the Build menu to simply package the solution. When the project is packaged, it creates the *.wsp* package in the solution directory in the BIN subfolder of the Build Configuration folder. For example, if you're in debug mode for the ProductExchangeModel created earlier in this chapter, the *.wsp* will be created in a location similar to the following:

```
C:\Source\ProductExchangeModel\ProductExchangeModel\bin\Debug\ProductExchangeModel.wsp
```

The *.wsp* package is the same as any other solution package you are familiar with in SharePoint. To move this BDC model to another environment, such as from a development server to a staging environment, you can deploy the *.wsp* package using Windows PowerShell or using STSAdm code.

Summary

In this chapter, you reviewed the various components of building a Business Data Connectivity (BDC) model and the Business Connectivity Services (BCS) connector inside Microsoft Visual Studio. First, you looked at the Business Data Connectivity Model project type and the user interface that Visual Studio offers to help configure the wizard. You then examined the requirements to create an external content type (ECT) with elements such as adding an identifier, adding method types, and configuring their type descriptors. You also saw how to create a C# class to define the object (Product) that represents the data being returned by the ECT. Finally, you learned how to add your own business logic to the generated C# code.

Appendix

BCS Model Infrastructure

In this appendix, you will:

- Review the hierarchy of Business Connectivity Services metadata objects

- Understand commonly used metadata objects and the relationships among them

In this appendix, you will look at a Business Data Connectivity (BDC) model file to understand its structure. Not all of the features available with Microsoft Business Connectivity Services (BCS) are able to be used by Microsoft Visual Studio or SharePoint Designer. Those familiar with creating the application definition file (ADF) for SharePoint 2007 will be aware that the ADF was created manually, which meant its creators were required to know its structure inside out. Thankfully, we seldom need to delve into this file now, but it is useful to know what is going on inside.

The model that you will look at is a single external content type (ECT) inside of a model. The ECT is for displaying external data. The ECT has full create, read, update and delete (CRUD) functionality. There are two Finder methods, and there are also filters applied to one of the Finder methods. To see the roles of each element of the model, you will also examine how what you view in the XML corresponds to its usage in SharePoint.

You can obtain the complete model from the source code.

Basic Structure

Figure A-1 shows the basic structure of the model.

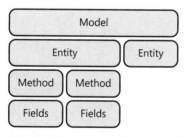

FIGURE A-1 A simplified view of the BDC model.

In Figure A-1, you can see that a model can contain multiple entities—an *entity* in the model refers to an ECT. Each entity can have one or more methods that provide functionality, such as getting all records, getting one record, or creating new records.

Model

The following code illustrates the model:

```
<Model>
  <AccessControlList />
  <LobSystems />
</Model>
```

Access Control List

Permissions to the model itself are configured from the first of many AccessControlList elements found in the model. An example of an access control list entity is shown below. This example grants all authenticated users permission to execute and select the ECT. If a user doesn't have permissions, the user will receive an "Access Denied" error message on the Web Part.

```
<AccessControlList>
  <AccessControlEntry Principal="NT Authority\Authenticated Users">
    <Right BdcRight="Execute" />
    <Right BdcRight="SelectableInClients" />
  </AccessControlEntry>
</AccessControlList>
```

You can view and change the settings in the Central Administration website. Navigate to a BDC model to view or set permissions, as shown in Figure A-2.

FIGURE A-2 You can view the access control list inside SharePoint.

LobSystems

The LobSystems element typically contains just one LobSystem. A LobSystem is the external system being accessed. You can see in the following code example that the LobSystem defined is connecting to a database. The other options available are DotNetAssembly, WCF, or Custom. The LobSystem Type affects the settings required in the LobSystem instance element.

```
<LobSystems>
  <LobSystem Type="Database" Name="Adventure Works">
    <Properties/>
    <AccessControlList/>
    <LobSystemInstances/>
    <Entities/>
  </LobSystem>
</LobSystems>
```

Properties

Most of the elements can accept properties to define behavior. An example of a behavior in the LobSystem is to set the wildcard character to use. The format is a name, a system type as attributes, and the desired value as the element's value.

```
<Properties>
    <Property Name="WildcardCharacter" Type="System.String">%</Property>
</Properties>
```

LobSystemInstances

The LobSystemInstances element contains typically just one LobSystemInstance, which is a single external system. You can see in this element the information that defines how to connect to the external system. In the following example, the external system is Microsoft SQL Server, and simple PassThrough authentication using trusted security is used. If you explicitly set SQL credentials, they would show here, or if you had used the Secure Store, you would have the properties defined to show the Secure Store ID that should be used:

```
<LobSystemInstances>
    <LobSystemInstance Name="Adventure Works">
      <Properties>
        <Property Name="AuthenticationMode" Type="System.String">PassThrough</Property>
        <Property Name="DatabaseAccessProvider" Type="System.String">SqlServer</Property>
        <Property Name="RdbConnection Data Source" Type="System.String">SP2010</Property>
        <Property Name="RdbConnection Initial Catalog"
Type="System.String">AdventureWorks</Property>
        <Property Name="RdbConnection Integrated Security" Type="System.String">SSPI</Property>
        <Property Name="RdbConnection Pooling" Type="System.String">True</Property>
        <Property Name="ShowInSearchUI" Type="System.String"></Property>
      </Properties>
    </LobSystemInstance>
  </LobSystemInstances>
```

You can edit these settings in the Central Administration website by navigating to the BCS service application and clicking the name of the external system from the External Systems View (in the ribbon). After you click the external system, you are taken to the view of the external system instances. When you click the name of the external system instance, you see the properties, as shown in Figure A-3. Having these settings editable in Central Administration is useful if you want to make any changes once the model has been deployed.

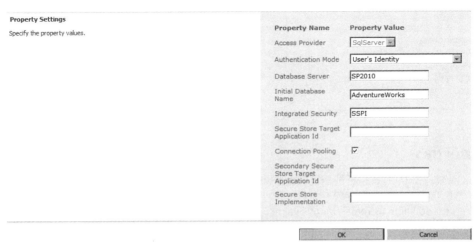

FIGURE A-3 In the external system instances section, you can edit the properties once the model has been deployed.

Entities Element

The Entities element is by far the largest of the elements. It contains the ECTs (entities):

```
<Entities>
  <Entity Namespace="http://www.adventureworks.com"
          Version="1.2.0.0"
          EstimatedInstanceCount="10000"
          Name="AdventureWorksProducts"
          DefaultDisplayName="Products">
  </Entity>
</Entities>
```

The version number is an important attribute to remember when working with a BDC model manually. SharePoint checks this version each time the model is imported. If it matches the existing version inside Central Administration, the ECT will not update with the changes. Here, you can also see the display name of the ECT for SharePoint users. For example, when you select the ECT to use on a Business Data Web Part, you will see the name, as shown in Figure A-4.

FIGURE A-4 Selecting an ECT is easy when it has a useful display name.

Entity

An entity is the ECT. It contains behavior and properties for the object that is being interacted with via BCS:

```
<Entity>
  <Properties/>
  <AccessControlList/>
  <Identifiers/>
  <Methods/>
</Entity>
```

The entity contains properties for functionality, such as setting the Title column:

```
<Properties>
      <Property Name="Title" Type="System.String">Name</Property>
</Properties>
```

Identifiers

To uniquely identify a record for the ECT, you need to have an identifier. The Identifiers element defines the TypeName and Name of the identifier:

```
<Identifiers>
    <Identifier TypeName="System.Int32" Name="ProductID" />
</Identifiers>
```

Methods Element

The Methods element contains the behavior of the ECT and, as the name implies, it contains all of the methods. For each method, such as Finder, SpecificFinder, Creator, Updater, and Delete, there is a method defined in the Methods element:

```
<Methods>
      <Method Name="Get Product Detail" DefaultDisplayName=" Get Product Detail ">
      <Method Name="Get All Products" DefaultDisplayName="Get All Products">
</Methods>
```

Method

A Method element contains all the necessary information to let SharePoint know how to handle the method, what type of method it is, if any filters are used, and what information gets passed in and out of the method. The following code illustrates an example:

```
<Method>
  <Properties/>
  <AccessControlList/>
  <FilterDescriptors/>
  <Parameters/>
  <MethodInstance/>
</Method>
```

Method Properties

The properties of the method define what needs to be called on the external system to perform the method's functionality. For example, the following properties define the required information for the method to select the product information from the SQL table:

```
<Properties>
    <Property Name="BackEndObject" Type="System.String">Product</Property>
    <Property Name="BackEndObjectType" Type="System.String">SqlServerTable</Property>
    <Property Name="RdbCommandText" Type="System.String">SELECT TOP(@ProductID) [ProductID] ,
[Name] , [Color] , [StandardCost] , [ModifiedDate] FROM [Production].[Product] WHERE [Name] LIKE
@Name) ORDER BY [ProductID]</Property>
    <Property Name="RdbCommandType" Type="System.Data.CommandType, System.Data, Version=2.0.0.0,
Culture=neutral, PublicKeyToken=b77a5c561934e089">Text</Property>
    <Property Name="Schema" Type="System.String">Production</Property>
  </Properties>
```

Filter Descriptors

Notice in the previous SQL statement the two parameters being passed in. The first is selecting the top X items , *TOP(@ProductID)*, and the second is using a where clause to find records matching the name, *WHERE [Name] LIKE @Name*. You can use a FilterDescriptors element to tell SharePoint that these values are filter values. The FilterDescriptors element defines the values' behavior with information such as filter type (Limit and Wildcard, in this case):

```
<FilterDescriptors>
    <FilterDescriptor Type="Wildcard" FilterField="Name" Name="Product Name">
      <Properties>
        <Property Name="CaseSensitive" Type="System.Boolean">false</Property>
        <Property Name="IsDefault" Type="System.Boolean">true</Property>
        <Property Name="UsedForDisambiguation" Type="System.Boolean">false</Property>
        <Property Name="UseValueAsDontCare" Type="System.Boolean">false</Property>
      </Properties>
    </FilterDescriptor>
    <FilterDescriptor Type="Limit" FilterField="ProductID" Name="Limit">
      <Properties>
        <Property Name="CaseSensitive" Type="System.Boolean">false</Property>
        <Property Name="IsDefault" Type="System.Boolean">false</Property>
        <Property Name="UsedForDisambiguation" Type="System.Boolean">false</Property>
      </Properties>
    </FilterDescriptor>
  </FilterDescriptors>
```

A filter will be shown in SharePoint depending on its type. In Figure A-5, you can see how to use the Wildcard filter on the business data list.

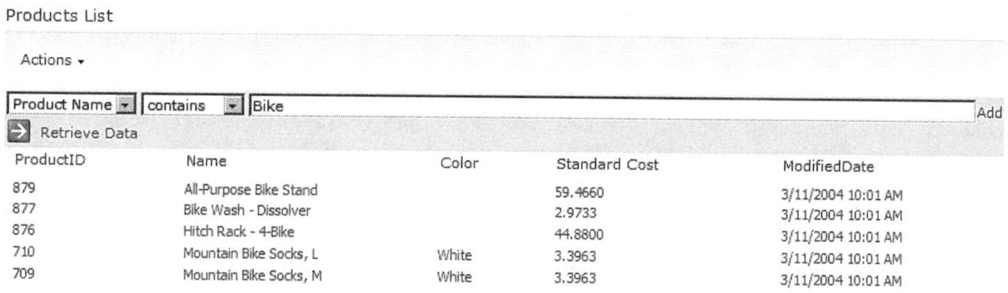

Products List

Actions ▾

Product Name ▾	contains ▾	Bike			Add
Retrieve Data					
ProductID	Name	Color	Standard Cost	ModifiedDate	
879	All-Purpose Bike Stand		59.4660	3/11/2004 10:01 AM	
877	Bike Wash - Dissolver		2.9733	3/11/2004 10:01 AM	
876	Hitch Rack - 4-Bike		44.8800	3/11/2004 10:01 AM	
710	Mountain Bike Socks, L	White	3.3963	3/11/2004 10:01 AM	
709	Mountain Bike Socks, M	White	3.3963	3/11/2004 10:01 AM	

FIGURE A-5 The Wildcard filter is a useful way to get the information you want.

You can change the Limit filter, which allows you to define how many records you want returned at a time for the external system, from the Edit View link on the Web Part (see Figure A-6).

☑ **Item Limit**

Specify the maximum number of items to retrieve from Adventure Works.

○ Do not limit the number of items displayed
◉ Limit the number of items displayed to:
[100]

FIGURE A-6 The Limit filter has a default value that can be changed to limit the records returned by the query.

Parameters

The parameters represent a very important piece of the BCS puzzle. The parameters describe the components being passed in and out of the method. A Finder method without any filters will contain just a return parameter. If a filter is defined, then the method needs to contain the information on the values that need to be passed into the method, so an additional In parameter will need to be defined, too.

This large section shows the parameters for the Finder method of the model. There are two In parameters, one for each filter, and also the Return parameter, which returns the matching records:

```
<Parameters>
  <Parameter Direction="In" Name="@Name">
    <TypeDescriptor>
  </Parameter>
  <Parameter Direction="In" Name="@ProductID">
    <TypeDescriptor>
  </Parameter>
  <Parameter Direction="Return" Name="Get All Products">
    <TypeDescriptor>
    </TypeDescriptor>
  </Parameter>
</Parameters>
```

Type Descriptor

A type descriptor defines the data going in and out of the methods and usually has a TypeName and a Name. You can add numerous properties to the type descriptor to alter its behavior:

```
<TypeDescriptor TypeName="System.String" Name="Name">
  <Properties>
    <Property Name="RequiredInForms" Type="System.Boolean">true</Property>
    <Property Name="ShowInPicker" Type="System.Boolean">true</Property>
    <Property Name="Size" Type="System.Int32">50</Property>
  </Properties>
  <Interpretation>
    <NormalizeString FromLOB="NormalizeToNull" ToLOB="NormalizeToEmptyString" />
  </Interpretation>
</TypeDescriptor>
```

Method Instance

The method instance is where the model defines the role of the method and its role for the ECT:

```
<MethodInstances>
  <MethodInstance Type="Finder" ReturnParameterName="Get All Products (Detailed)" Name="Get All Products (Detailed)">
    <AccessControlList />
  </MethodInstance>
</MethodInstances>
```

Index

Symbols

About the Authors

 **PENELOPE COVENTRY** is a multiple-year recipient of Microsoft's Most Valuable Professional (MVP) for Microsoft SharePoint Server and an independent consultant based in the United Kingdom, with more than 30 years of industry experience. She focuses on the design, implementation, and development of SharePoint technology-based solutions. She has worked with SharePoint since 2001. Most recently, she has worked for the international financial services group Aviva PLC, as well as provided consultancy services to Microsoft Gold partners ICS Solutions and Combined Knowledge.

Penny has authored and coauthored a number of books. They include both editions of *Microsoft Office SharePoint Designer Step by Step*, *Microsoft SharePoint 2010 Administrator's Companion*, *Microsoft Office SharePoint Server 2007 Administrator's Companion*, *Microsoft SharePoint Products and Technologies Resources Kit*, *Microsoft SharePoint Foundation 2010 Inside Out*, *Microsoft SharePoint Foundation 2010 Step by Step*, and both editions of *Microsoft Windows SharePoint Services Step by Step*.

Penny is frequently seen at TechEd, either as a technical learning guide or on the SharePoint Ask-the-Experts panels. She also speaks at events, such as the International SharePoint Conference, Australia and New Zealand SharePoint conferences, SharePoint Best Practices conferences, the Swedish SharePoint and Exchange Forum, SharePoint Summit in Toronto, SharePoint User Group UK meetings, and UK and Belgium SharePoint Saturdays.

Penny lives in Hinckley, Leicestershire, England, with her husband, Peter, and dog, Poppy.

 **BRETT LONSDALE** is a UK-based SharePoint developer, trainer, and author specializing in Business Connectivity Services. Brett is a cofounder of Lightning Tools, which provides third-party Web Parts and tools to help make building SharePoint solutions a simpler task. BCS Meta Man is one of the tools that help with the connectivity to external data sources such as Oracle, SQL, and other data sources. Brett is often seen at SharePoint conferences worldwide speaking on his specialist subjects of Business Connectivity Services, SharePoint security, and content aggregation.

Along with this book, Brett also coauthored *Developer's Guide to the SharePoint 2007 Business Data Catalog*, and he has contributed to *Microsoft Office SharePoint Server 2007 Administrator's Companion*, *Microsoft SharePoint 2010 Administrator's Companion*, and *Microsoft SharePoint Foundation 2010 Step by Step*.

As one of the cofounders of the UK SharePoint training company Combined Knowledge, he still enjoys teaching SharePoint when he gets the opportunity to do so. With little time available to teach entire five-day courses, Brett enjoys contributing to the SharePoint community through the SharePoint Pod Show at *www.sharepointpodshow.com*, along with cohosts Rob Foster, Jeremy Thake, and Nick Swan. Interviews with other SharePoint administrators, developers, and end users are recorded by the SharePoint Pod Show and made available to download, providing a great source of learning material.

In his spare time, Brett enjoys spending time with his young daughter, Rio, and his girlfriend, Sara. Brett is also learning the Filipino martial art of Doce Pares to maintain fitness as well as learn a new skill.

You can find blogs authored by Brett and other Lightning Tools employees at *www.lightningtools.com/blog*, and you can find Brett on Twitter at *brettlonsdale*.

 **PHILL DUFFY** has been working with SharePoint for five years and currently works for Lightning Tools as a product manager. Previously, Phill was a developer at Lightning Tools, where he worked on the company's popular BCS Meta Man tool. Phill enjoys speaking at conferences when he can. His speaking adventures have taken him to SPTechCon Boston and San Francisco, UK and the Netherlands SharePoint Saturdays, and the San Diego and London SharePoint Best Practices Conferences. Phill is an MCTS Application Developer for SharePoint 2007 and 2010.